SZERO

18

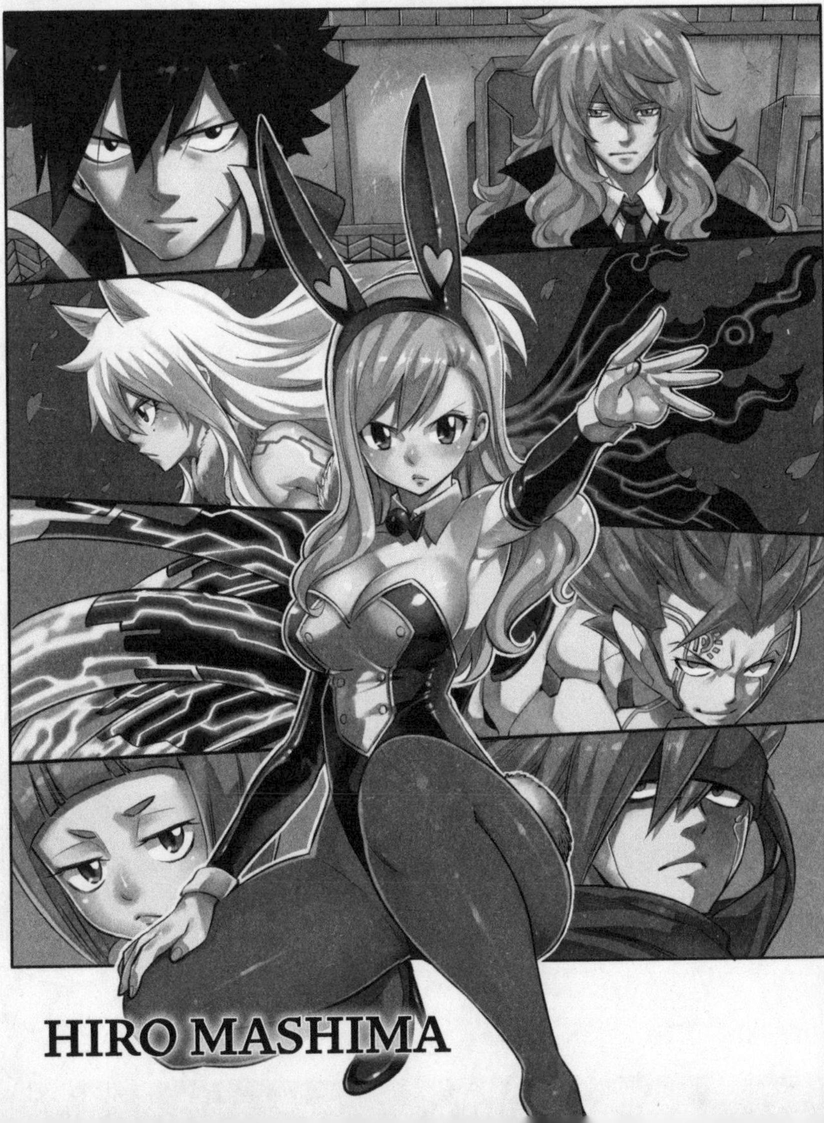

HIRO MASHIMA

EDENS ZERO 18 contents

CHAPTER 150: WEISZ VS. NASSEH

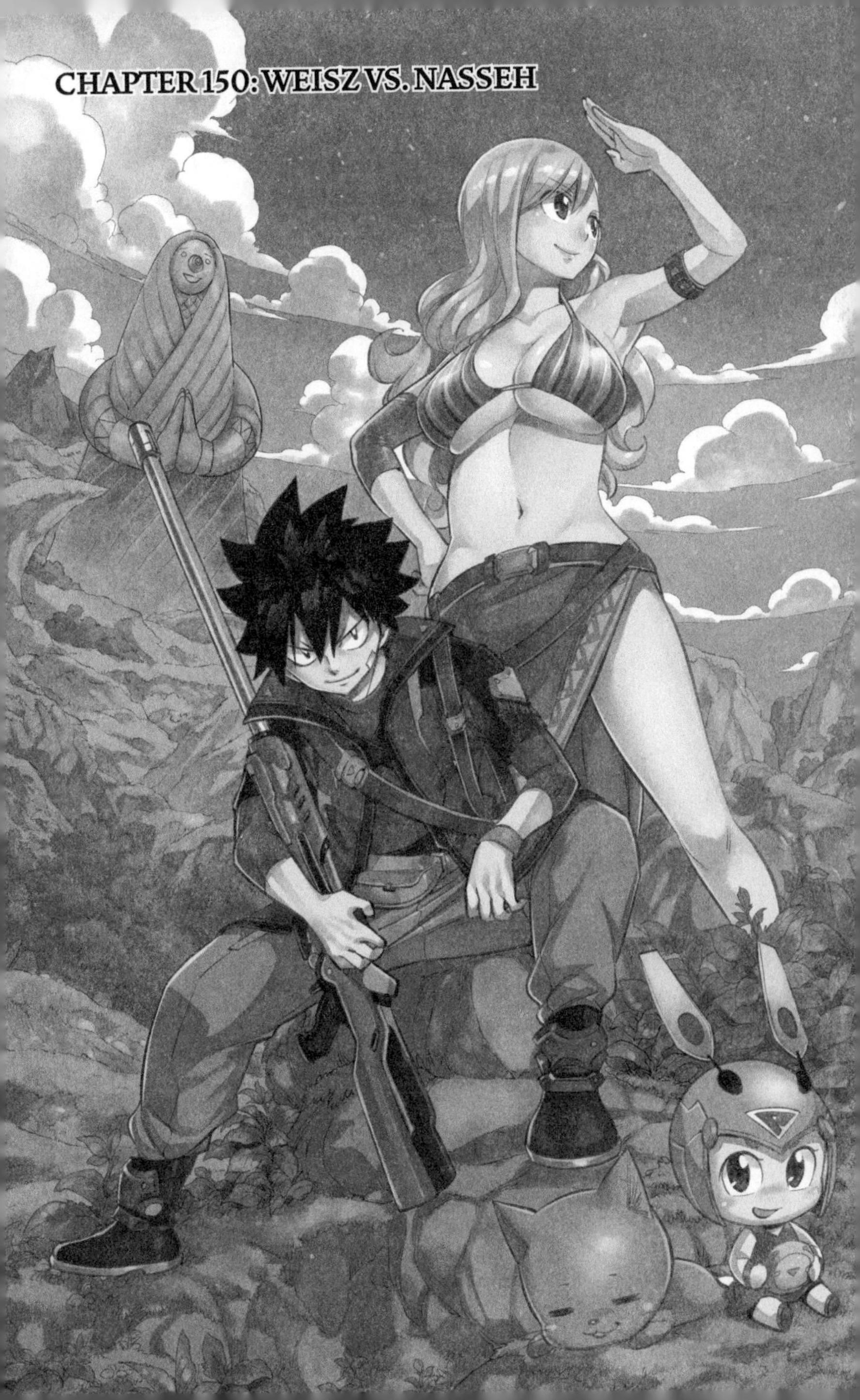

EDENSZERO

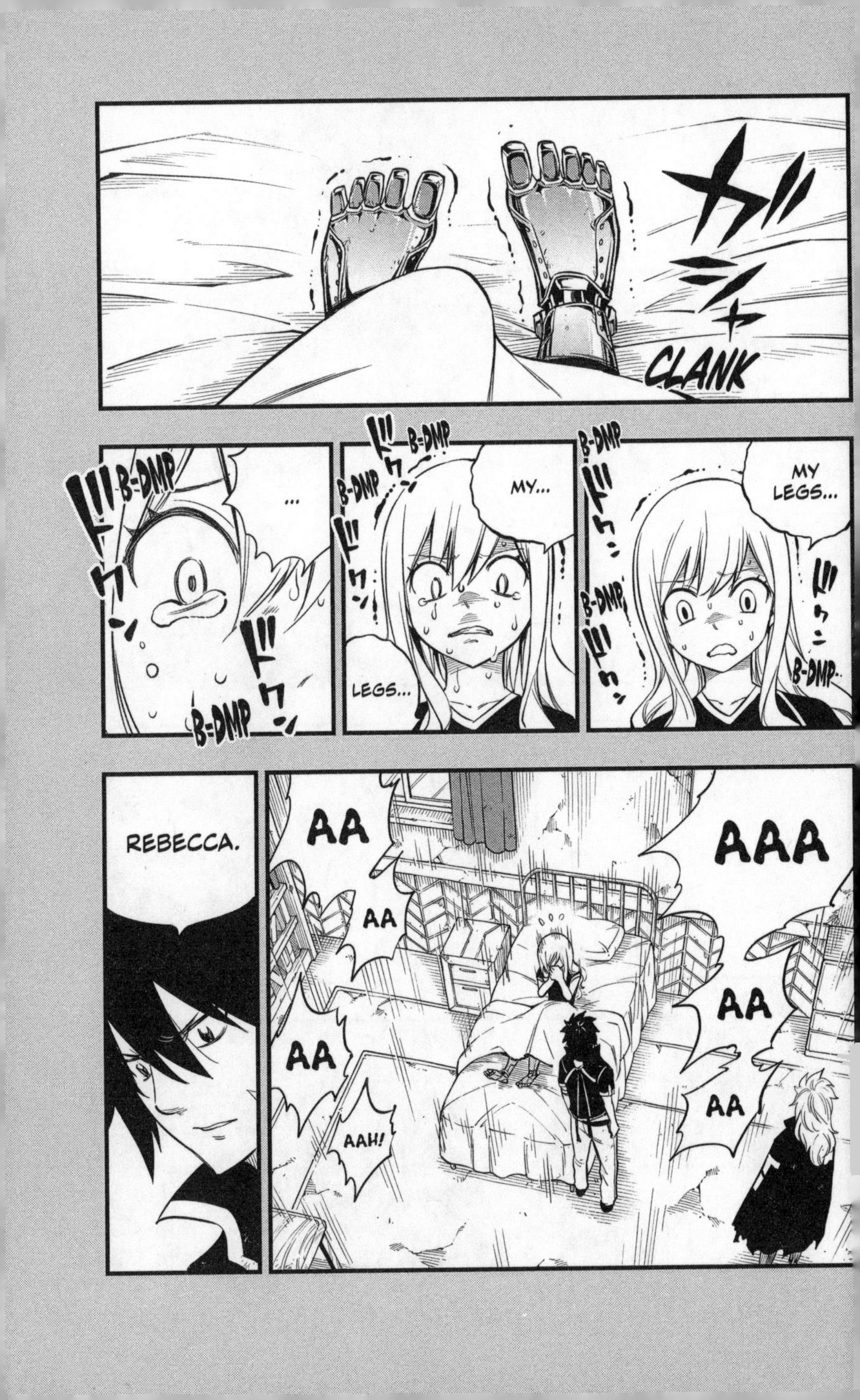
CLANK
B-DMP
MY LEGS...
B-DMP
B-DMP...
B-DMP
B-DMP
MY...
LEGS...
B-DMP
...
B-DMP
AAA
AA
AA
AA
AA
AAH!
AA
AA
REBECCA.

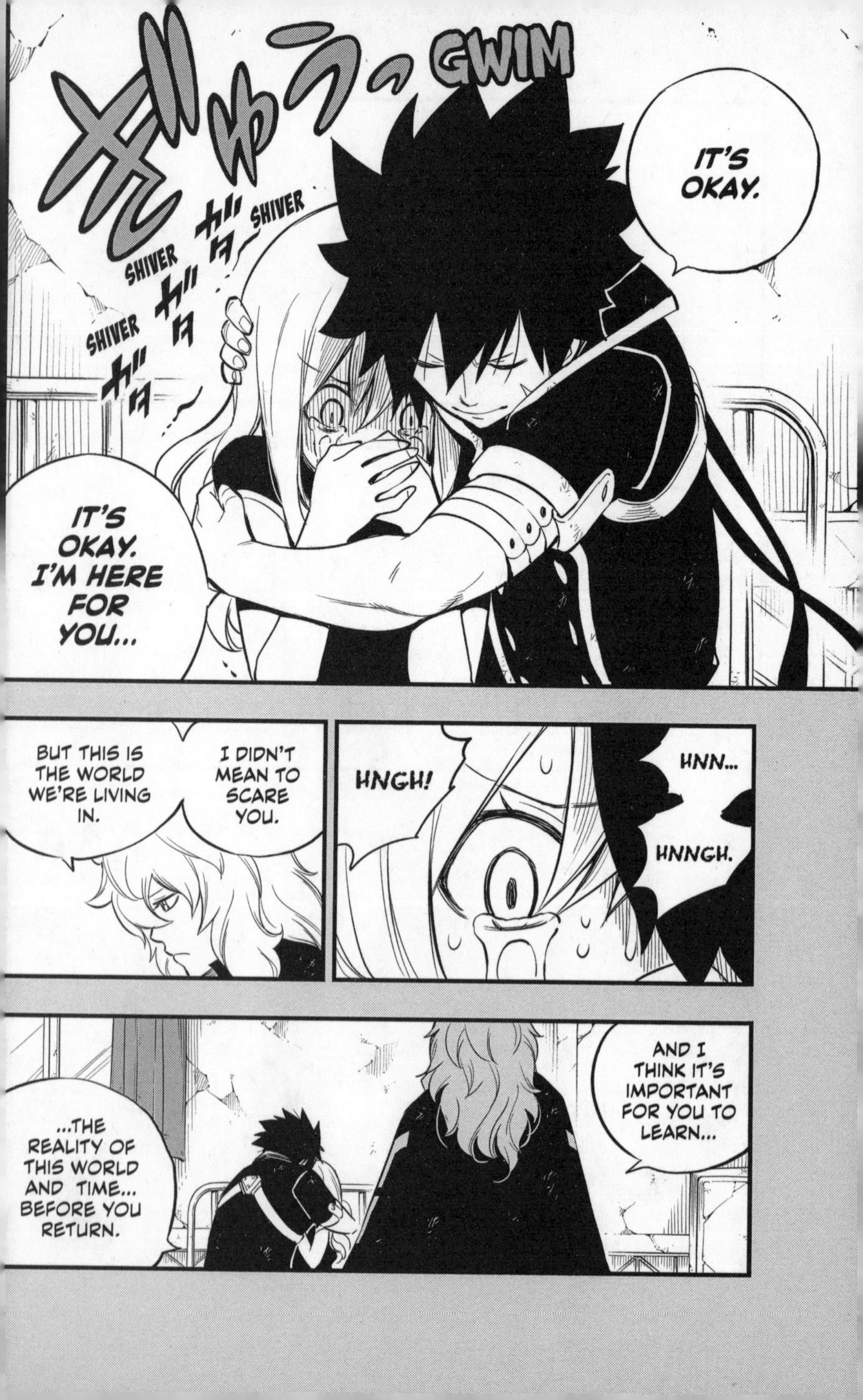
GWIM
IT'S OKAY.
SHIVER
SHIVER
SHIVER
IT'S OKAY. I'M HERE FOR YOU...
HNN...
HNNGH.
HNGH!
I DIDN'T MEAN TO SCARE YOU.
BUT THIS IS THE WORLD WE'RE LIVING IN.
AND I THINK IT'S IMPORTANT FOR YOU TO LEARN...
...THE REALITY OF THIS WORLD AND TIME... BEFORE YOU RETURN.

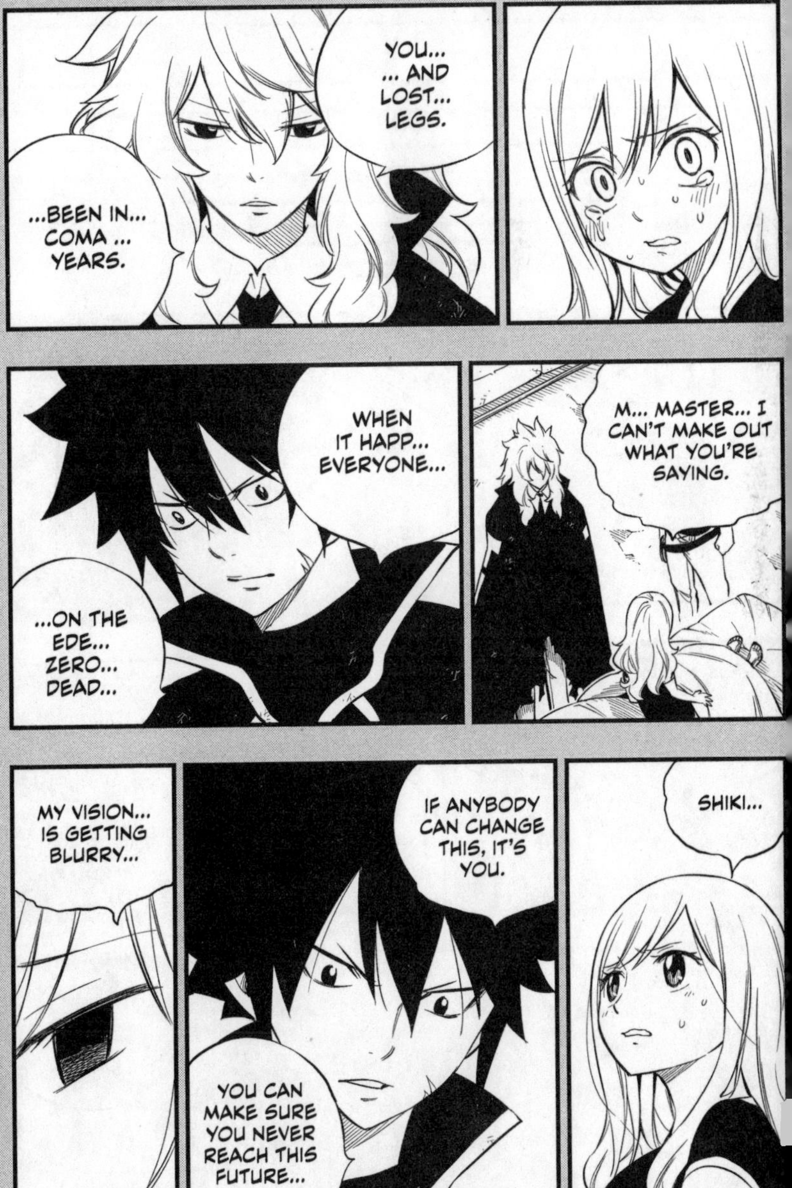
YOU... ... AND LOST... LEGS.
...BEEN IN... COMA ... YEARS.
M... MASTER... I CAN'T MAKE OUT WHAT YOU'RE SAYING.
WHEN IT HAPP... EVERYONE...
...ON THE EDE... ZERO... DEAD...
SHIKI...
IF ANYBODY CAN CHANGE THIS, IT'S YOU.
YOU CAN MAKE SURE YOU NEVER REACH THIS FUTURE...
MY VISION... IS GETTING BLURRY...

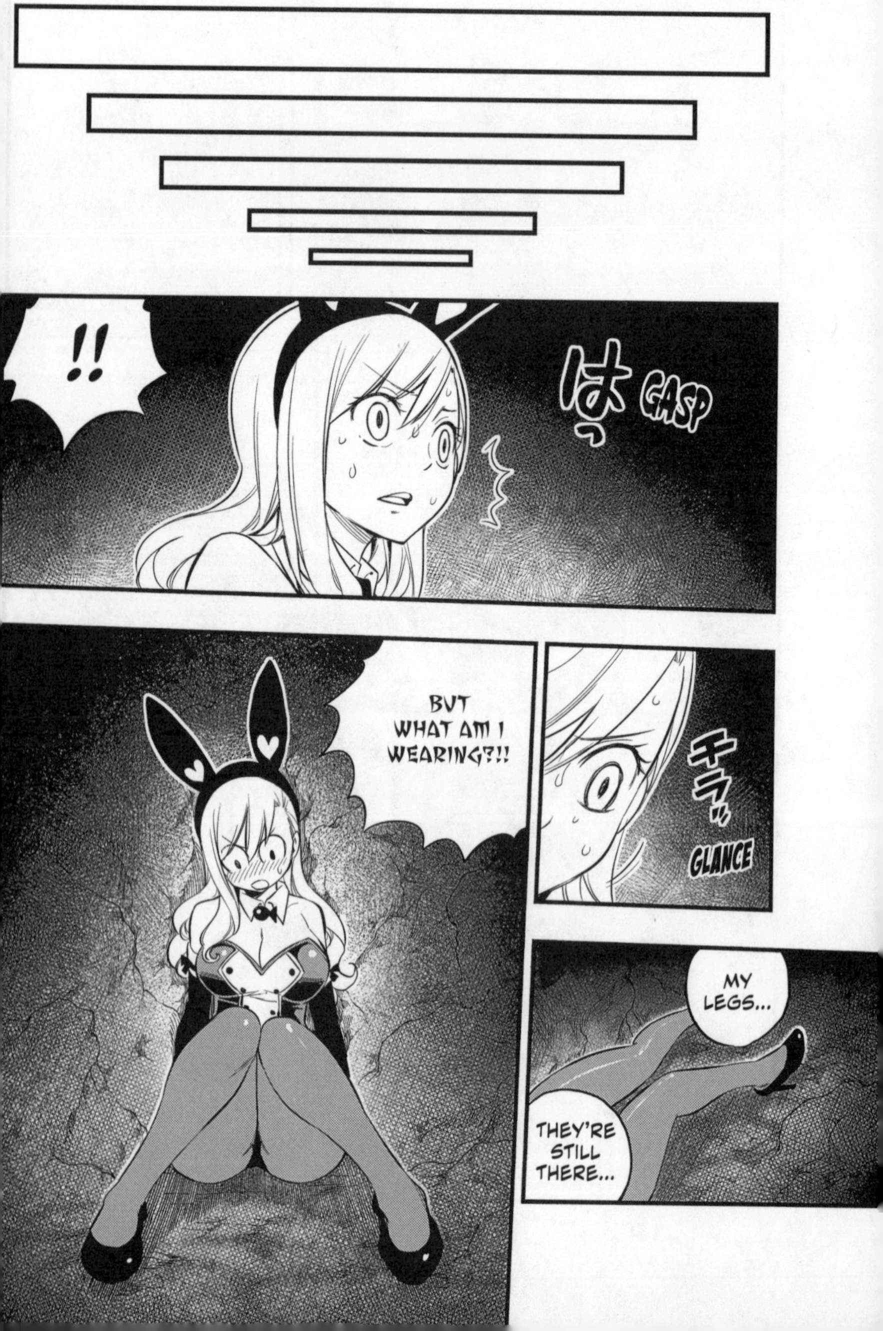
はっ GASP
!!
チラッ GLANCE
MY LEGS...
THEY'RE STILL THERE...
BUT WHAT AM I WEARING?!!

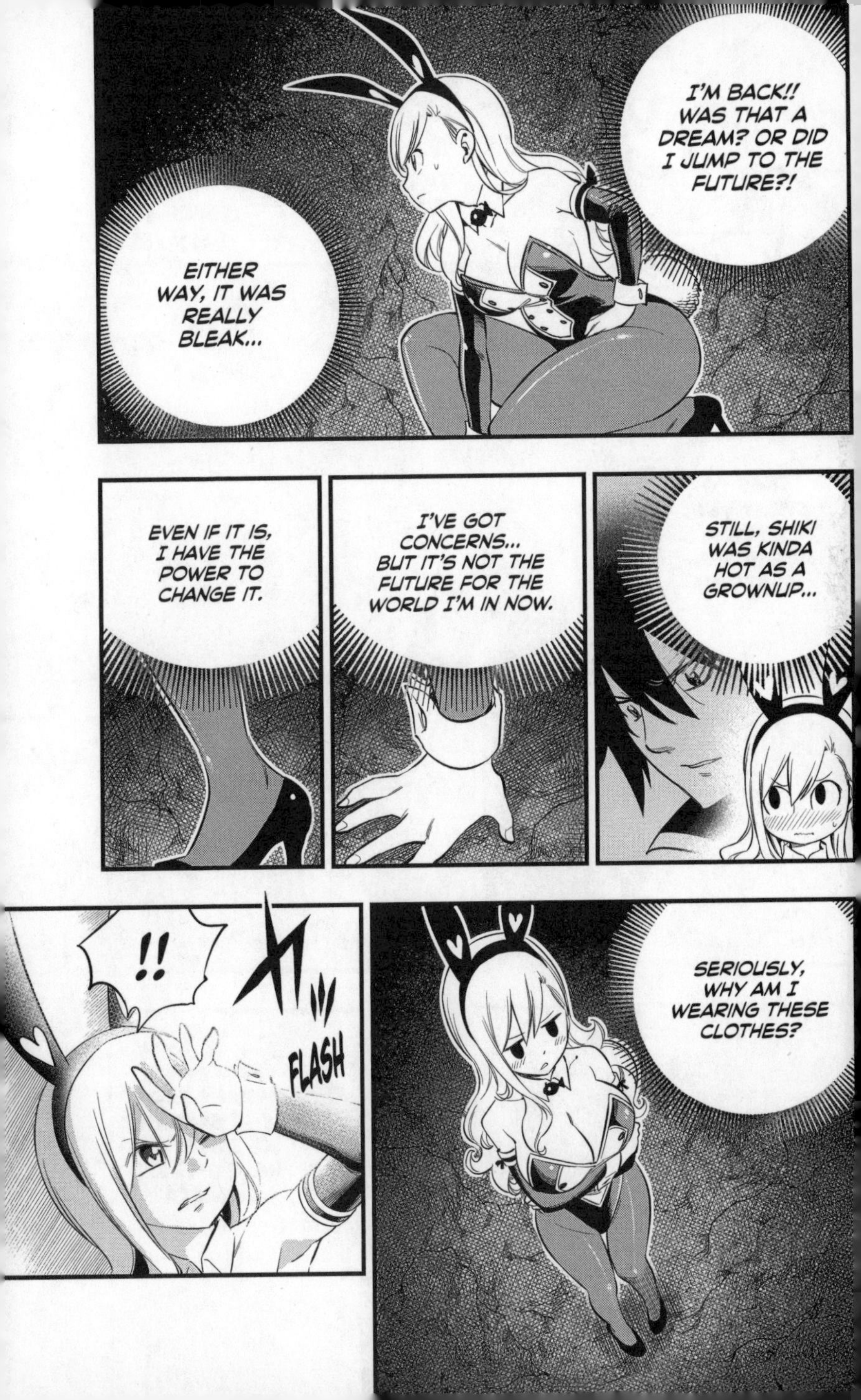
I'M BACK!! WAS THAT A DREAM? OR DID I JUMP TO THE FUTURE?!
EITHER WAY, IT WAS REALLY BLEAK...
STILL, SHIKI WAS KINDA HOT AS A GROWNUP...
I'VE GOT CONCERNS... BUT IT'S NOT THE FUTURE FOR THE WORLD I'M IN NOW.
EVEN IF IT IS, I HAVE THE POWER TO CHANGE IT.
SERIOUSLY, WHY AM I WEARING THESE CLOTHES?
!!
FLASH

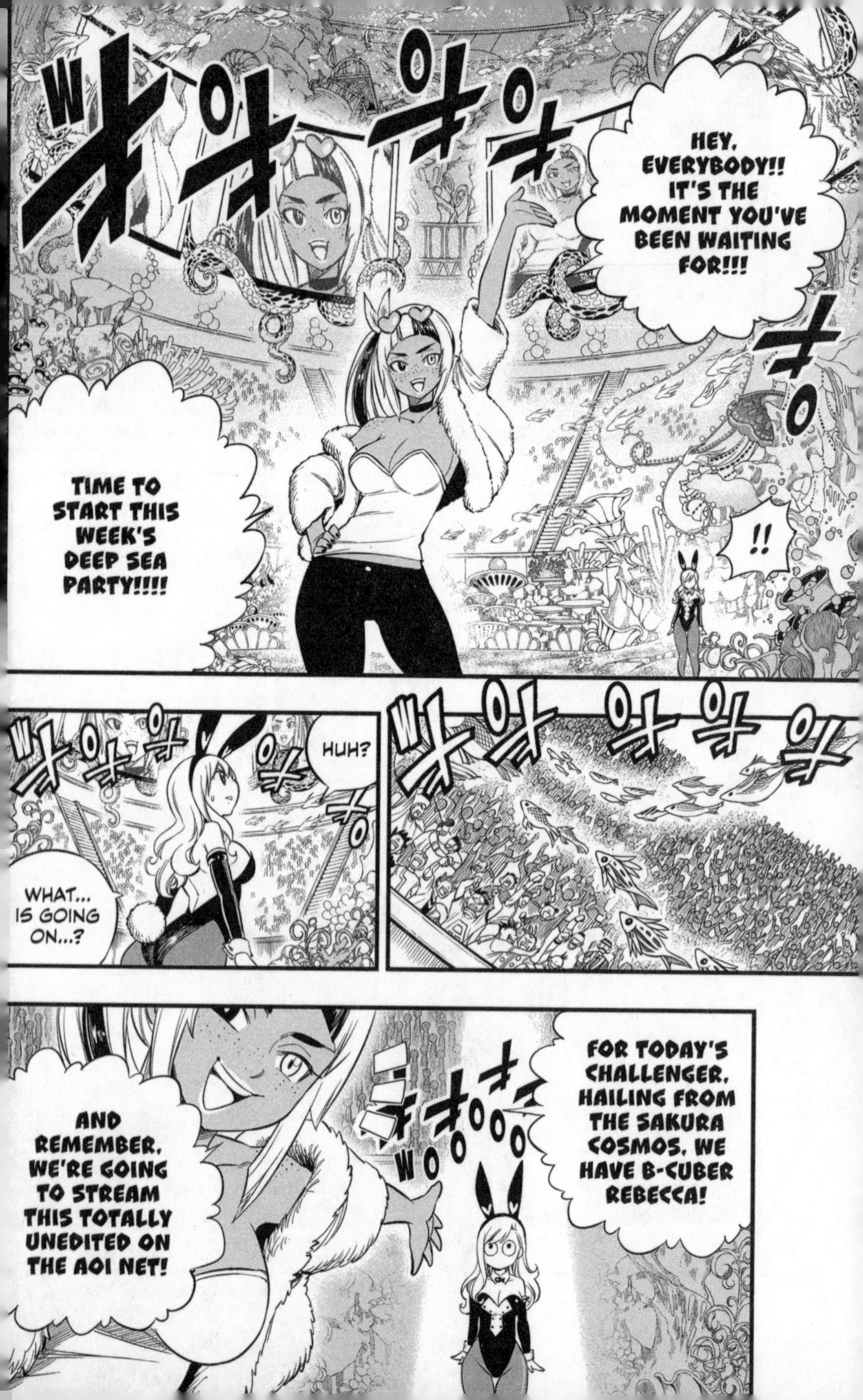
HEY, EVERYBODY!! IT'S THE MOMENT YOU'VE BEEN WAITING FOR!!!
TIME TO START THIS WEEK'S DEEP SEA PARTY!!!!
!!
HUH?
WHAT... IS GOING ON...?
FOR TODAY'S CHALLENGER, HAILING FROM THE SAKURA COSMOS, WE HAVE B-CUBER REBECCA!
AND REMEMBER, WE'RE GOING TO STREAM THIS TOTALLY UNEDITED ON THE AOI NET!

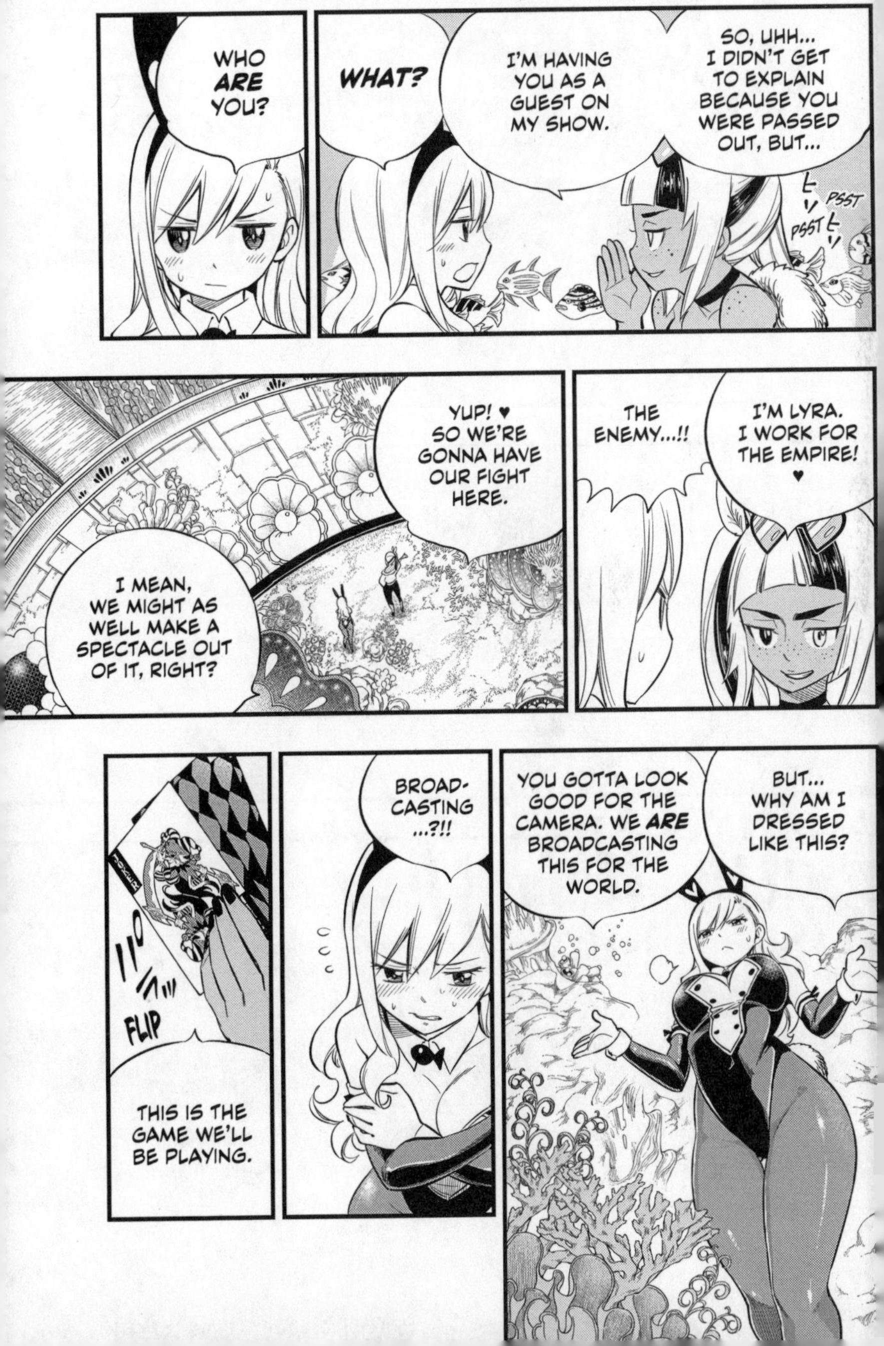
SO, UHH... I DIDN'T GET TO EXPLAIN BECAUSE YOU WERE PASSED OUT, BUT...
PSST PSST
I'M HAVING YOU AS A GUEST ON MY SHOW.
WHAT?
WHO ARE YOU?
I'M LYRA. I WORK FOR THE EMPIRE! ♥
THE ENEMY...!!
YUP! ♥ SO WE'RE GONNA HAVE OUR FIGHT HERE.
I MEAN, WE MIGHT AS WELL MAKE A SPECTACLE OUT OF IT, RIGHT?
BUT... WHY AM I DRESSED LIKE THIS?
YOU GOTTA LOOK GOOD FOR THE CAMERA. WE ARE BROADCASTING THIS FOR THE WORLD.
BROAD-CASTING ...?!!
FLIP
THIS IS THE GAME WE'LL BE PLAYING.

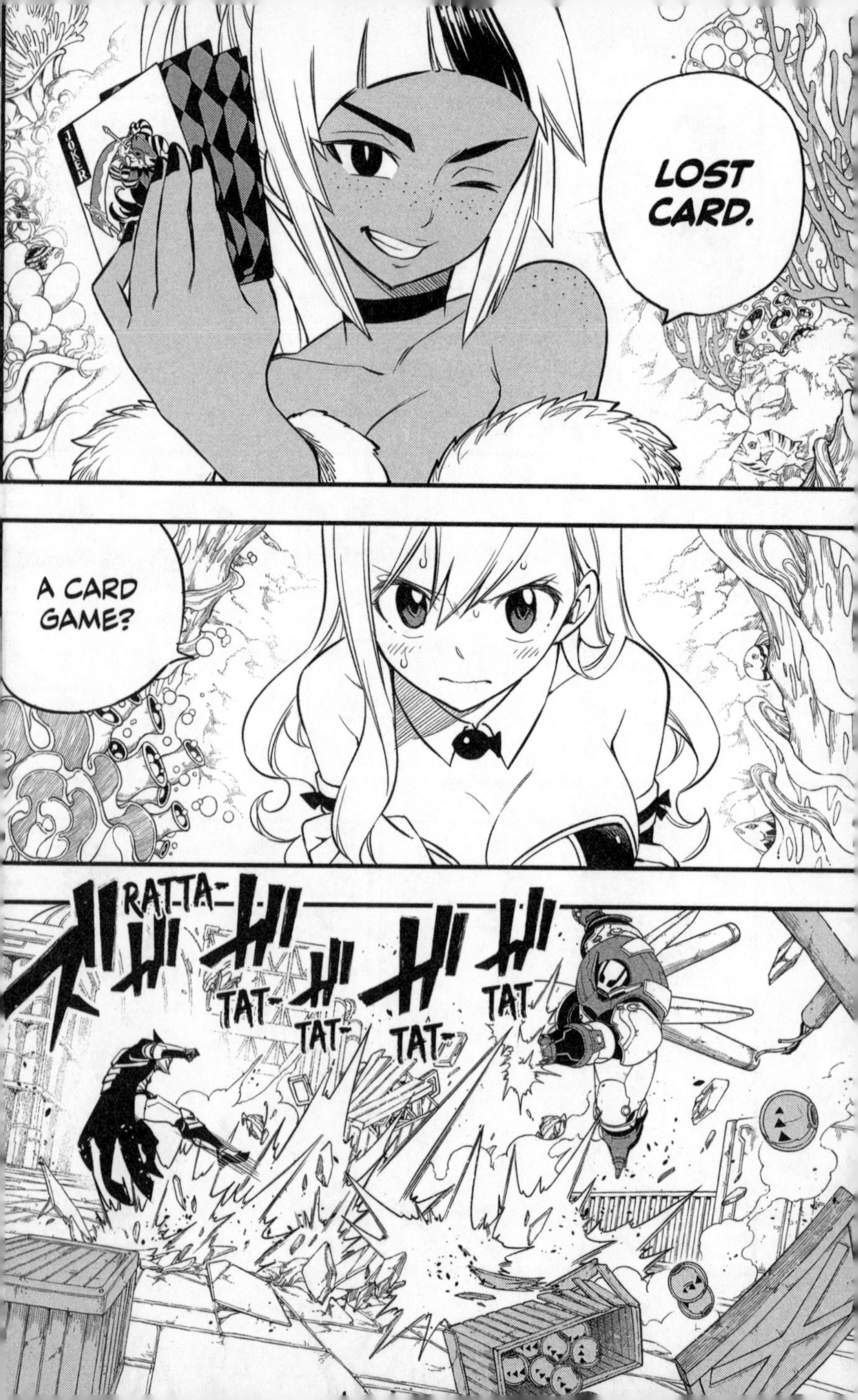
LOST CARD.
A CARD GAME?
RATTA-
TAT-
TAT-
TAT-
TAT

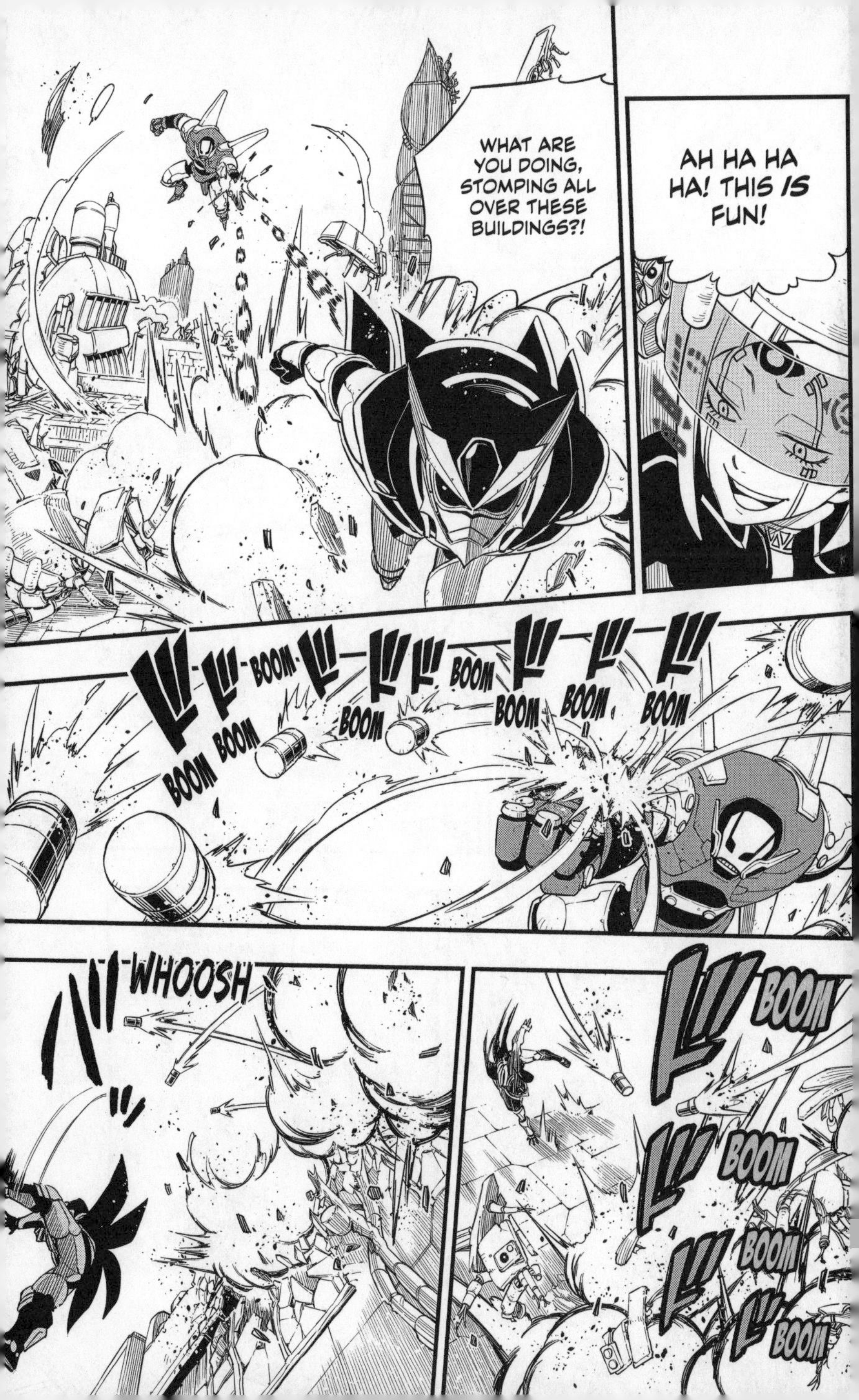
AH HA HA HA! THIS *IS* FUN!
WHAT ARE YOU DOING, STOMPING ALL OVER THESE BUILDINGS?!
BOOM
BOOM
BOOM
BOOM
BOOM
BOOM
BOOM
BOOM
BOOM
BOOM
BOOM
BOOM
BOOM
WHOOSH

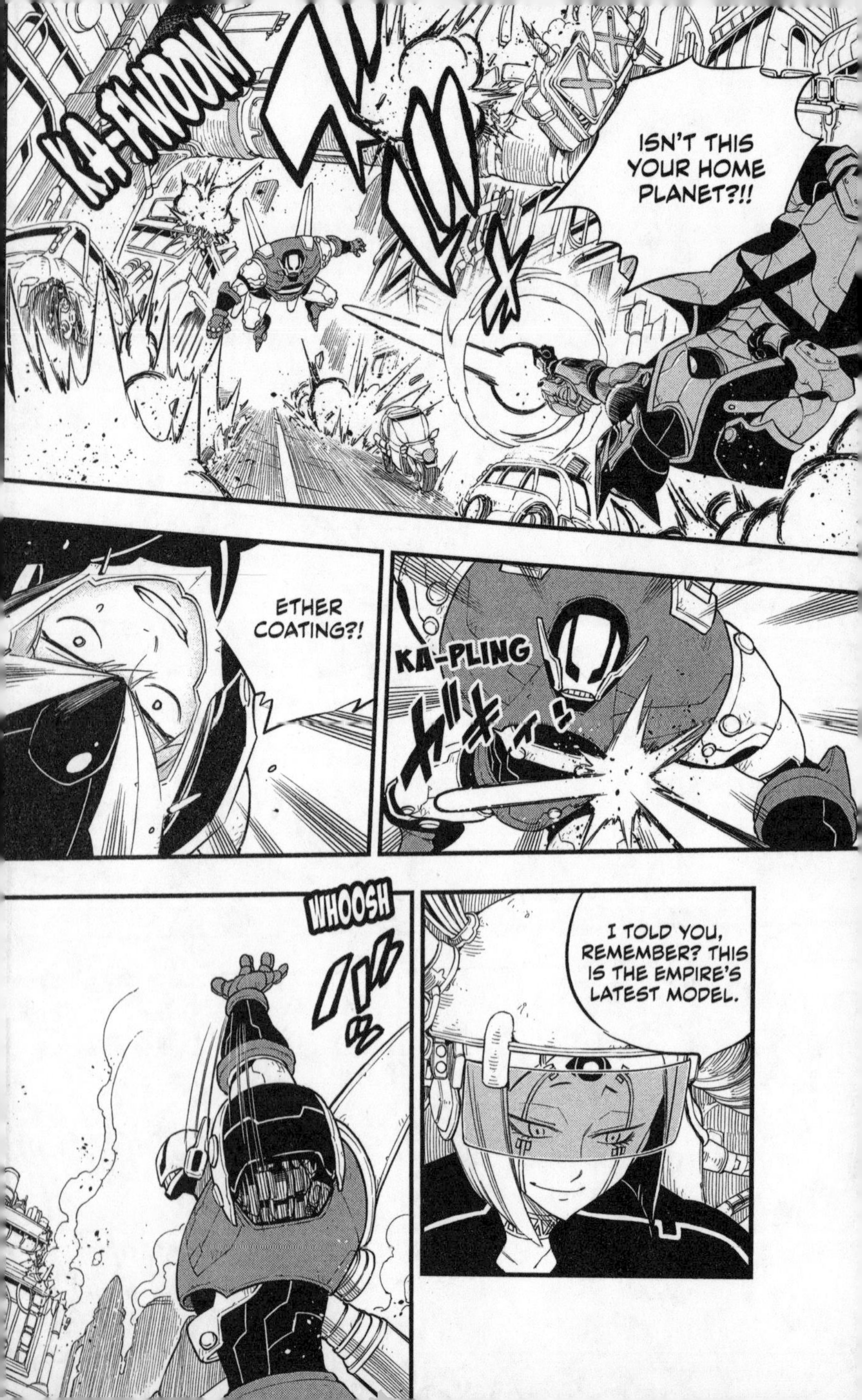
ISN'T THIS YOUR HOME PLANET?!!
KA-FWOOM
KA-PLING
ETHER COATING?!
I TOLD YOU, REMEMBER? THIS IS THE EMPIRE'S LATEST MODEL.
WHOOSH

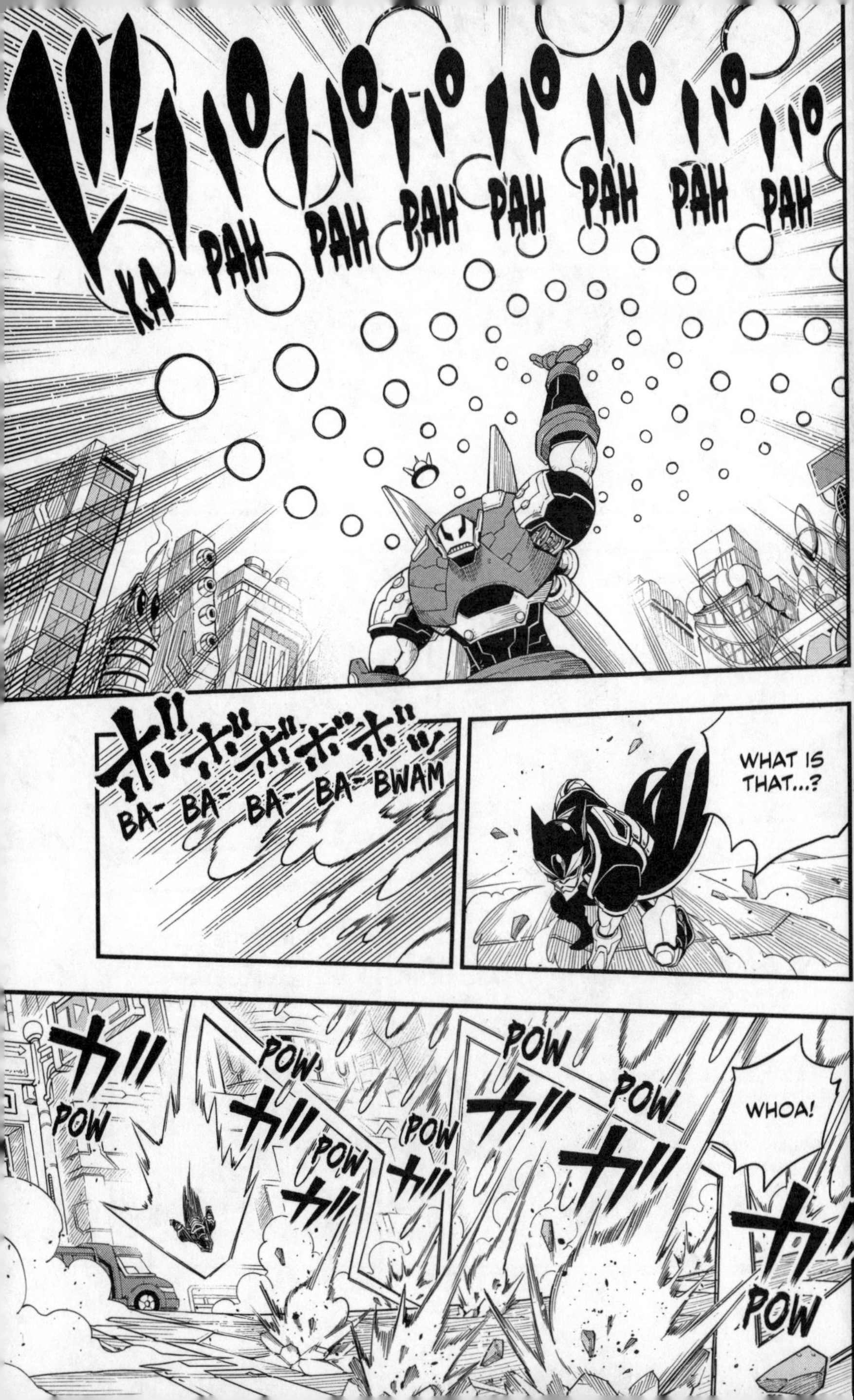
KA PAH PAH PAH PAH PAH PAH PAH
WHAT IS THAT...?
BA- BA- BA- BA- BWAM
WHOA!
POW POW POW POW POW POW POW

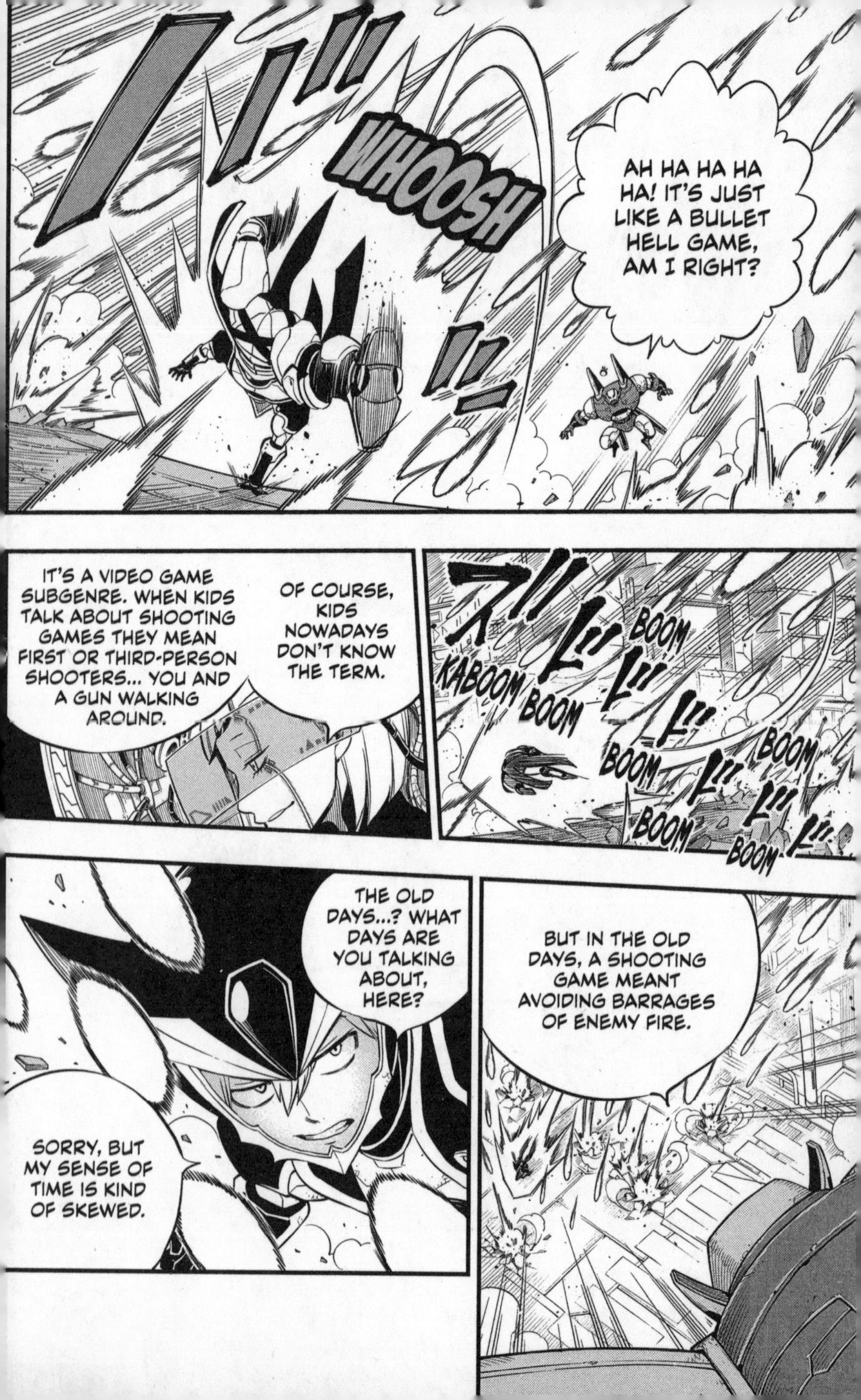
AH HA HA HA HA! IT'S JUST LIKE A BULLET HELL GAME, AM I RIGHT?
WHOOSH
BOOM
KABOOM
BOOM
BOOM
BOOM
BOOM
BOOM
OF COURSE, KIDS NOWADAYS DON'T KNOW THE TERM.
IT'S A VIDEO GAME SUBGENRE. WHEN KIDS TALK ABOUT SHOOTING GAMES THEY MEAN FIRST OR THIRD-PERSON SHOOTERS... YOU AND A GUN WALKING AROUND.
BUT IN THE OLD DAYS, A SHOOTING GAME MEANT AVOIDING BARRAGES OF ENEMY FIRE.
THE OLD DAYS...? WHAT DAYS ARE YOU TALKING ABOUT, HERE?
SORRY, BUT MY SENSE OF TIME IS KIND OF SKEWED.

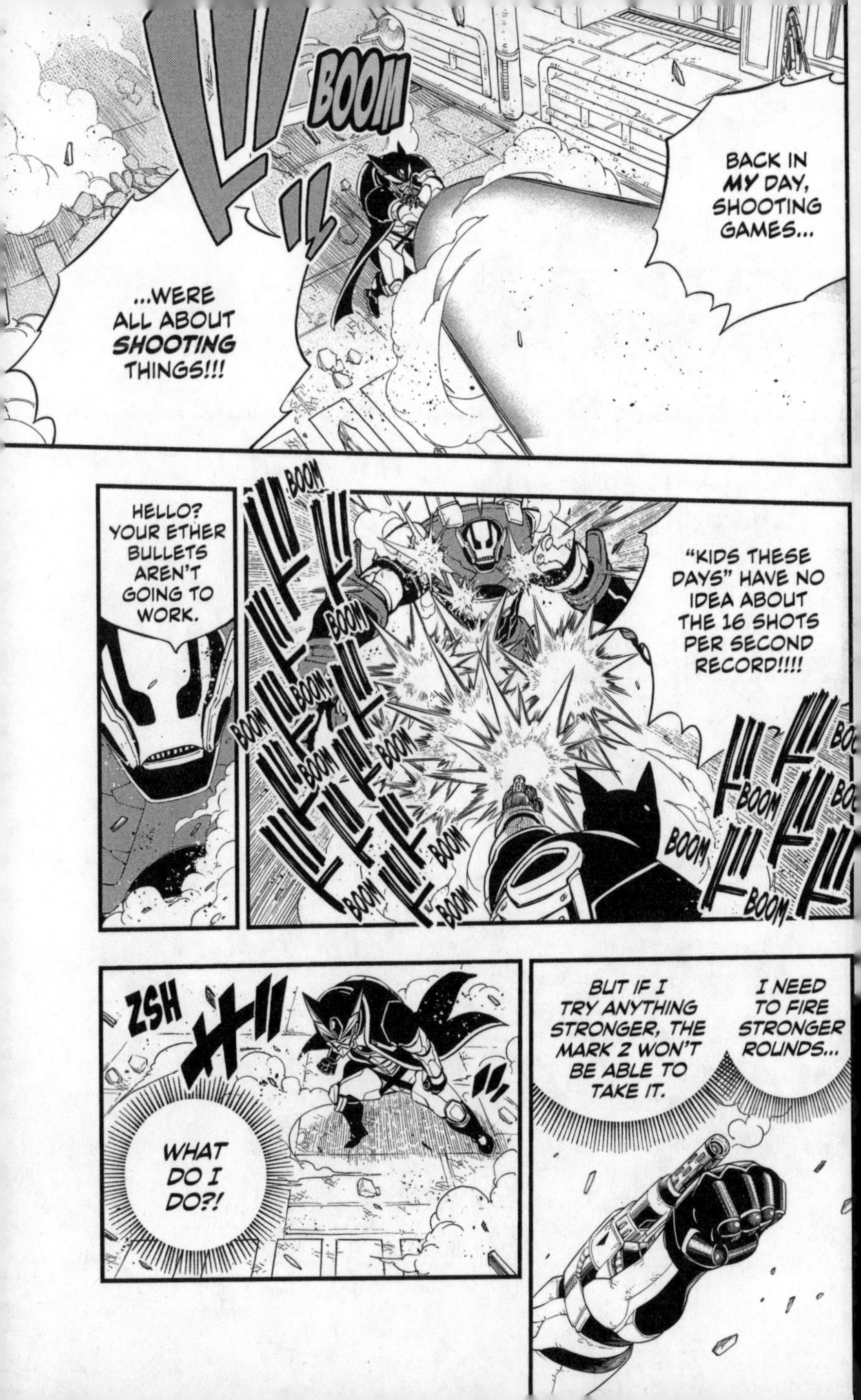

BOOM
BACK IN MY DAY, SHOOTING GAMES...
...WERE ALL ABOUT SHOOTING THINGS!!!
BOOM
"KIDS THESE DAYS" HAVE NO IDEA ABOUT THE 16 SHOTS PER SECOND RECORD!!!!
BOOM
BOOM
BOOM
BOOM
BOOM
BOOM
BOOM
BOOM
BOOM
BOOM
BOOM
HELLO? YOUR ETHER BULLETS AREN'T GOING TO WORK.
I NEED TO FIRE STRONGER ROUNDS...
BUT IF I TRY ANYTHING STRONGER, THE MARK 2 WON'T BE ABLE TO TAKE IT.
ZSH
WHAT DO I DO?!

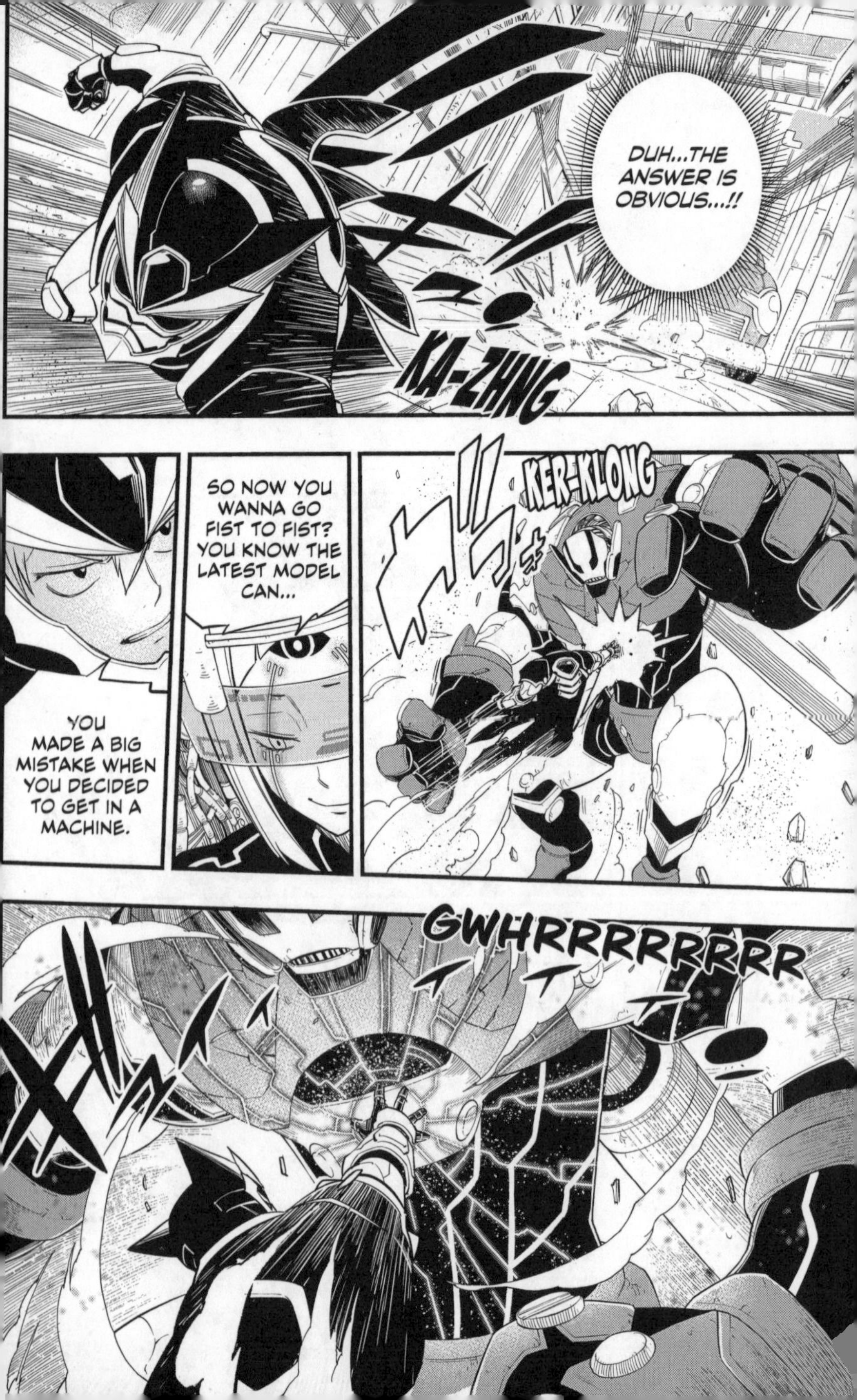
DUH...THE ANSWER IS OBVIOUS...!!
KA-ZHNG
KER-KLONG
SO NOW YOU WANNA GO FIST TO FIST? YOU KNOW THE LATEST MODEL CAN...
YOU MADE A BIG MISTAKE WHEN YOU DECIDED TO GET IN A MACHINE.
GWHRRRRRRRRR

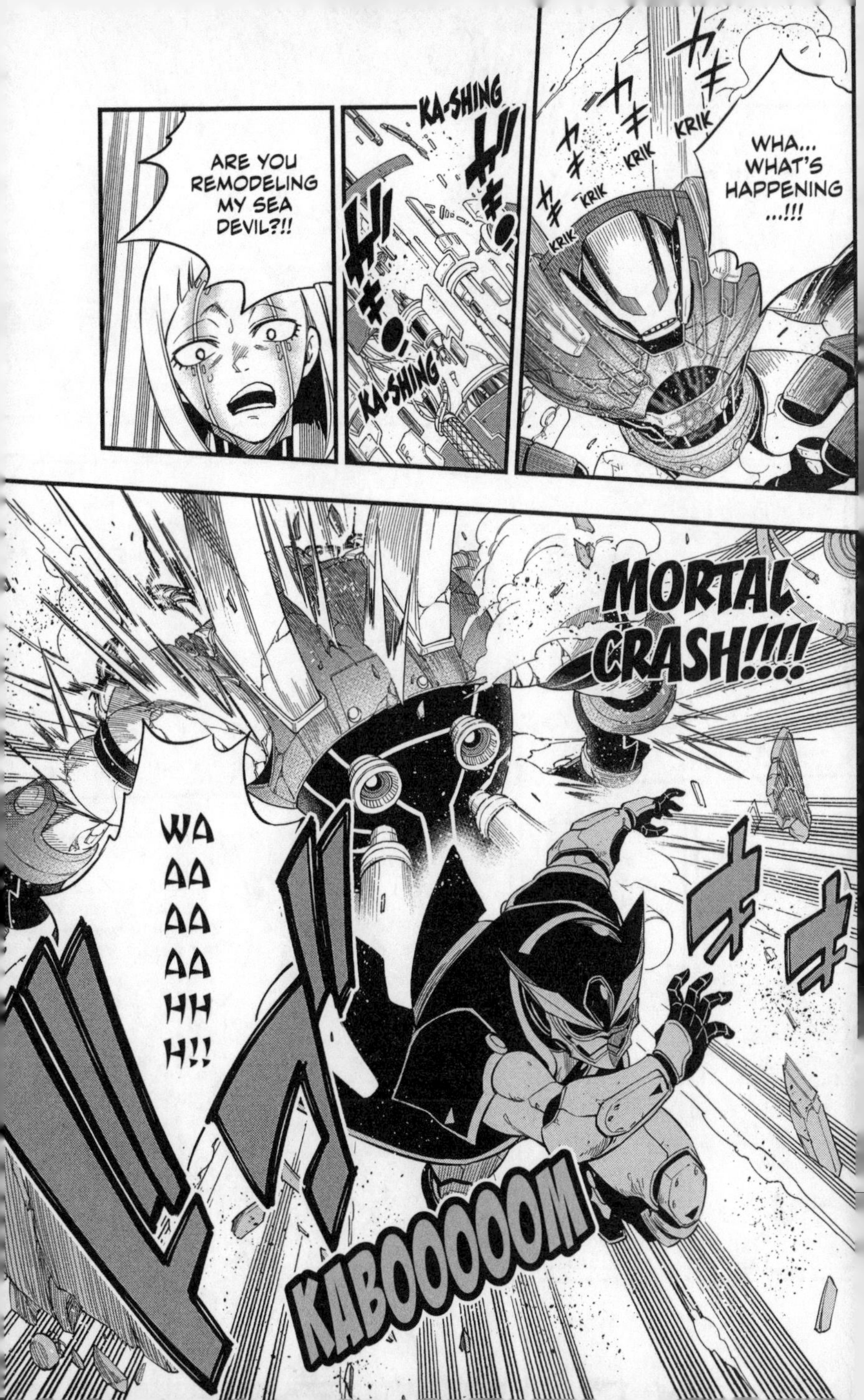
KRIK
KRIK
KRIK
KRIK
WHA... WHAT'S HAPPENING ...!!!
KA-SHING
KA-SHING
ARE YOU REMODELING MY SEA DEVIL?!!
MORTAL CRASH!!!!
WAAAAAAAAHHH!!
KABOOOOOM

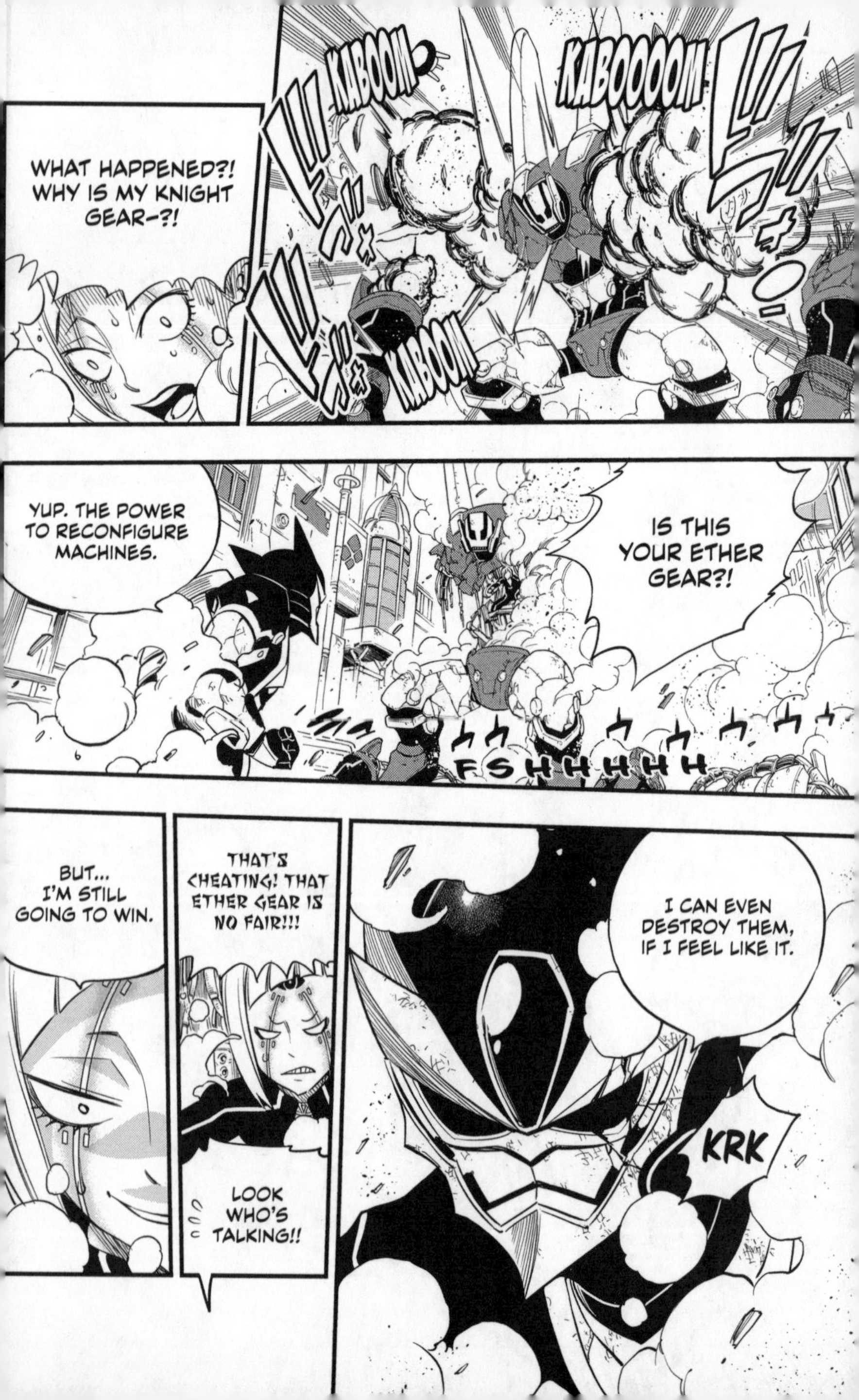
KABOOOOM
KABOOM
KABOOM
WHAT HAPPENED?! WHY IS MY KNIGHT GEAR-?!
IS THIS YOUR ETHER GEAR?!
YUP. THE POWER TO RECONFIGURE MACHINES.
FSHHHHHH
I CAN EVEN DESTROY THEM, IF I FEEL LIKE IT.
KRK
THAT'S CHEATING! THAT ETHER GEAR IS NO FAIR!!!
LOOK WHO'S TALKING!!
BUT... I'M STILL GOING TO WIN.

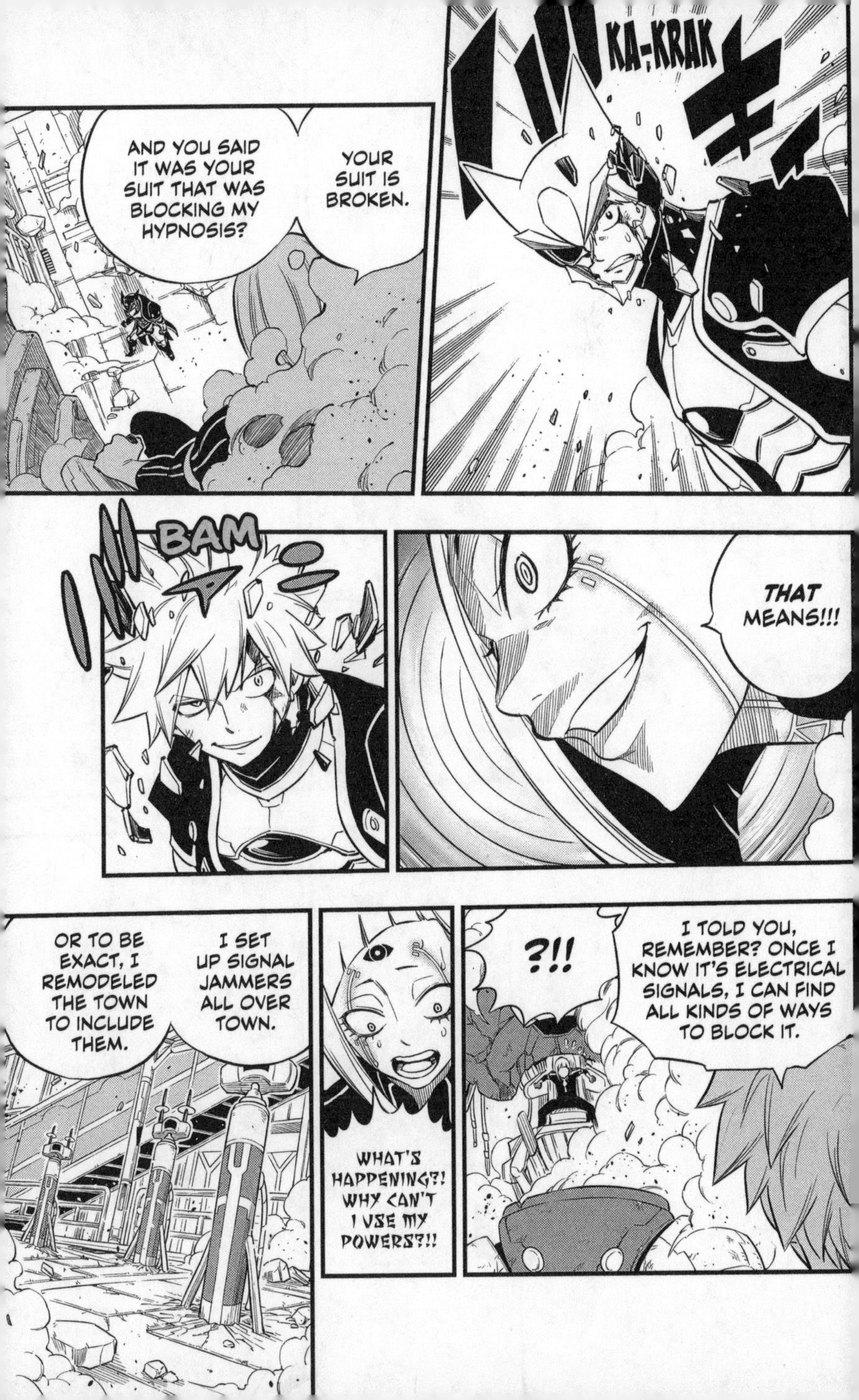
KA-KRAK
YOUR SUIT IS BROKEN.
AND YOU SAID IT WAS YOUR SUIT THAT WAS BLOCKING MY HYPNOSIS?
THAT MEANS!!!
BAM
?!!
I TOLD YOU, REMEMBER? ONCE I KNOW IT'S ELECTRICAL SIGNALS, I CAN FIND ALL KINDS OF WAYS TO BLOCK IT.
WHAT'S HAPPENING?! WHY CAN'T I USE MY POWERS?!!
I SET UP SIGNAL JAMMERS ALL OVER TOWN.
OR TO BE EXACT, I REMODELED THE TOWN TO INCLUDE THEM.

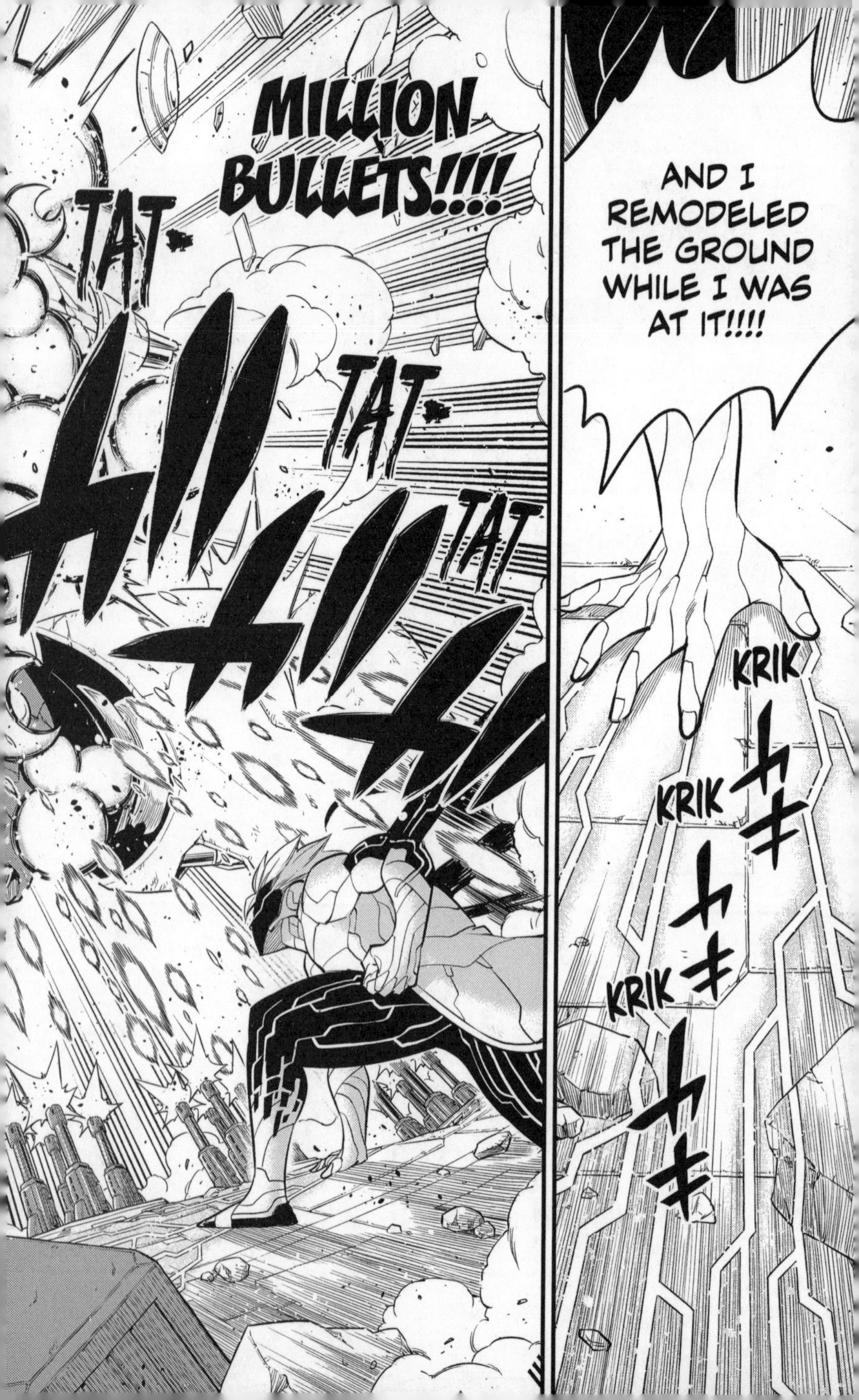
AND I REMODELED THE GROUND WHILE I WAS AT IT!!!!
KRIK
KRIK
KRIK
MILLION BULLETS!!!!
TAT
TAT
TAT

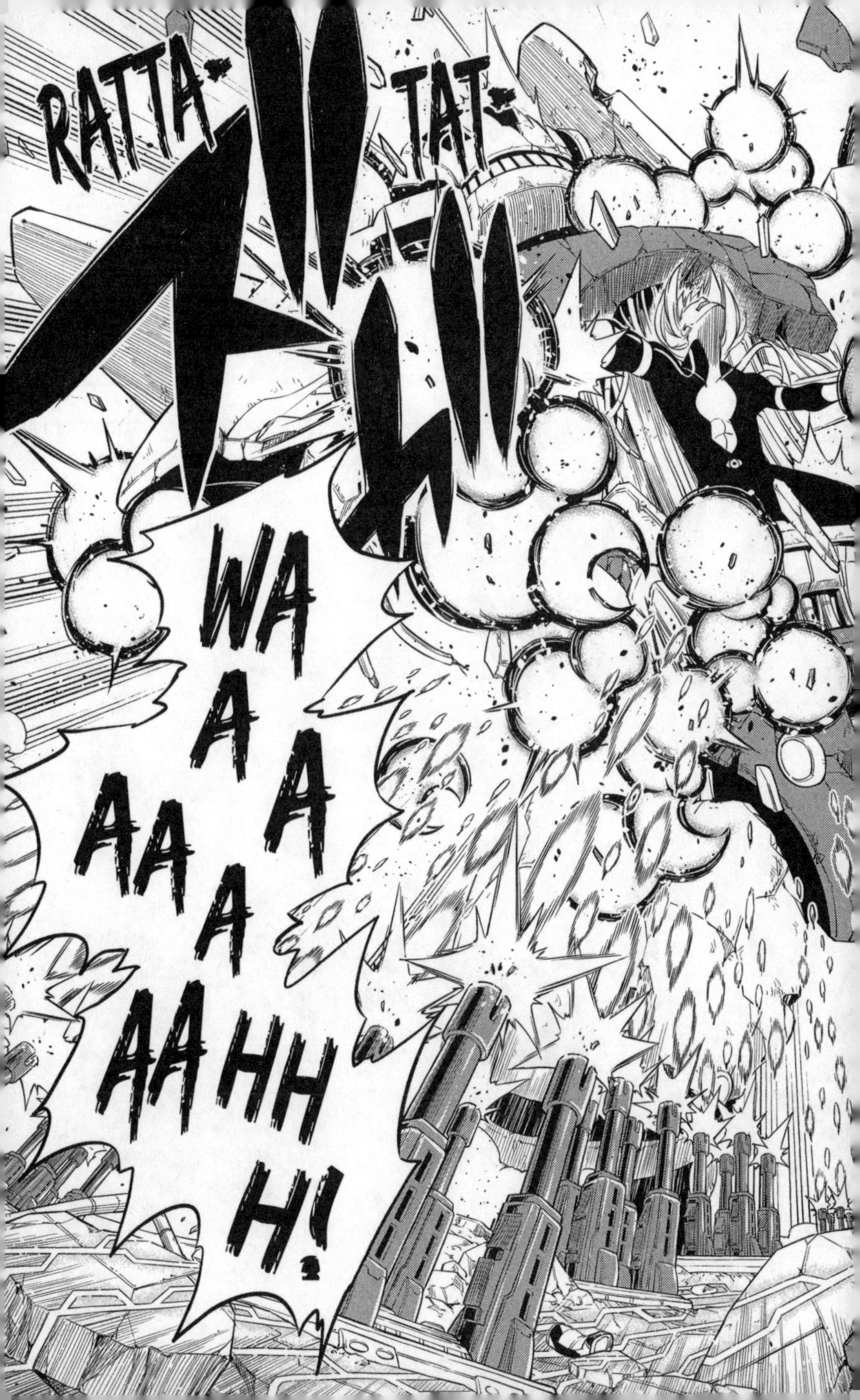
RATTA-TAT-
WAAAAAAAAHHH!

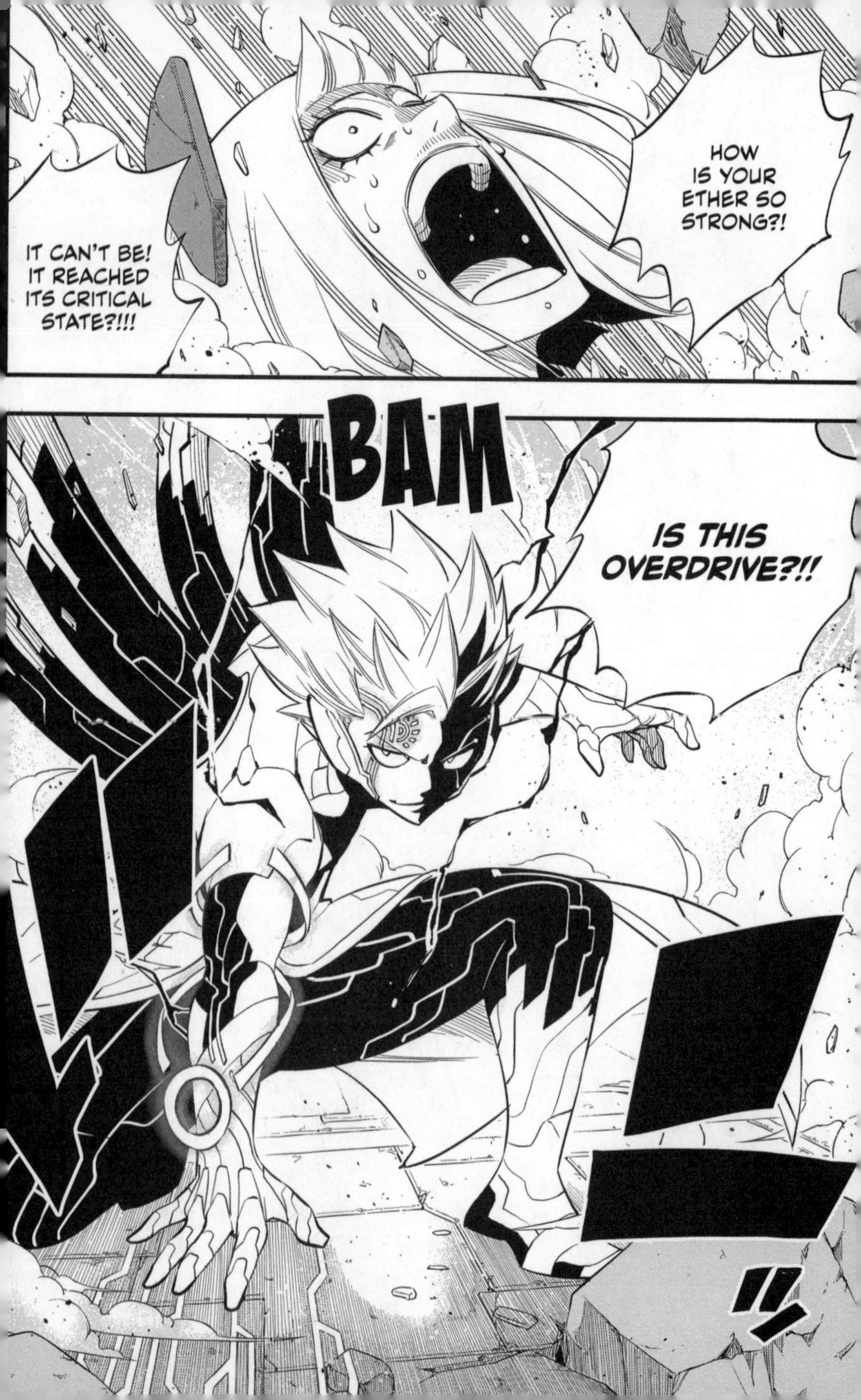
HOW IS YOUR ETHER SO STRONG?!
IT CAN'T BE! IT REACHED ITS CRITICAL STATE?!!!
BAM
IS THIS OVERDRIVE?!!

EDENS ZERO

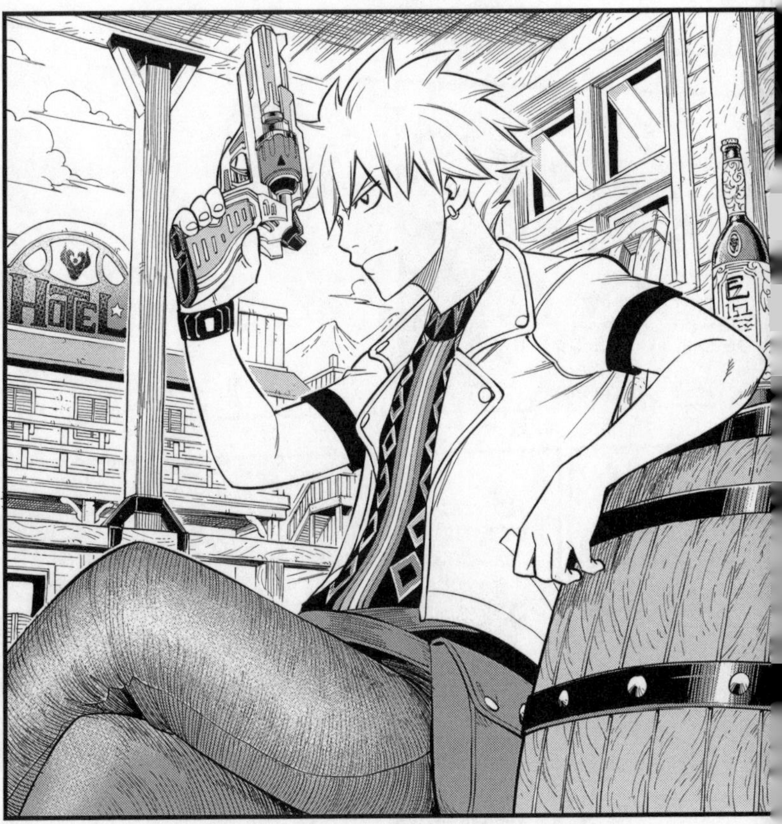
HOTEL

CHAPTER 151: HANDPRINTS

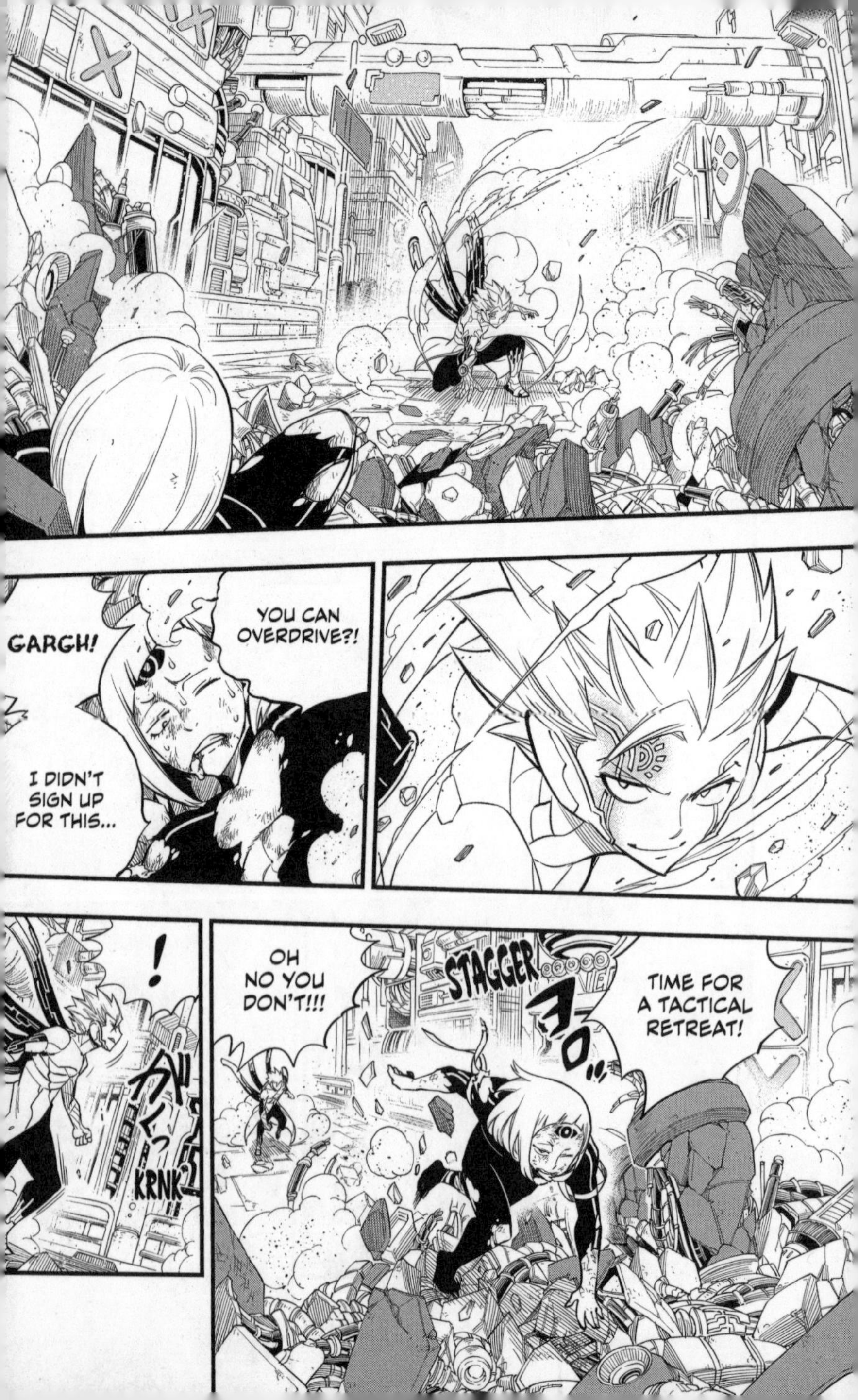
YOU CAN OVERDRIVE?!
GARGH!
I DIDN'T SIGN UP FOR THIS...
TIME FOR A TACTICAL RETREAT!
STAGGER
OH NO YOU DON'T!!!
!
KRNK

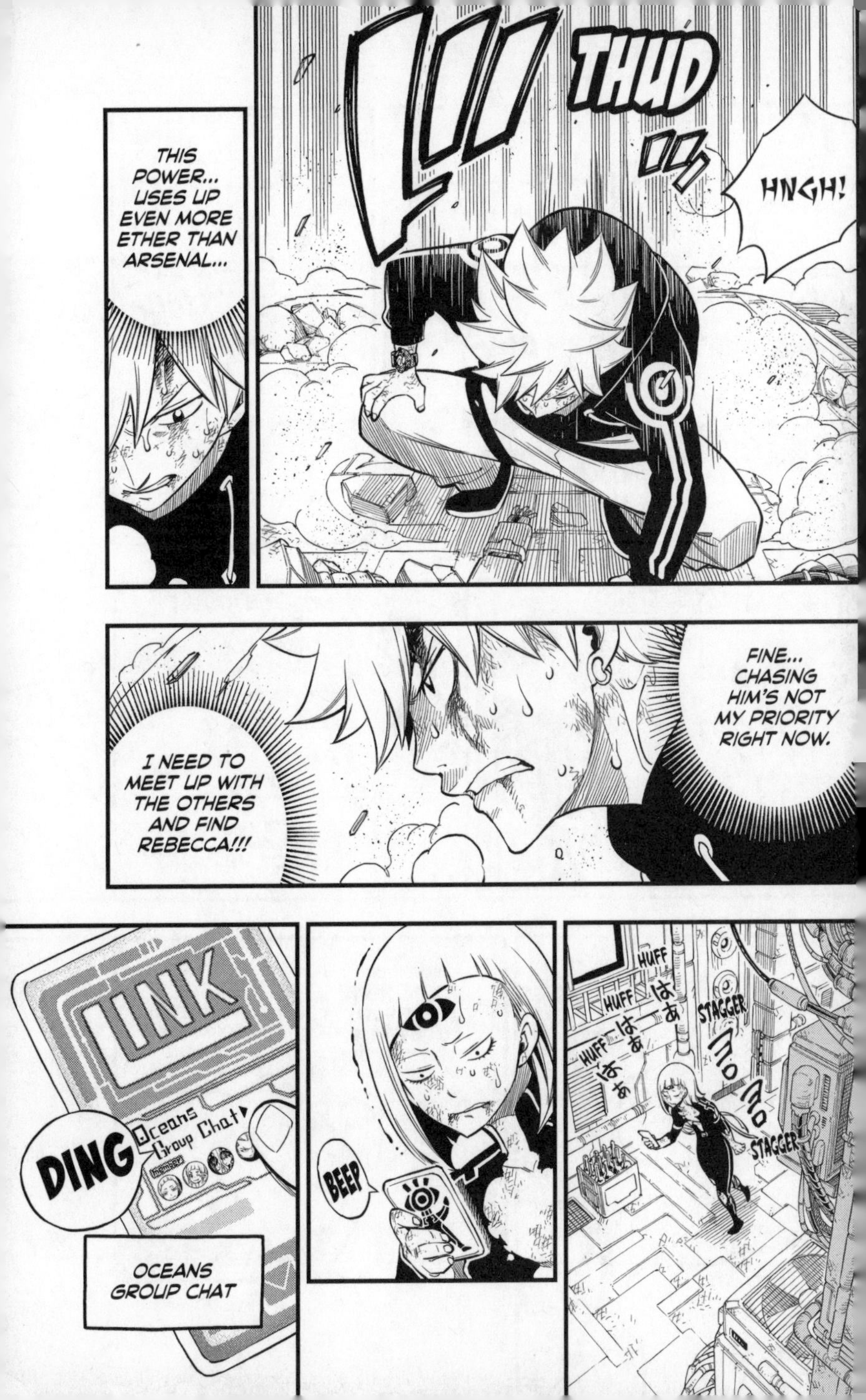
THUD
HNGH!
THIS POWER... USES UP EVEN MORE ETHER THAN ARSENAL...
FINE... CHASING HIM'S NOT MY PRIORITY RIGHT NOW.
I NEED TO MEET UP WITH THE OTHERS AND FIND REBECCA!!!
HUFF
HUFF
HUFF
はあ
はあ
はあ
STAGGER
STAGGER
BEEP
LINK
Oceans Group Chat
DING
OCEANS GROUP CHAT

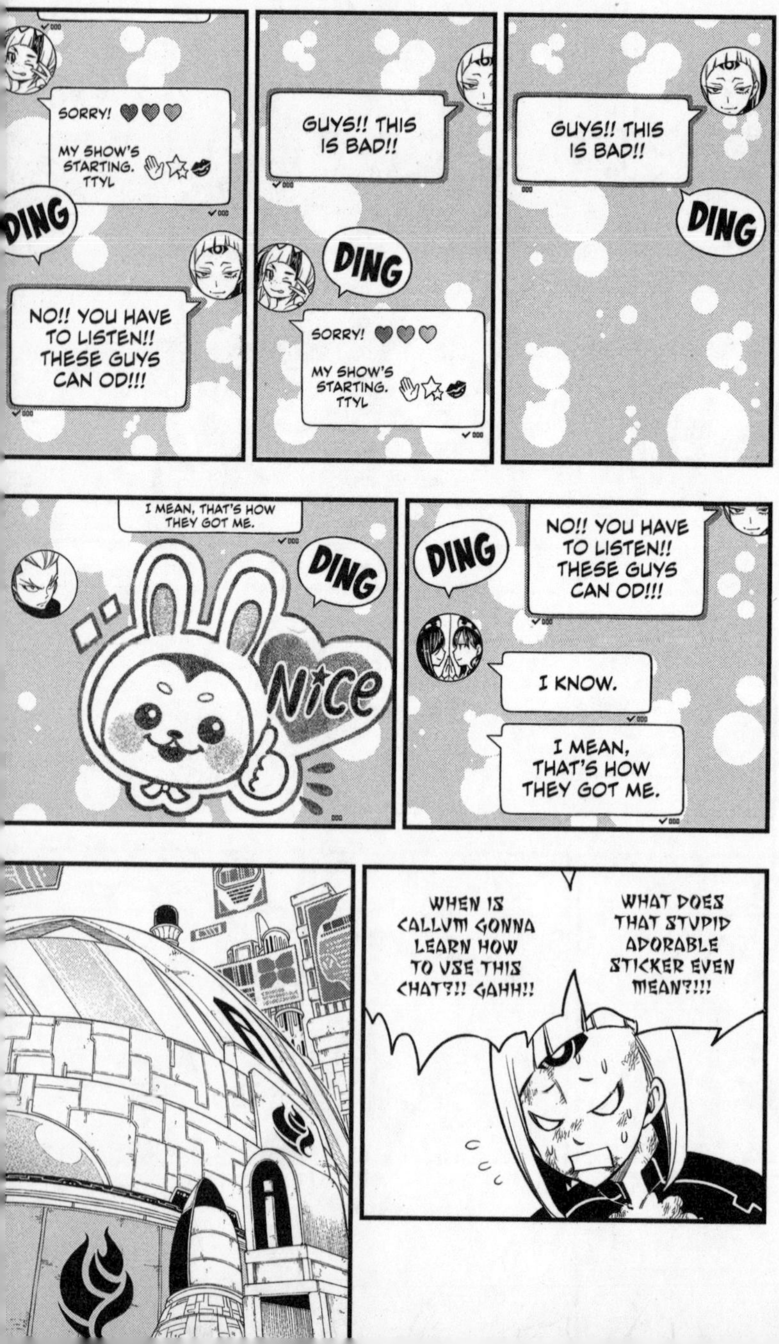
GUYS!! THIS IS BAD!!
DING
GUYS!! THIS IS BAD!!
DING
SORRY!
MY SHOW'S STARTING. TTYL
SORRY!
MY SHOW'S STARTING. TTYL
DING
NO!! YOU HAVE TO LISTEN!! THESE GUYS CAN OD!!!
DING
NO!! YOU HAVE TO LISTEN!! THESE GUYS CAN OD!!!
I KNOW.
I MEAN, THAT'S HOW THEY GOT ME.
I MEAN, THAT'S HOW THEY GOT ME.
DING
Nice
WHAT DOES THAT STUPID ADORABLE STICKER EVEN MEAN?!!!
WHEN IS CALLUM GONNA LEARN HOW TO USE THIS CHAT?!! GAHH!!

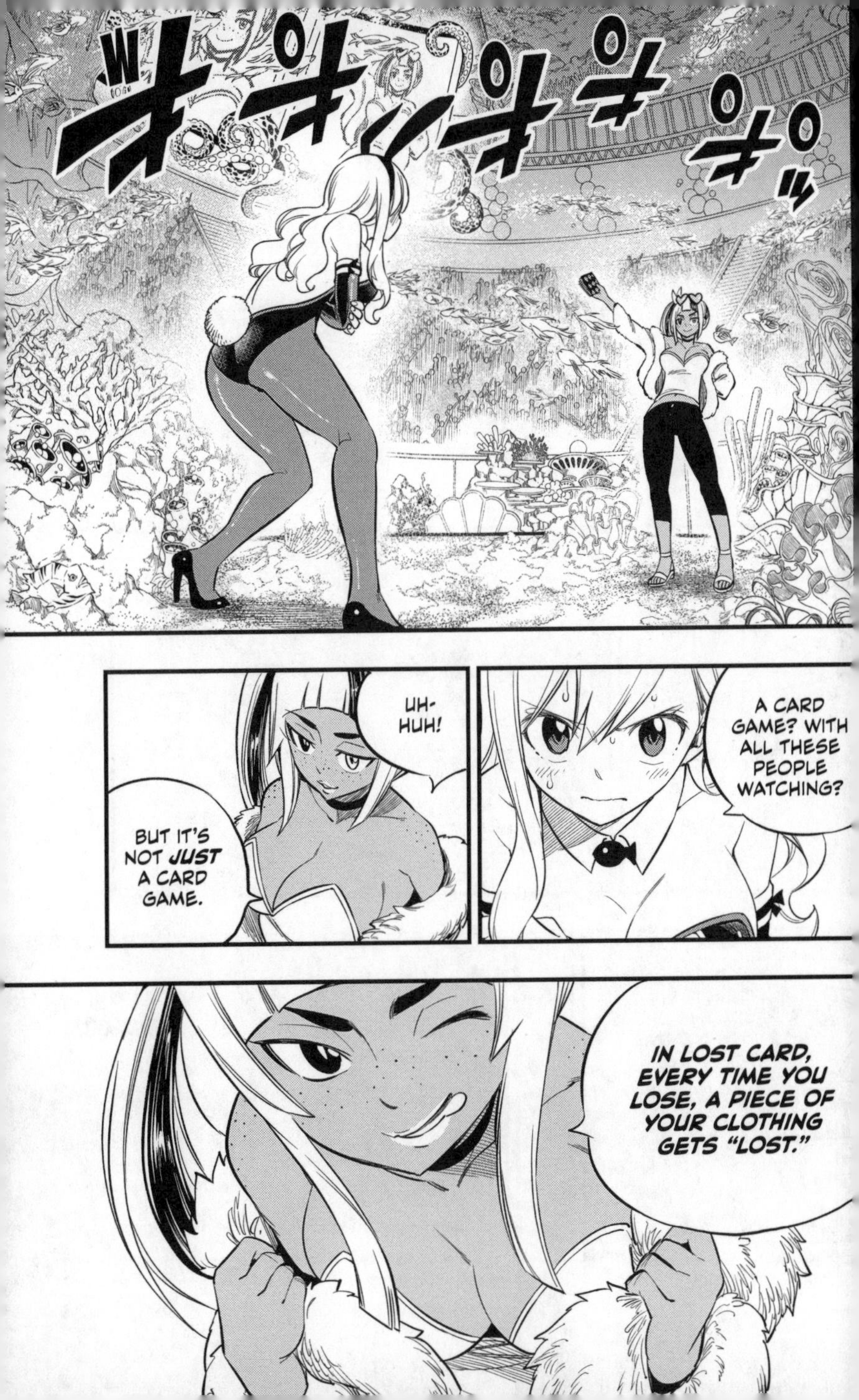
A CARD GAME? WITH ALL THESE PEOPLE WATCHING?
UH-HUH!
BUT IT'S NOT *JUST* A CARD GAME.
IN LOST CARD, EVERY TIME YOU LOSE, A PIECE OF YOUR CLOTHING GETS "LOST."

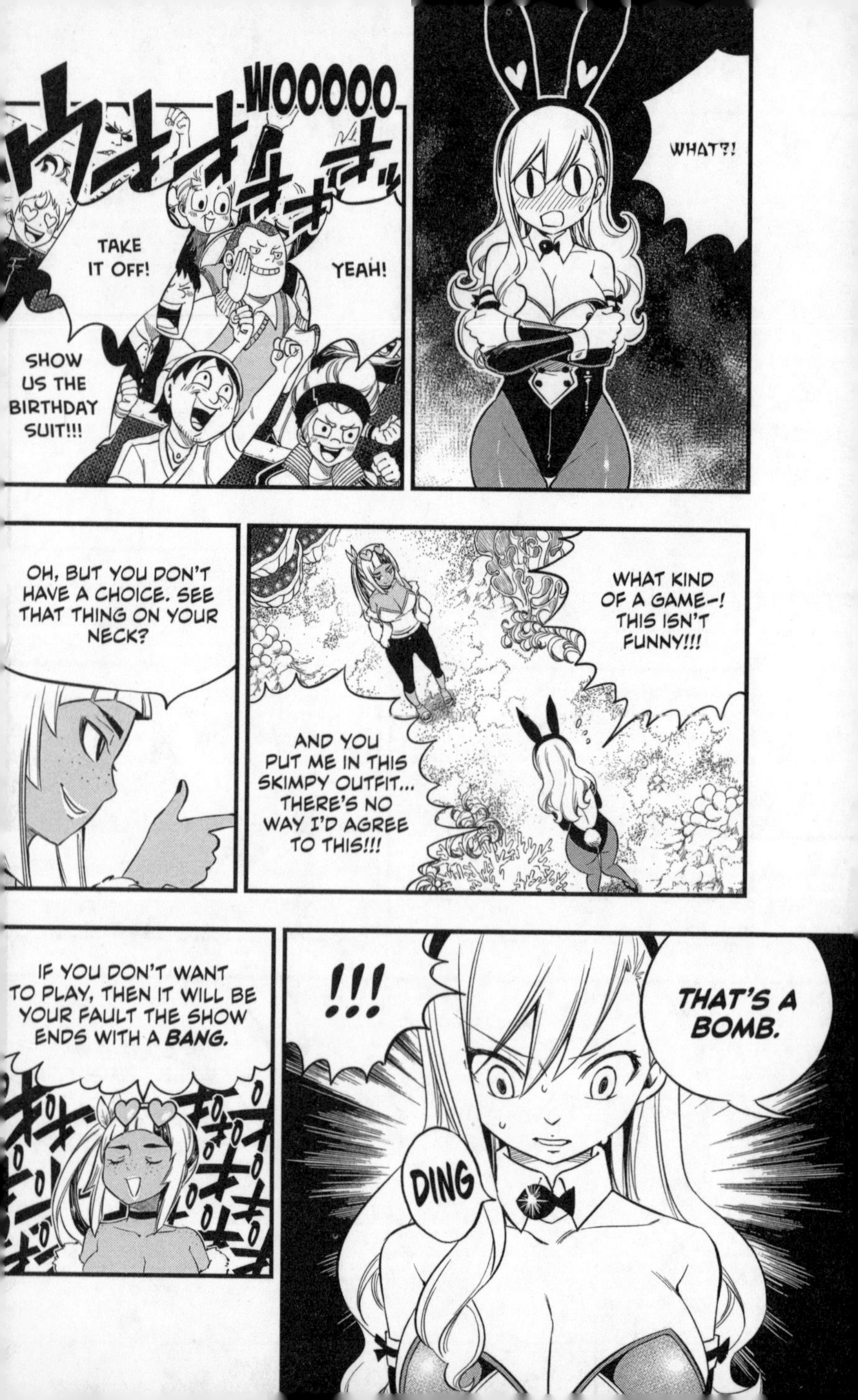
WHAT?!
WOOOOO
YEAH!
TAKE IT OFF!
SHOW US THE BIRTHDAY SUIT!!!
WHAT KIND OF A GAME—! THIS ISN'T FUNNY!!!
AND YOU PUT ME IN THIS SKIMPY OUTFIT... THERE'S NO WAY I'D AGREE TO THIS!!!
OH, BUT YOU DON'T HAVE A CHOICE. SEE THAT THING ON YOUR NECK?
THAT'S A BOMB.
!!!
DING
IF YOU DON'T WANT TO PLAY, THEN IT WILL BE YOUR FAULT THE SHOW ENDS WITH A *BANG.*

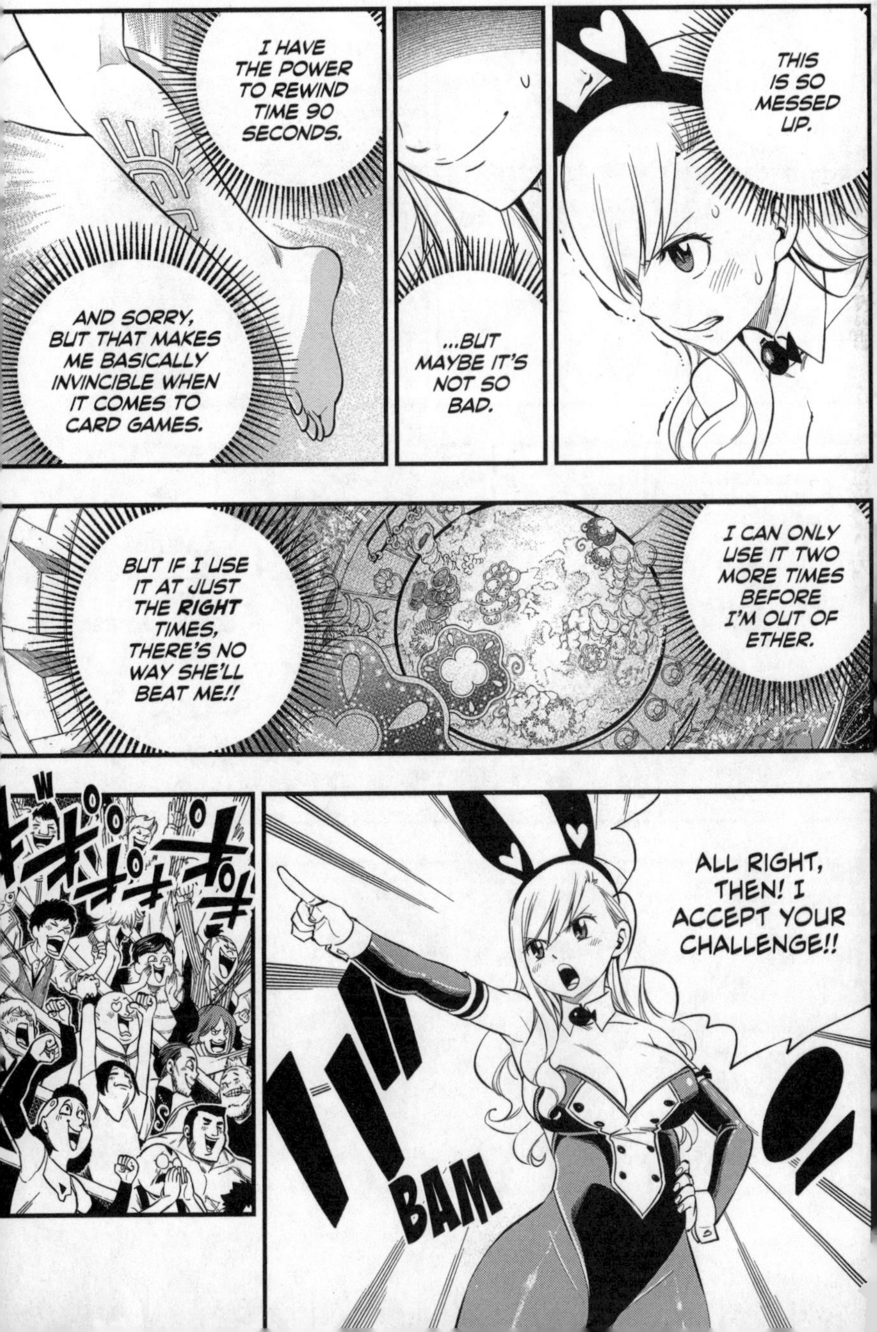
THIS IS SO MESSED UP.
...BUT MAYBE IT'S NOT SO BAD.
I HAVE THE POWER TO REWIND TIME 90 SECONDS.
AND SORRY, BUT THAT MAKES ME BASICALLY INVINCIBLE WHEN IT COMES TO CARD GAMES.
I CAN ONLY USE IT TWO MORE TIMES BEFORE I'M OUT OF ETHER.
BUT IF I USE IT AT JUST THE **RIGHT** TIMES, THERE'S NO WAY SHE'LL BEAT ME!!
ALL RIGHT, THEN! I ACCEPT YOUR CHALLENGE!!
BAM
WOOO

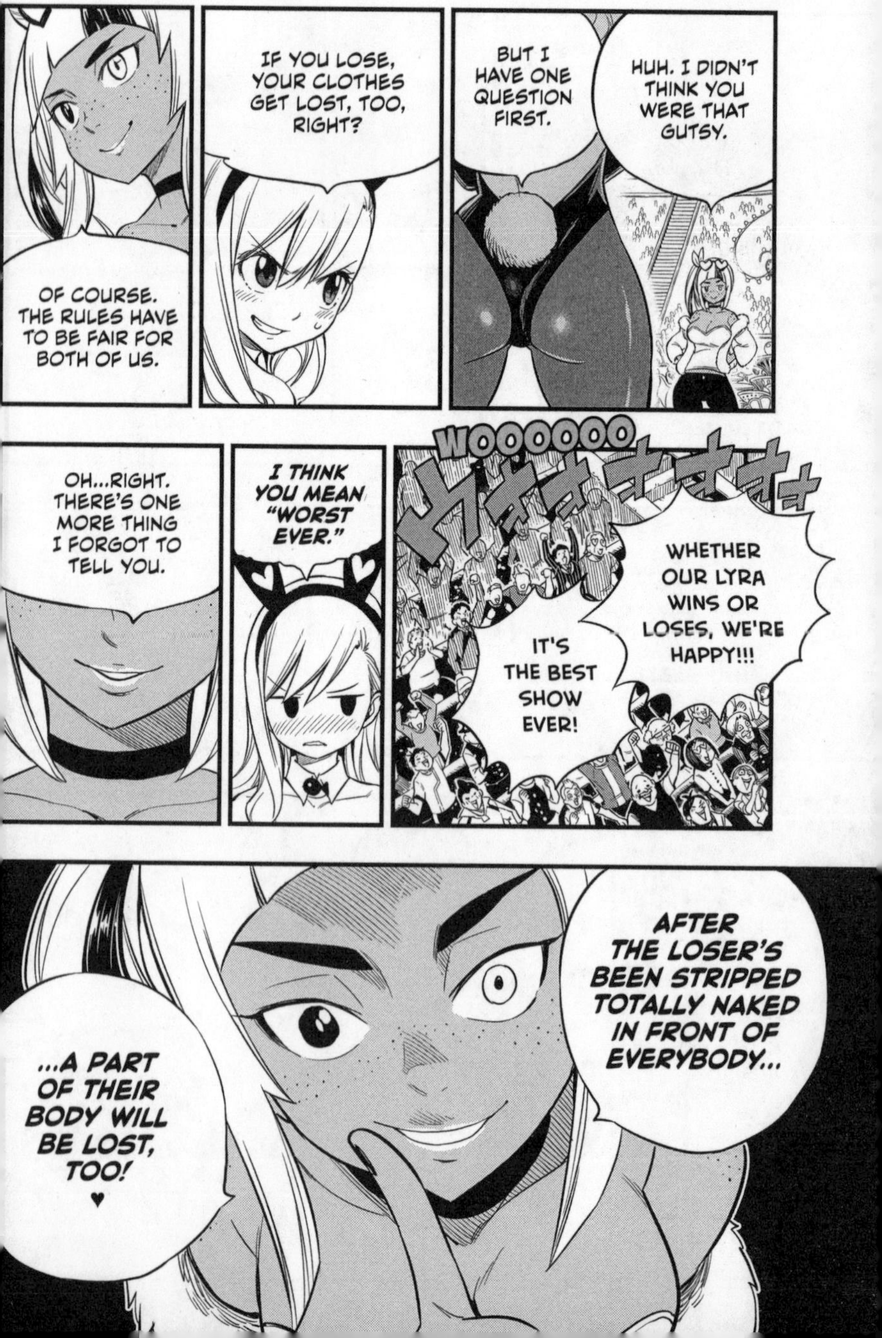
HUH. I DIDN'T THINK YOU WERE THAT GUTSY.
BUT I HAVE ONE QUESTION FIRST.
IF YOU LOSE, YOUR CLOTHES GET LOST, TOO, RIGHT?
OF COURSE. THE RULES HAVE TO BE FAIR FOR BOTH OF US.
WOOOOOO
WHETHER OUR LYRA WINS OR LOSES, WE'RE HAPPY!!!
IT'S THE BEST SHOW EVER!
I THINK YOU MEAN "WORST EVER."
OH...RIGHT. THERE'S ONE MORE THING I FORGOT TO TELL YOU.
AFTER THE LOSER'S BEEN STRIPPED TOTALLY NAKED IN FRONT OF EVERYBODY...
...A PART OF THEIR BODY WILL BE LOST, TOO! ♥

CLANK

WHAT?

SHUDDER

A PART OF...MY BODY?

SHIVER

SHIVER

SHIVER

SHIVER

CRASH

PKT

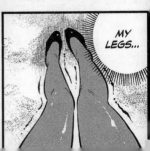

MY LEGS...

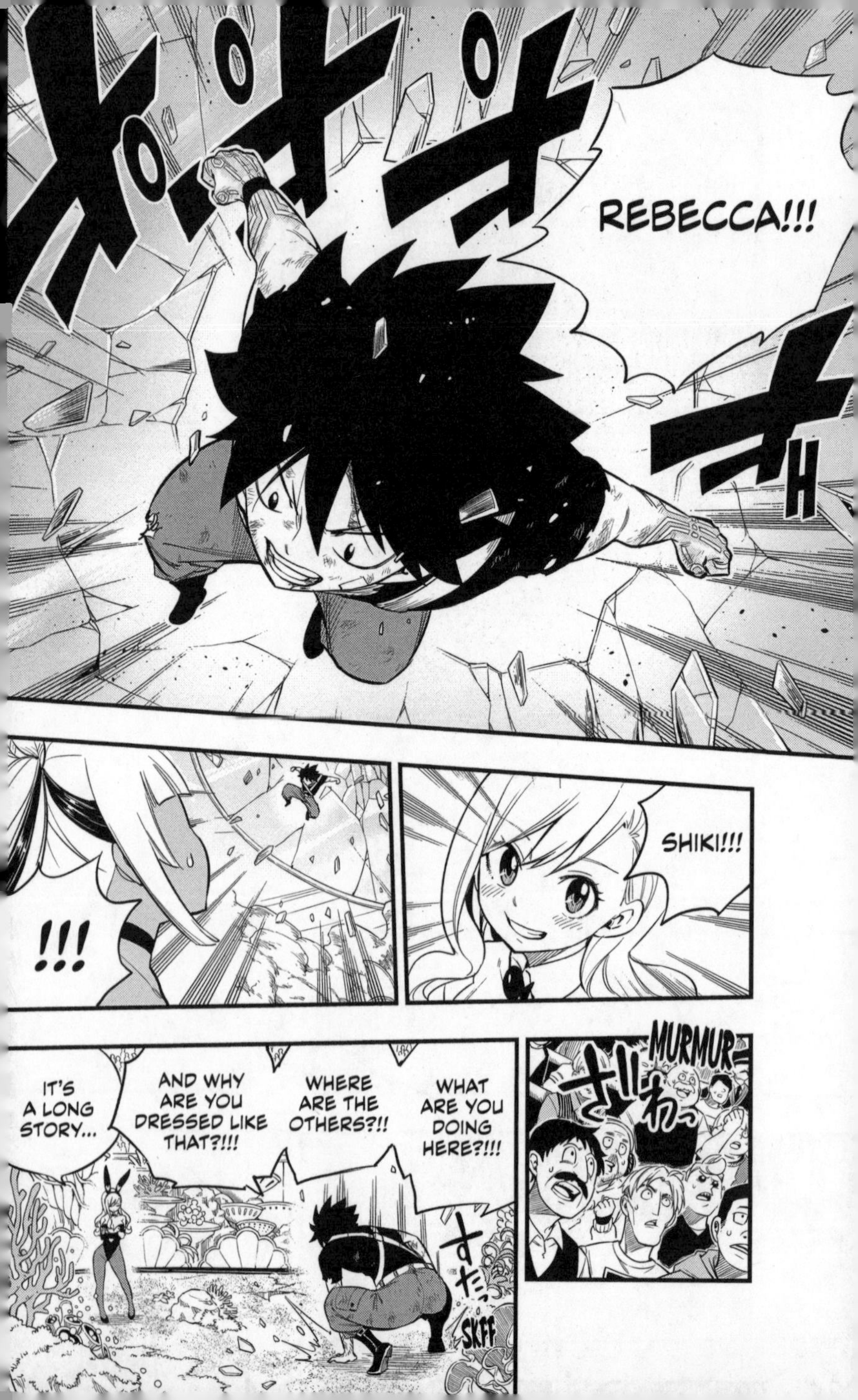
REBECCA!!!
SHIKI!!!
!!!
MURMUR
WHAT ARE YOU DOING HERE?!!!
WHERE ARE THE OTHERS?!!
AND WHY ARE YOU DRESSED LIKE THAT?!!!
IT'S A LONG STORY...
SKFF

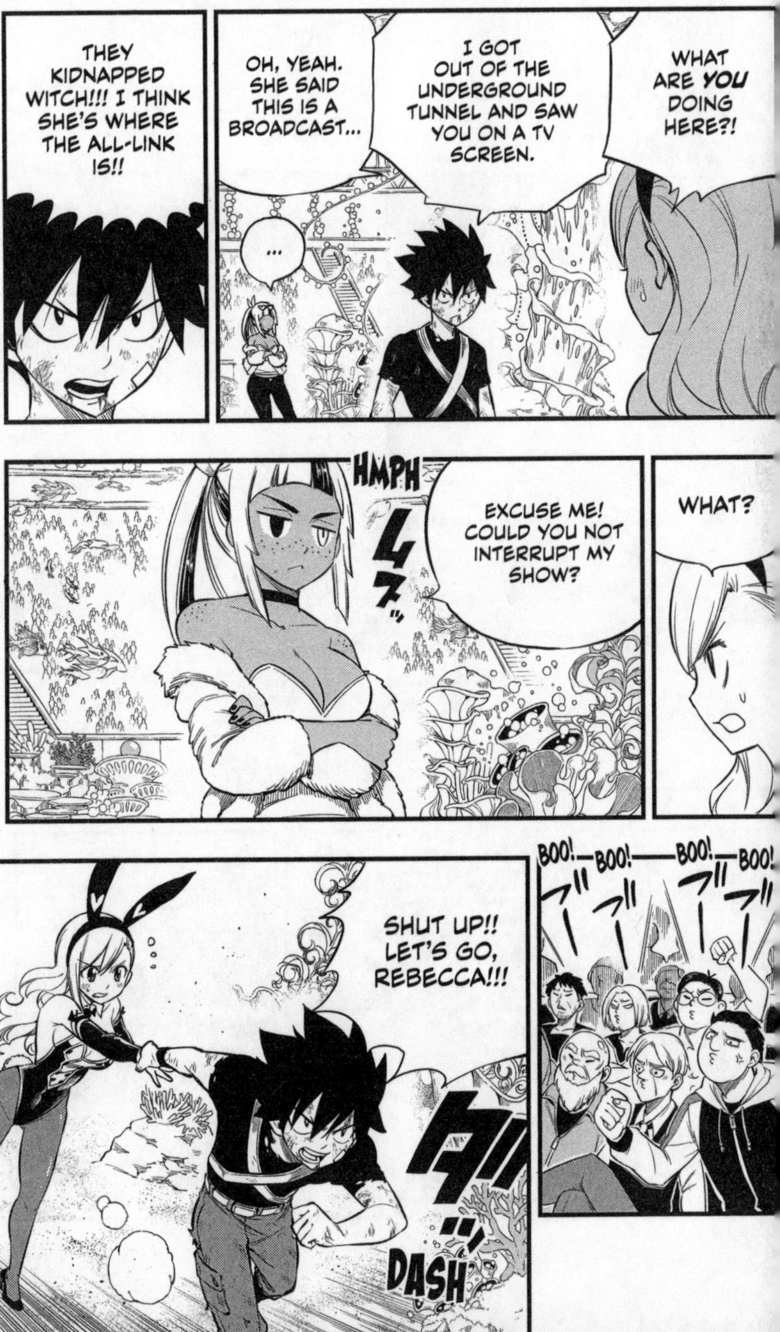
WHAT ARE YOU DOING HERE?!
I GOT OUT OF THE UNDERGROUND TUNNEL AND SAW YOU ON A TV SCREEN.
OH, YEAH. SHE SAID THIS IS A BROADCAST...
...
THEY KIDNAPPED WITCH!!! I THINK SHE'S WHERE THE ALL-LINK IS!!
WHAT?
EXCUSE ME! COULD YOU NOT INTERRUPT MY SHOW?
HMPH
BOO! BOO! BOO! BOO!
SHUT UP!! LET'S GO, REBECCA!!!
DASH

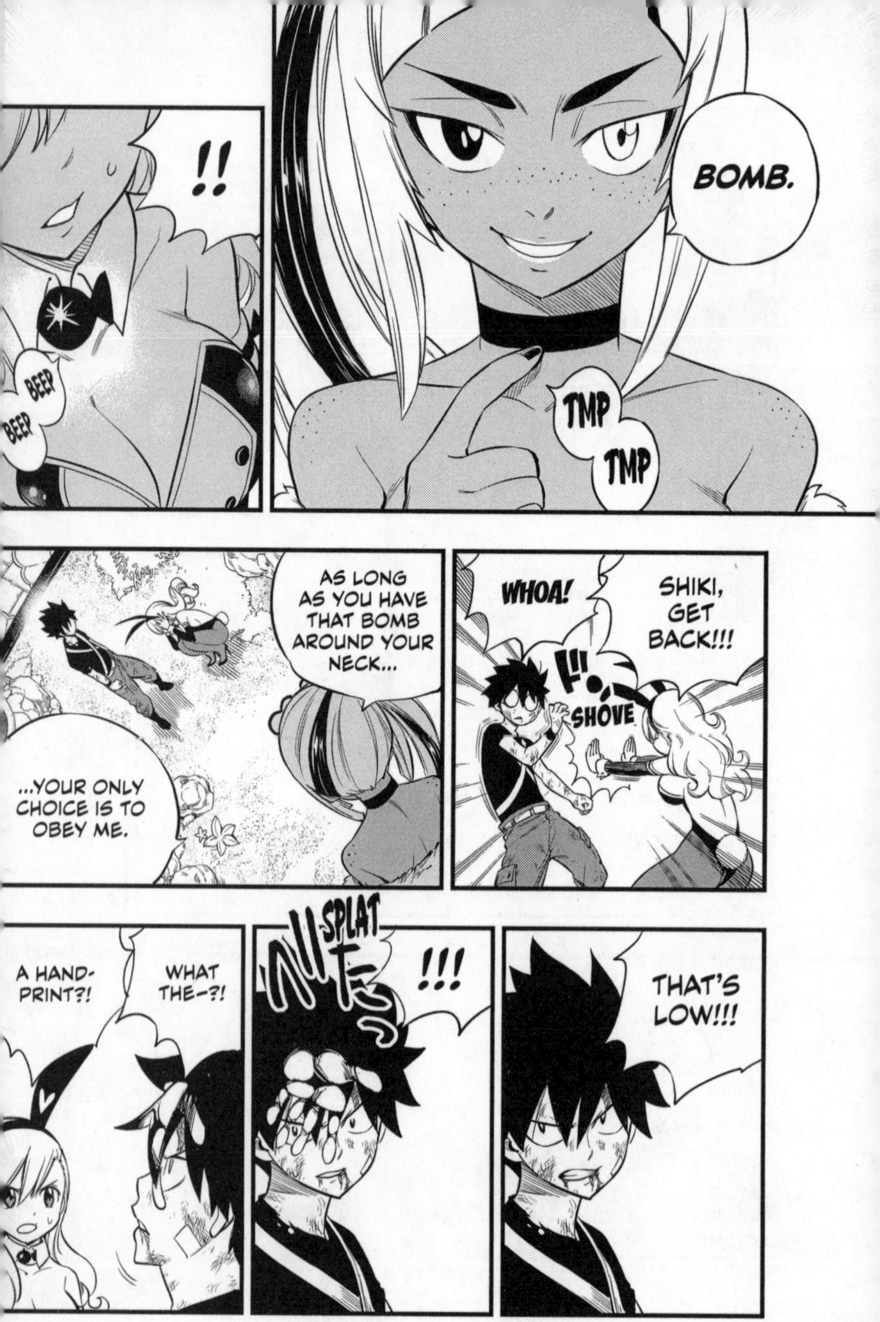
BOMB.
TMP
TMP
!!
BEEP
BEEP
SHIKI, GET BACK!!!
WHOA!
SHOVE
AS LONG AS YOU HAVE THAT BOMB AROUND YOUR NECK...
...YOUR ONLY CHOICE IS TO OBEY ME.
THAT'S LOW!!!
SPLAT
!!!
WHAT THE-?!
A HAND-PRINT?!

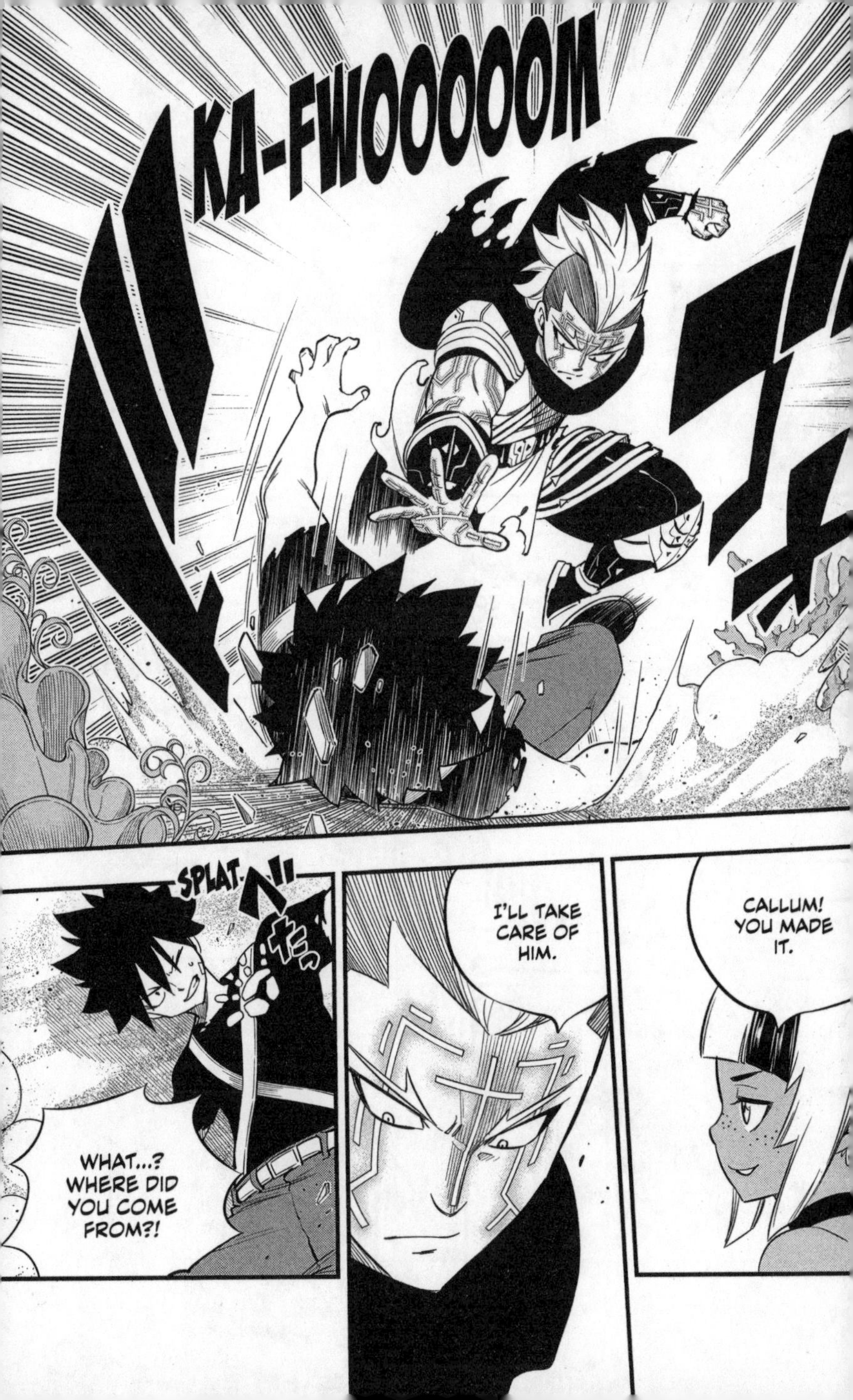
KA-FWOOOOOM
CALLUM! YOU MADE IT.
I'LL TAKE CARE OF HIM.
SPLAT
WHAT...? WHERE DID YOU COME FROM?!

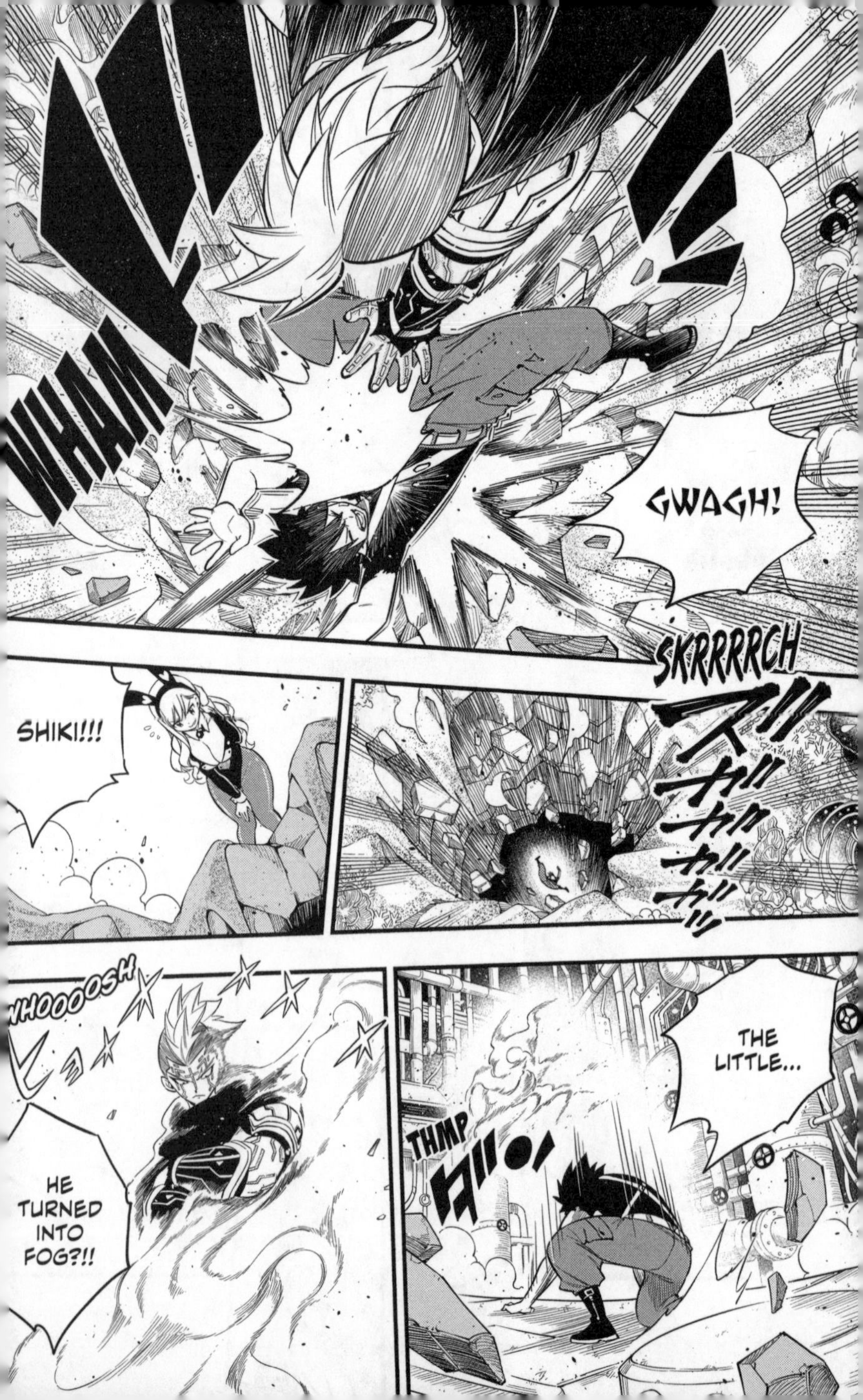
GWAGH!
WHAM
SKRRRRCH
SHIKI!!!
THE LITTLE...
THMP
WHOOOOSH
HE TURNED INTO FOG?!!

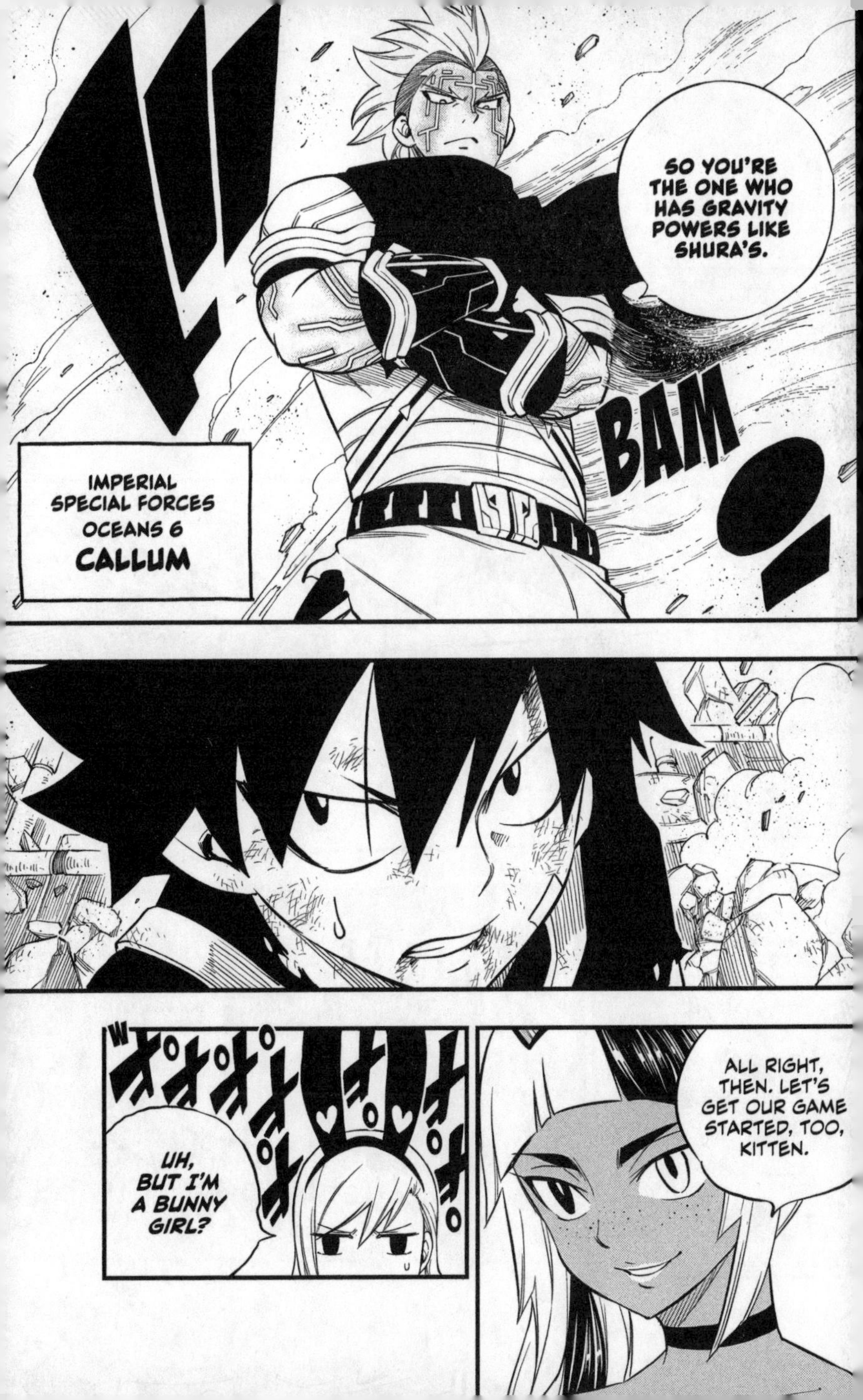
SO YOU'RE THE ONE WHO HAS GRAVITY POWERS LIKE SHURA'S.
BAM
IMPERIAL SPECIAL FORCES OCEANS 6 CALLUM
ALL RIGHT, THEN. LET'S GET OUR GAME STARTED, TOO, KITTEN.
UH, BUT I'M A BUNNY GIRL?

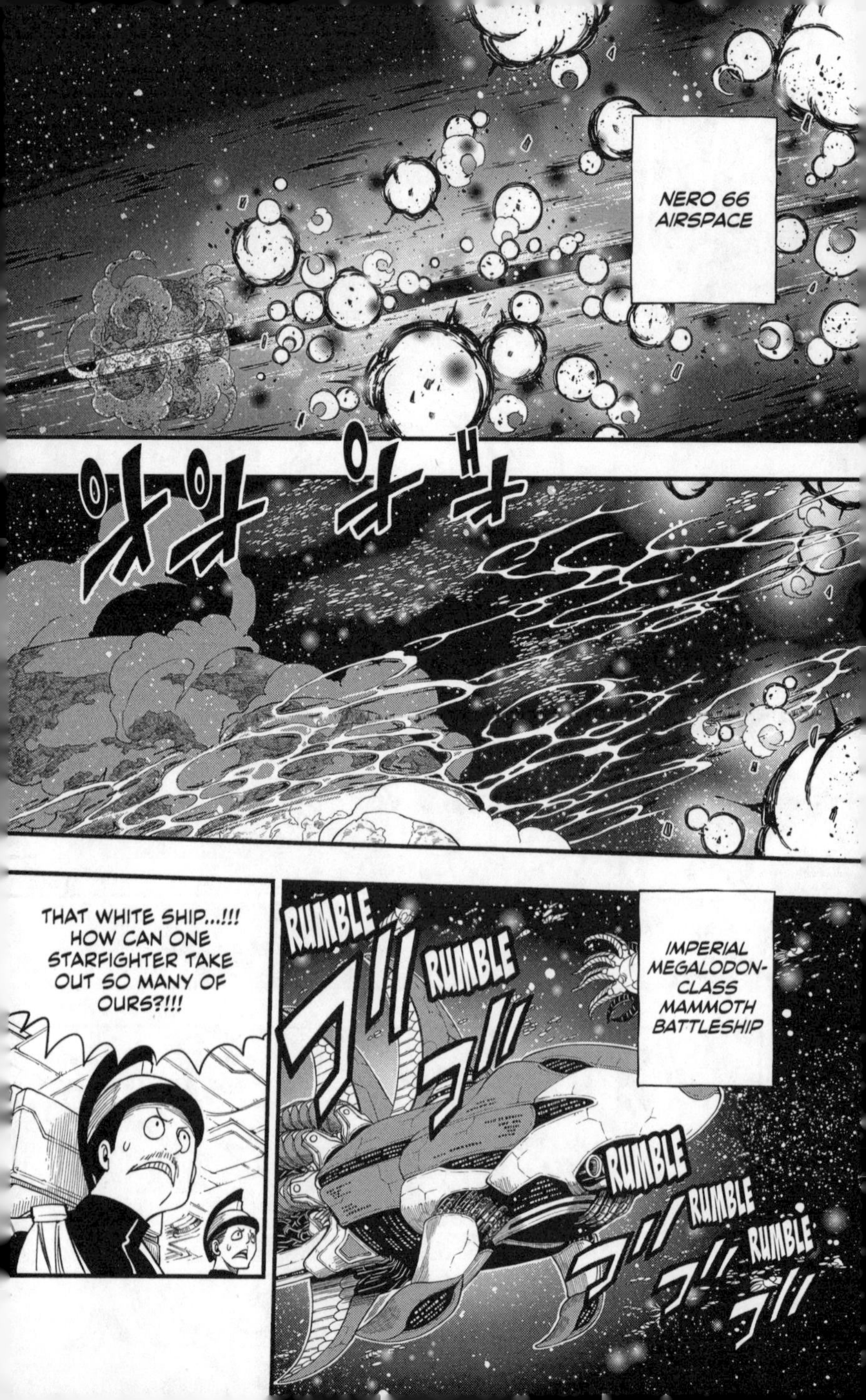
NERO 66 AIRSPACE
IMPERIAL MEGALODON-CLASS MAMMOTH BATTLESHIP
RUMBLE
RUMBLE
RUMBLE
RUMBLE
RUMBLE
THAT WHITE SHIP...!!! HOW CAN ONE STARFIGHTER TAKE OUT SO MANY OF OURS?!!!

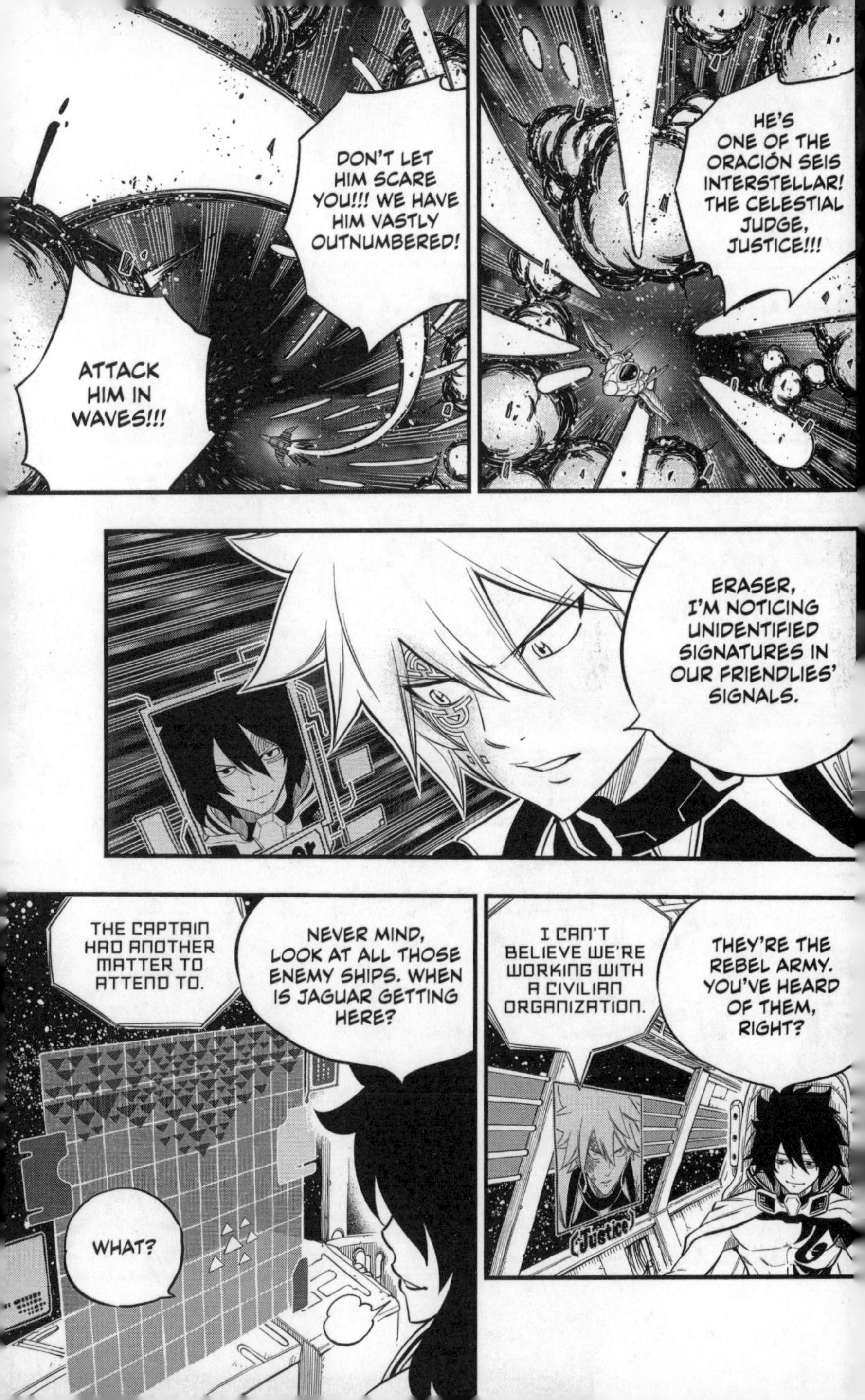
HE'S ONE OF THE ORACIÓN SEIS INTERSTELLAR! THE CELESTIAL JUDGE, JUSTICE!!!
DON'T LET HIM SCARE YOU!!! WE HAVE HIM VASTLY OUTNUMBERED!
ATTACK HIM IN WAVES!!!
ERASER, I'M NOTICING UNIDENTIFIED SIGNATURES IN OUR FRIENDLIES' SIGNALS.
THEY'RE THE REBEL ARMY. YOU'VE HEARD OF THEM, RIGHT?
I CAN'T BELIEVE WE'RE WORKING WITH A CIVILIAN ORGANIZATION.
Justice
NEVER MIND, LOOK AT ALL THOSE ENEMY SHIPS. WHEN IS JAGUAR GETTING HERE?
THE CAPTAIN HAD ANOTHER MATTER TO ATTEND TO.
WHAT?

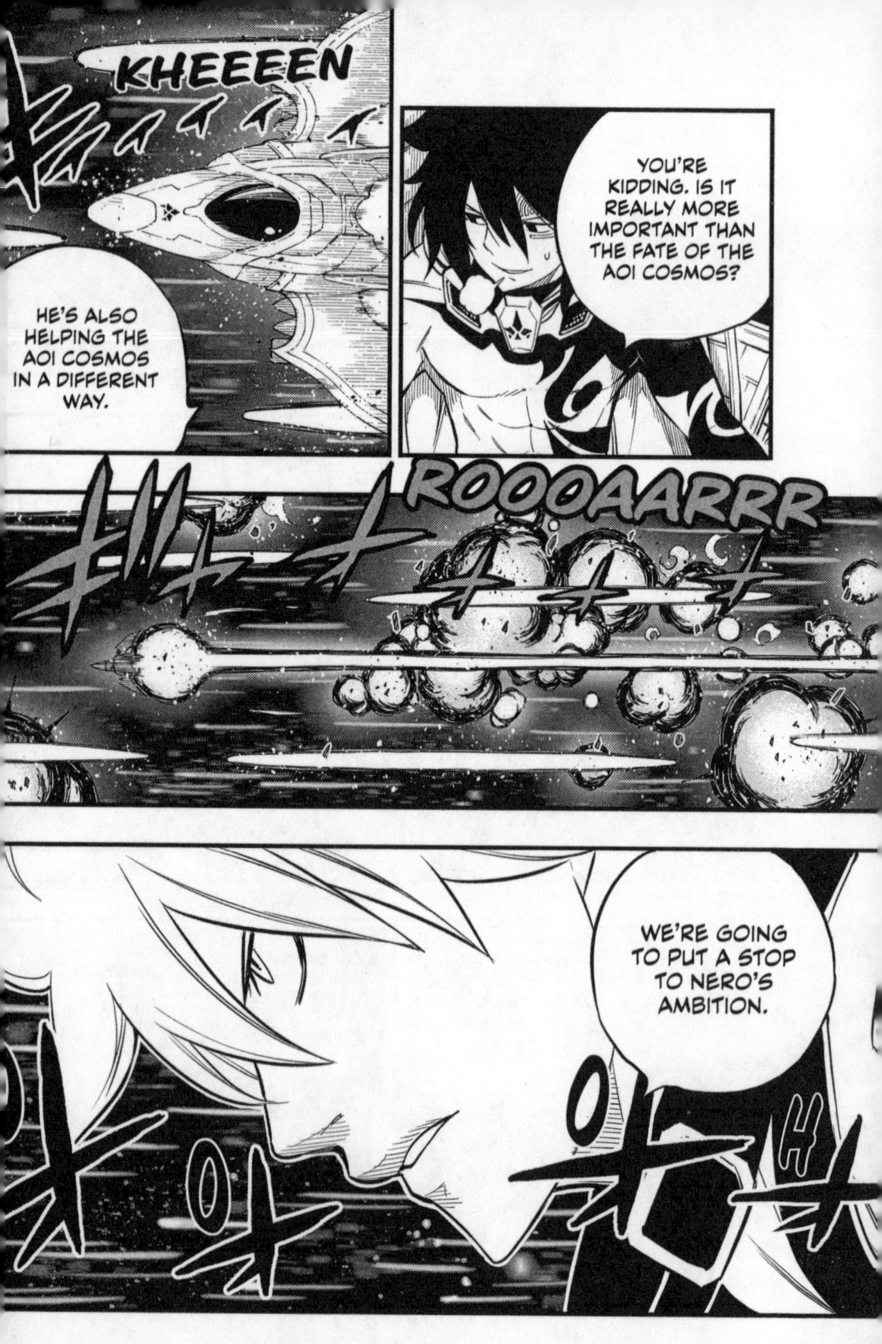
YOU'RE KIDDING. IS IT REALLY MORE IMPORTANT THAN THE FATE OF THE AOI COSMOS?
KHEEEEN
HE'S ALSO HELPING THE AOI COSMOS IN A DIFFERENT WAY.
ROOOAARRR
WE'RE GOING TO PUT A STOP TO NERO'S AMBITION.

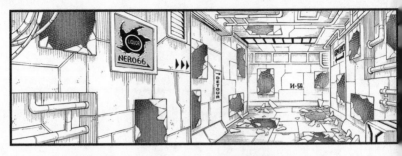

I APPEAR TO HAVE ESCAPED THE MIRROR...

I MUST FIND THE OTHERS...

GRR...

I....

FREEZE!!!

CLACK

SOMEONE'S THERE!!!

!!

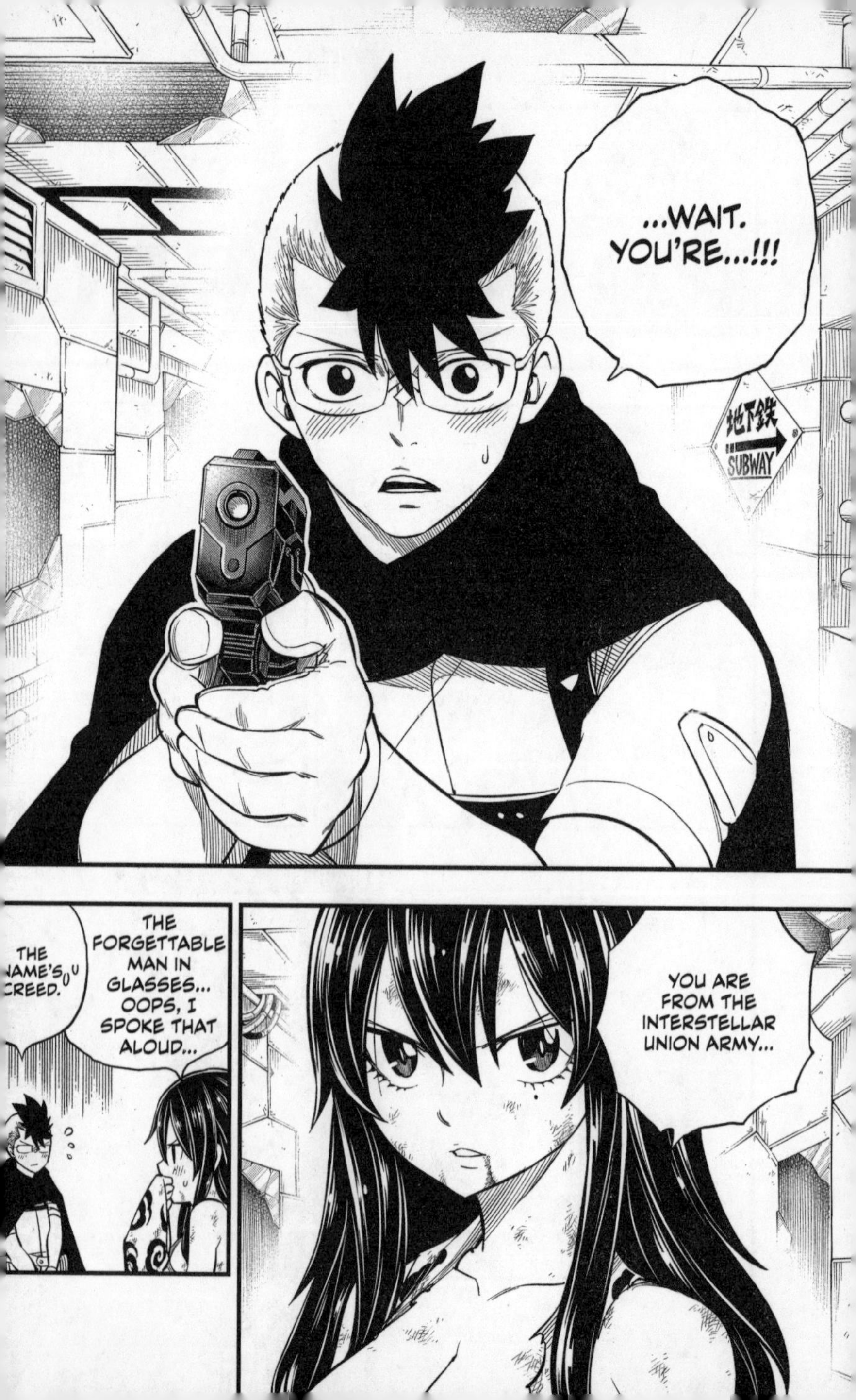
...WAIT. YOU'RE...!!!
地下鉄
SUBWAY
YOU ARE FROM THE INTERSTELLAR UNION ARMY...
THE FORGETTABLE MAN IN GLASSES... OOPS, I SPOKE THAT ALOUD...
THE NAME'S CREED.

EDENS ZERO

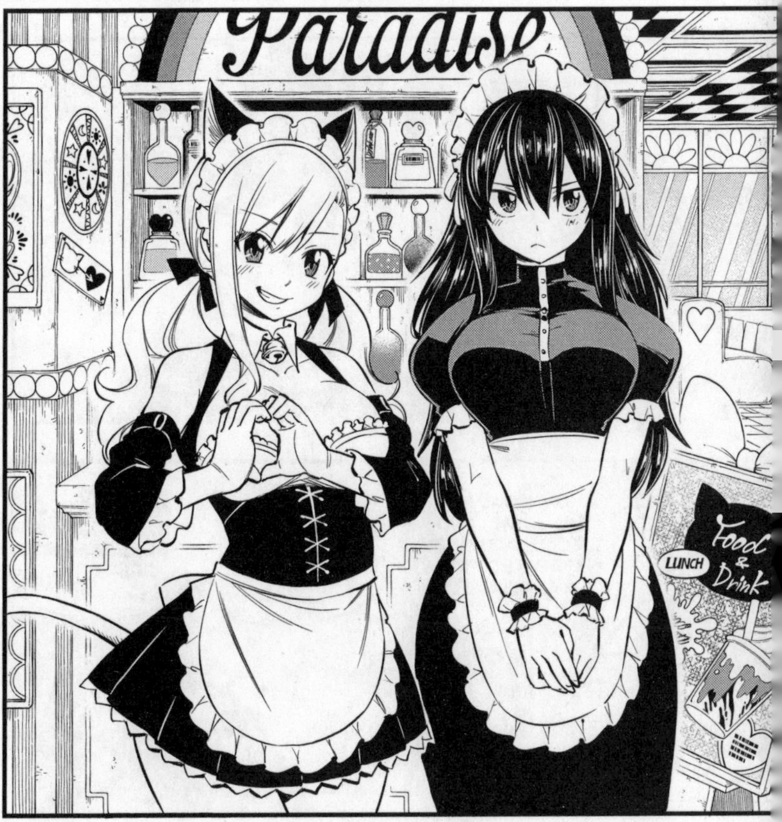
Paradise
LUNCH
Food & Drink

CHAPTER 152: LOST CARD

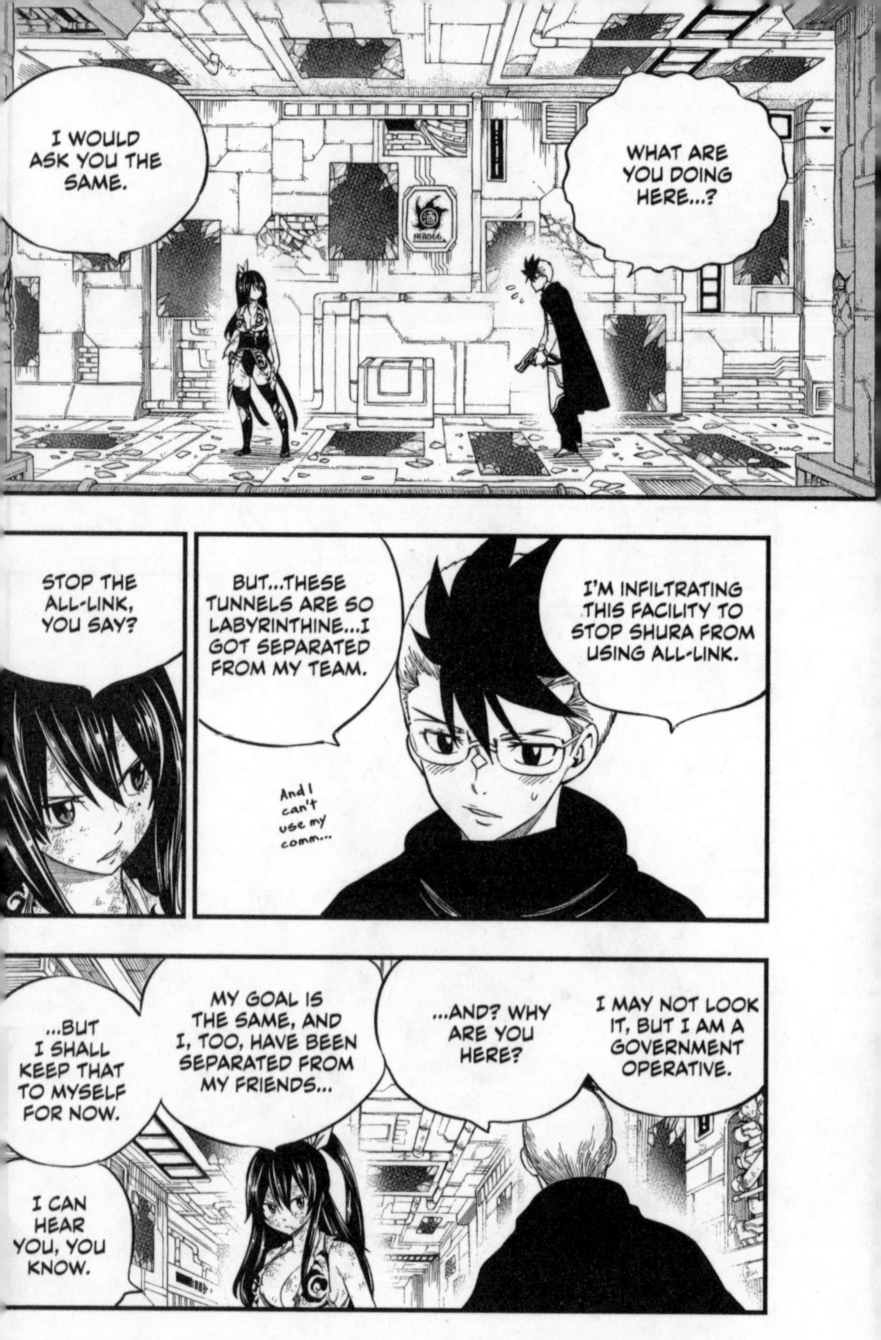
WHAT ARE YOU DOING HERE...?
I WOULD ASK YOU THE SAME.
I'M INFILTRATING THIS FACILITY TO STOP SHURA FROM USING ALL-LINK.
BUT...THESE TUNNELS ARE SO LABYRINTHINE...I GOT SEPARATED FROM MY TEAM.
And I can't use my comm...
STOP THE ALL-LINK, YOU SAY?
I MAY NOT LOOK IT, BUT I AM A GOVERNMENT OPERATIVE.
...AND? WHY ARE YOU HERE?
MY GOAL IS THE SAME, AND I, TOO, HAVE BEEN SEPARATED FROM MY FRIENDS...
...BUT I SHALL KEEP THAT TO MYSELF FOR NOW.
I CAN HEAR YOU, YOU KNOW.

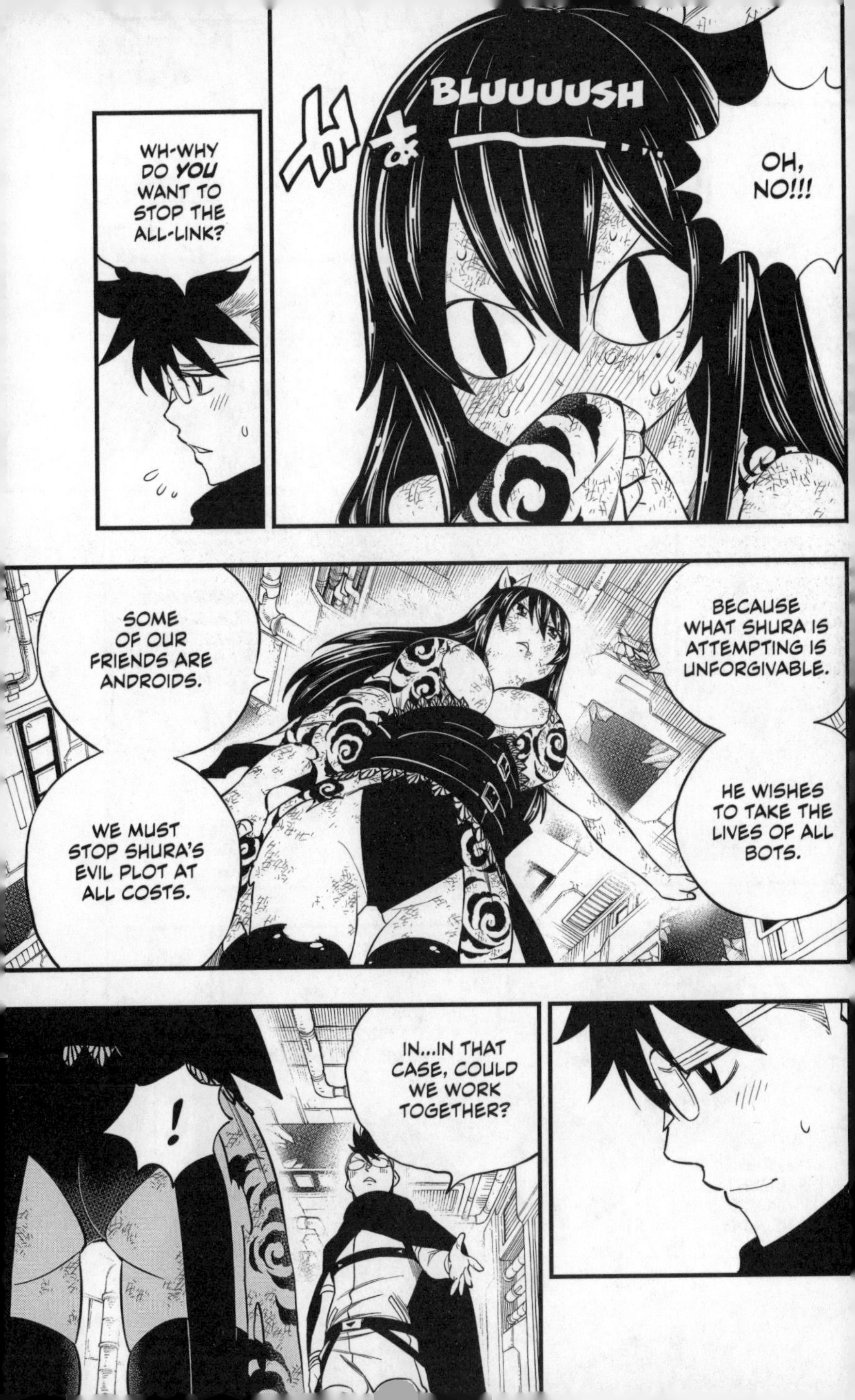
BLUUUUSH
OH, NO!!!
WH-WHY DO *YOU* WANT TO STOP THE ALL-LINK?
BECAUSE WHAT SHURA IS ATTEMPTING IS UNFORGIVABLE.
HE WISHES TO TAKE THE LIVES OF ALL BOTS.
SOME OF OUR FRIENDS ARE ANDROIDS.
WE MUST STOP SHURA'S EVIL PLOT AT ALL COSTS.
IN...IN THAT CASE, COULD WE WORK TOGETHER?
!

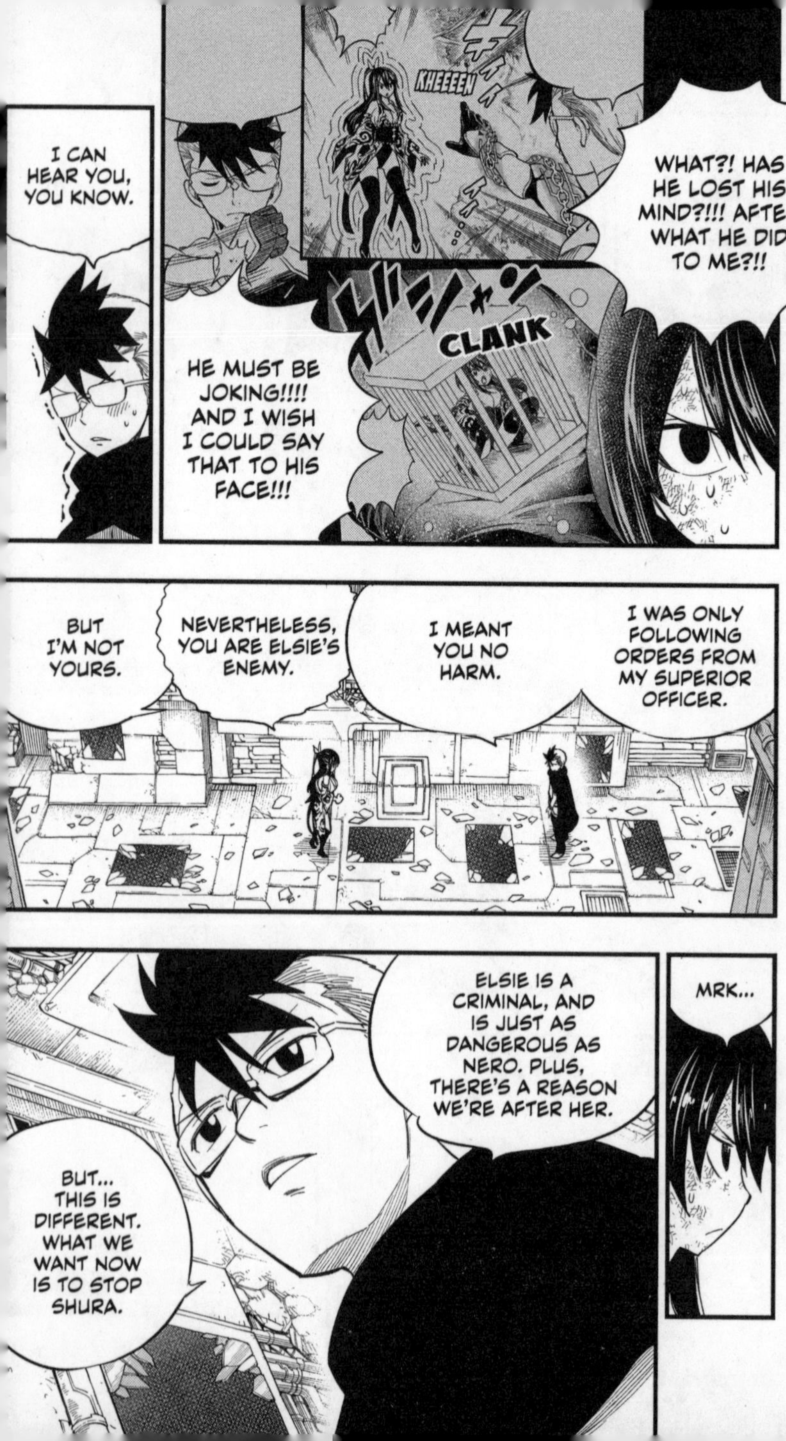
KHEEEEN
WHAT?! HAS HE LOST HIS MIND?!!! AFTER WHAT HE DID TO ME?!!
CLANK
HE MUST BE JOKING!!!! AND I WISH I COULD SAY THAT TO HIS FACE!!!
I CAN HEAR YOU, YOU KNOW.
I WAS ONLY FOLLOWING ORDERS FROM MY SUPERIOR OFFICER.
I MEANT YOU NO HARM.
NEVERTHELESS, YOU ARE ELSIE'S ENEMY.
BUT I'M NOT YOURS.
MRK...
ELSIE IS A CRIMINAL, AND IS JUST AS DANGEROUS AS NERO. PLUS, THERE'S A REASON WE'RE AFTER HER.
BUT... THIS IS DIFFERENT. WHAT WE WANT NOW IS TO STOP SHURA.

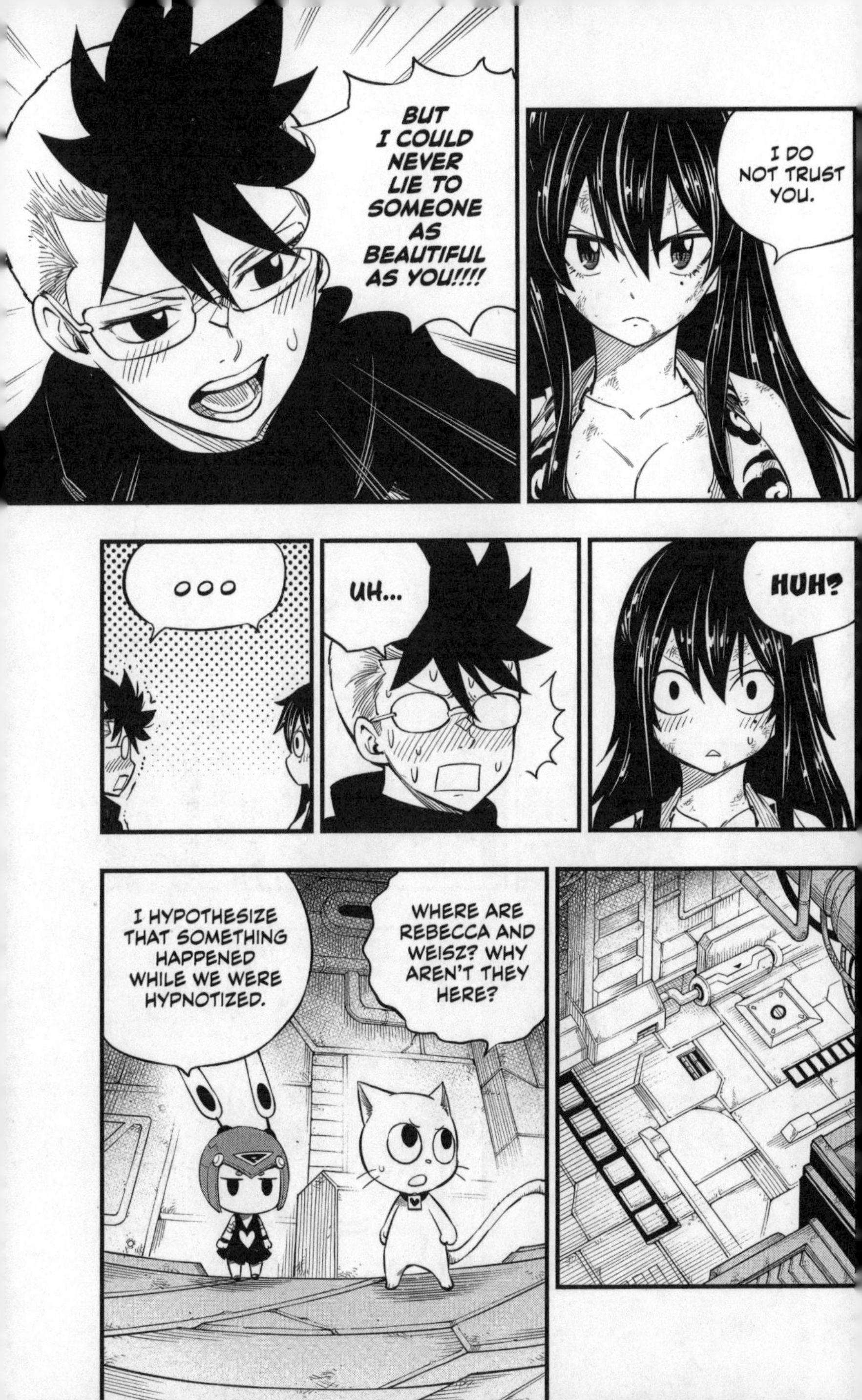
I DO NOT TRUST YOU.
BUT I COULD NEVER LIE TO SOMEONE AS BEAUTIFUL AS YOU!!!!
HUH?
UH...
ooo
WHERE ARE REBECCA AND WEISZ? WHY AREN'T THEY HERE?
I HYPOTHESIZE THAT SOMETHING HAPPENED WHILE WE WERE HYPNOTIZED.

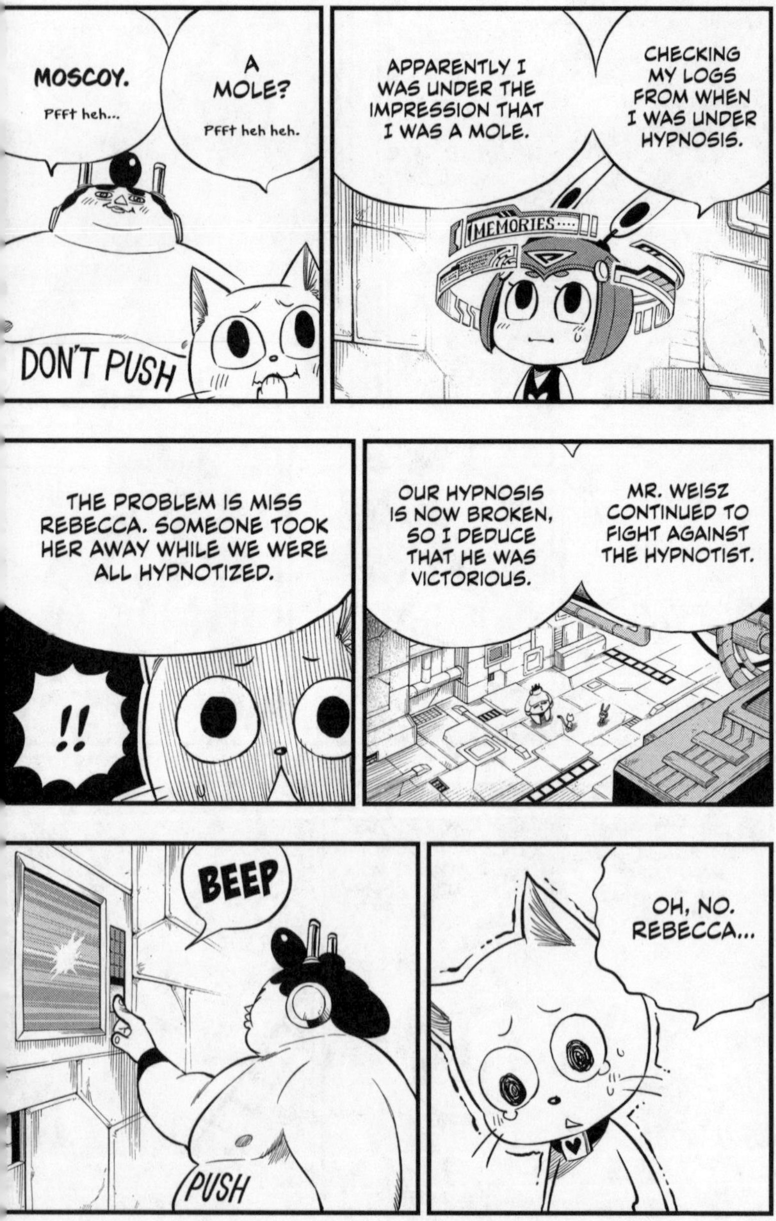

CHECKING MY LOGS FROM WHEN I WAS UNDER HYPNOSIS.
APPARENTLY I WAS UNDER THE IMPRESSION THAT I WAS A MOLE.
MEMORIES....
A MOLE?
Pfft heh heh.
MOSCOY.
Pfft heh...
DON'T PUSH
MR. WEISZ CONTINUED TO FIGHT AGAINST THE HYPNOTIST.
OUR HYPNOSIS IS NOW BROKEN, SO I DEDUCE THAT HE WAS VICTORIOUS.
THE PROBLEM IS MISS REBECCA. SOMEONE TOOK HER AWAY WHILE WE WERE ALL HYPNOTIZED.
!!
OH, NO. REBECCA...
BEEP
PUSH

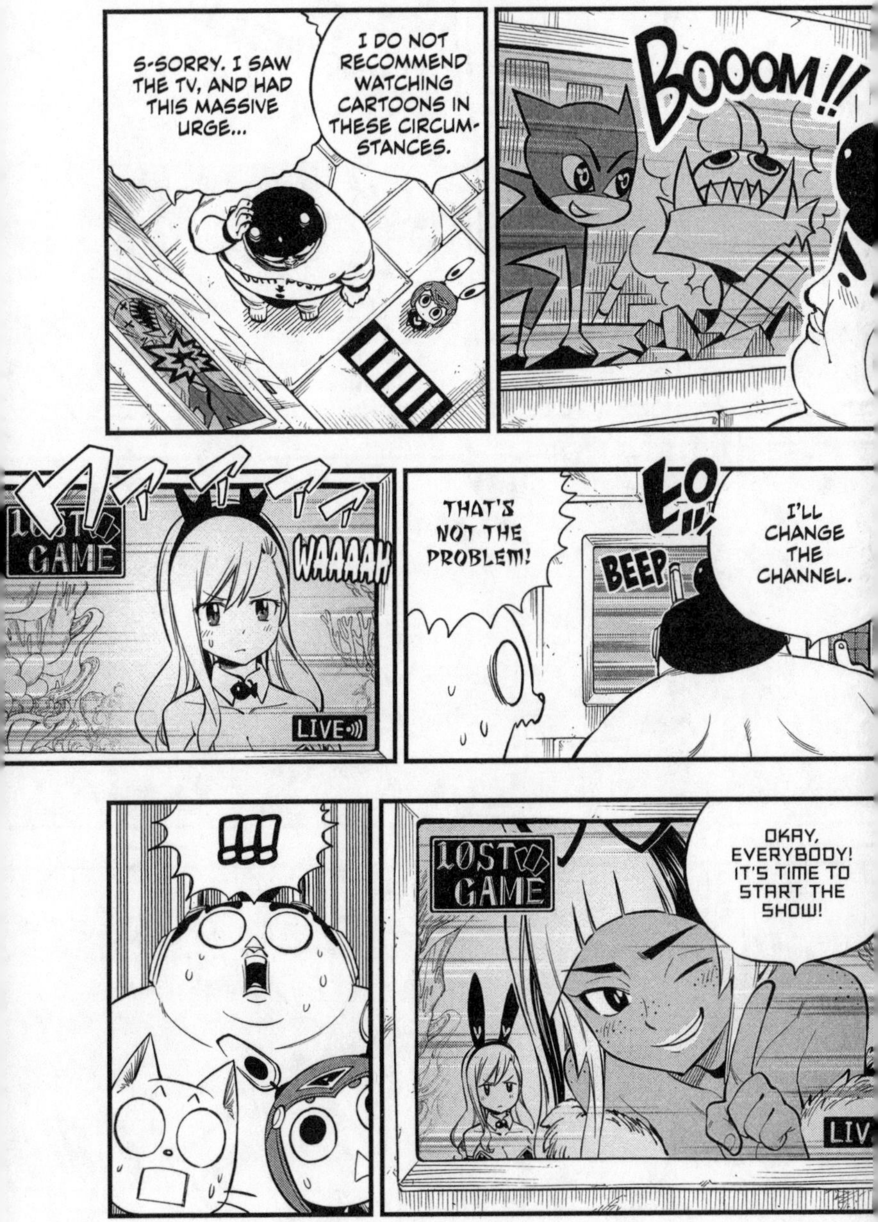
BOOOM!!
I DO NOT RECOMMEND WATCHING CARTOONS IN THESE CIRCUM-STANCES.
S-SORRY. I SAW THE TV, AND HAD THIS MASSIVE URGE...
I'LL CHANGE THE CHANNEL.
BEEP
THAT'S NOT THE PROBLEM!
WAAAAH
LOST GAME
LIVE
OKAY, EVERYBODY! IT'S TIME TO START THE SHOW!
LOST GAME
LIV
!!!

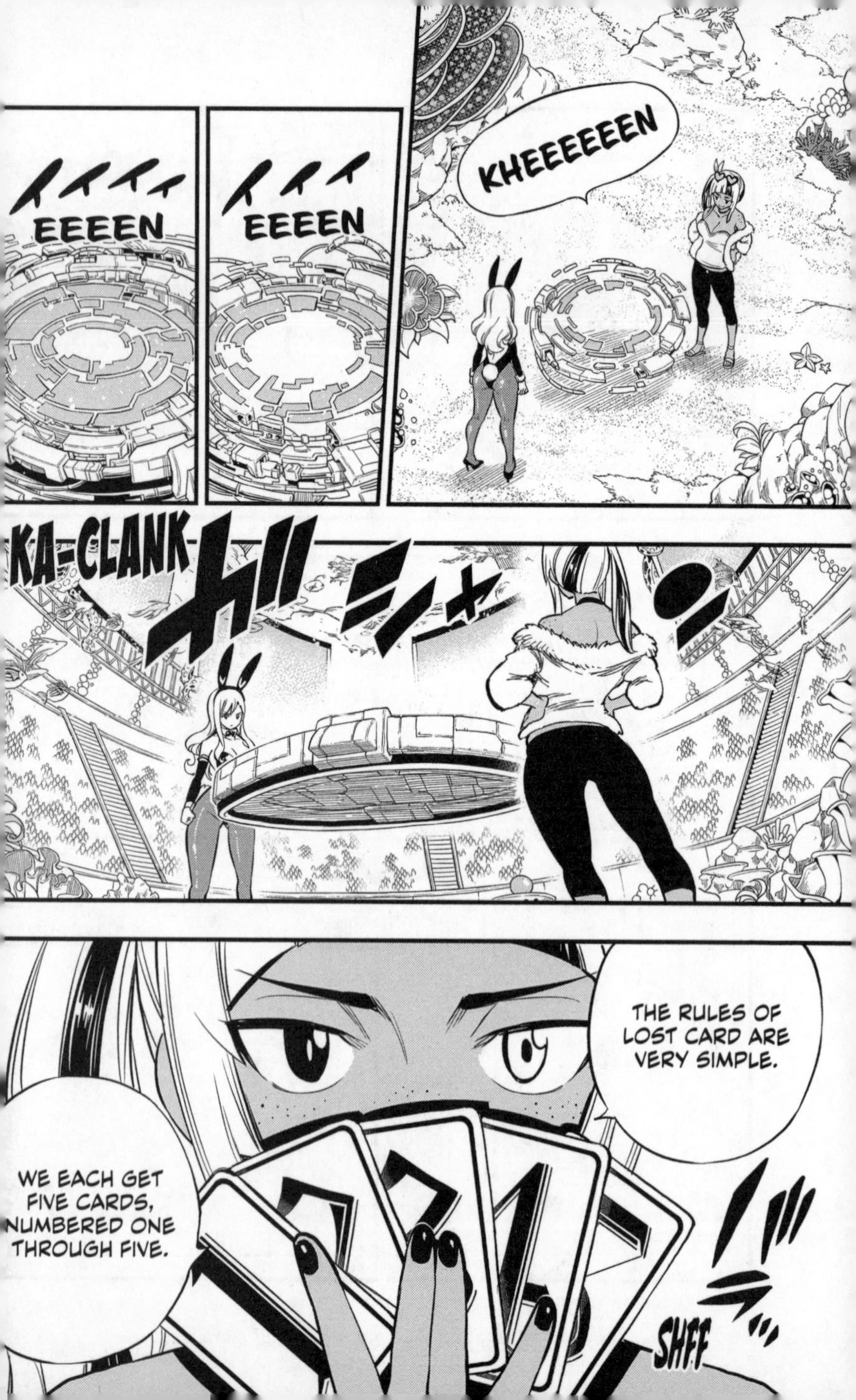
KHEEEEEEN
イイイ
EEEEN
イイイ
EEEEN
KA-CLANK
THE RULES OF LOST CARD ARE VERY SIMPLE.
WE EACH GET FIVE CARDS, NUMBERED ONE THROUGH FIVE.
SHFF

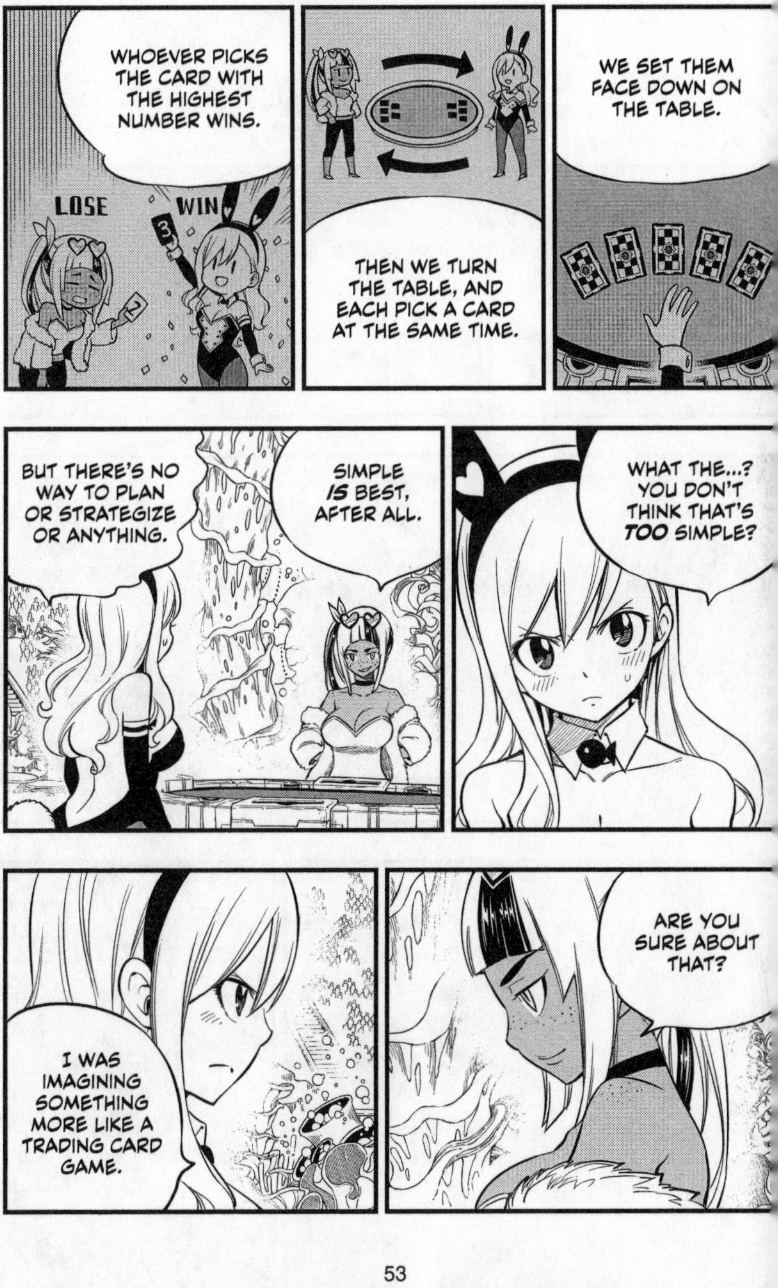
WE SET THEM FACE DOWN ON THE TABLE.
THEN WE TURN THE TABLE, AND EACH PICK A CARD AT THE SAME TIME.
WHOEVER PICKS THE CARD WITH THE HIGHEST NUMBER WINS.
WIN
LOSE
WHAT THE...? YOU DON'T THINK THAT'S *TOO* SIMPLE?
SIMPLE *IS* BEST, AFTER ALL.
BUT THERE'S NO WAY TO PLAN OR STRATEGIZE OR ANYTHING.
ARE YOU SURE ABOUT THAT?
I WAS IMAGINING SOMETHING MORE LIKE A TRADING CARD GAME.

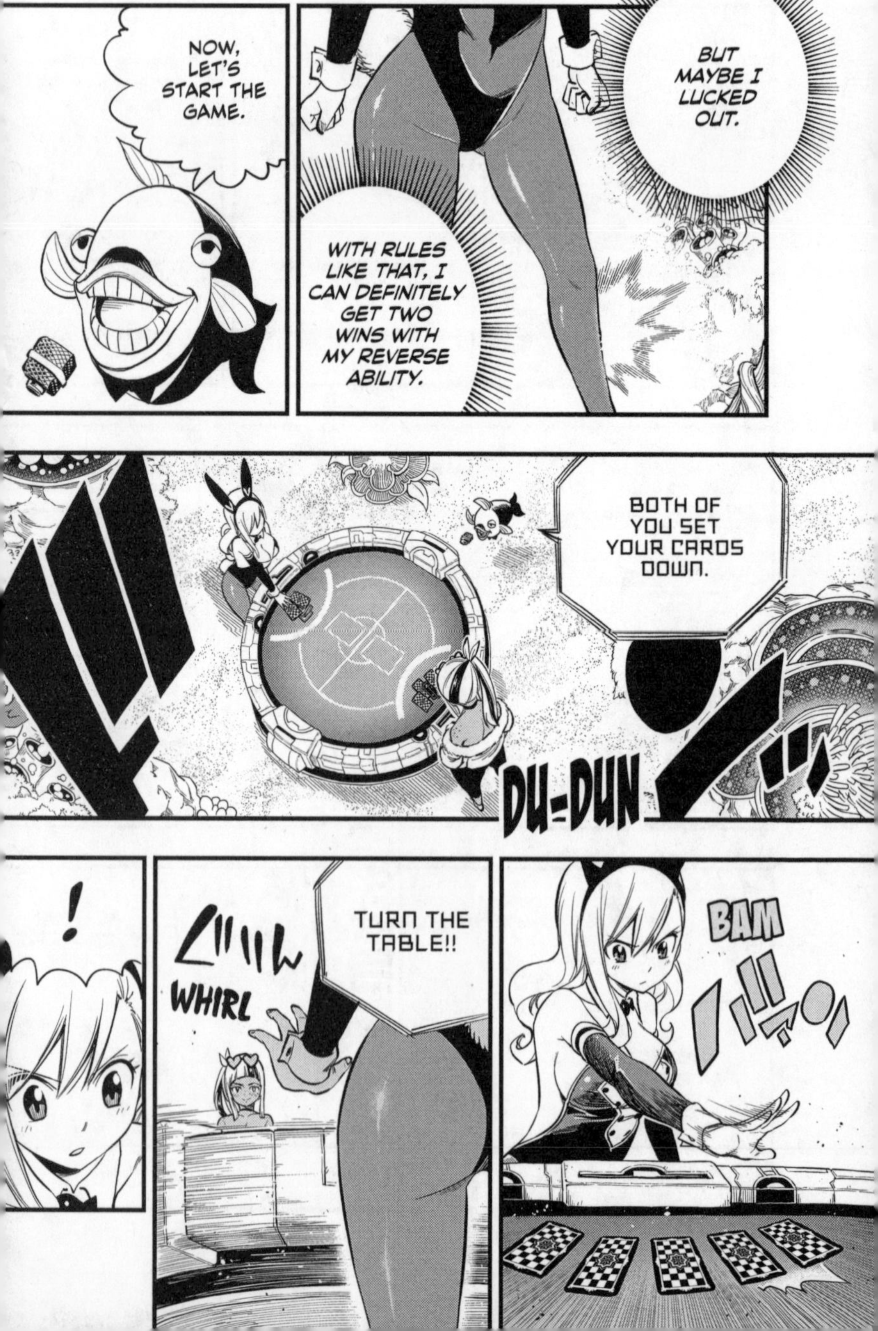
BUT MAYBE I LUCKED OUT.
WITH RULES LIKE THAT, I CAN DEFINITELY GET TWO WINS WITH MY REVERSE ABILITY.
NOW, LET'S START THE GAME.
BOTH OF YOU SET YOUR CARDS DOWN.
DU-DUN
BAM
TURN THE TABLE!!
WHIRL
!

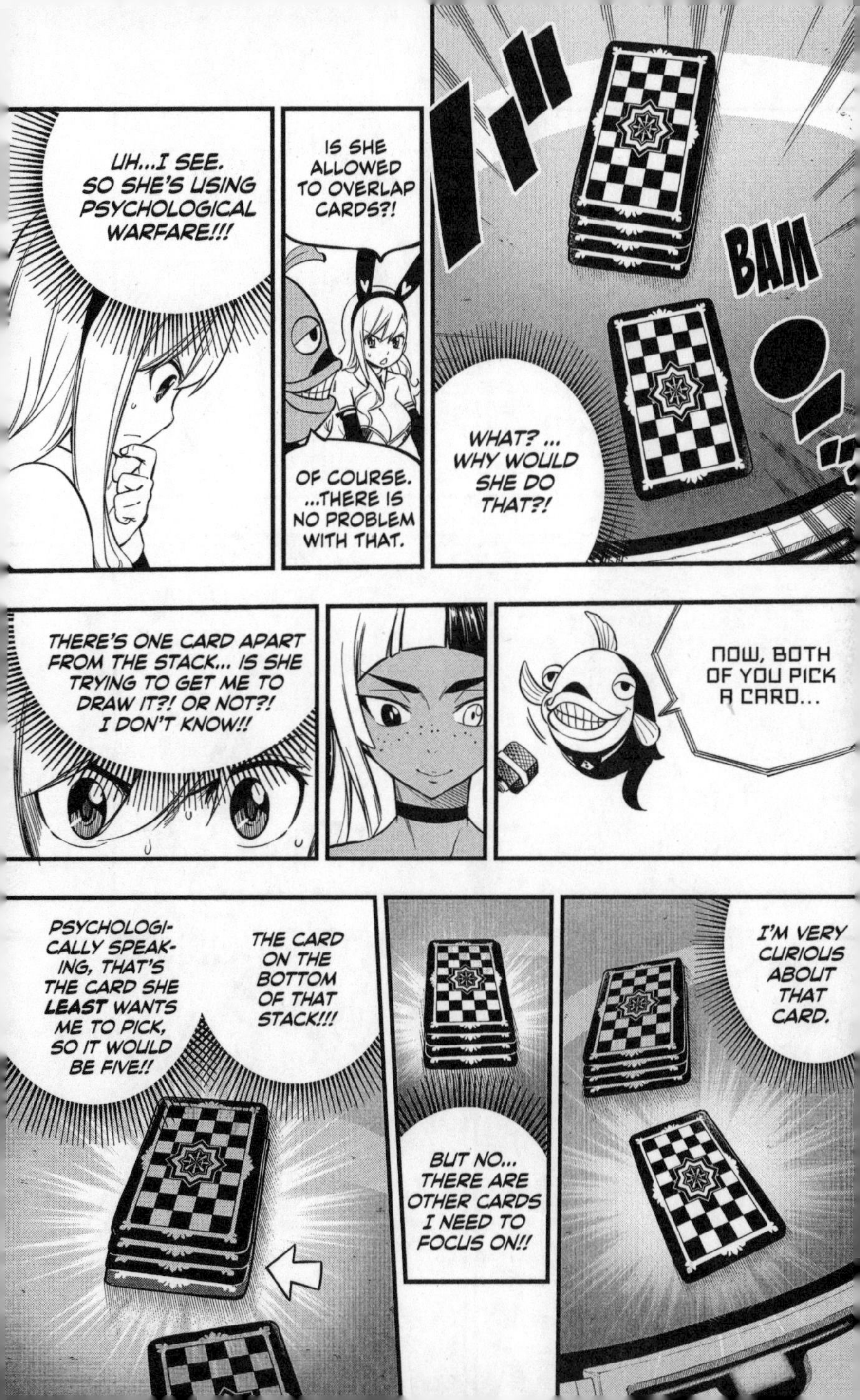
BAM
WHAT? ... WHY WOULD SHE DO THAT?!
IS SHE ALLOWED TO OVERLAP CARDS?!
OF COURSE. ...THERE IS NO PROBLEM WITH THAT.
UH...I SEE. SO SHE'S USING PSYCHOLOGICAL WARFARE!!!
NOW, BOTH OF YOU PICK A CARD...
THERE'S ONE CARD APART FROM THE STACK... IS SHE TRYING TO GET ME TO DRAW IT?! OR NOT?! I DON'T KNOW!!
I'M VERY CURIOUS ABOUT THAT CARD.
BUT NO... THERE ARE OTHER CARDS I NEED TO FOCUS ON!!
THE CARD ON THE BOTTOM OF THAT STACK!!!
PSYCHOLOGI-CALLY SPEAK-ING, THAT'S THE CARD SHE **LEAST** WANTS ME TO PICK, SO IT WOULD BE FIVE!!

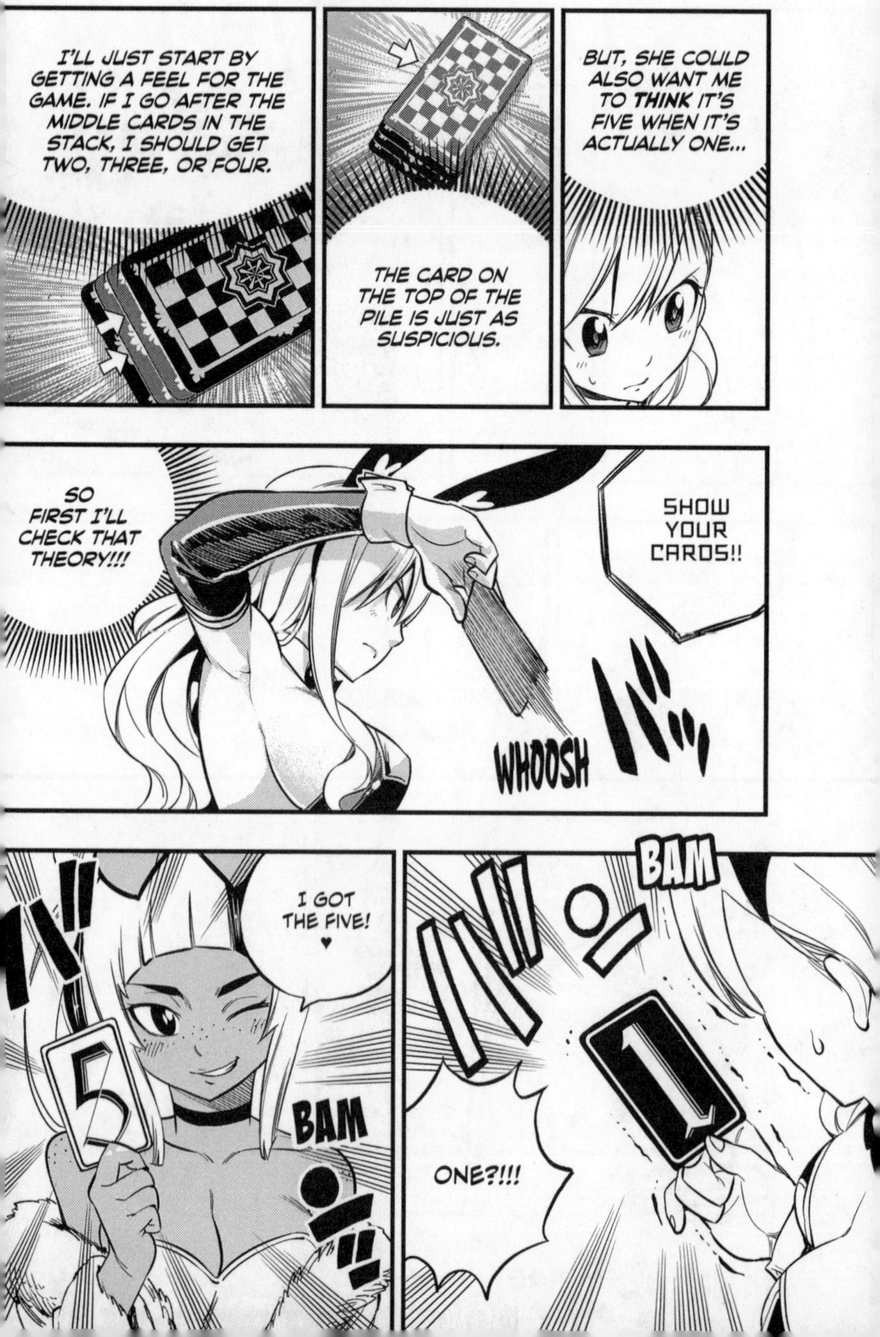
BUT, SHE COULD ALSO WANT ME TO **THINK** IT'S FIVE WHEN IT'S ACTUALLY ONE...
THE CARD ON THE TOP OF THE PILE IS JUST AS SUSPICIOUS.
I'LL JUST START BY GETTING A FEEL FOR THE GAME. IF I GO AFTER THE MIDDLE CARDS IN THE STACK, I SHOULD GET TWO, THREE, OR FOUR.
SHOW YOUR CARDS!!
WHOOSH
SO FIRST I'LL CHECK THAT THEORY!!!
BAM
ONE?!!!
I GOT THE FIVE! ♥
BAM

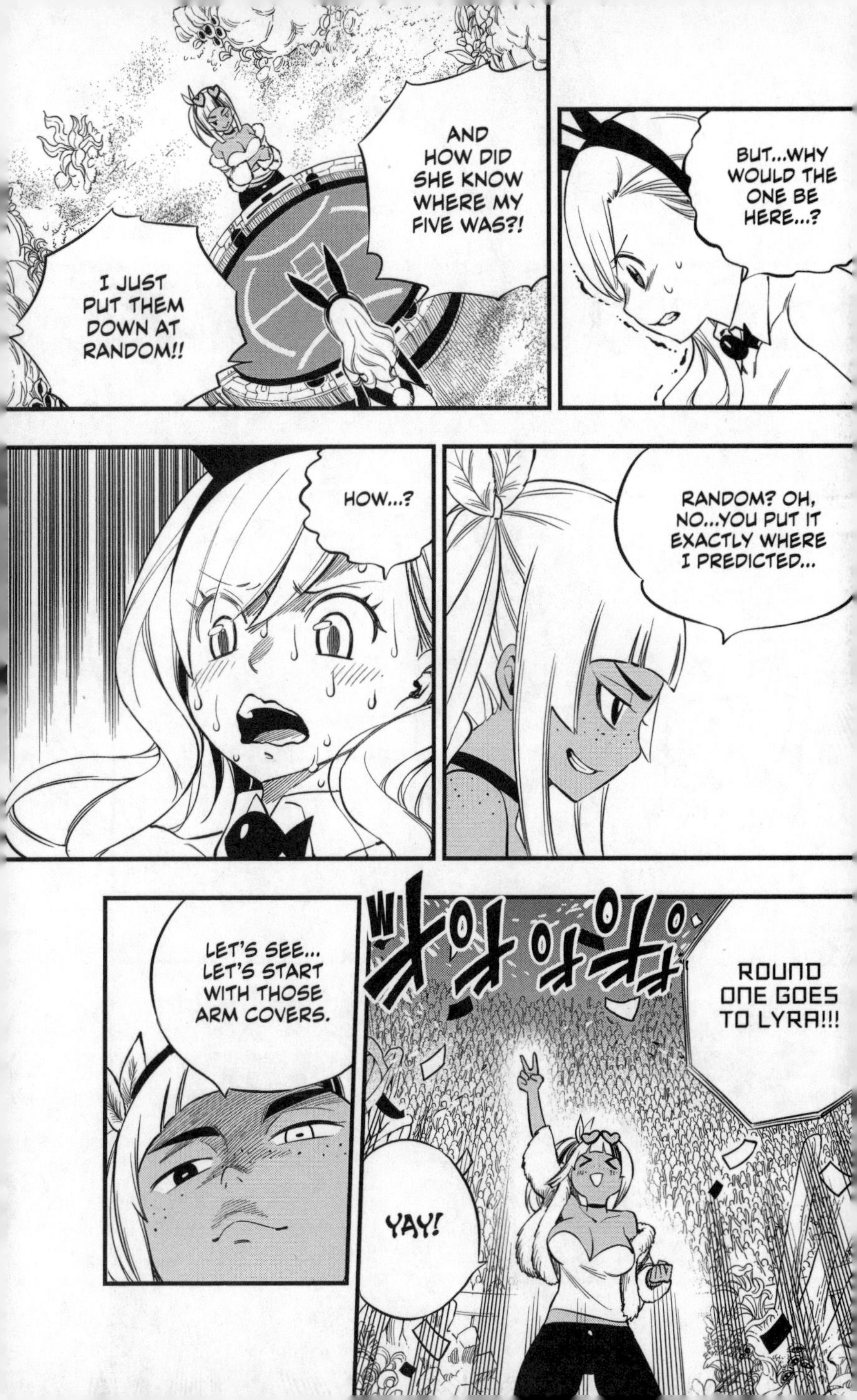
BUT...WHY WOULD THE ONE BE HERE...?
AND HOW DID SHE KNOW WHERE MY FIVE WAS?!
I JUST PUT THEM DOWN AT RANDOM!!
RANDOM? OH, NO...YOU PUT IT EXACTLY WHERE I PREDICTED...
HOW...?
ROUND ONE GOES TO LYRA!!!
YAY!
LET'S SEE... LET'S START WITH THOSE ARM COVERS.

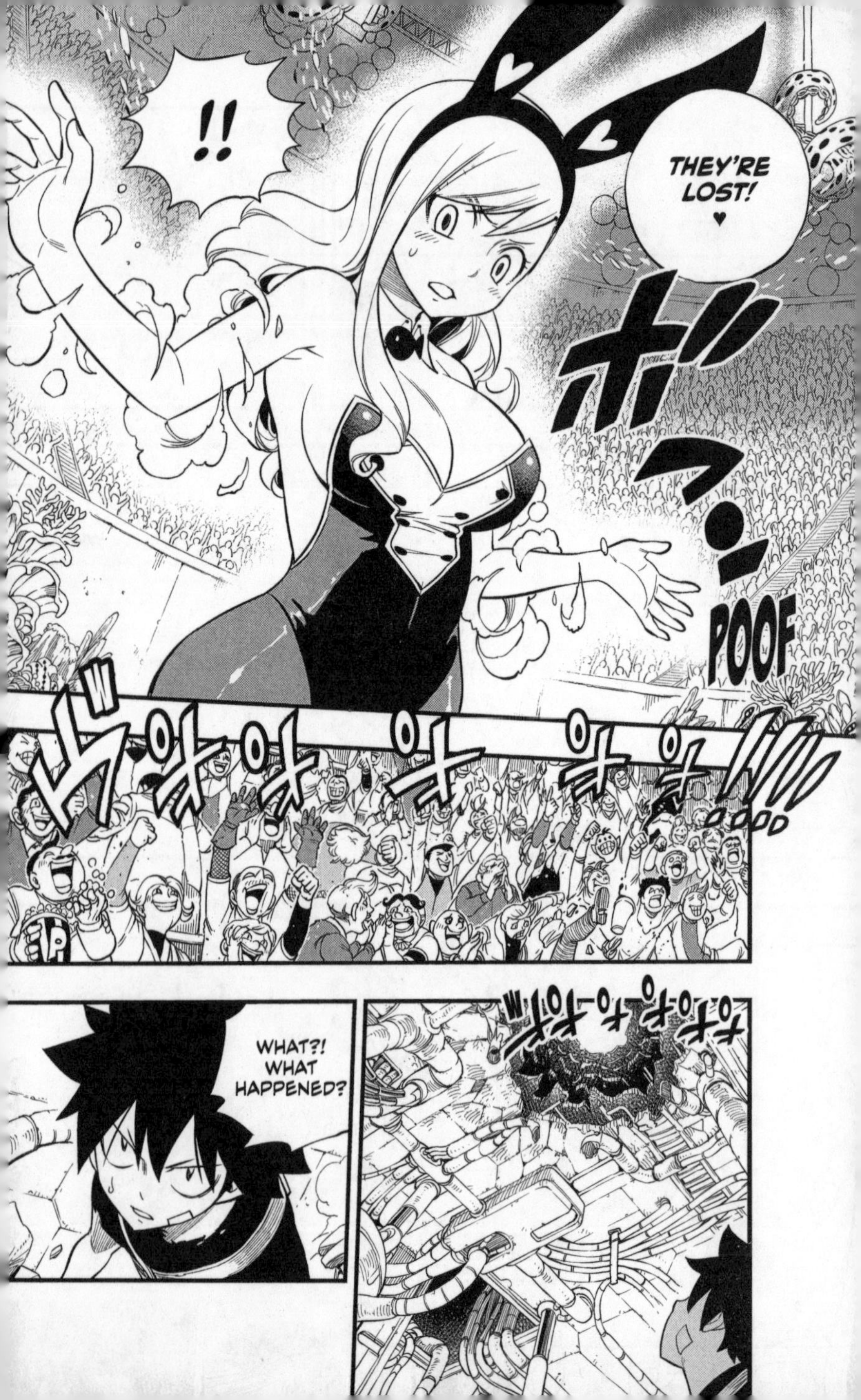
THEY'RE LOST! ♥
!!
POOF
W
OOOO
W
WHAT?! WHAT HAPPENED?

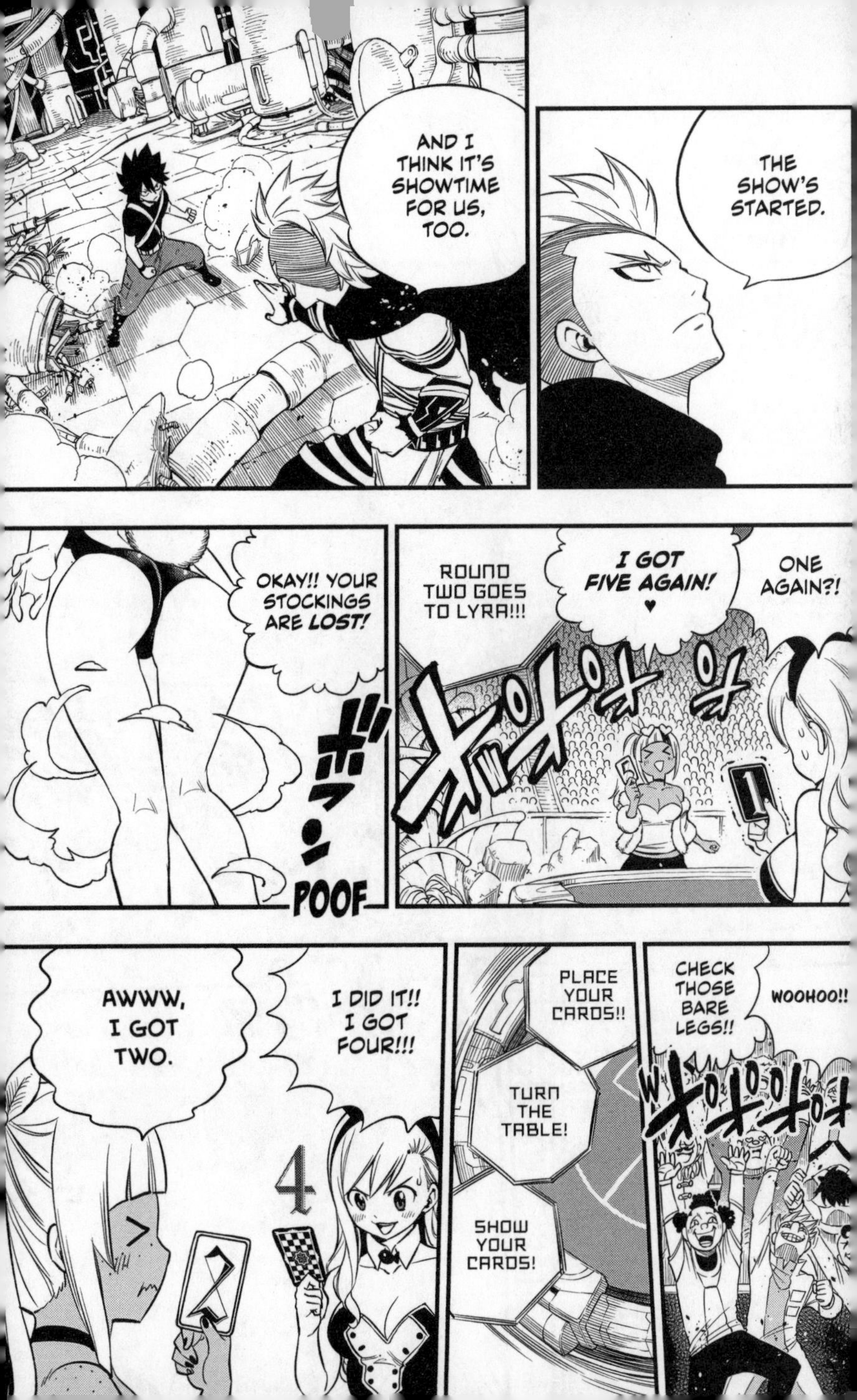
THE SHOW'S STARTED.
AND I THINK IT'S SHOWTIME FOR US, TOO.
ONE AGAIN?!
I GOT FIVE AGAIN! ♥
ROUND TWO GOES TO LYRA!!!
OKAY!! YOUR STOCKINGS ARE LOST!
POOF
WOOHOO!!
CHECK THOSE BARE LEGS!!
PLACE YOUR CARDS!!
TURN THE TABLE!
SHOW YOUR CARDS!
I DID IT!! I GOT FOUR!!!
AWWW, I GOT TWO.

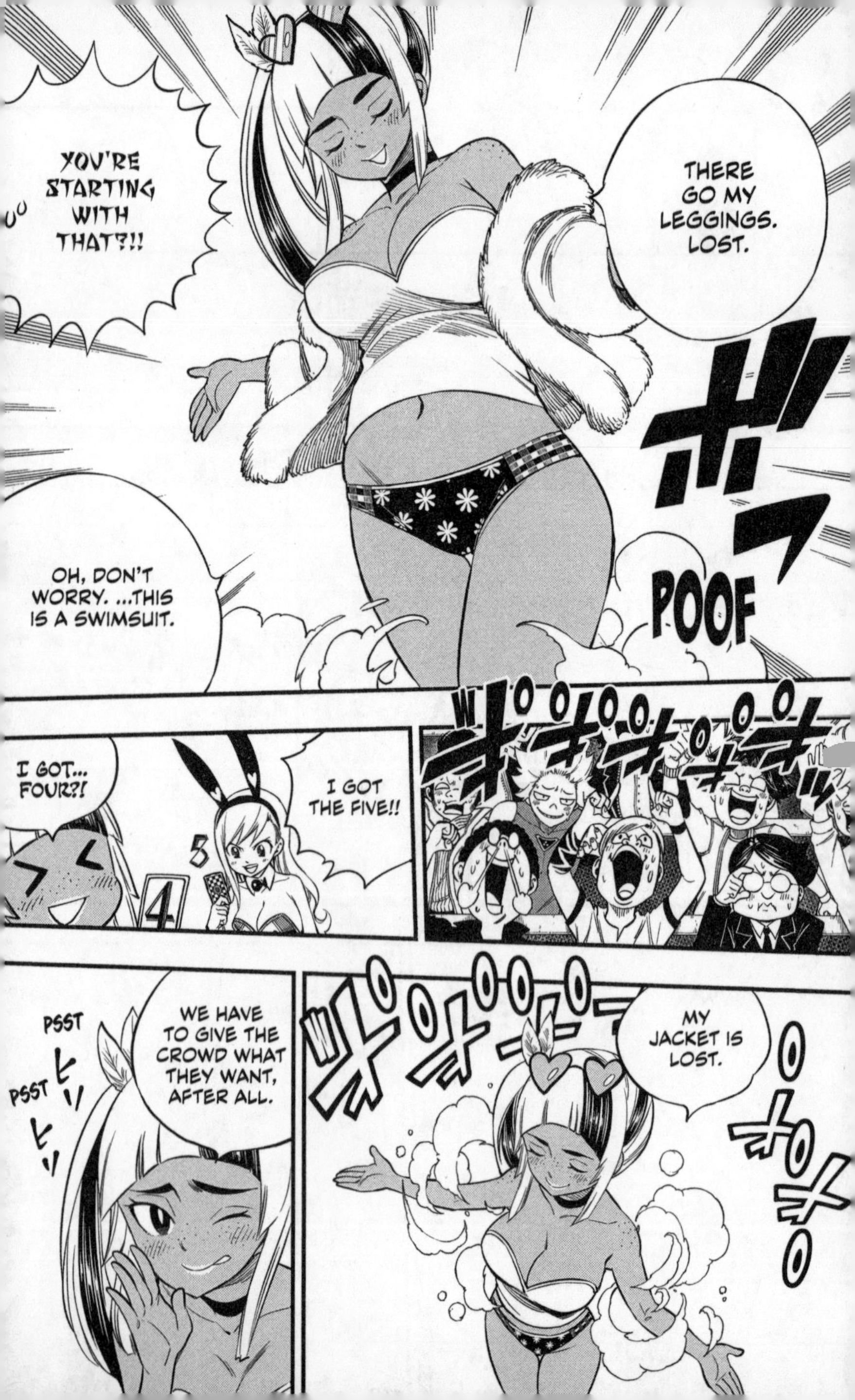

THERE GO MY LEGGINGS. LOST.
POOF
YOU'RE STARTING WITH THAT?!!
OH, DON'T WORRY. ...THIS IS A SWIMSUIT.
WOOOOOO
I GOT THE FIVE!!
5
4
I GOT... FOUR?!
MY JACKET IS LOST.
WE HAVE TO GIVE THE CROWD WHAT THEY WANT, AFTER ALL.
PSST
PSST

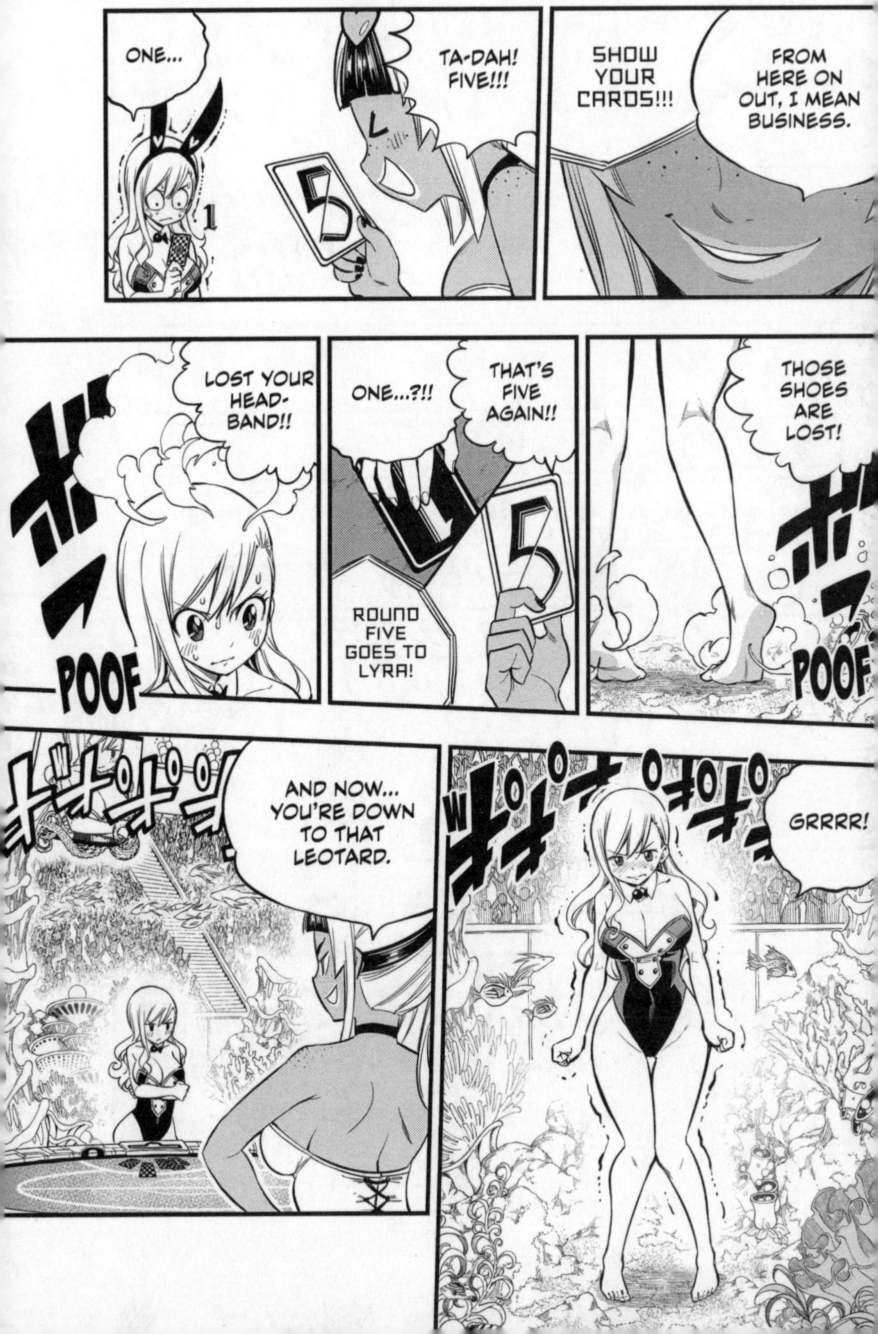
FROM HERE ON OUT, I MEAN BUSINESS.
SHOW YOUR CARDS!!!
TA-DAH! FIVE!!!
ONE...
THOSE SHOES ARE LOST!
POOF
THAT'S FIVE AGAIN!!
ONE...?!!
ROUND FIVE GOES TO LYRA!
LOST YOUR HEAD-BAND!!
POOF
GRRRR!
AND NOW... YOU'RE DOWN TO THAT LEOTARD.

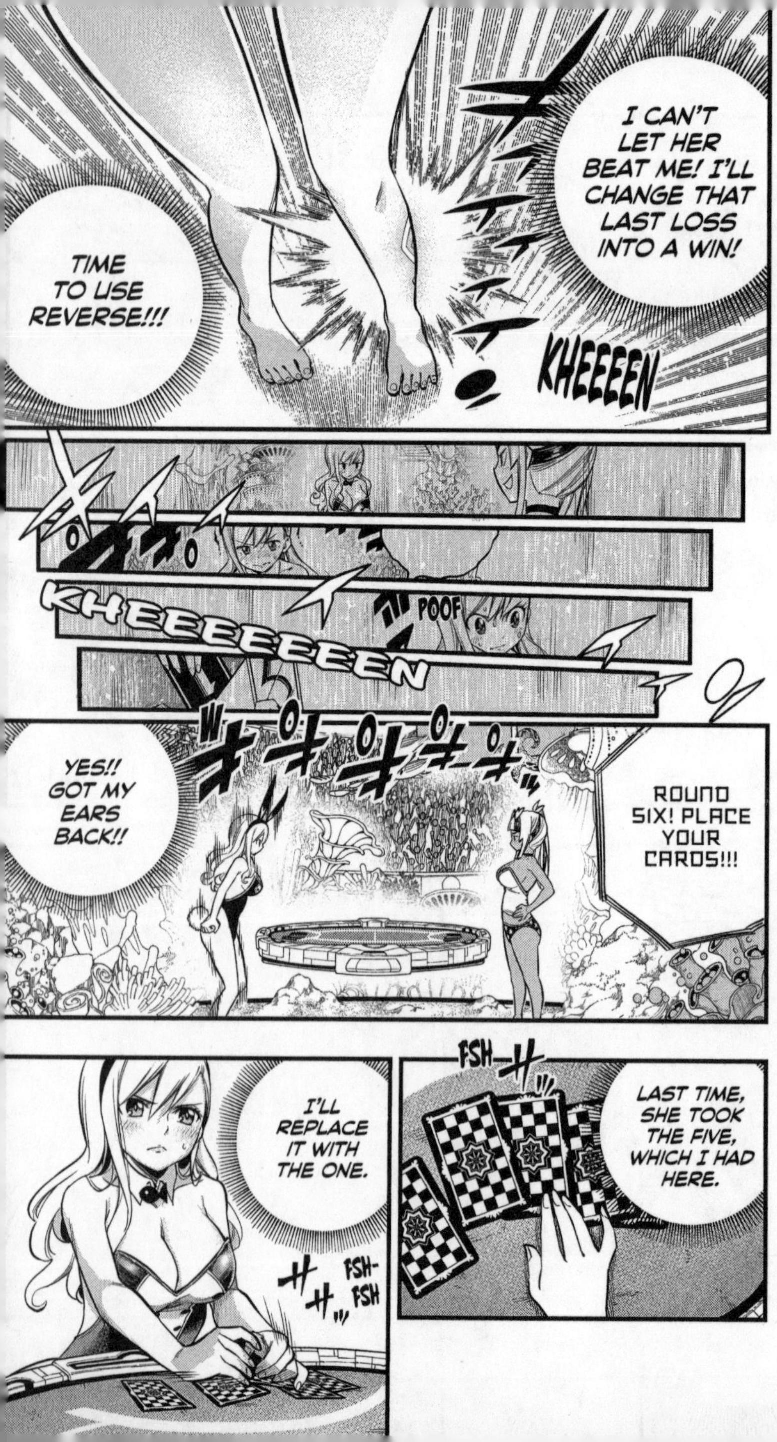
I CAN'T LET HER BEAT ME! I'LL CHANGE THAT LAST LOSS INTO A WIN!
TIME TO USE REVERSE!!!
KHEEEEN
KHEEEEEEEEEN
POOF
ROUND SIX! PLACE YOUR CARDS!!!
YES!! GOT MY EARS BACK!!
FSH
LAST TIME, SHE TOOK THE FIVE, WHICH I HAD HERE.
I'LL REPLACE IT WITH THE ONE.
FSH-FSH

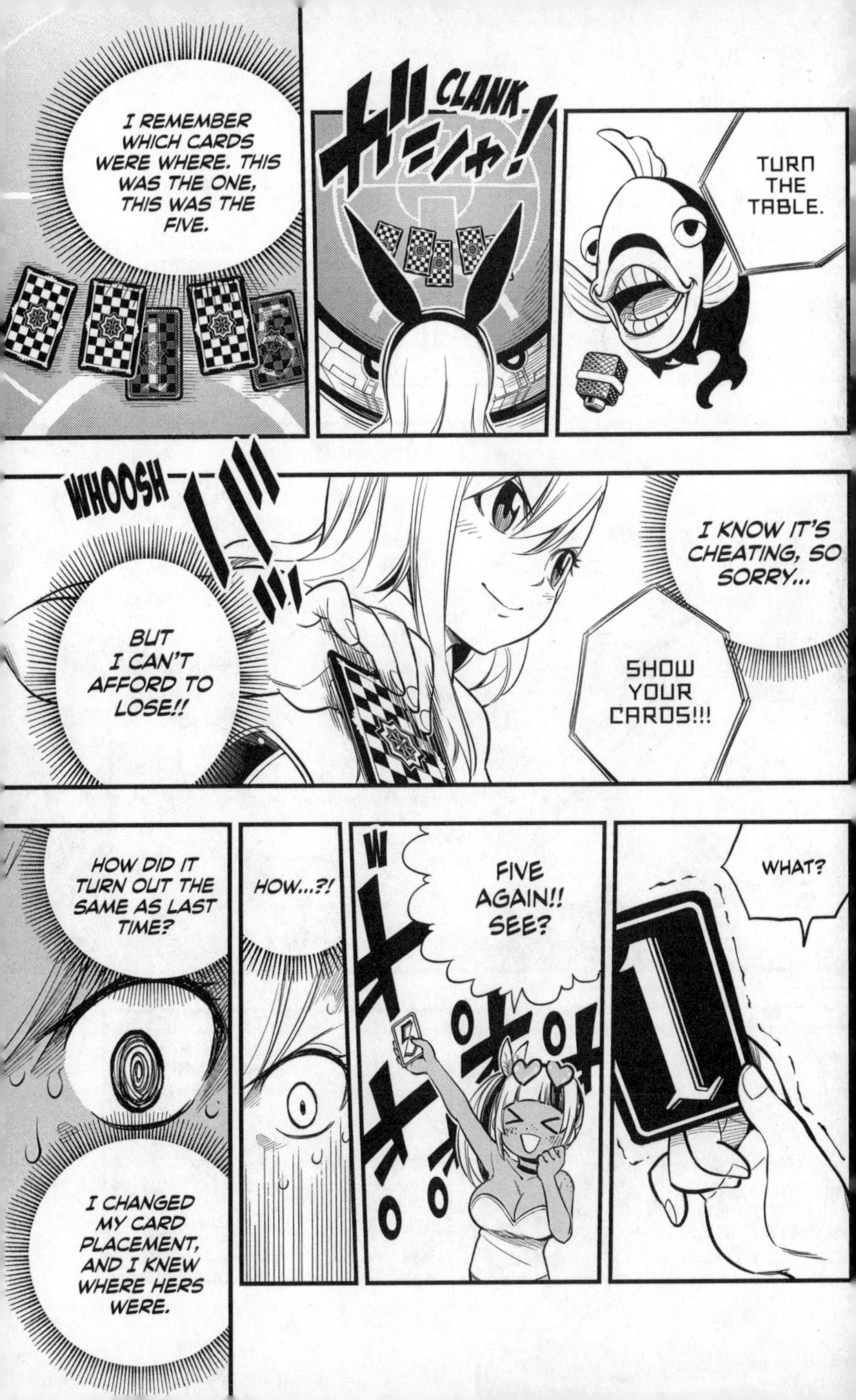
TURN THE TABLE.
CLANK
I REMEMBER WHICH CARDS WERE WHERE. THIS WAS THE ONE, THIS WAS THE FIVE.
I KNOW IT'S CHEATING, SO SORRY...
SHOW YOUR CARDS!!!
WHOOSH
BUT I CAN'T AFFORD TO LOSE!!
WHAT?
FIVE AGAIN!! SEE?
HOW...?!
HOW DID IT TURN OUT THE SAME AS LAST TIME?
I CHANGED MY CARD PLACEMENT, AND I KNEW WHERE HERS WERE.

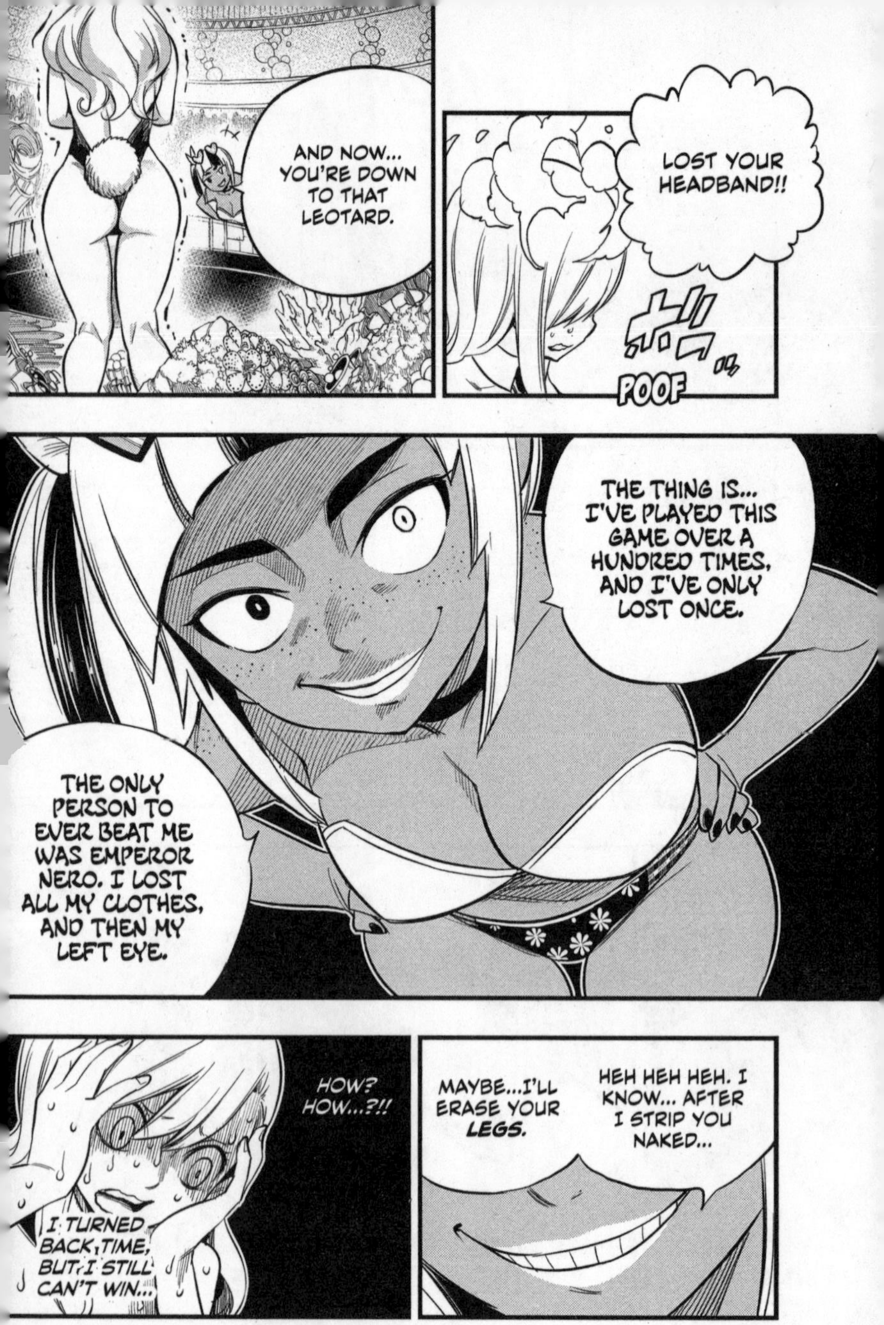
LOST YOUR HEADBAND!!
POOF
AND NOW... YOU'RE DOWN TO THAT LEOTARD.
THE THING IS... I'VE PLAYED THIS GAME OVER A HUNDRED TIMES, AND I'VE ONLY LOST ONCE.
THE ONLY PERSON TO EVER BEAT ME WAS EMPEROR NERO. I LOST ALL MY CLOTHES, AND THEN MY LEFT EYE.
HEH HEH HEH. I KNOW... AFTER I STRIP YOU NAKED...
MAYBE...I'LL ERASE YOUR *LEGS.*
HOW? HOW...?!!
I TURNED BACK TIME, BUT I STILL CAN'T WIN...

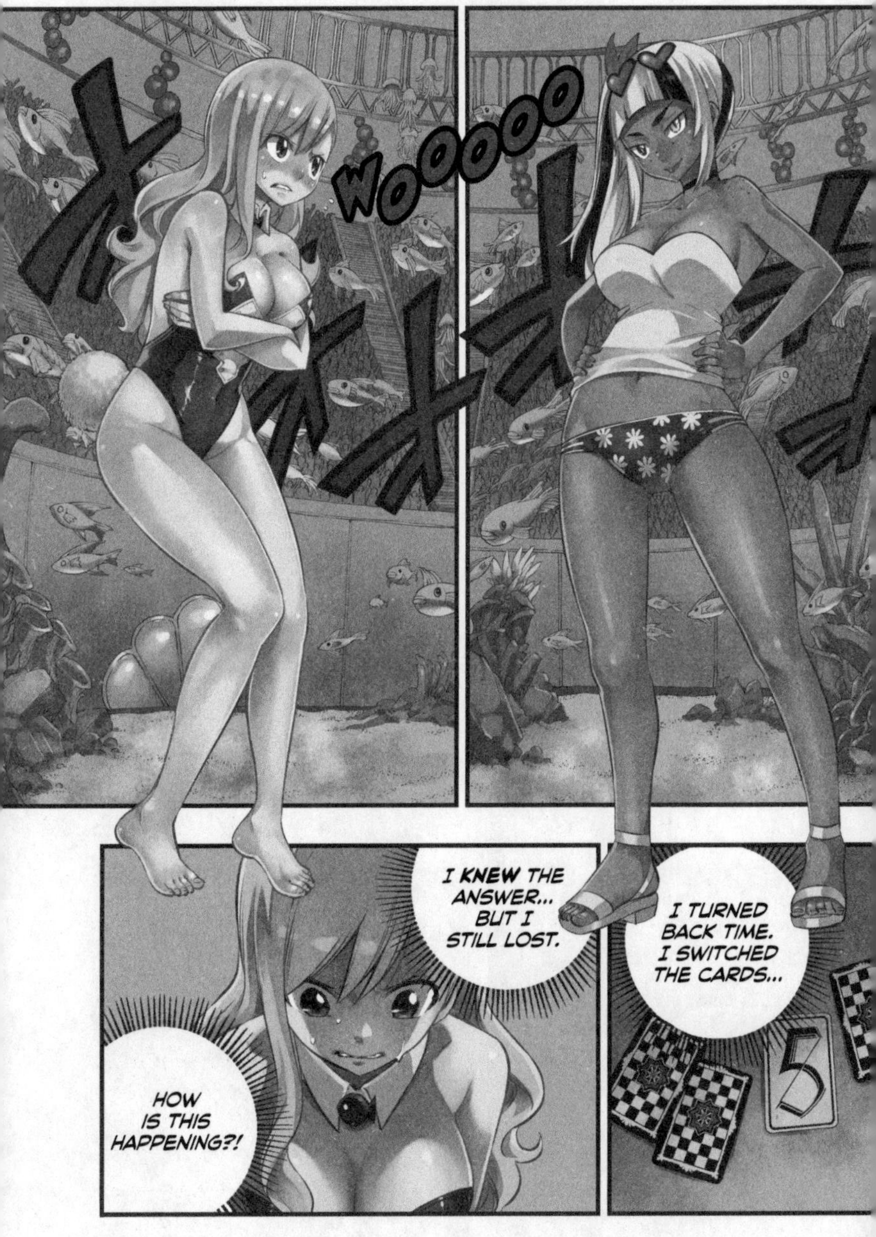
WOOOOO
I TURNED BACK TIME. I SWITCHED THE CARDS...
I KNEW THE ANSWER... BUT I STILL LOST.
HOW IS THIS HAPPENING?!

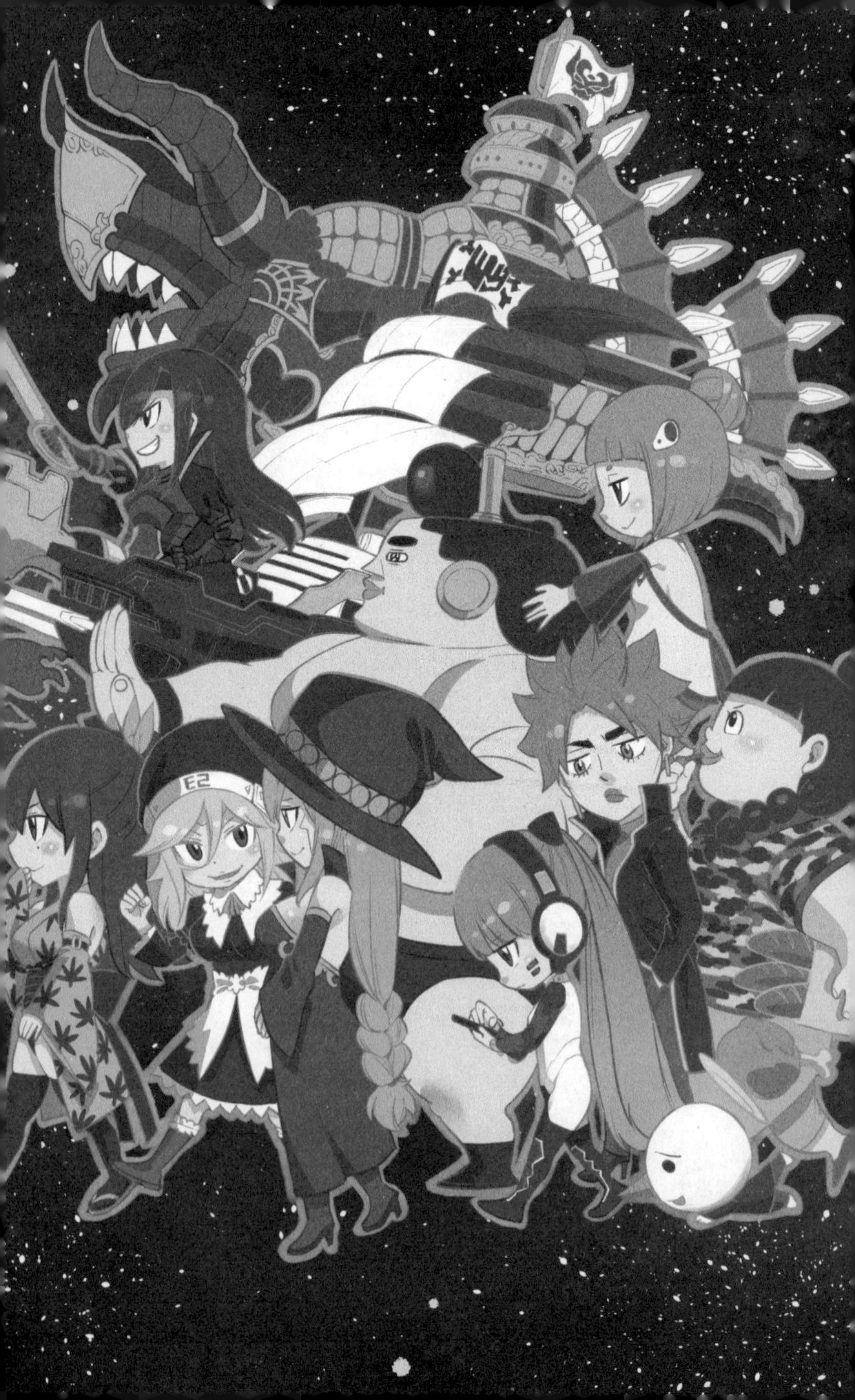

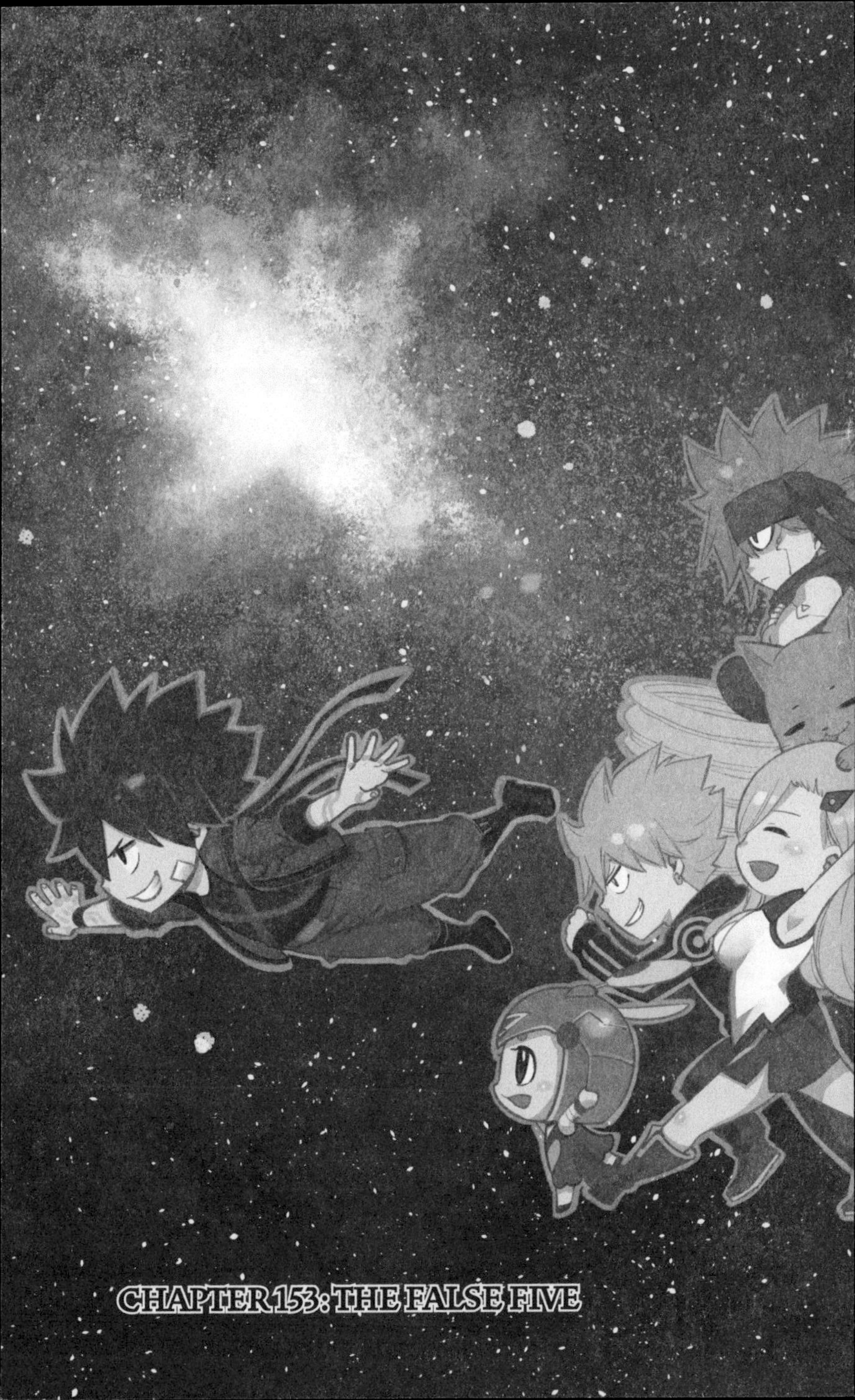
CHAPTER 153: THE FALSE FIVE

WELCOME TO THE NEXT INSTALLMENT OF...

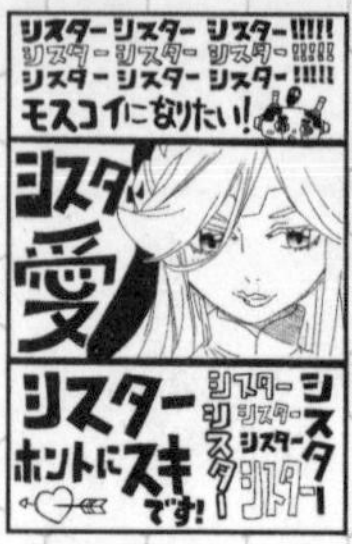
シスター シスター シスター!!!!!
シスター シスター シスター!!!!!
シスター シスター シスター!!!!!
モスコイになりたい!
シスター
愛
シスター
ホントにスキです!

(MOSCO MARK 2-SAN, KYOTO)

▶THIS IS INCREDIBLE! IT'S OVERFLOWING WITH LOVE... OR LIKE A DAM HAS BURST?! EVEN YOUR PEN NAME!!

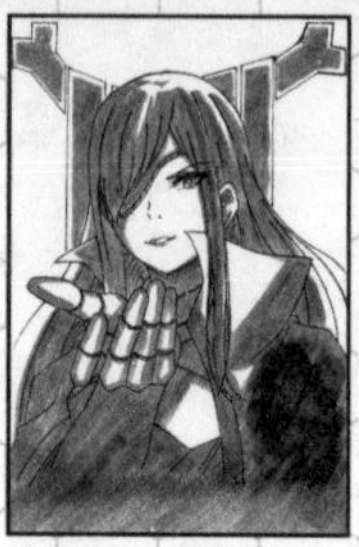

(KURODO NISHIZAKI-SAN, SAITAMA)

▲WHY DO I FEEL SO INTIMIDATED? IT'S SUCH A QUIET PICTURE, BUT ITS AURA!

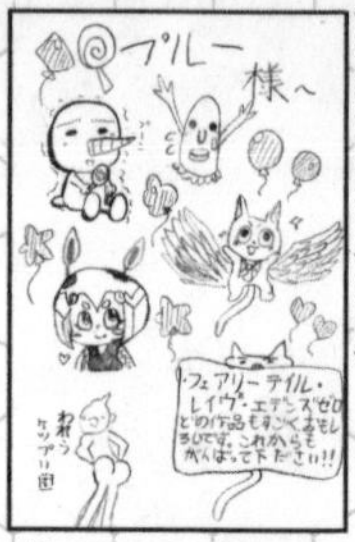
プルー
様へ

(MOCHISUKE-SAN, CHIBA)

▲A MASSIVE ASSEMBLY OF MASCOT CHARACTERS... OR SO I THOUGHT, BUT THEN I NOTICED A WEIRD ONE!

(YUTA HAMADA-SAN, OSAKA)

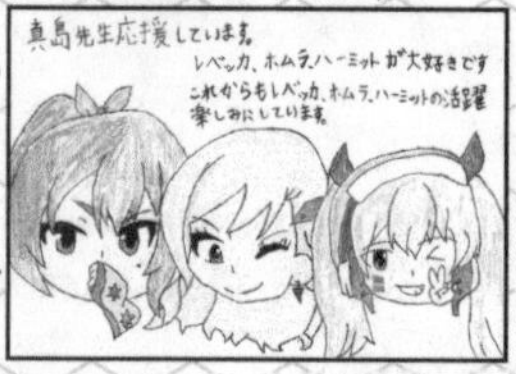
真島先生応援しています。

▶THE THREE OF THEM LINED UP TOGETHER LOOK LIKE A ROW OF MOCHI DUMPLINGS. IT'S HEARTWARMING.

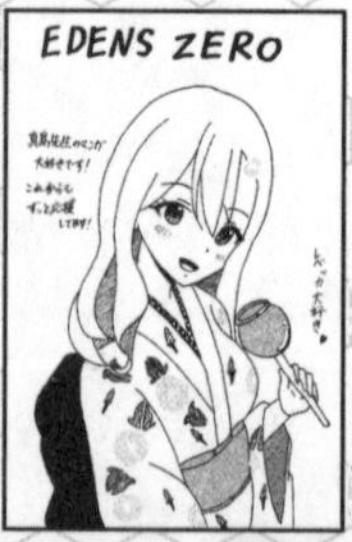
EDENS ZERO

(YUKI TAKEISHI-SAN, HYOGO)

◀IT LOOKS LIKE A PHOTOGRAPH TAKEN DURING A SUMMER FESTIVAL. I LOVE HOW THIS PICTURE IS SO ALIVE!

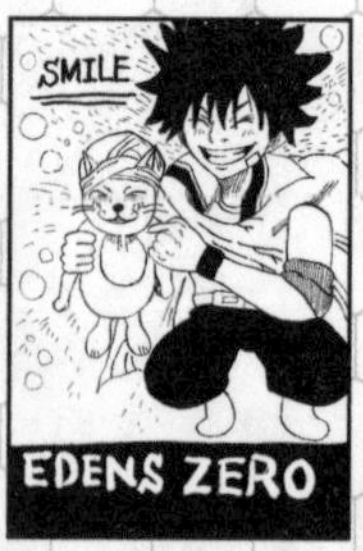
SMILE
EDENS ZERO

(TAKUMI TOKINAGA-SAN, KANAGAWA)

▲IN A SENSE, IT'S THE STRONGEST WEAPON THERE IS: A SMILE. IF WE CAN SMILE TOGETHER, THEN WE'RE ALREADY FRIENDS!

MASHIMA'S ONE-HIT KO

(YU MIYATA-SAN, AICHI)

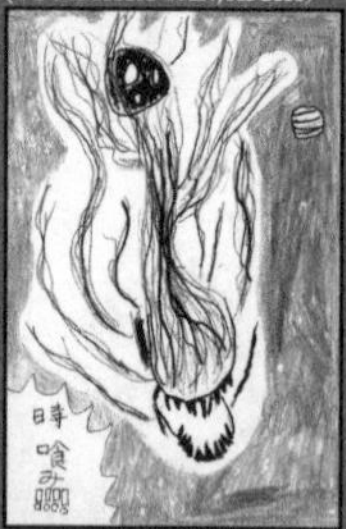

▲I DIDN'T THINK ANYONE WOULD EVER DRAW ME A CHRONOPHAGE. IT'S A THING NOW! THANK YOU, I LOVE IT!

EZ DRAWING

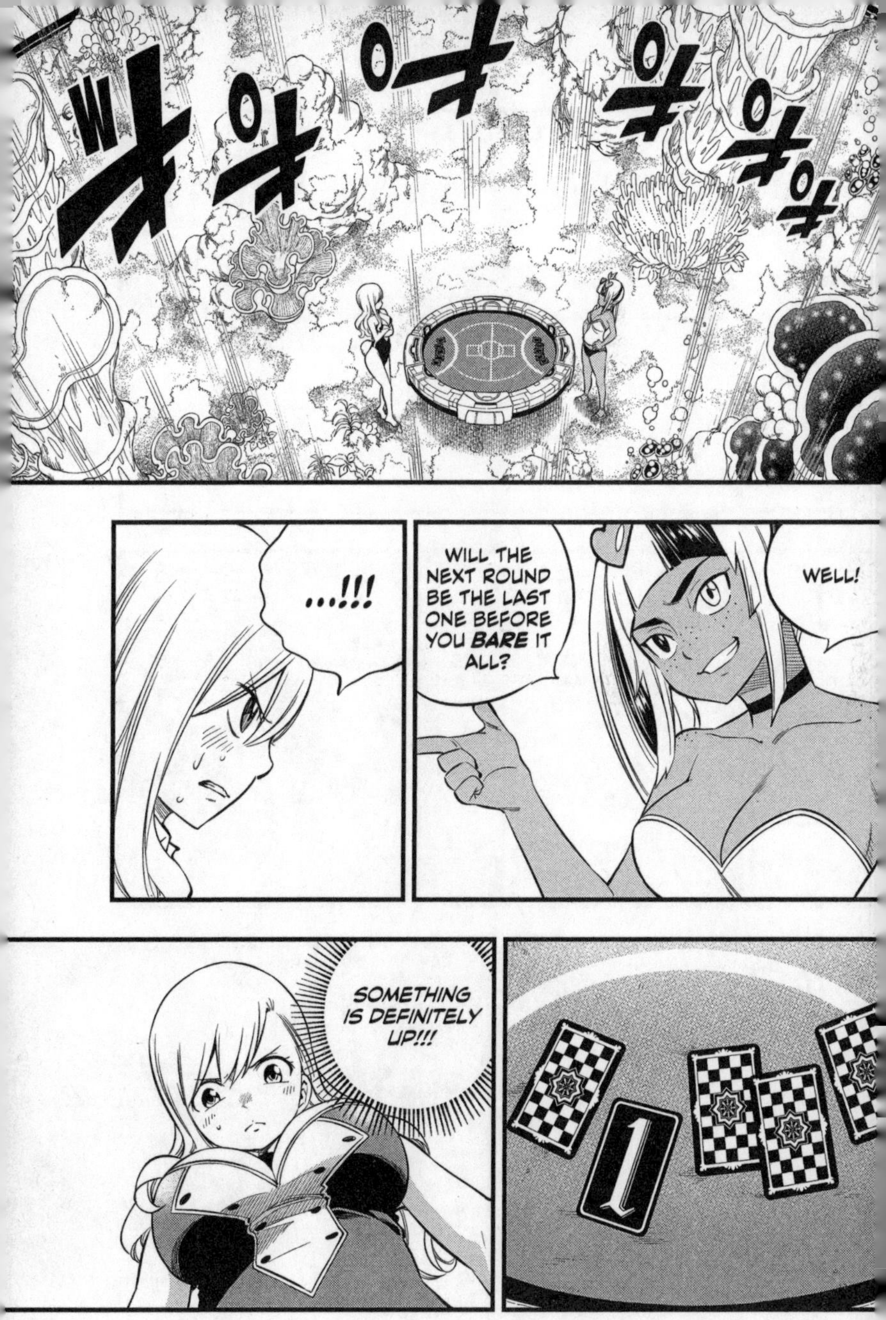
WELL!
WILL THE NEXT ROUND BE THE LAST ONE BEFORE YOU *BARE* IT ALL?
...!!!
SOMETHING IS DEFINITELY UP!!!

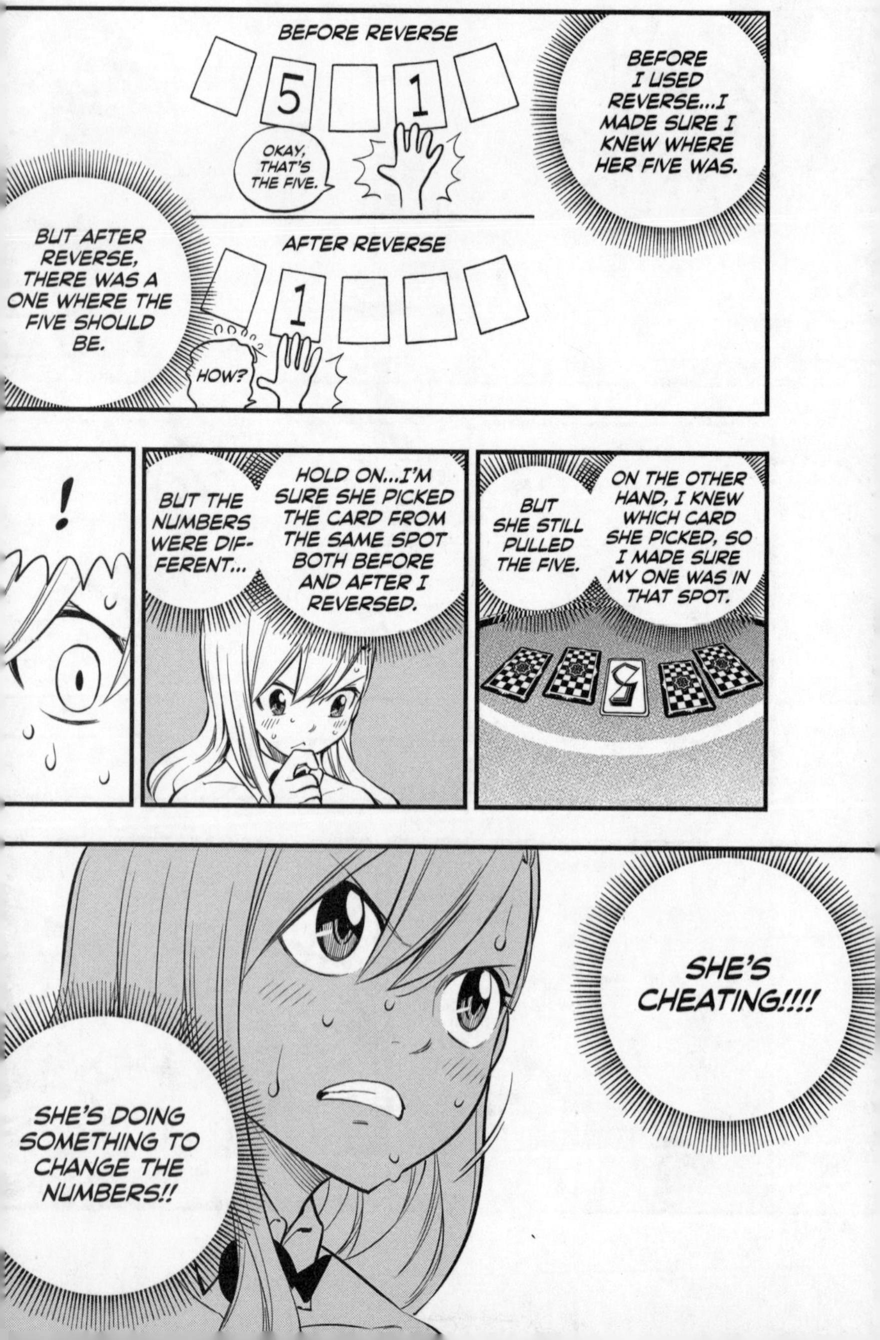

BEFORE I USED REVERSE...I MADE SURE I KNEW WHERE HER FIVE WAS.
BEFORE REVERSE
5
1
OKAY, THAT'S THE FIVE.
AFTER REVERSE
1
BUT AFTER REVERSE, THERE WAS A ONE WHERE THE FIVE SHOULD BE.
HOW?
ON THE OTHER HAND, I KNEW WHICH CARD SHE PICKED, SO I MADE SURE MY ONE WAS IN THAT SPOT.
BUT SHE STILL PULLED THE FIVE.
HOLD ON...I'M SURE SHE PICKED THE CARD FROM THE SAME SPOT BOTH BEFORE AND AFTER I REVERSED.
BUT THE NUMBERS WERE DIF-FERENT...
!
SHE'S CHEATING!!!!
SHE'S DOING SOMETHING TO CHANGE THE NUMBERS!!

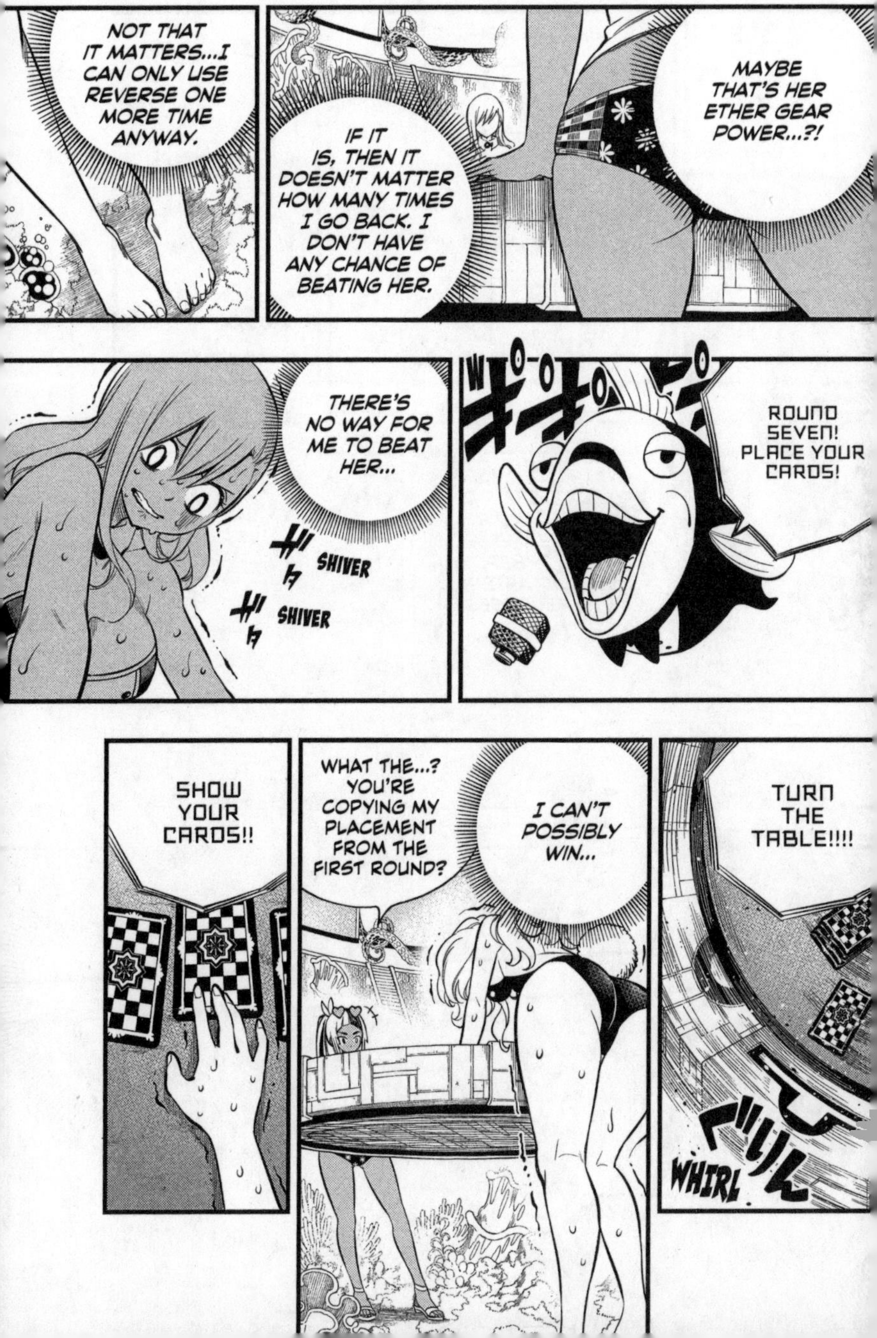
MAYBE THAT'S HER ETHER GEAR POWER...?!
IF IT IS, THEN IT DOESN'T MATTER HOW MANY TIMES I GO BACK. I DON'T HAVE ANY CHANCE OF BEATING HER.
NOT THAT IT MATTERS...I CAN ONLY USE REVERSE ONE MORE TIME ANYWAY.
ROUND SEVEN! PLACE YOUR CARDS!
THERE'S NO WAY FOR ME TO BEAT HER...
SHIVER
SHIVER
TURN THE TABLE!!!!
WHIRL
WHAT THE...? YOU'RE COPYING MY PLACEMENT FROM THE FIRST ROUND?
I CAN'T POSSIBLY WIN...
SHOW YOUR CARDS!!

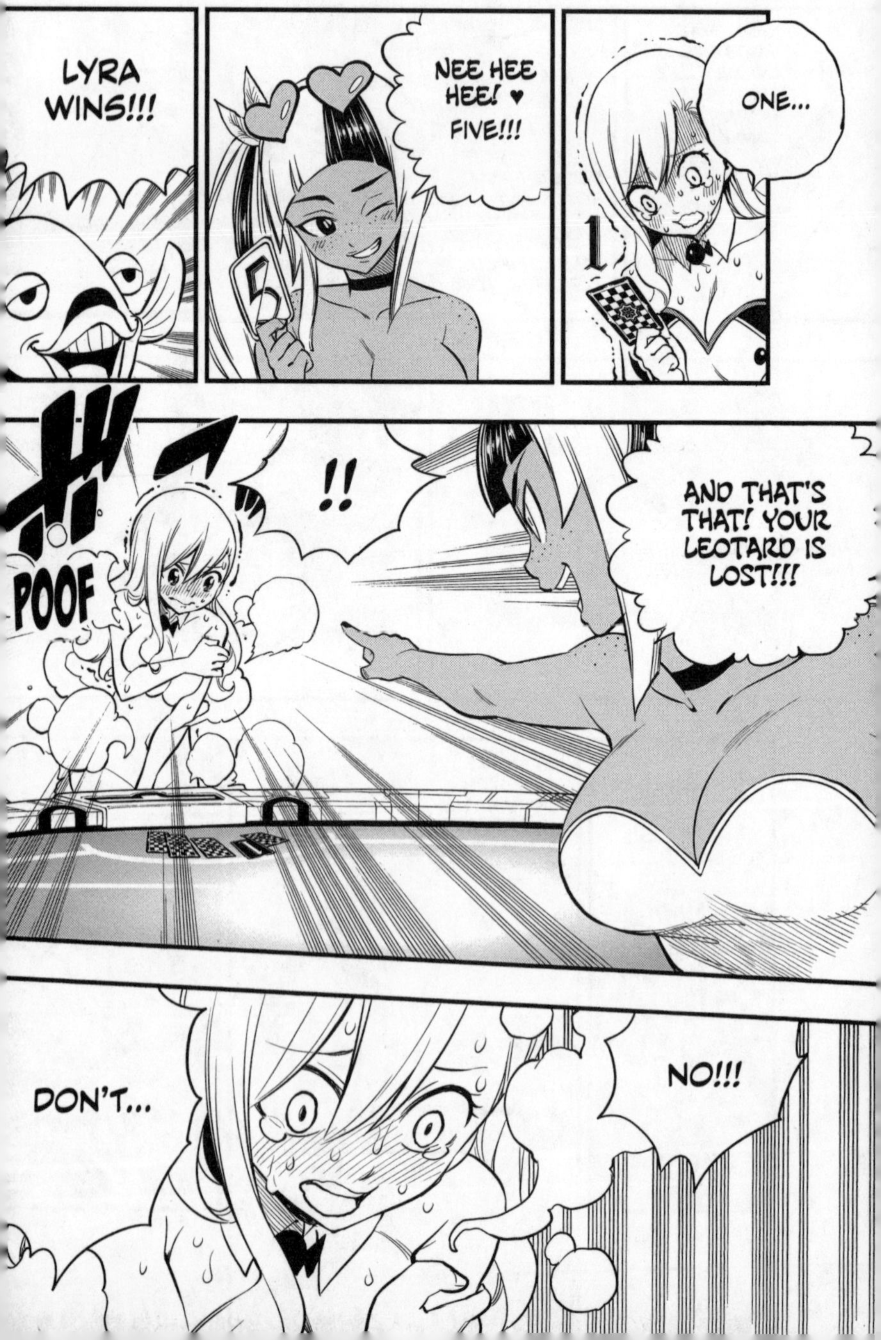
ONE...
NEE HEE HEE! ♥ FIVE!!!
LYRA WINS!!!
AND THAT'S THAT! YOUR LEOTARD IS LOST!!!
!!
POOF
NO!!!
DON'T...

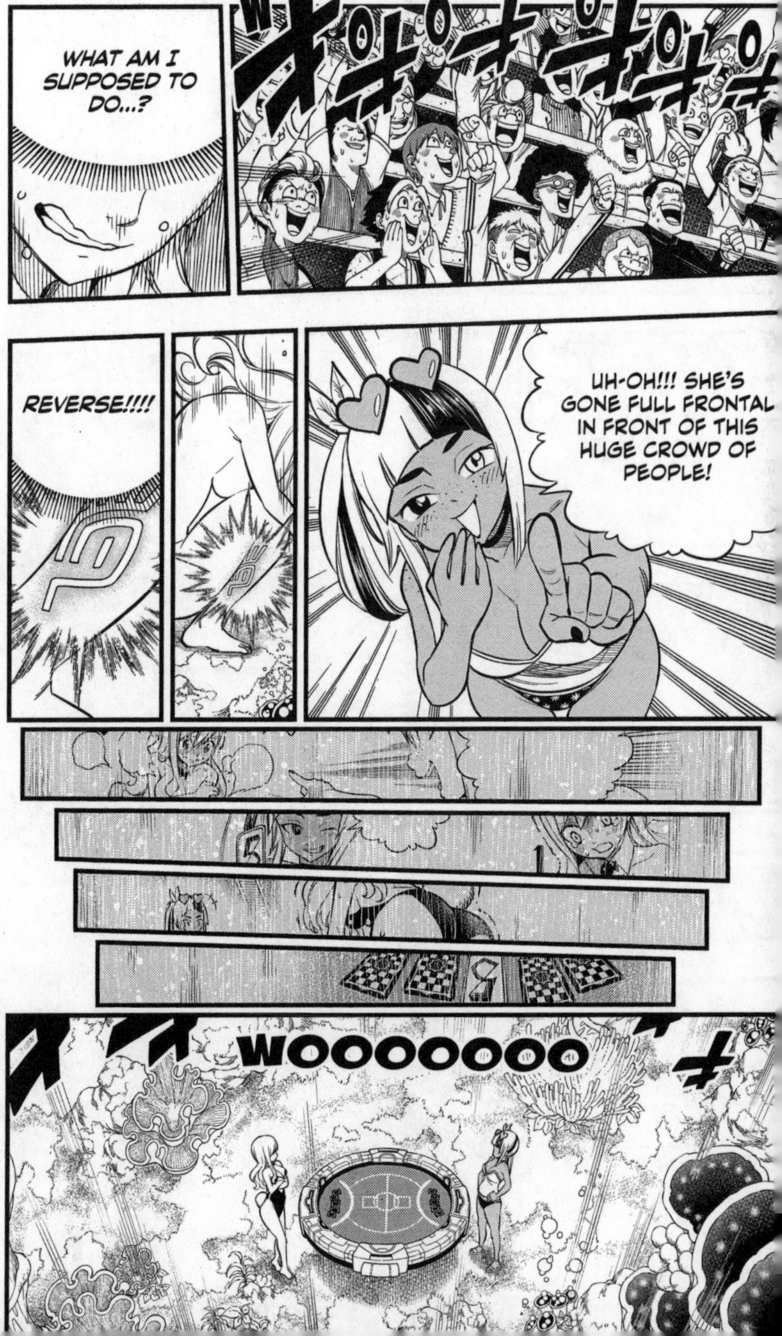
WHAT AM I SUPPOSED TO DO...?
UH-OH!!! SHE'S GONE FULL FRONTAL IN FRONT OF THIS HUGE CROWD OF PEOPLE!
REVERSE!!!!
WOOOOOOO

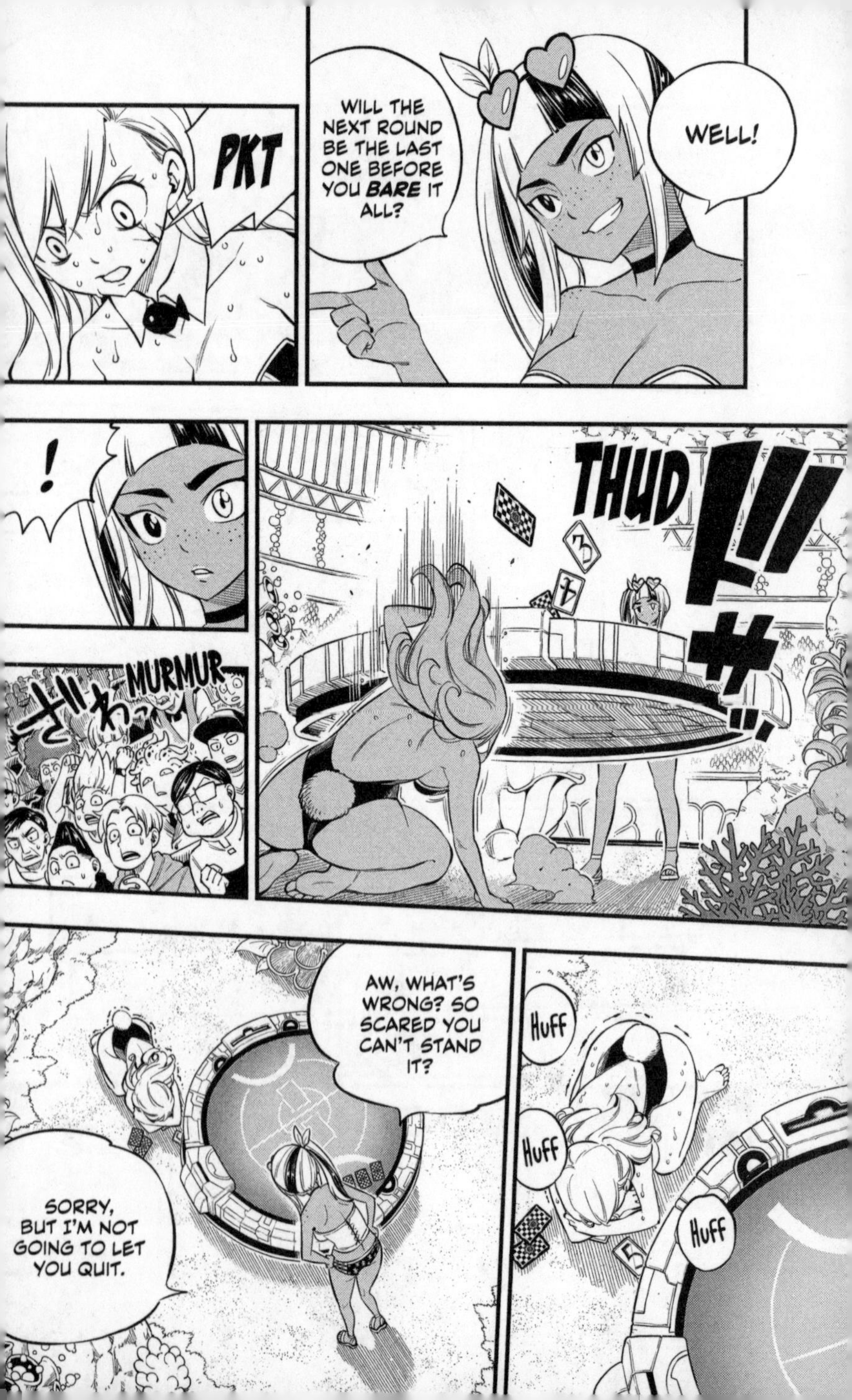
WELL!
WILL THE NEXT ROUND BE THE LAST ONE BEFORE YOU *BARE* IT ALL?
PKT
THUD
!
MURMUR
ざわっ
Huff
Huff
Huff
AW, WHAT'S WRONG? SO SCARED YOU CAN'T STAND IT?
SORRY, BUT I'M NOT GOING TO LET YOU QUIT.

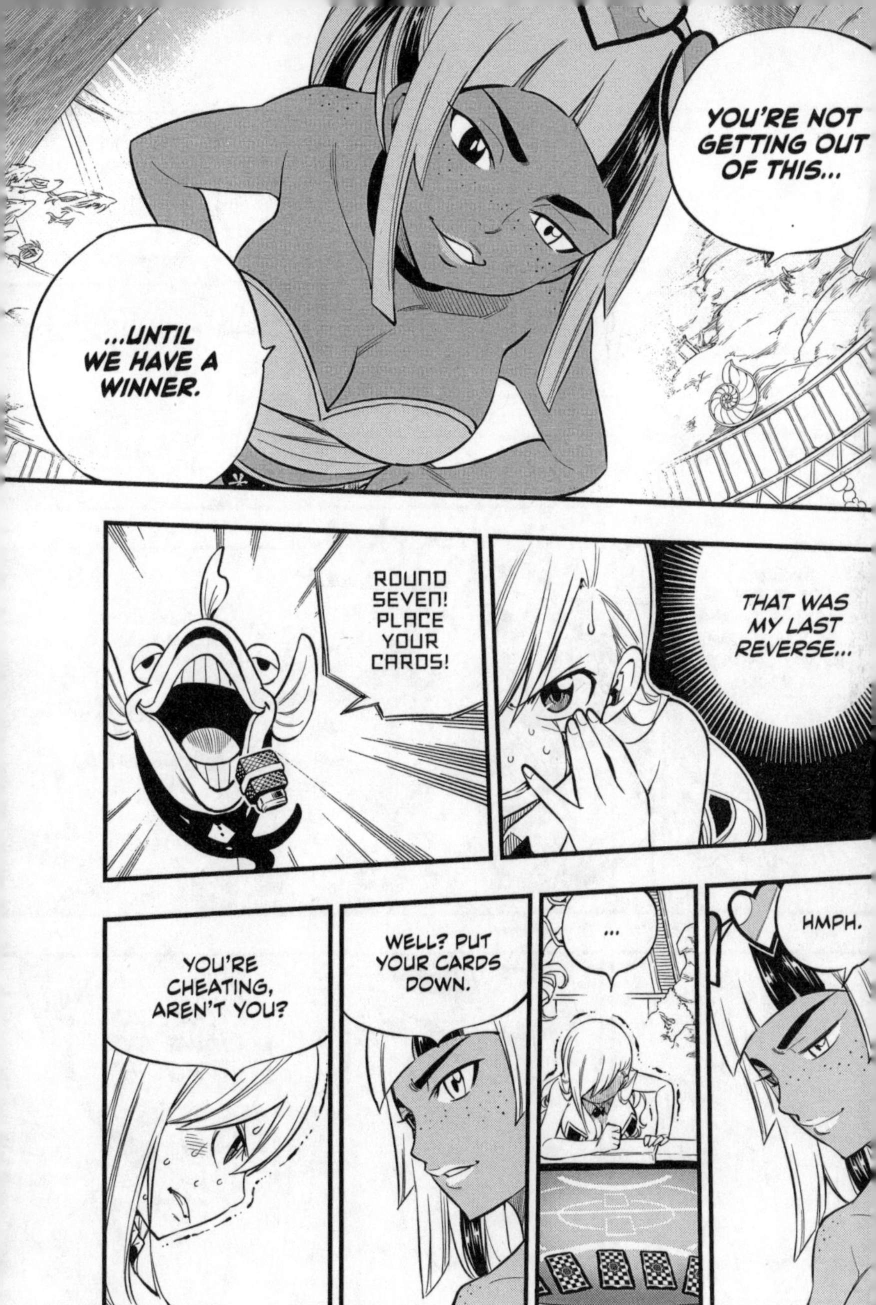
YOU'RE NOT GETTING OUT OF THIS...
...UNTIL WE HAVE A WINNER.
THAT WAS MY LAST REVERSE...
ROUND SEVEN! PLACE YOUR CARDS!
HMPH.
...
WELL? PUT YOUR CARDS DOWN.
YOU'RE CHEATING, AREN'T YOU?

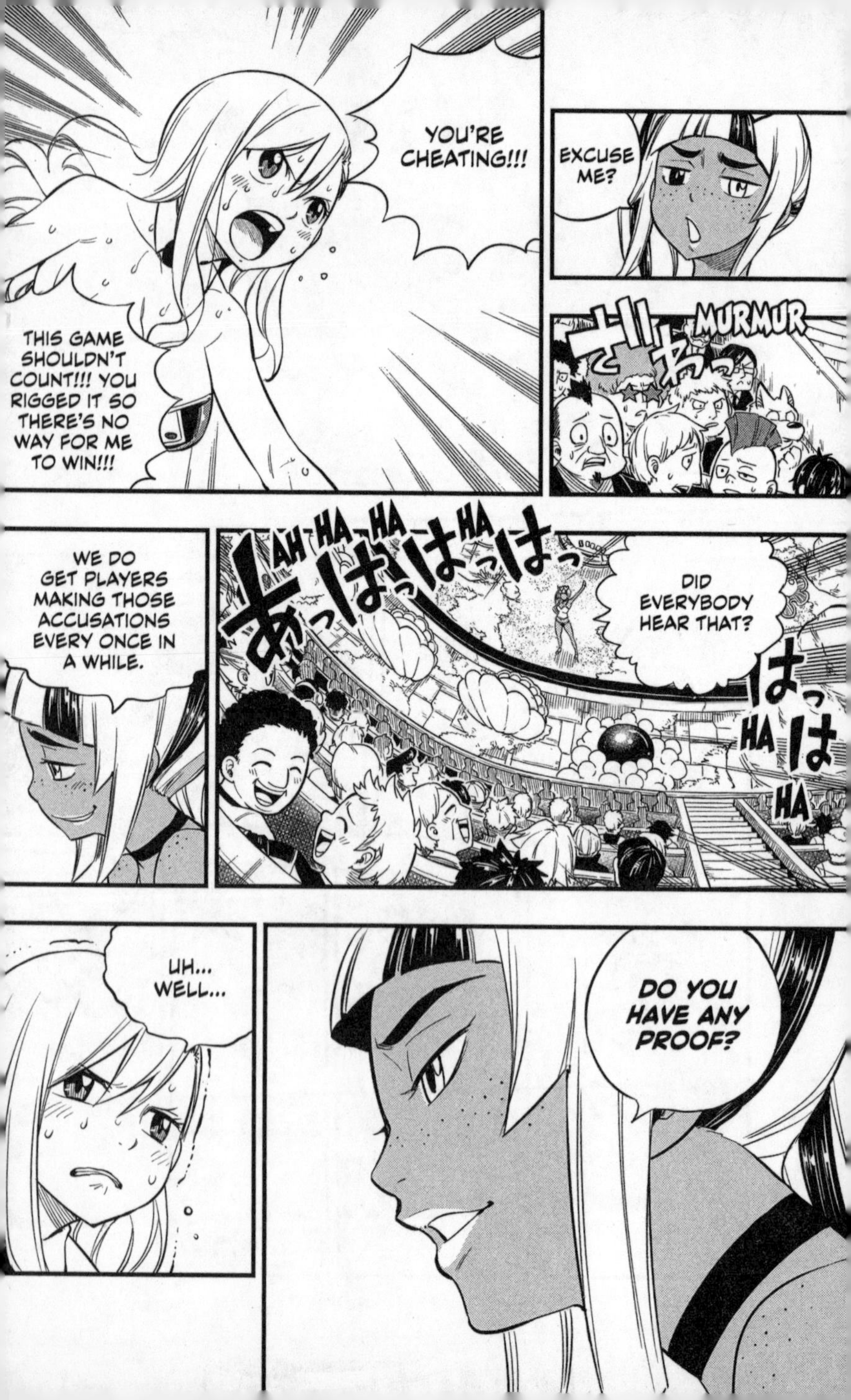
EXCUSE ME?
MURMUR
YOU'RE CHEATING!!!
THIS GAME SHOULDN'T COUNT!!! YOU RIGGED IT SO THERE'S NO WAY FOR ME TO WIN!!!
AH HA HA HA
DID EVERYBODY HEAR THAT?
HA HA
WE DO GET PLAYERS MAKING THOSE ACCUSATIONS EVERY ONCE IN A WHILE.
DO YOU HAVE ANY PROOF?
UH... WELL...

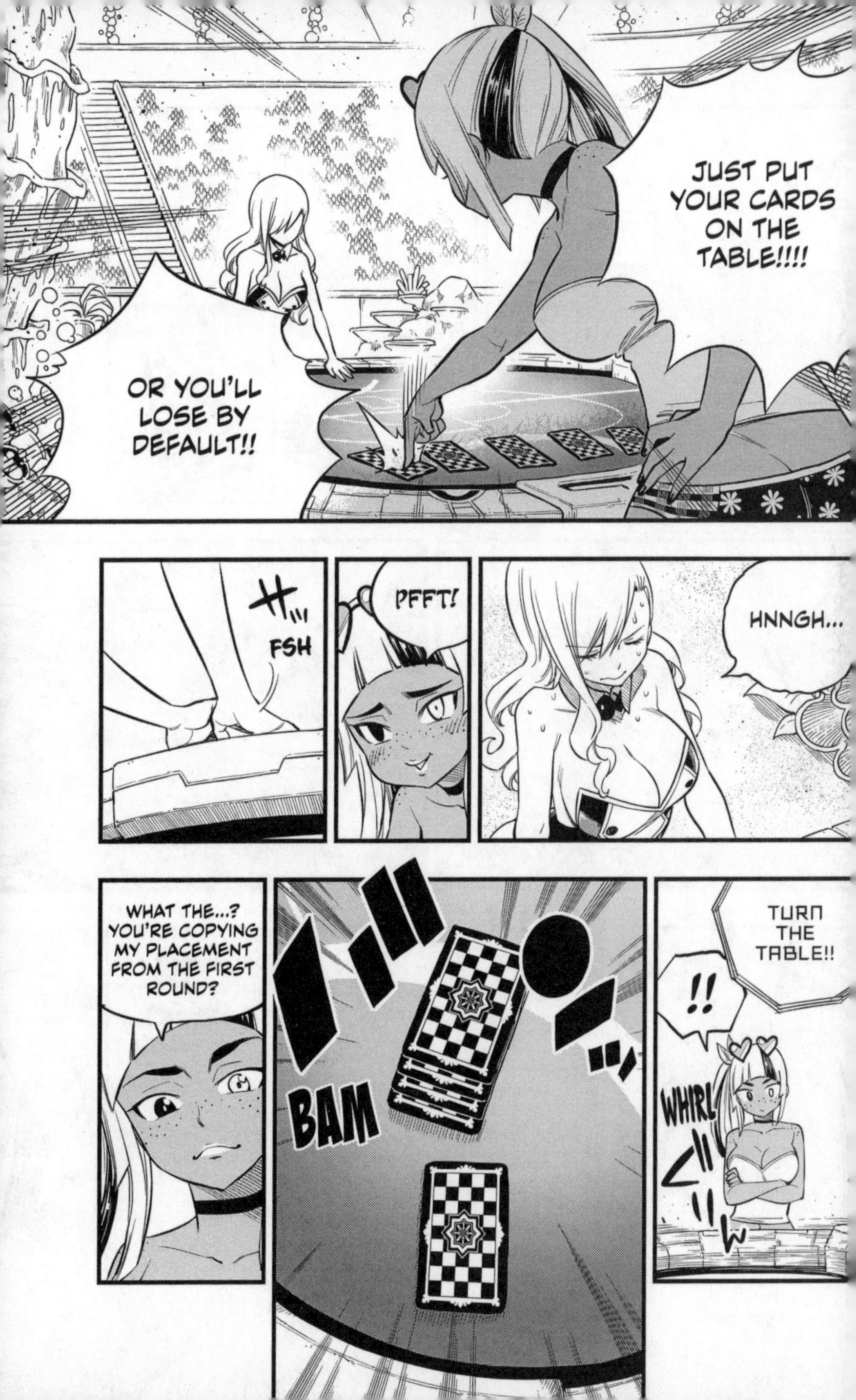
JUST PUT YOUR CARDS ON THE TABLE!!!!
OR YOU'LL LOSE BY DEFAULT!!
HNNGH...
PFFT!
FSH
TURN THE TABLE!!
!!
WHIRL
BAM
WHAT THE...? YOU'RE COPYING MY PLACEMENT FROM THE FIRST ROUND?

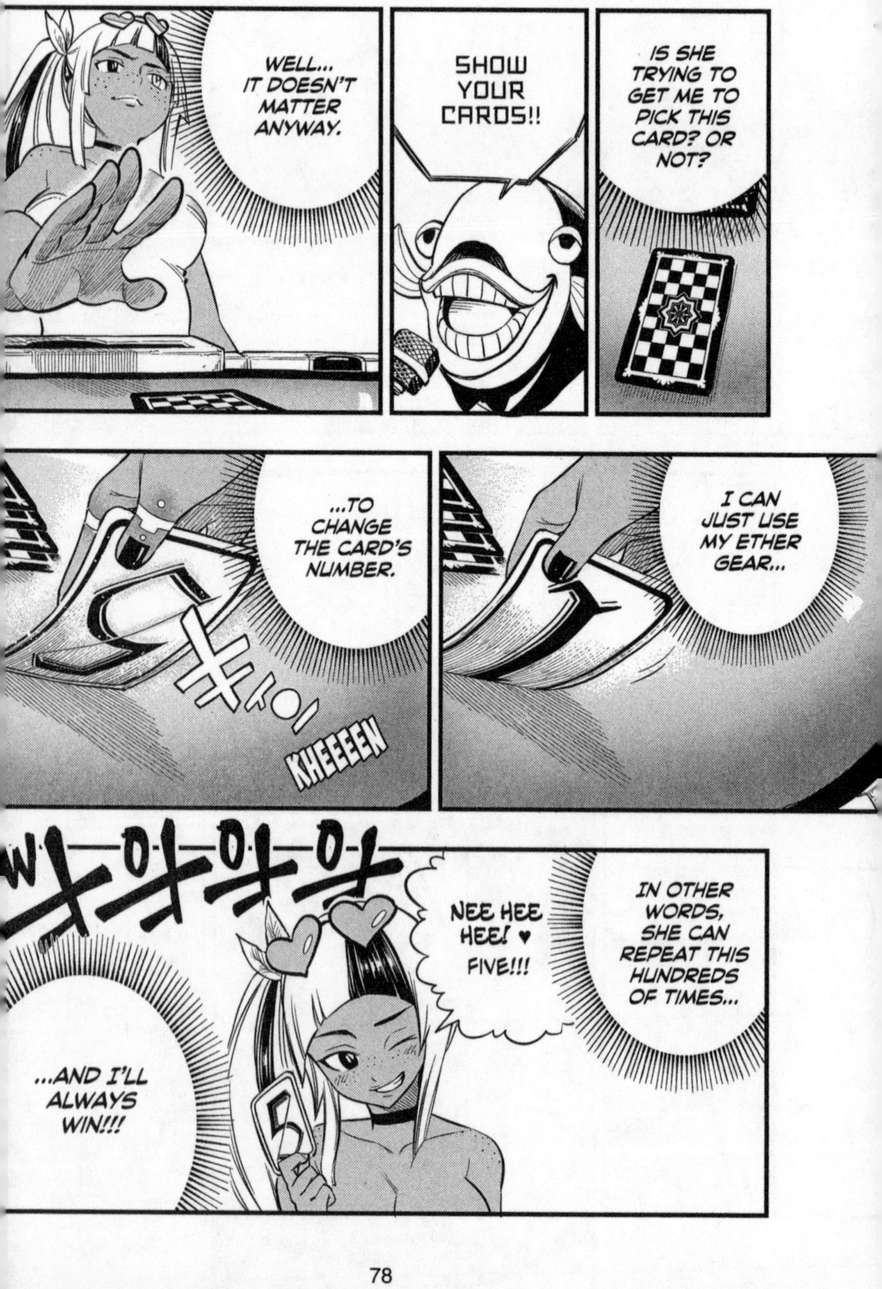
IS SHE TRYING TO GET ME TO PICK THIS CARD? OR NOT?
SHOW YOUR CARDS!!
WELL... IT DOESN'T MATTER ANYWAY.
I CAN JUST USE MY ETHER GEAR...
...TO CHANGE THE CARD'S NUMBER.
KHEEEEN
IN OTHER WORDS, SHE CAN REPEAT THIS HUNDREDS OF TIMES...
NEE HEE HEE! ♥ FIVE!!!
...AND I'LL ALWAYS WIN!!!

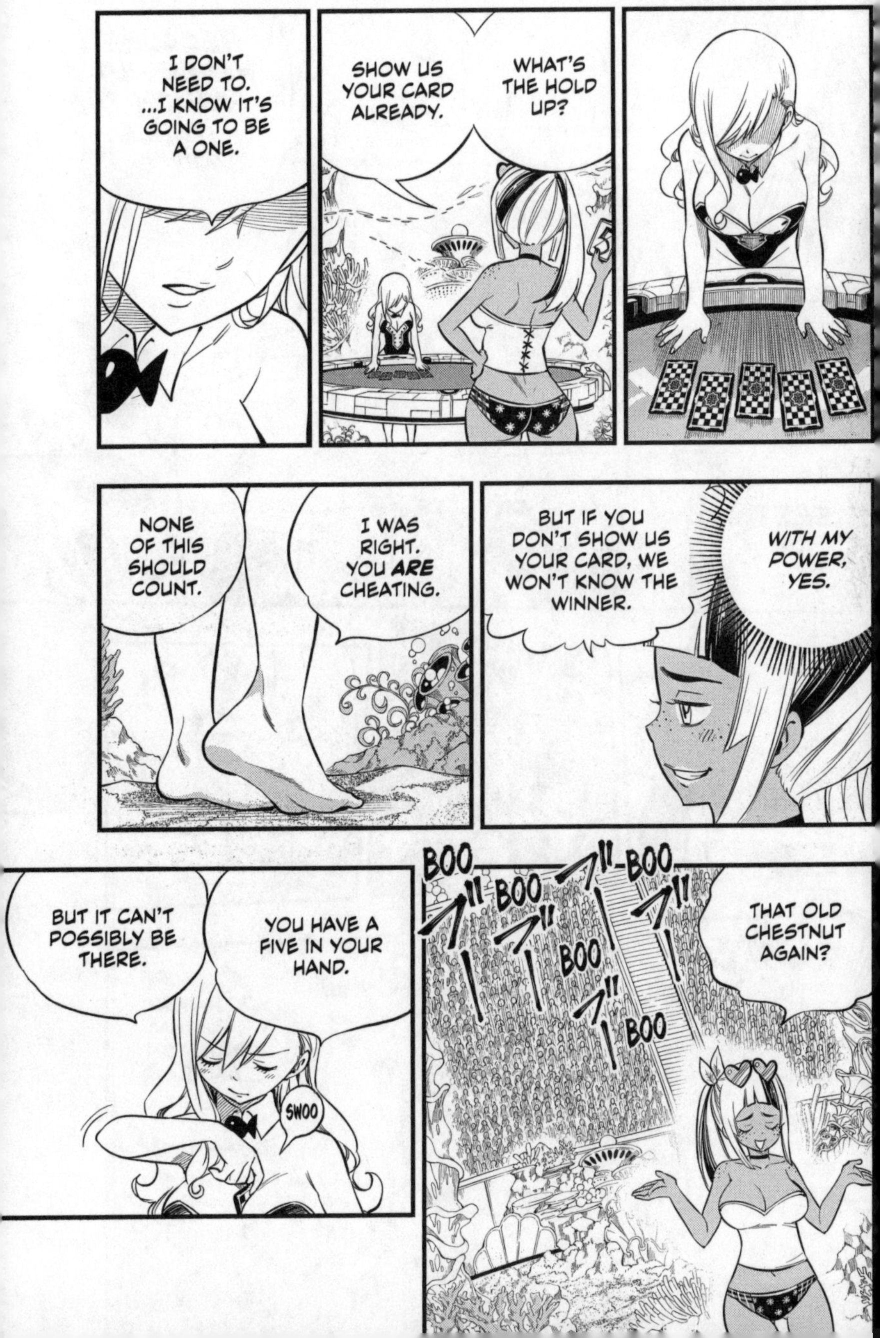
WHAT'S THE HOLD UP?
SHOW US YOUR CARD ALREADY.
I DON'T NEED TO. ...I KNOW IT'S GOING TO BE A ONE.
WITH MY POWER, YES.
BUT IF YOU DON'T SHOW US YOUR CARD, WE WON'T KNOW THE WINNER.
I WAS RIGHT. YOU *ARE* CHEATING.
NONE OF THIS SHOULD COUNT.
BOO BOO BOO BOO BOO
THAT OLD CHESTNUT AGAIN?
YOU HAVE A FIVE IN YOUR HAND.
BUT IT CAN'T POSSIBLY BE THERE.
SWOO

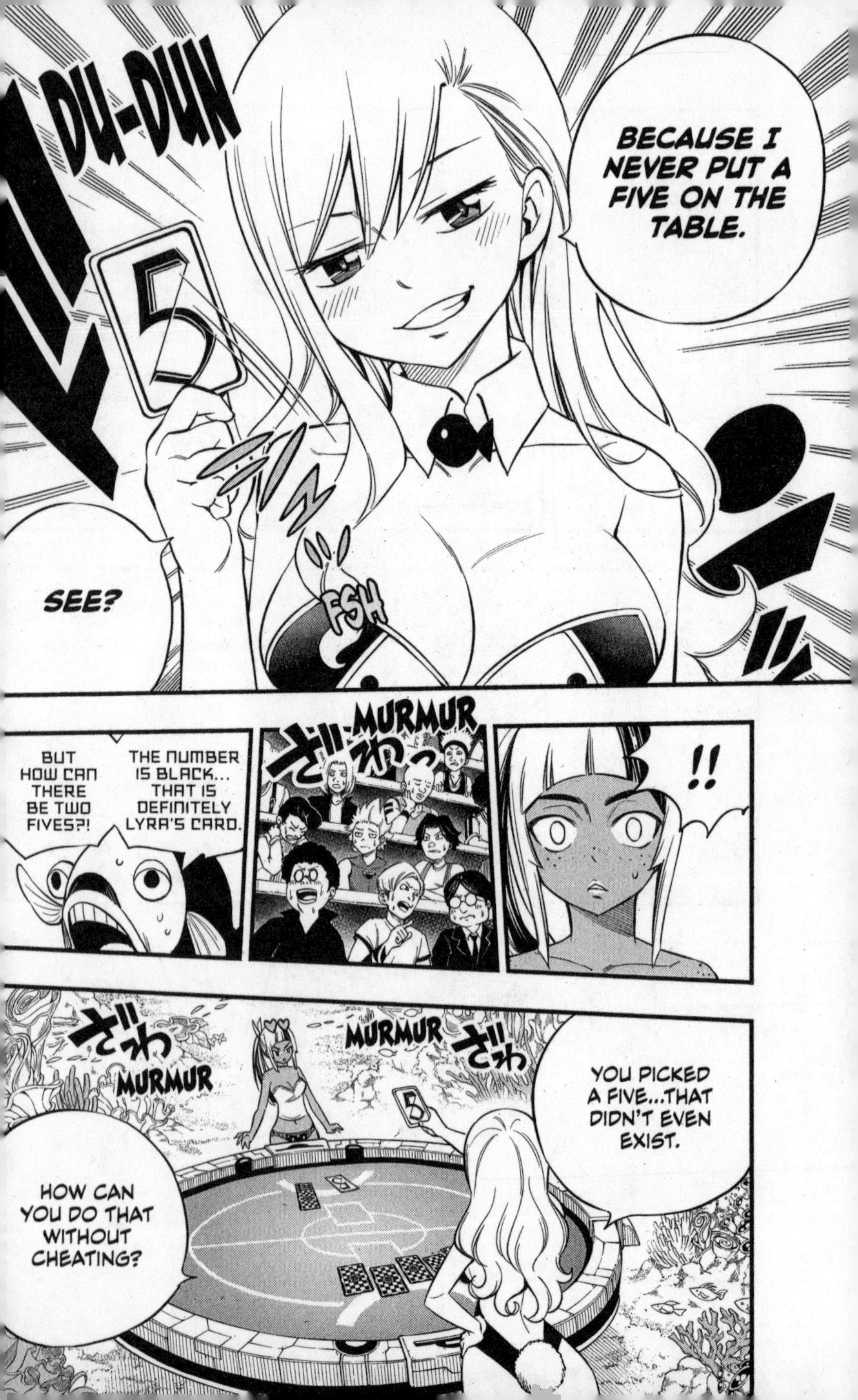
BECAUSE I NEVER PUT A FIVE ON THE TABLE.
DU-DUN
FSH
SEE?
!!
MURMUR
ざわっ
THE NUMBER IS BLACK... THAT IS DEFINITELY LYRA'S CARD.
BUT HOW CAN THERE BE TWO FIVES?!
YOU PICKED A FIVE...THAT DIDN'T EVEN EXIST.
ざわ
MURMUR
ざわ
MURMUR
HOW CAN YOU DO THAT WITHOUT CHEATING?

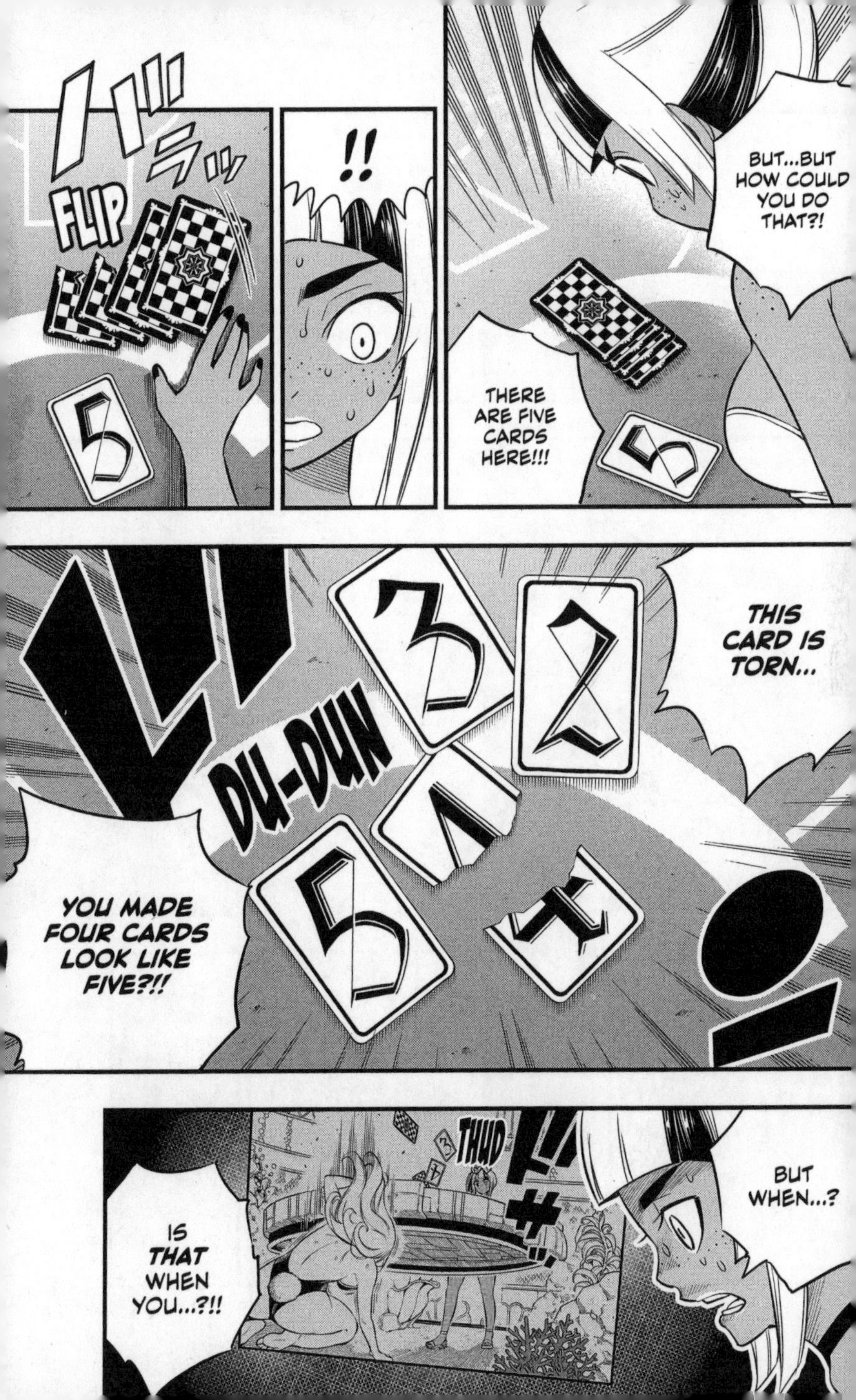
BUT...BUT HOW COULD YOU DO THAT?!
THERE ARE FIVE CARDS HERE!!!
!!
FLIP
5
THIS CARD IS TORN...
DU-DUN
3
2
5
4
YOU MADE FOUR CARDS LOOK LIKE FIVE?!!
BUT WHEN...?
THUD
IS THAT WHEN YOU...?!!

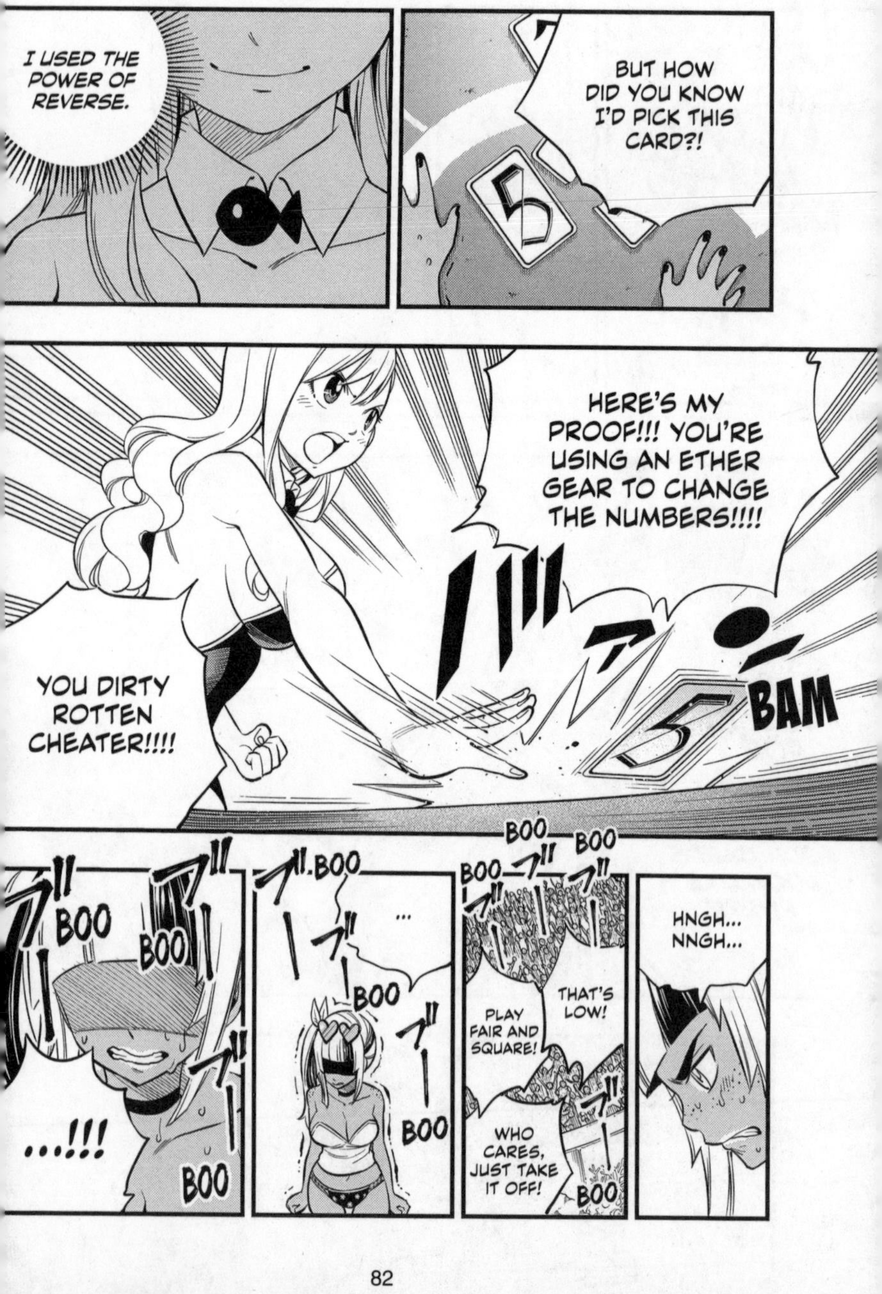
BUT HOW DID YOU KNOW I'D PICK THIS CARD?!
I USED THE POWER OF REVERSE.
HERE'S MY PROOF!!! YOU'RE USING AN ETHER GEAR TO CHANGE THE NUMBERS!!!!
BAM
YOU DIRTY ROTTEN CHEATER!!!!
HNGH... NNGH...
BOO
BOO
BOO
THAT'S LOW!
PLAY FAIR AND SQUARE!
WHO CARES, JUST TAKE IT OFF!
BOO
BOO
...
BOO
BOO
BOO
BOO
...!!!
BOO

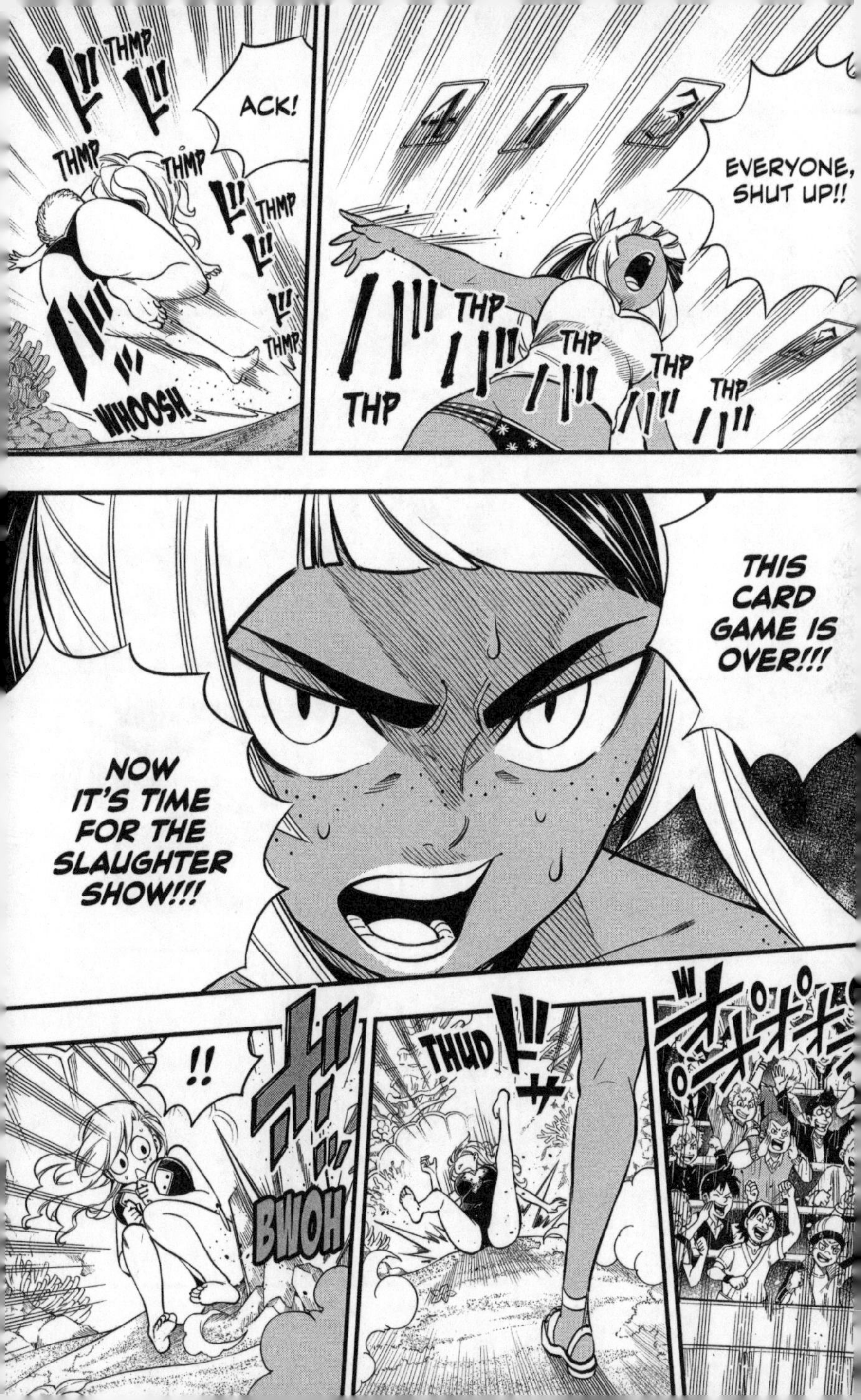
EVERYONE, SHUT UP!!
THP
THP
THP
THP
THP
THMP
THMP
ACK!
THMP
THMP
THMP
WHOOSH
THIS CARD GAME IS OVER!!!
NOW IT'S TIME FOR THE SLAUGHTER SHOW!!!
THUD
!!
BWOH

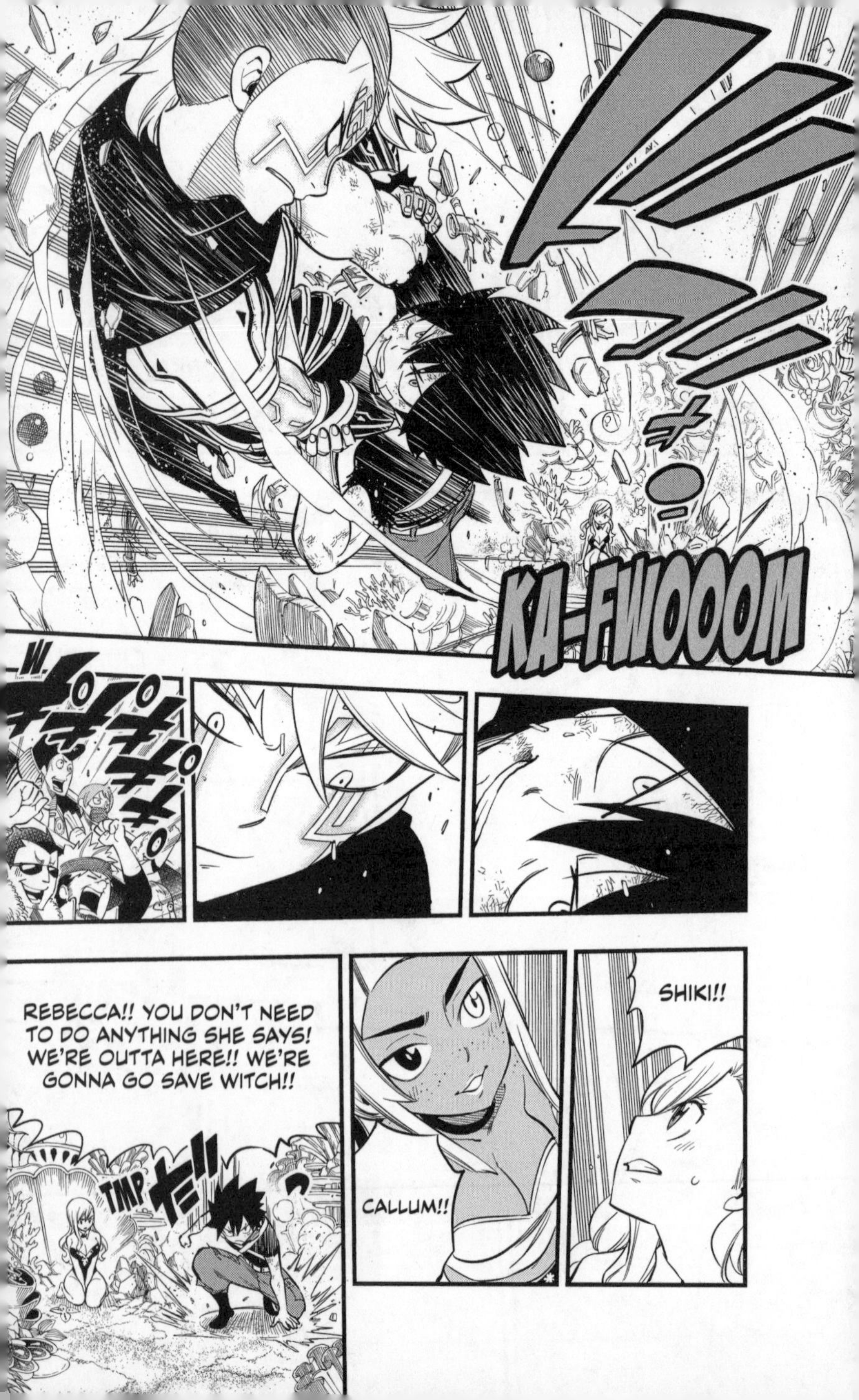
KA-FWOOOM
SHIKI!!
CALLUM!!
REBECCA!! YOU DON'T NEED TO DO ANYTHING SHE SAYS! WE'RE OUTTA HERE!! WE'RE GONNA GO SAVE WITCH!!
TMP

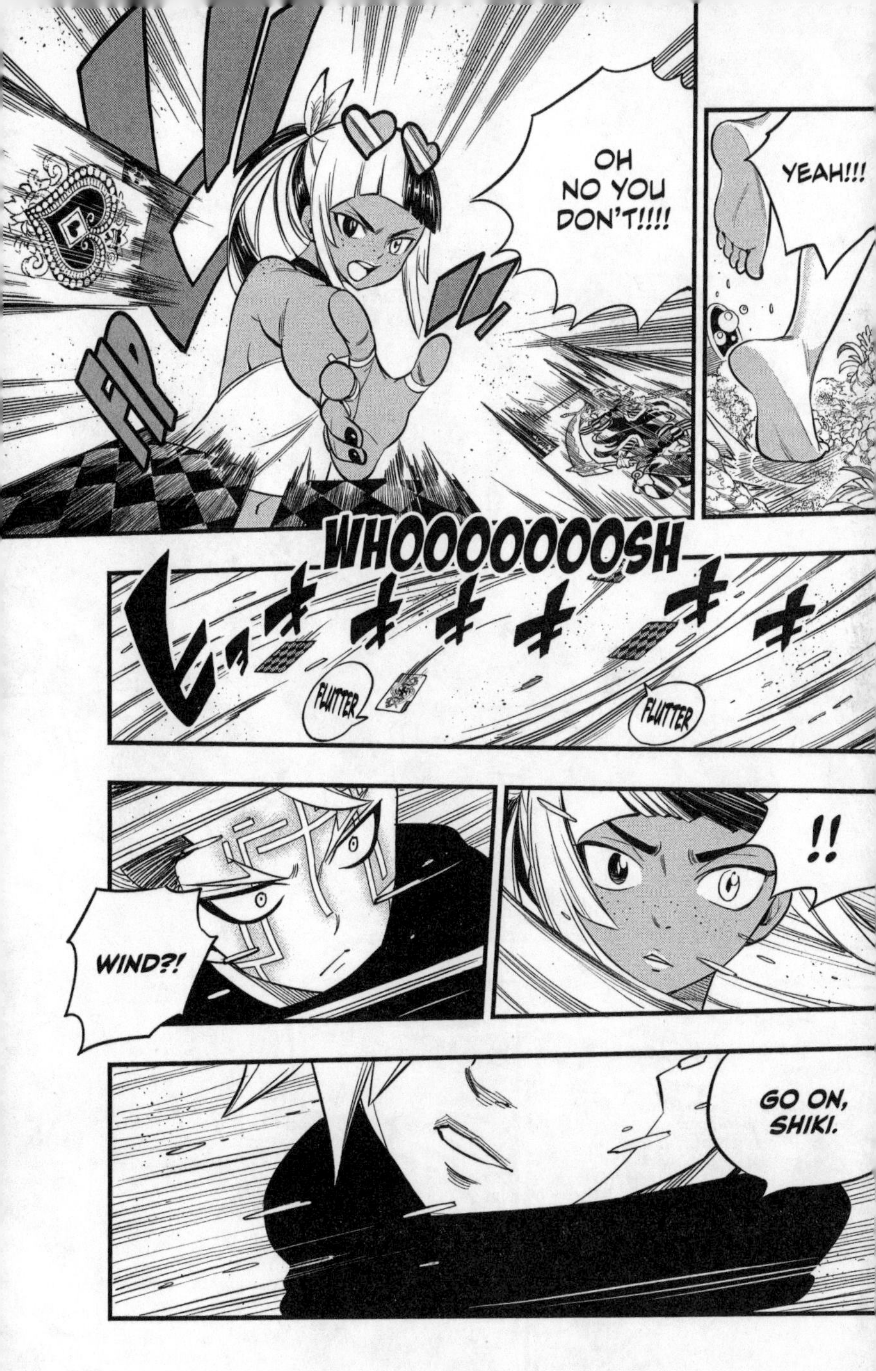
YEAH!!!
OH NO YOU DON'T!!!!
FIP
WHOOOOOOOOSH
FLUTTER
FLUTTER
!!
WIND?!
GO ON, SHIKI.

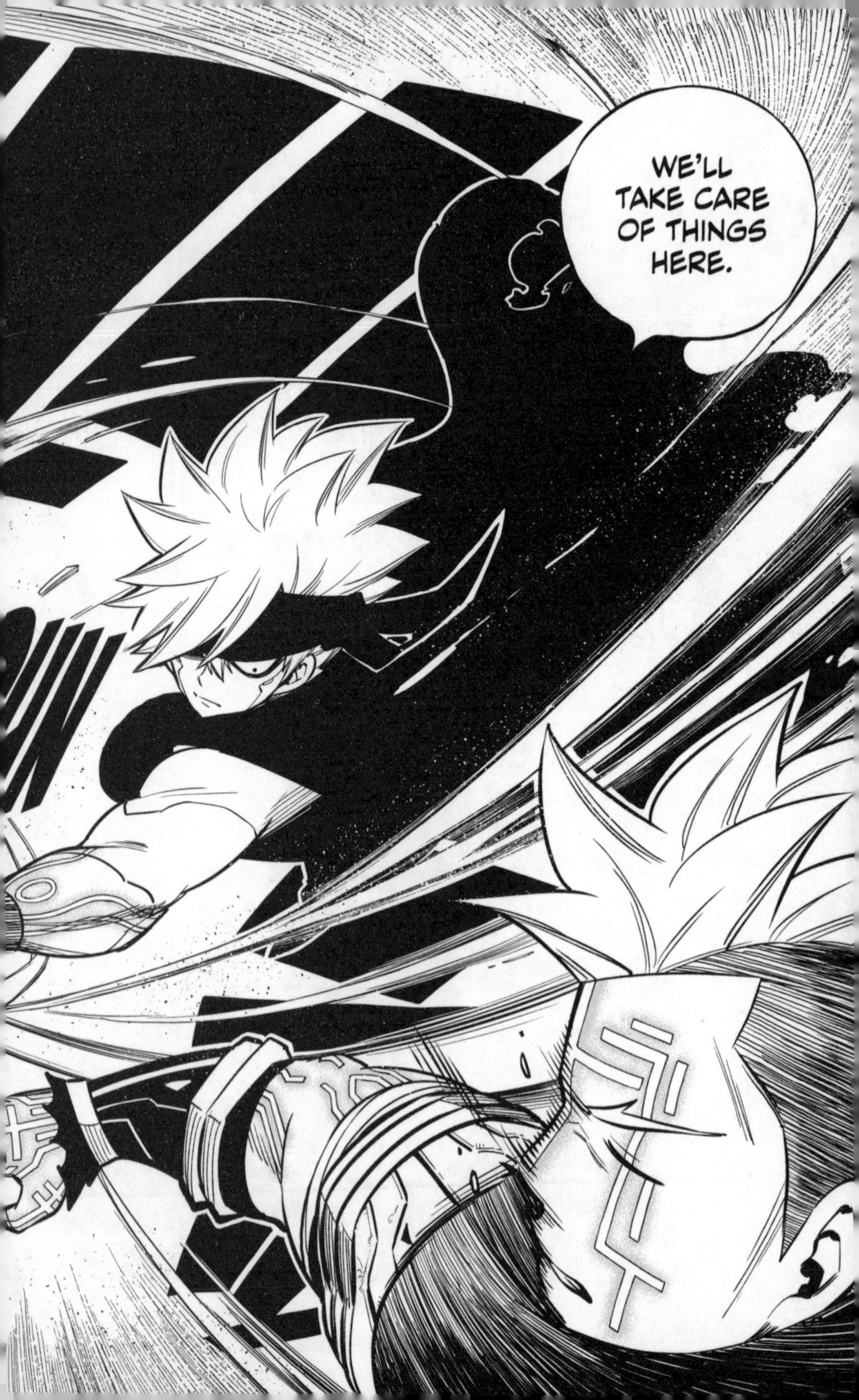
WE'LL TAKE CARE OF THINGS HERE.

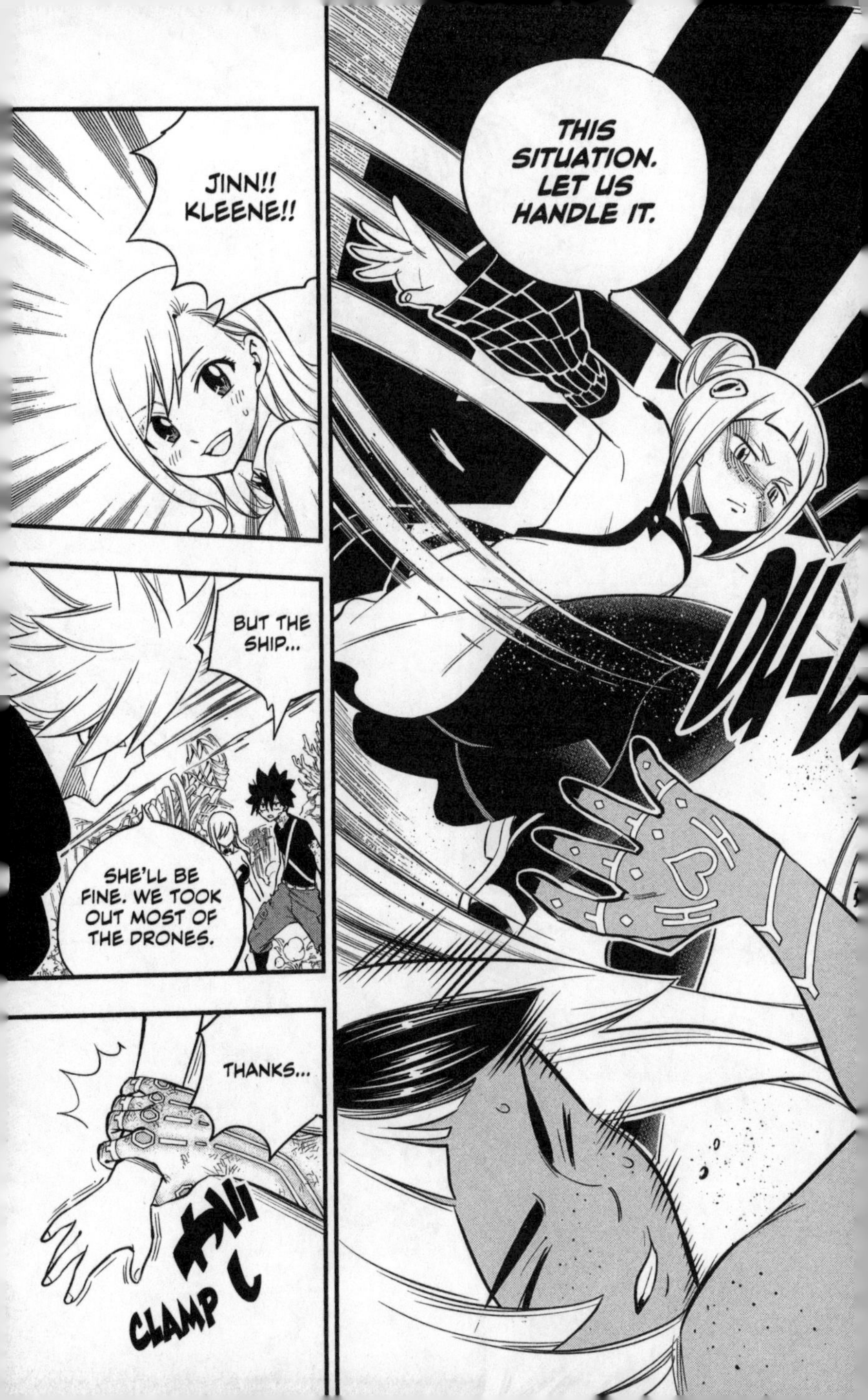
THIS SITUATION. LET US HANDLE IT.
JINN!! KLEENE!!
BUT THE SHIP...
SHE'LL BE FINE. WE TOOK OUT MOST OF THE DRONES.
THANKS...
CLAMP

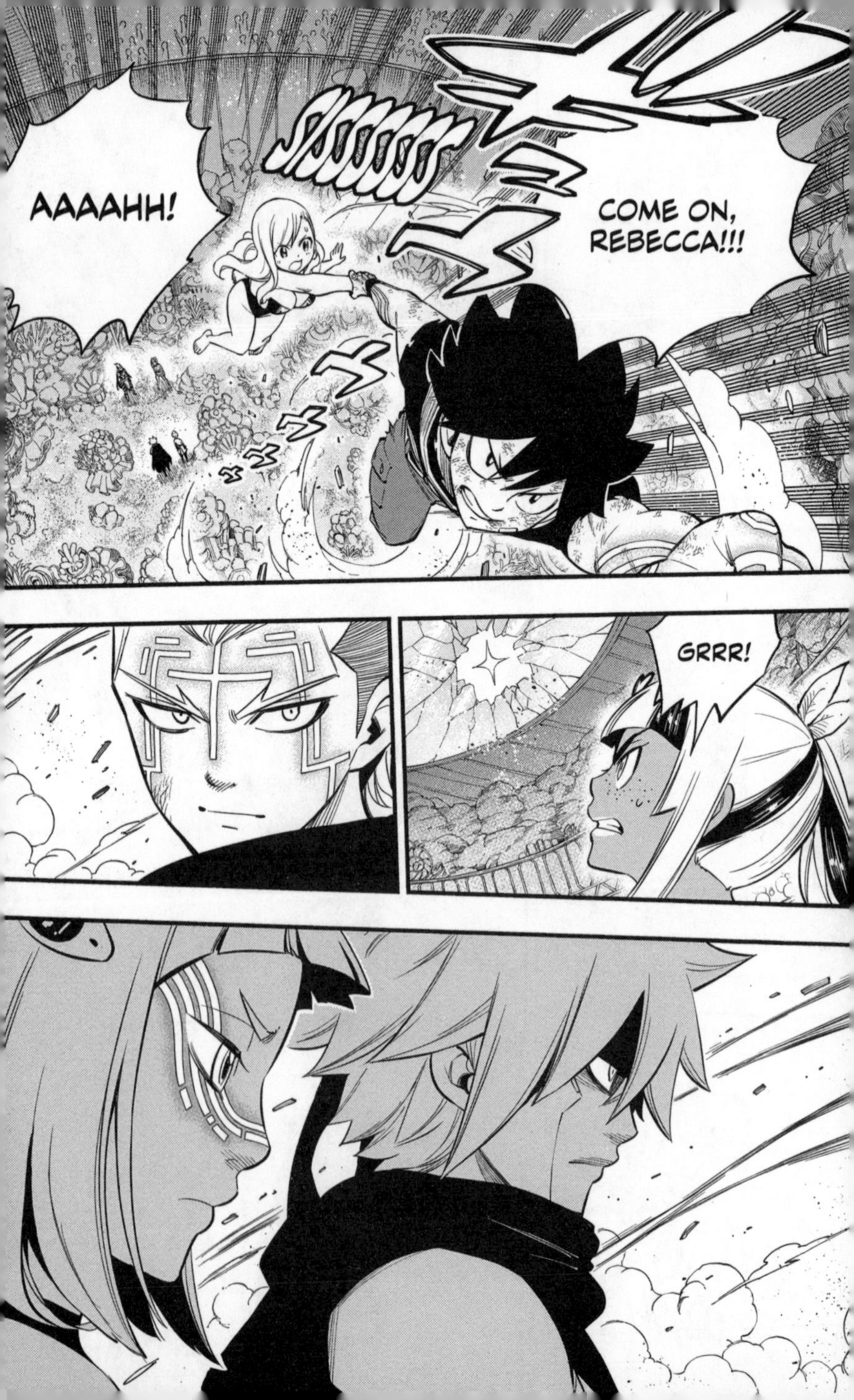
COME ON, REBECCA!!!
AAAAHH!
GRRR!

EDENS ZERO

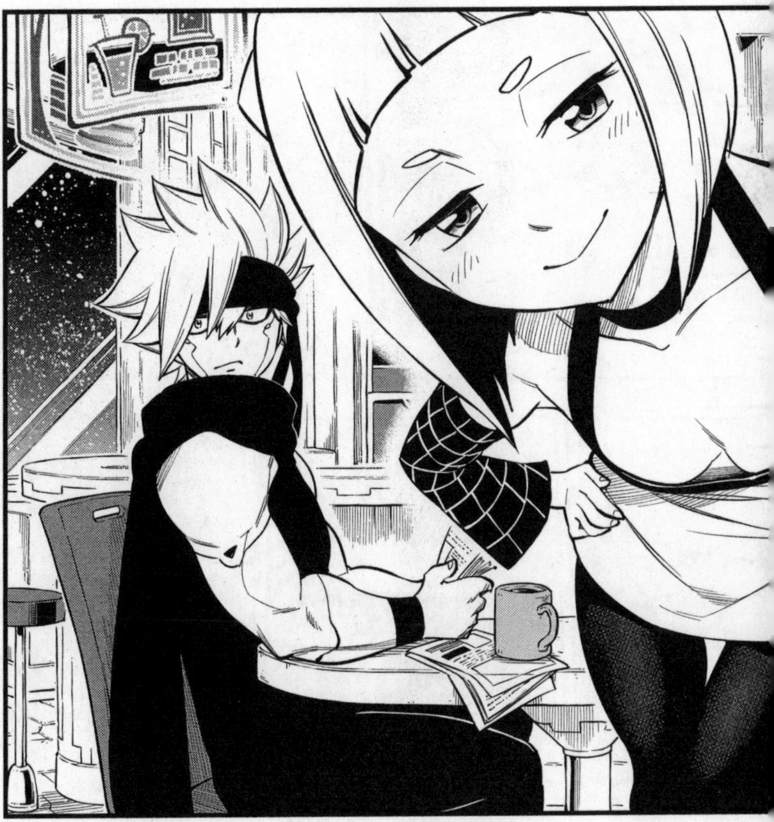

CHAPTER 154: SKYMECH NINJUTSU

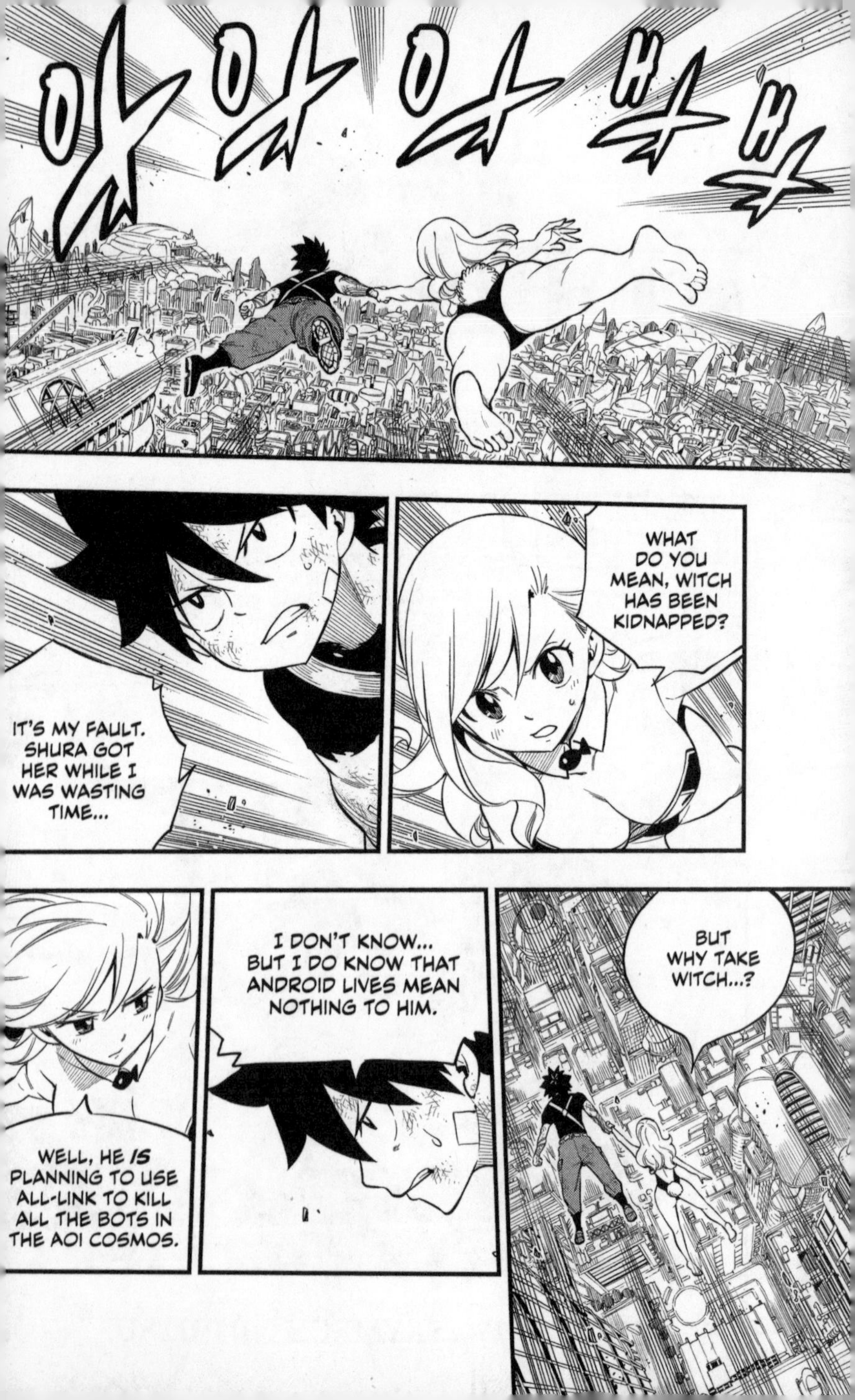
WHAT DO YOU MEAN, WITCH HAS BEEN KIDNAPPED?
IT'S MY FAULT. SHURA GOT HER WHILE I WAS WASTING TIME...
BUT WHY TAKE WITCH...?
I DON'T KNOW... BUT I DO KNOW THAT ANDROID LIVES MEAN NOTHING TO HIM.
WELL, HE *IS* PLANNING TO USE ALL-LINK TO KILL ALL THE BOTS IN THE AOI COSMOS.

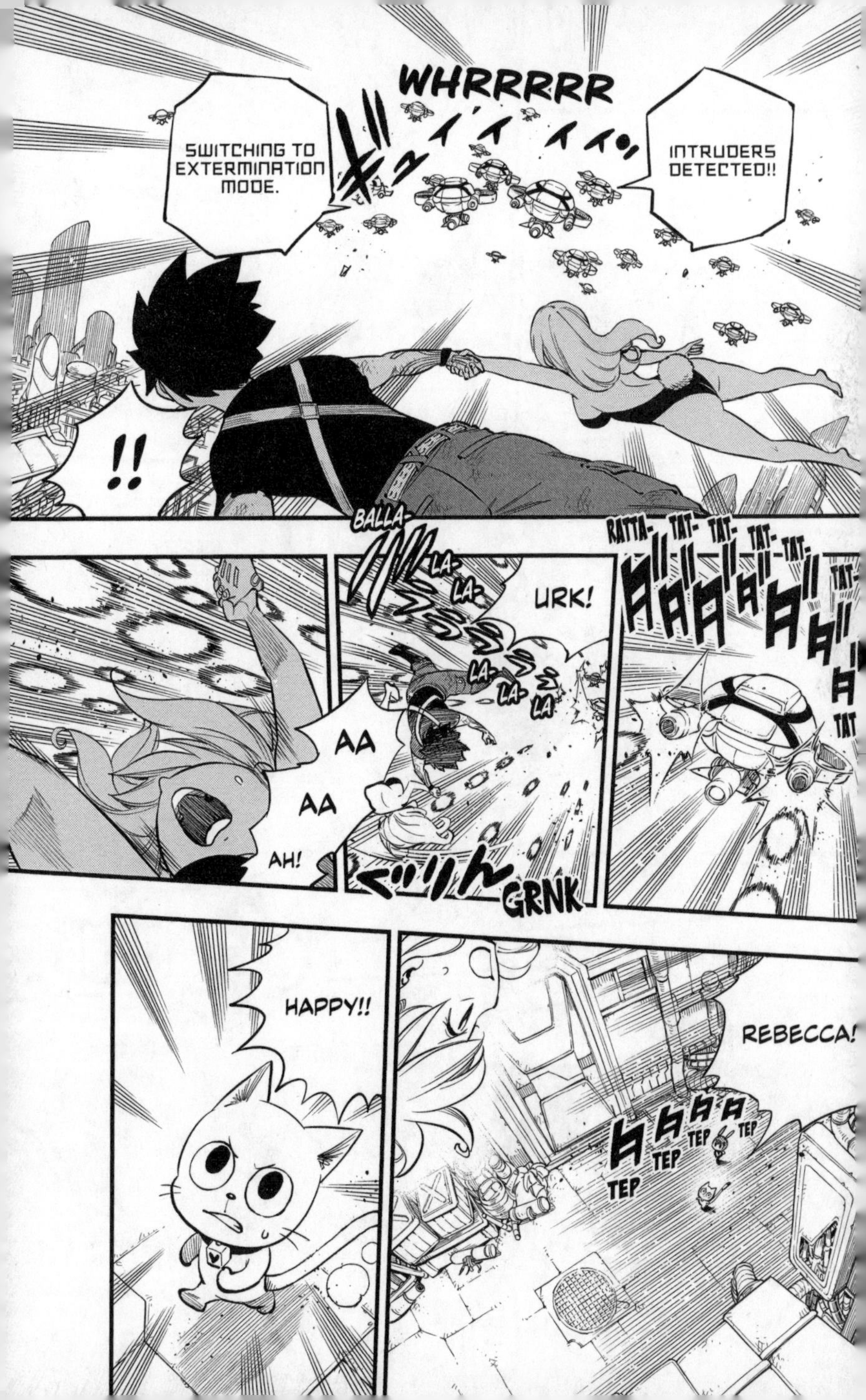
INTRUDERS DETECTED!!
WHRRRRR
SWITCHING TO EXTERMINATION MODE.
!!
RATTA-TAT-TAT-TAT-TAT-TAT-TAT
BALLA-LA-LA-LA-LA-LA
URK!
GRNK
AA
AA
AH!
REBECCA!
TEP TEP TEP TEP TEP
HAPPY!!

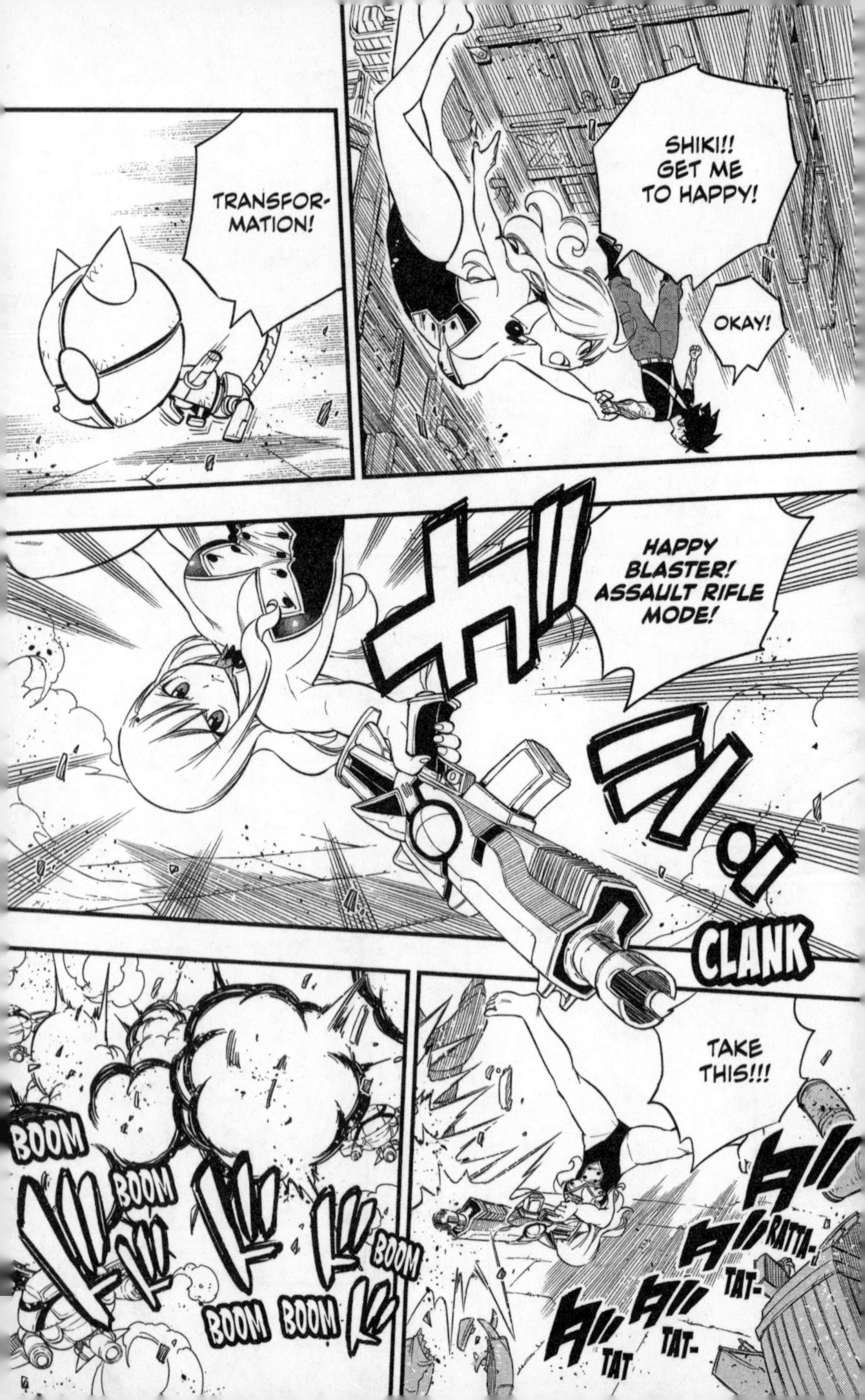
SHIKI!! GET ME TO HAPPY!
OKAY!
TRANSFOR-MATION!
HAPPY BLASTER! ASSAULT RIFLE MODE!
CLANK
TAKE THIS!!!
RATTA-TAT-TAT-TAT
BOOM
BOOM
BOOM
BOOM
BOOM

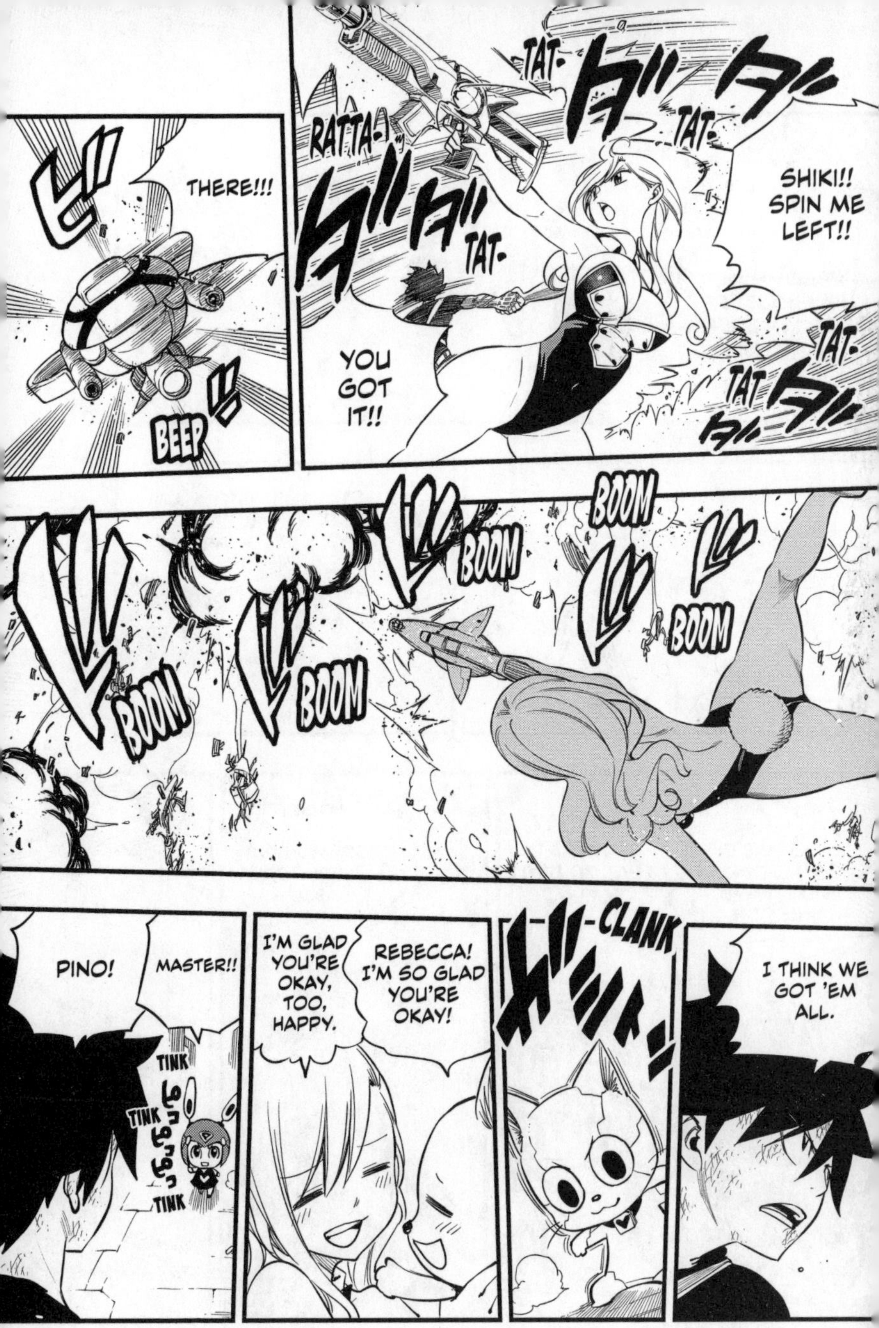
TAT-
TAT-
SHIKI!! SPIN ME LEFT!!
RATTA-
TAT-
YOU GOT IT!!
TAT-
TAT
THERE!!!
BEEP
BOOM
BOOM
BOOM
BOOM
BOOM
I THINK WE GOT 'EM ALL.
-CLANK
REBECCA! I'M SO GLAD YOU'RE OKAY!
I'M GLAD YOU'RE OKAY, TOO, HAPPY.
MASTER!!
PINO!
TINK
TINK
TINK

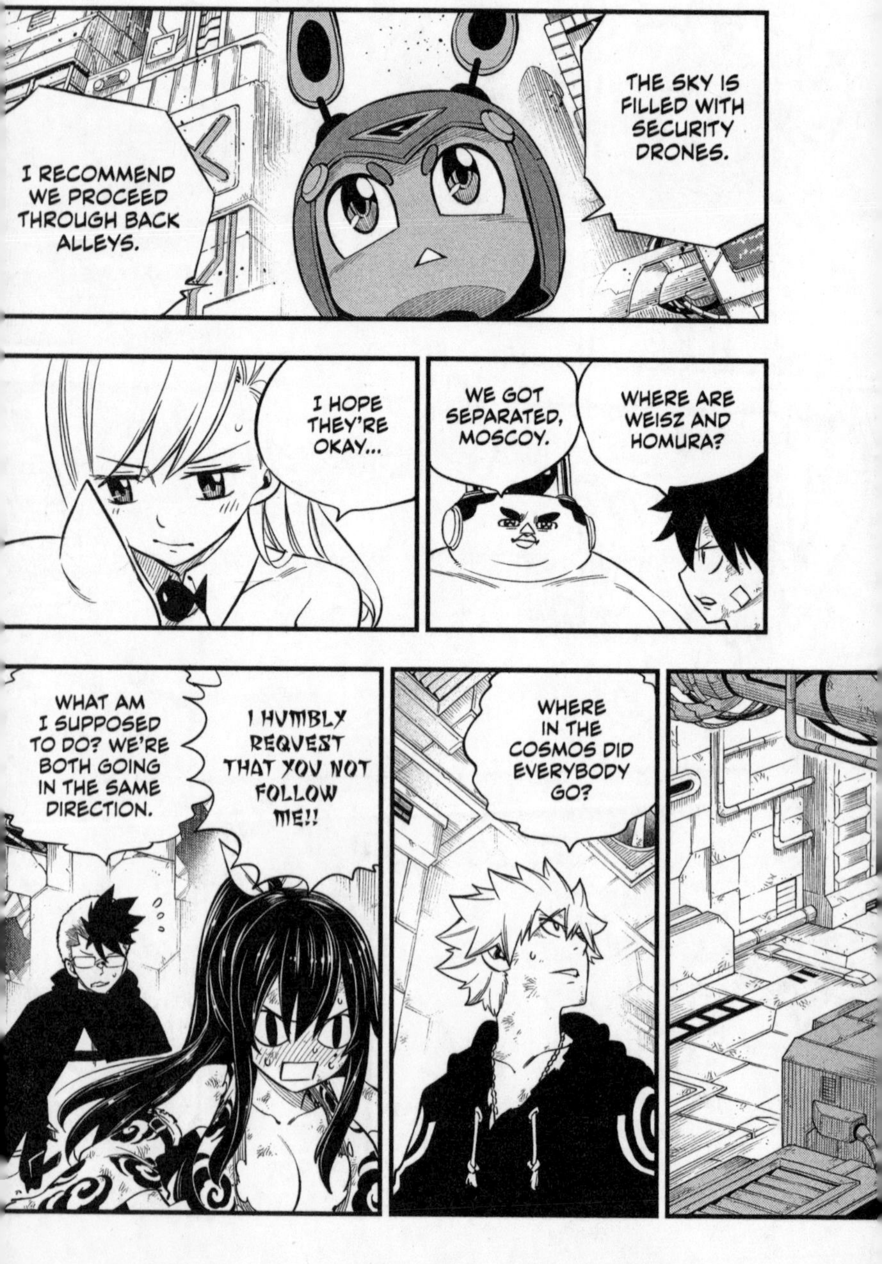
THE SKY IS FILLED WITH SECURITY DRONES.
I RECOMMEND WE PROCEED THROUGH BACK ALLEYS.
WHERE ARE WEISZ AND HOMURA?
WE GOT SEPARATED, MOSCOY.
I HOPE THEY'RE OKAY...
WHERE IN THE COSMOS DID EVERYBODY GO?
I HUMBLY REQUEST THAT YOU NOT FOLLOW ME!!
WHAT AM I SUPPOSED TO DO? WE'RE BOTH GOING IN THE SAME DIRECTION.

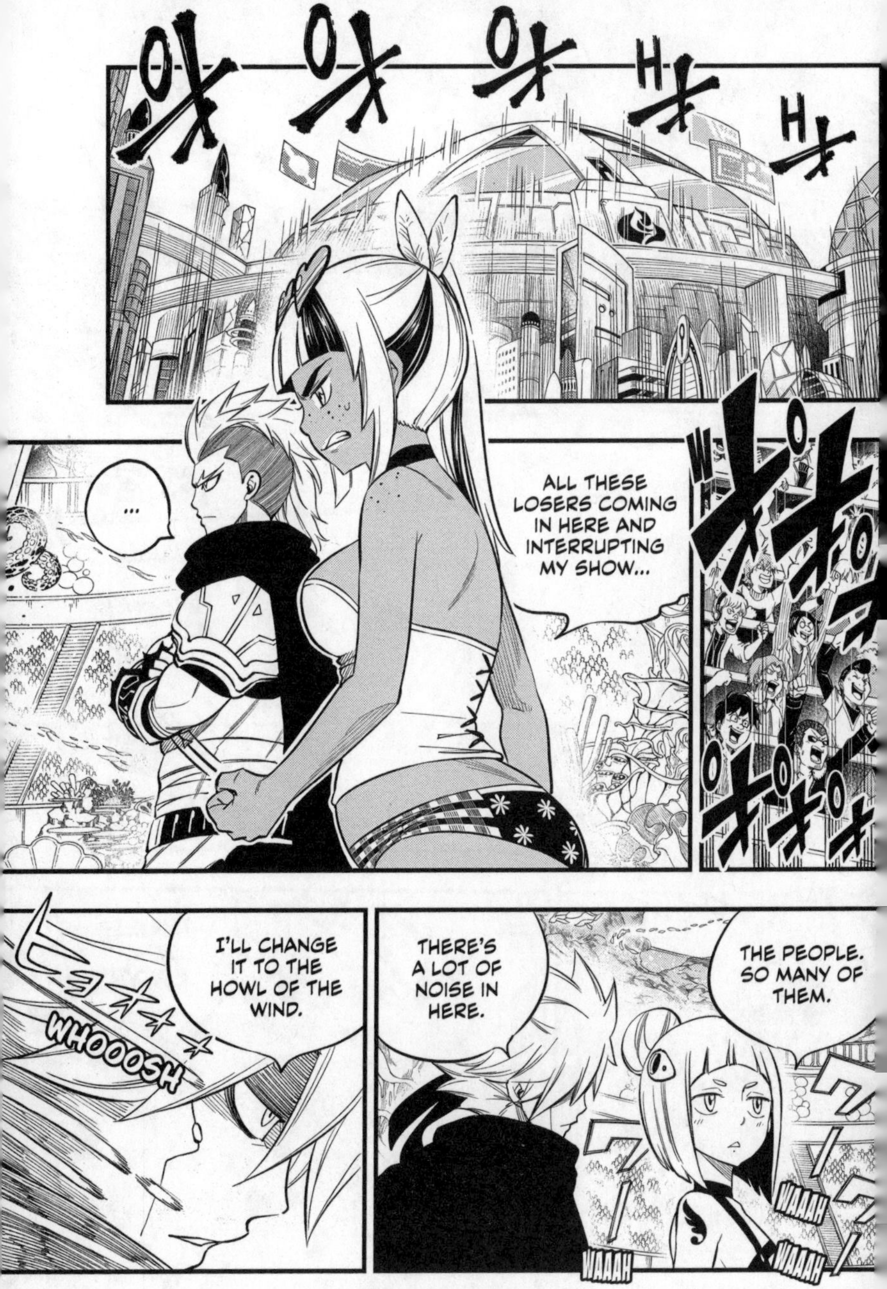
ALL THESE LOSERS COMING IN HERE AND INTERRUPTING MY SHOW...
...
THE PEOPLE. SO MANY OF THEM.
THERE'S A LOT OF NOISE IN HERE.
WAAAH
WAAAH
WAAAH
I'LL CHANGE IT TO THE HOWL OF THE WIND.
WHOOOSH

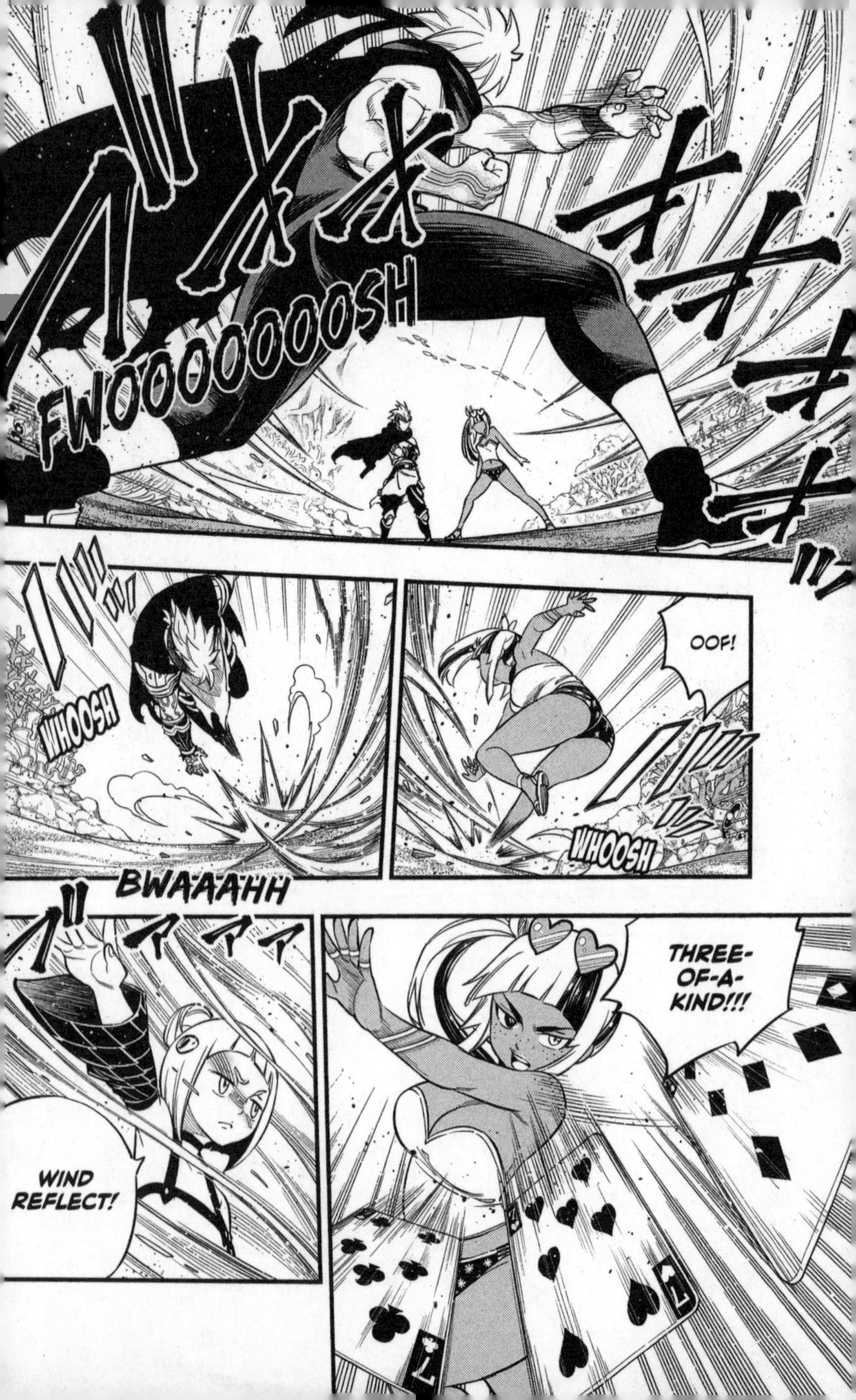
FWOOOOOOOOSH
OOF!
WHOOSH
WHOOSH
THREE-OF-A-KIND!!!
BWAAAHH
WIND REFLECT!

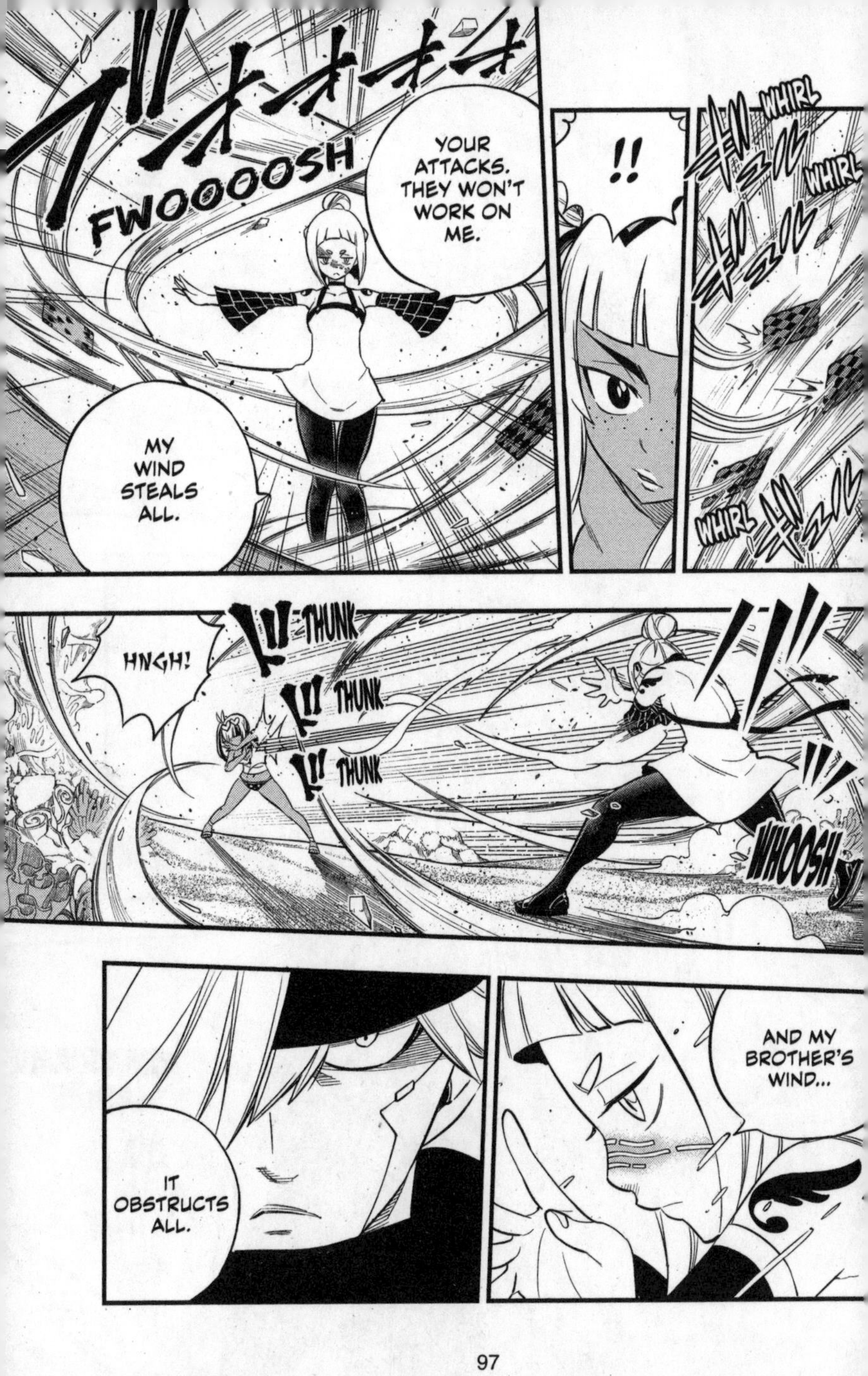
WHIRL
WHIRL
WHIRL
!!
FWOOOOSH
YOUR ATTACKS. THEY WON'T WORK ON ME.
MY WIND STEALS ALL.
THUNK
HNGH!
THUNK
THUNK
WHOOSH
AND MY BROTHER'S WIND...
IT OBSTRUCTS ALL.

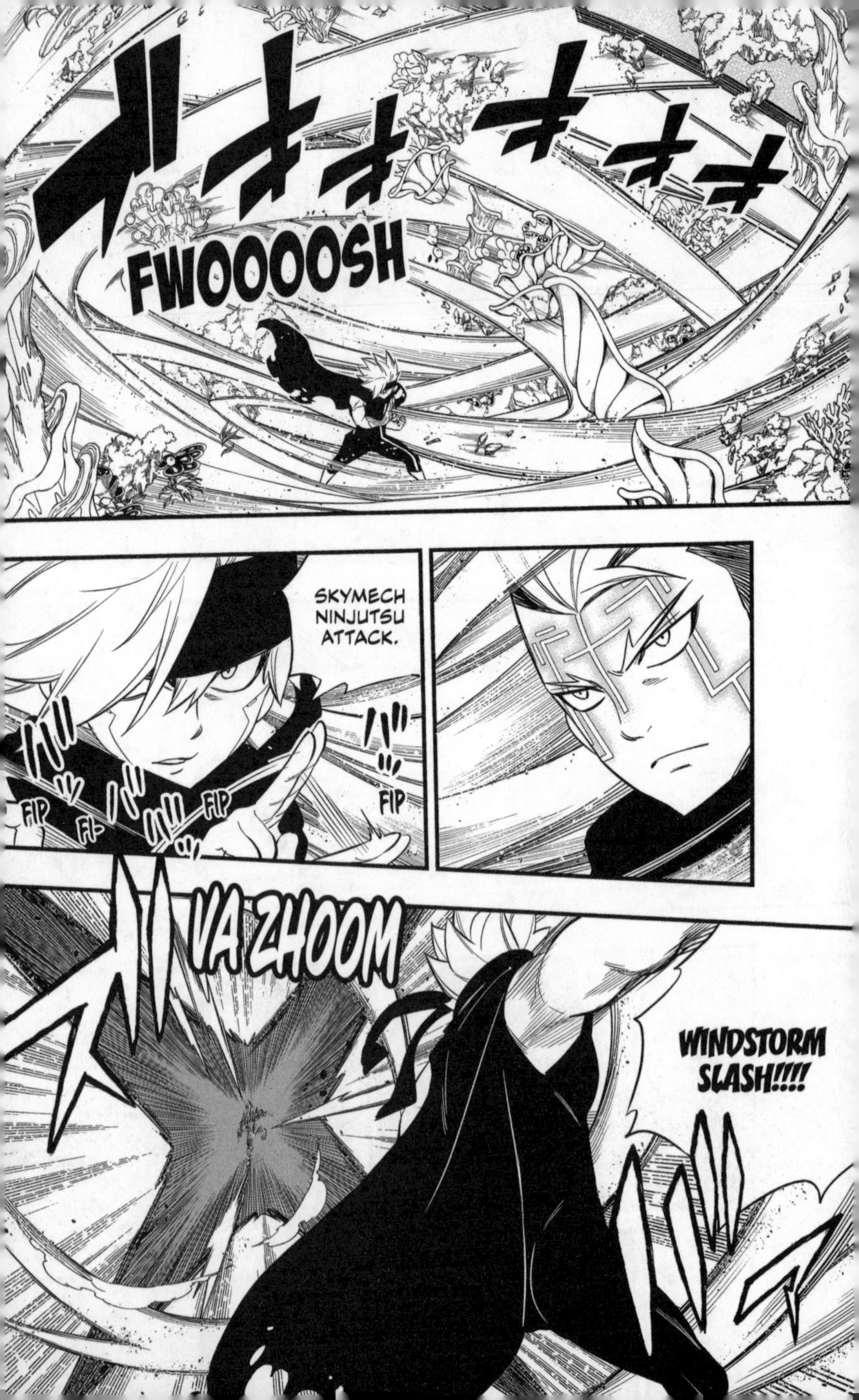
FWOOOOSH
SKYMECH NINJUTSU ATTACK.
FIP
FIP
FI-
FIP
VA ZHOOM
WINDSTORM SLASH!!!!

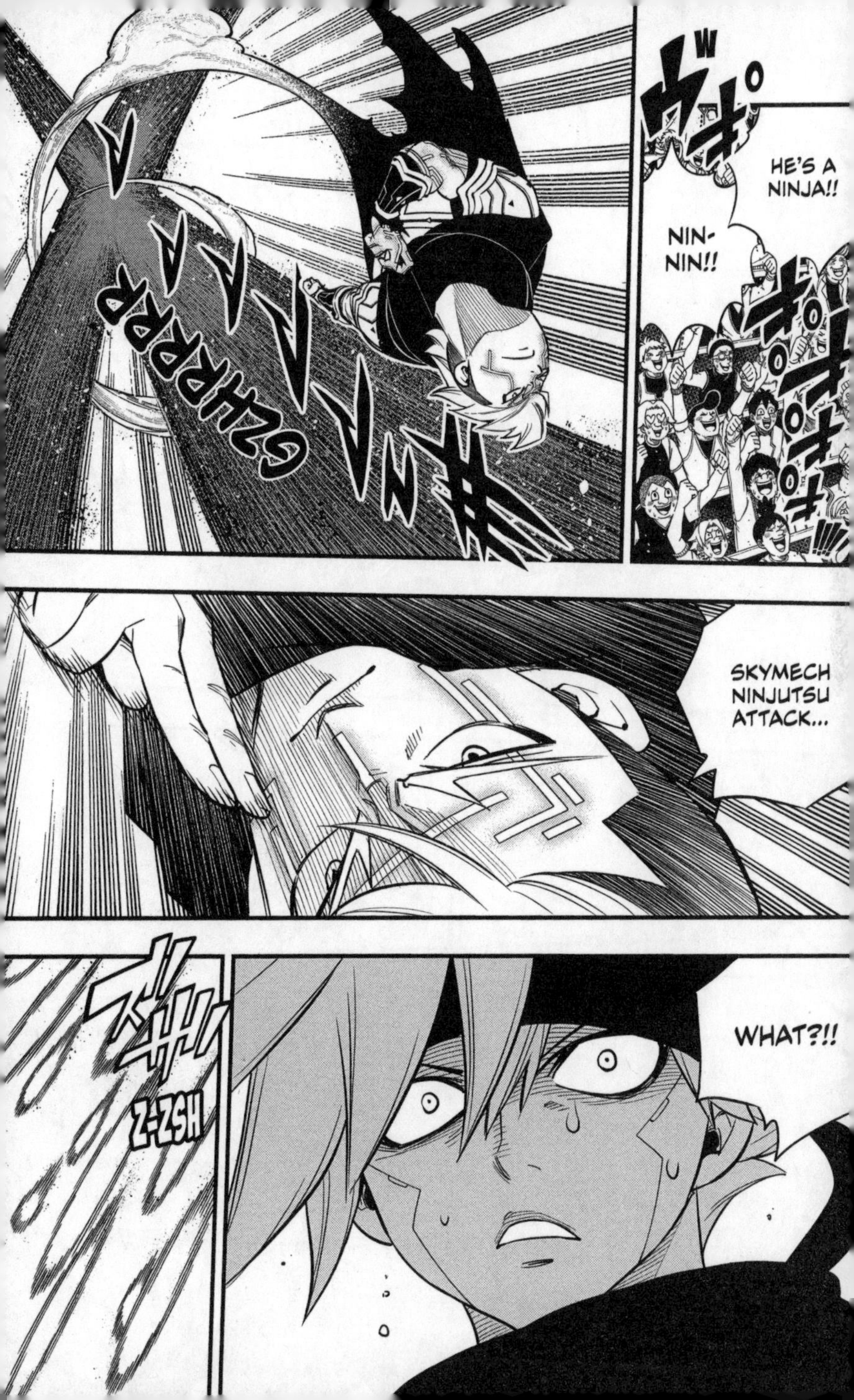
HE'S A NINJA!!
NIN-NIN!!
GZHRPP
SKYMECH NINJUTSU ATTACK...
WHAT?!!
Z-ZSH

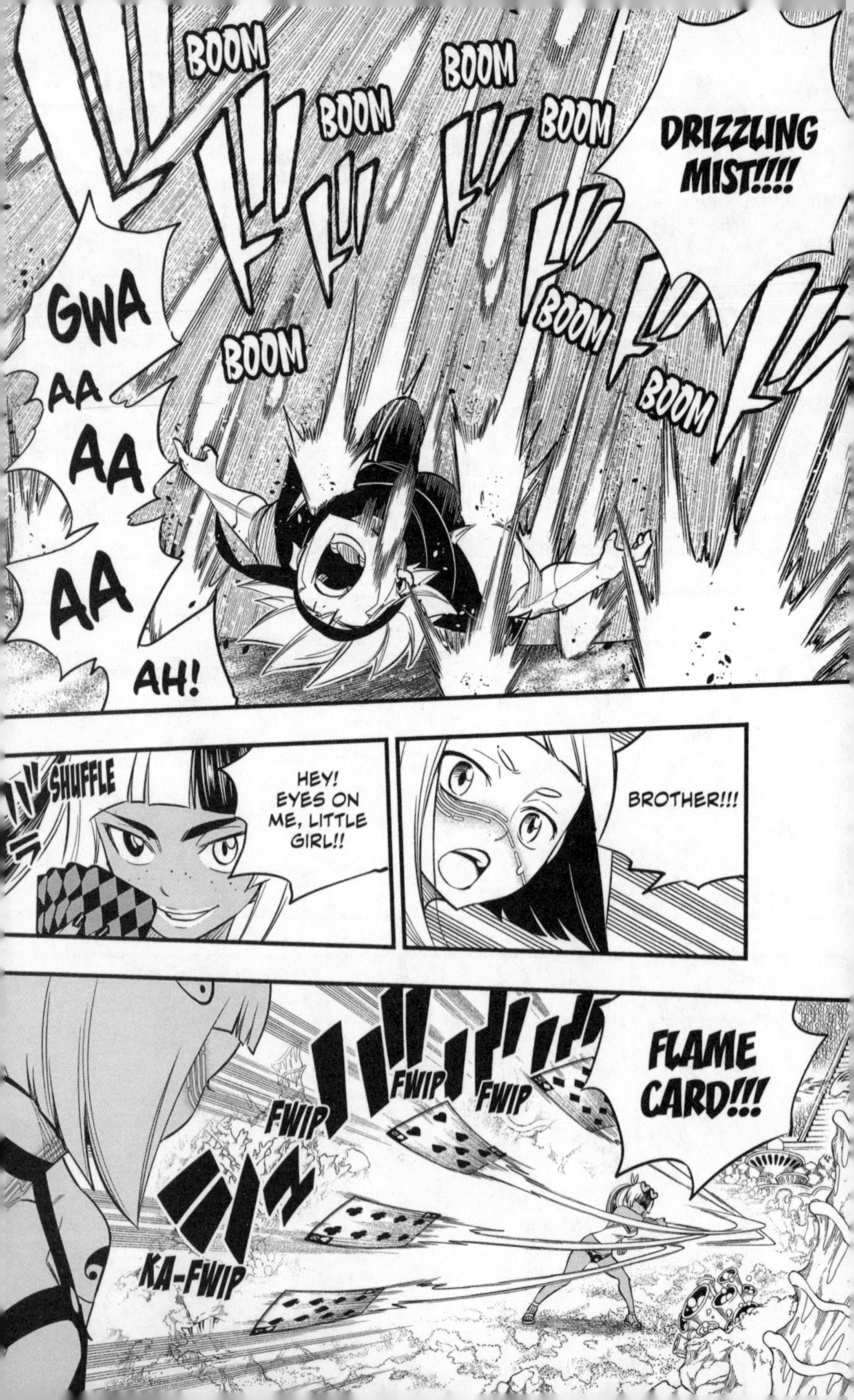
DRIZZLING MIST!!!!
BOOM
BOOM
BOOM
BOOM
BOOM
BOOM
BOOM
GWA AA AA AA AH!
BROTHER!!!
HEY! EYES ON ME, LITTLE GIRL!!
SHUFFLE
FLAME CARD!!!
FWIP
FWIP
FWIP
KA-FWIP

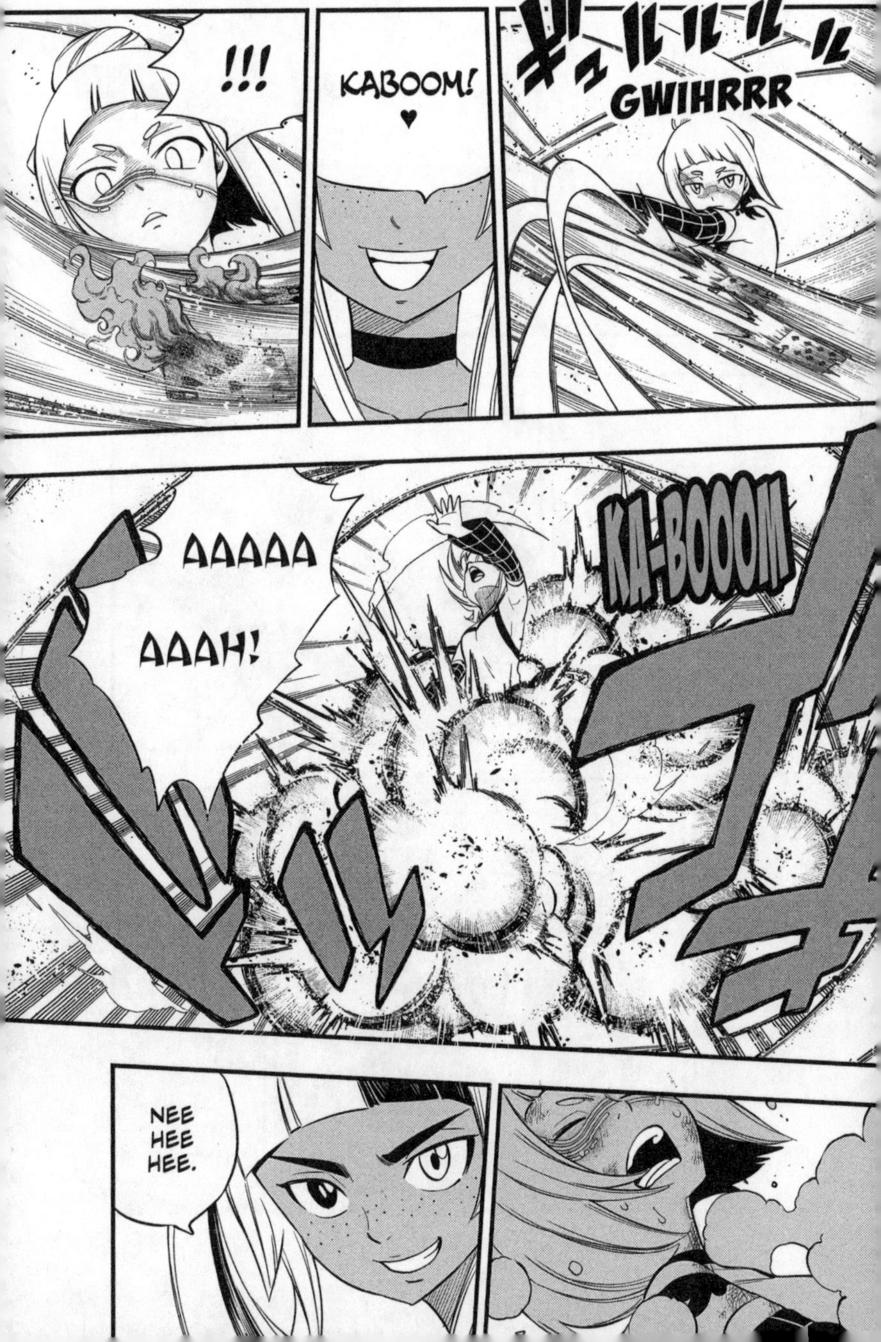
GWIHRRR
KABOOM! ♥
!!!
KA-BOOOM
AAAAA AAAH!
NEE HEE HEE.

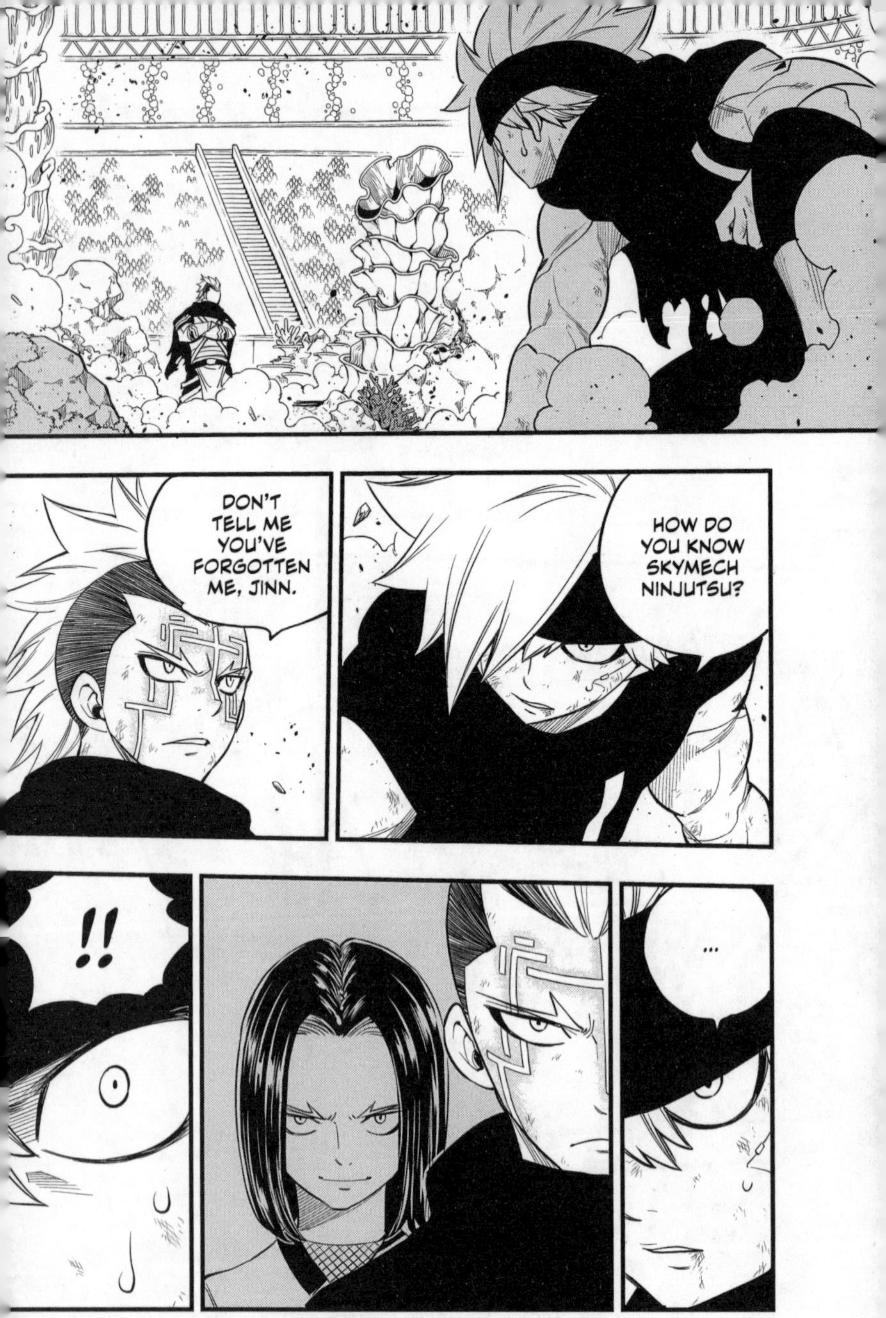
HOW DO YOU KNOW SKYMECH NINJUTSU?
DON'T TELL ME YOU'VE FORGOTTEN ME, JINN.
...
!!

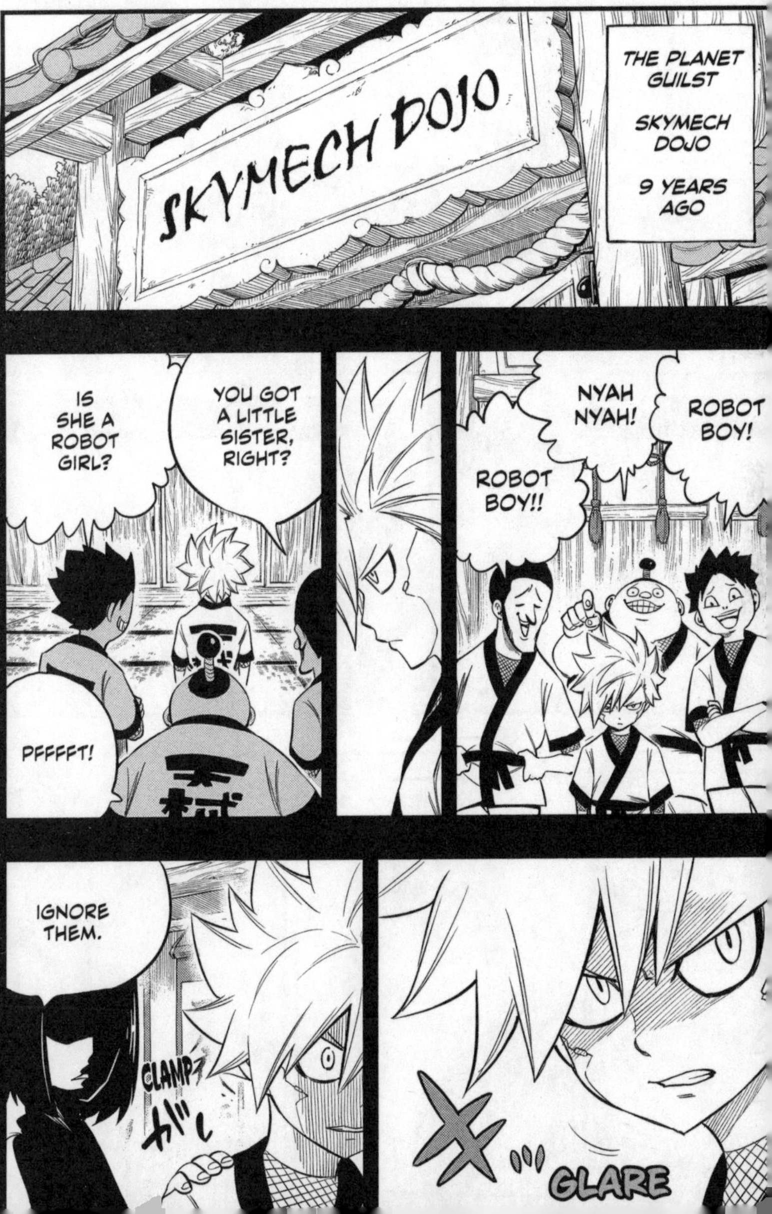
THE PLANET GUILST
SKYMECH DOJO
9 YEARS AGO
SKYMECH DOJO
ROBOT BOY!
NYAH NYAH!
ROBOT BOY!!
YOU GOT A LITTLE SISTER, RIGHT?
IS SHE A ROBOT GIRL?
PFFFFT!
GLARE
IGNORE THEM.
CLAMP

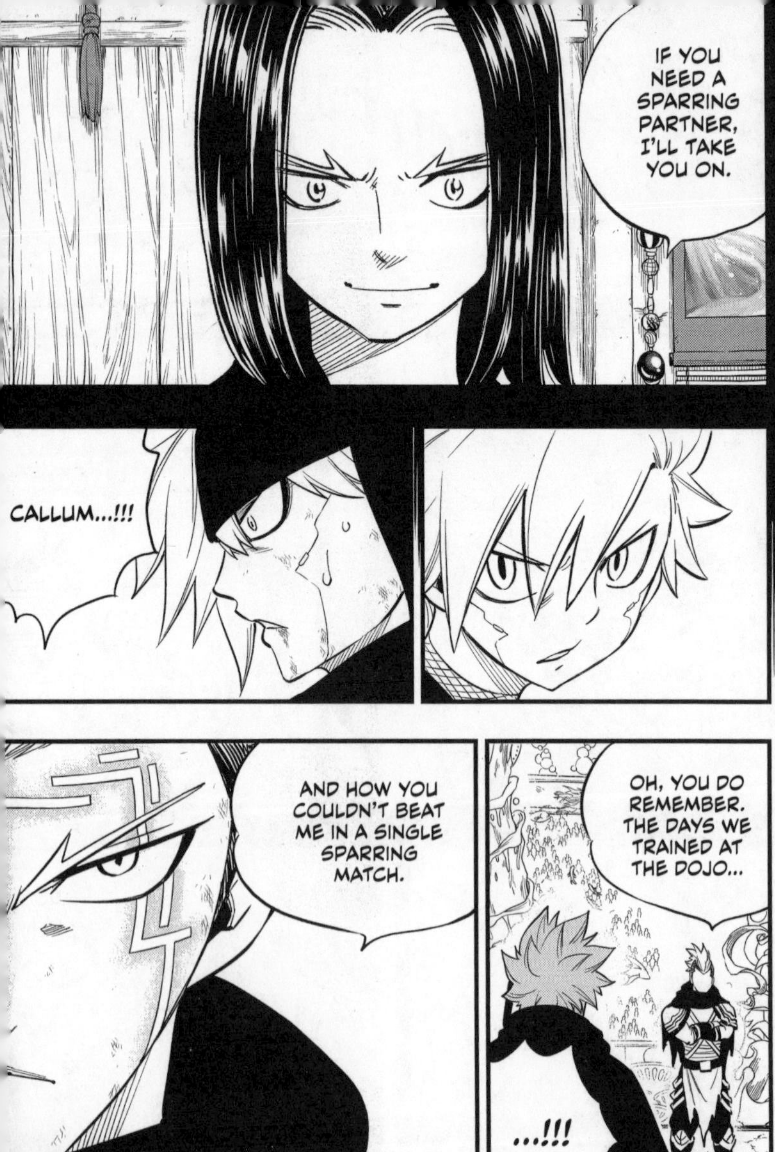
IF YOU NEED A SPARRING PARTNER, I'LL TAKE YOU ON.
CALLUM...!!!
OH, YOU DO REMEMBER. THE DAYS WE TRAINED AT THE DOJO...
...!!!
AND HOW YOU COULDN'T BEAT ME IN A SINGLE SPARRING MATCH.

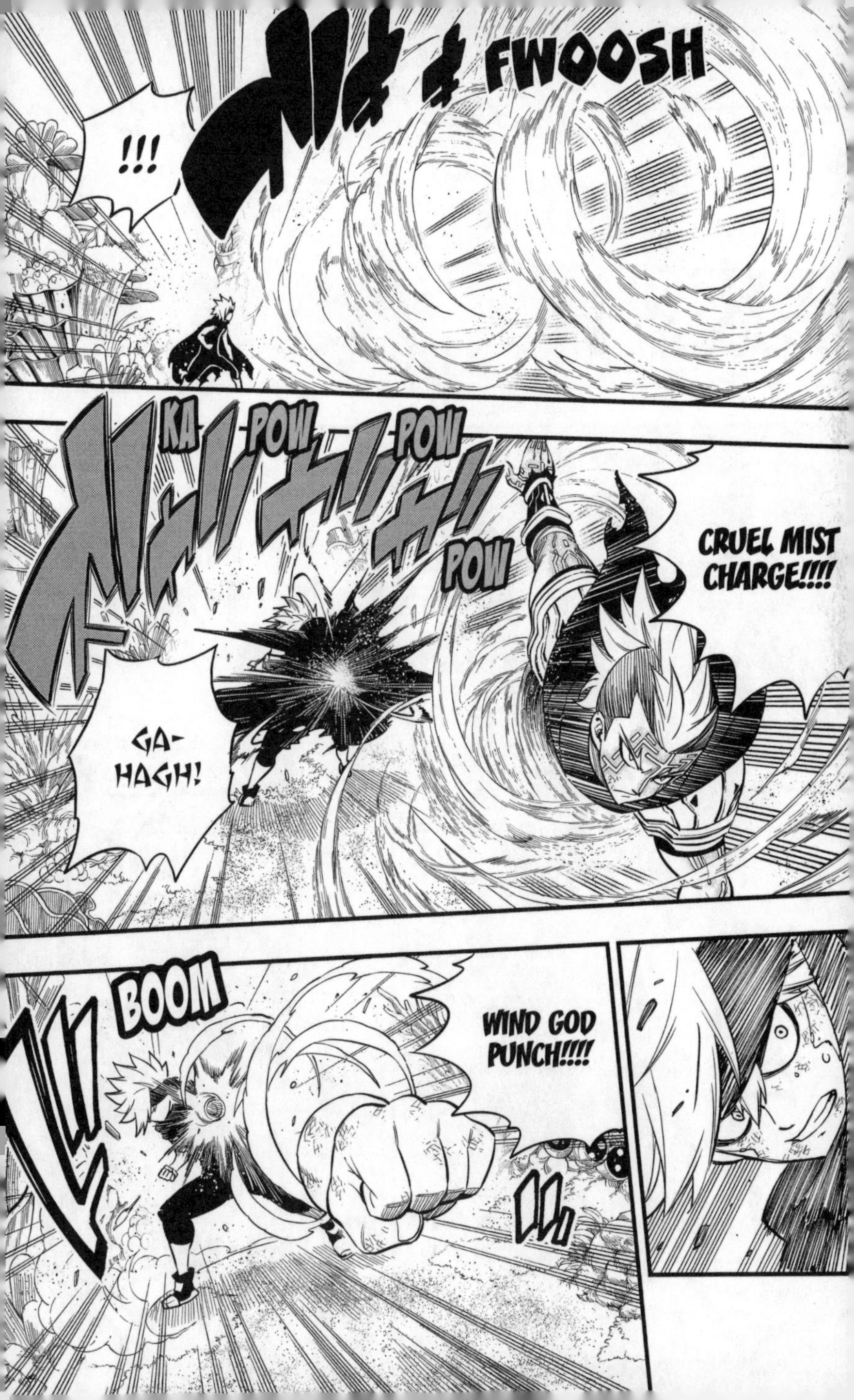
FWOOSH
!!!
CRUEL MIST CHARGE!!!!
KA POW POW POW
GA-HAGH!
WIND GOD PUNCH!!!!
BOOM

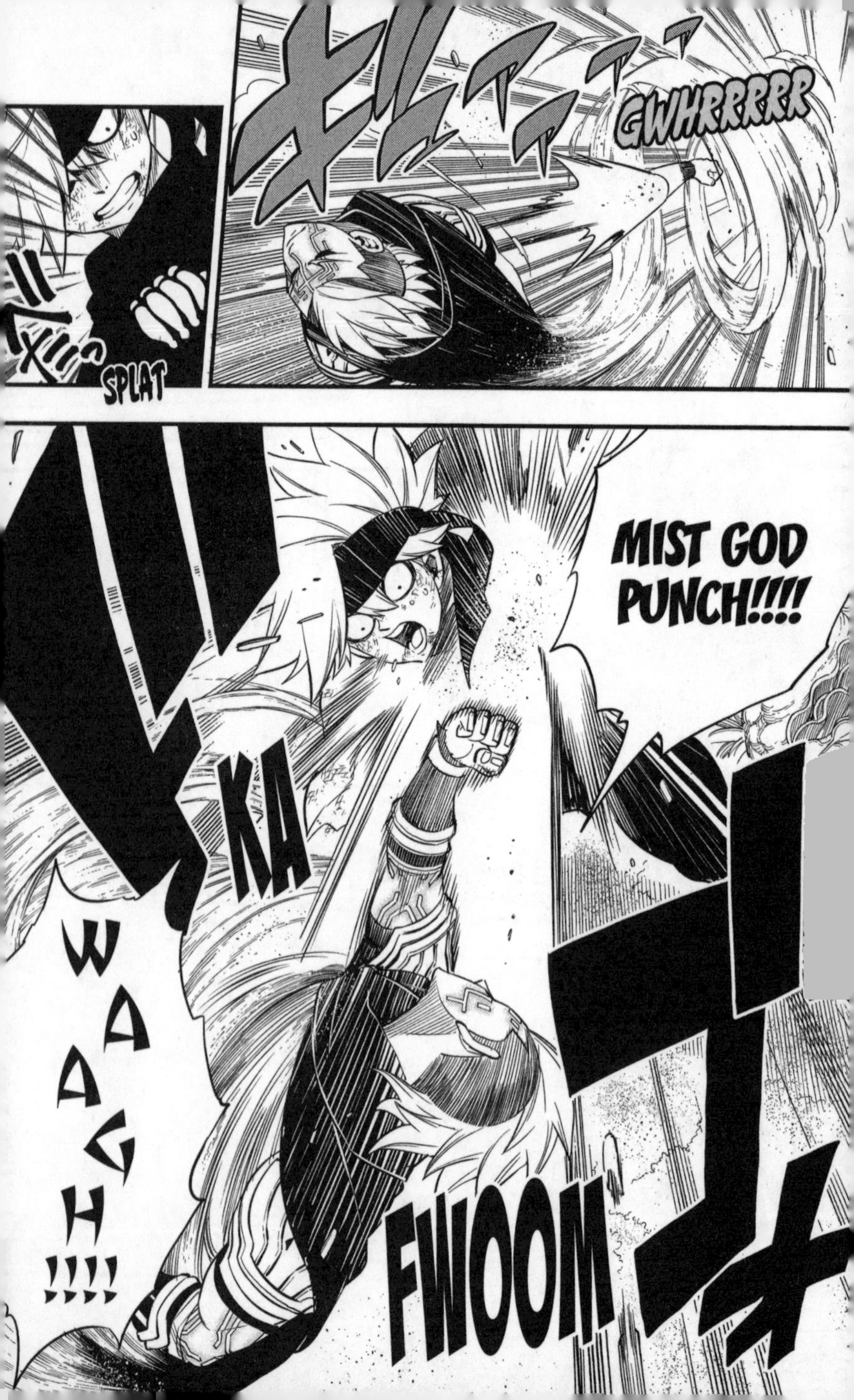
GWHRRRRR
SPLAT
MIST GOD PUNCH!!!!
KA
FWOOM
WAAGH!!!!

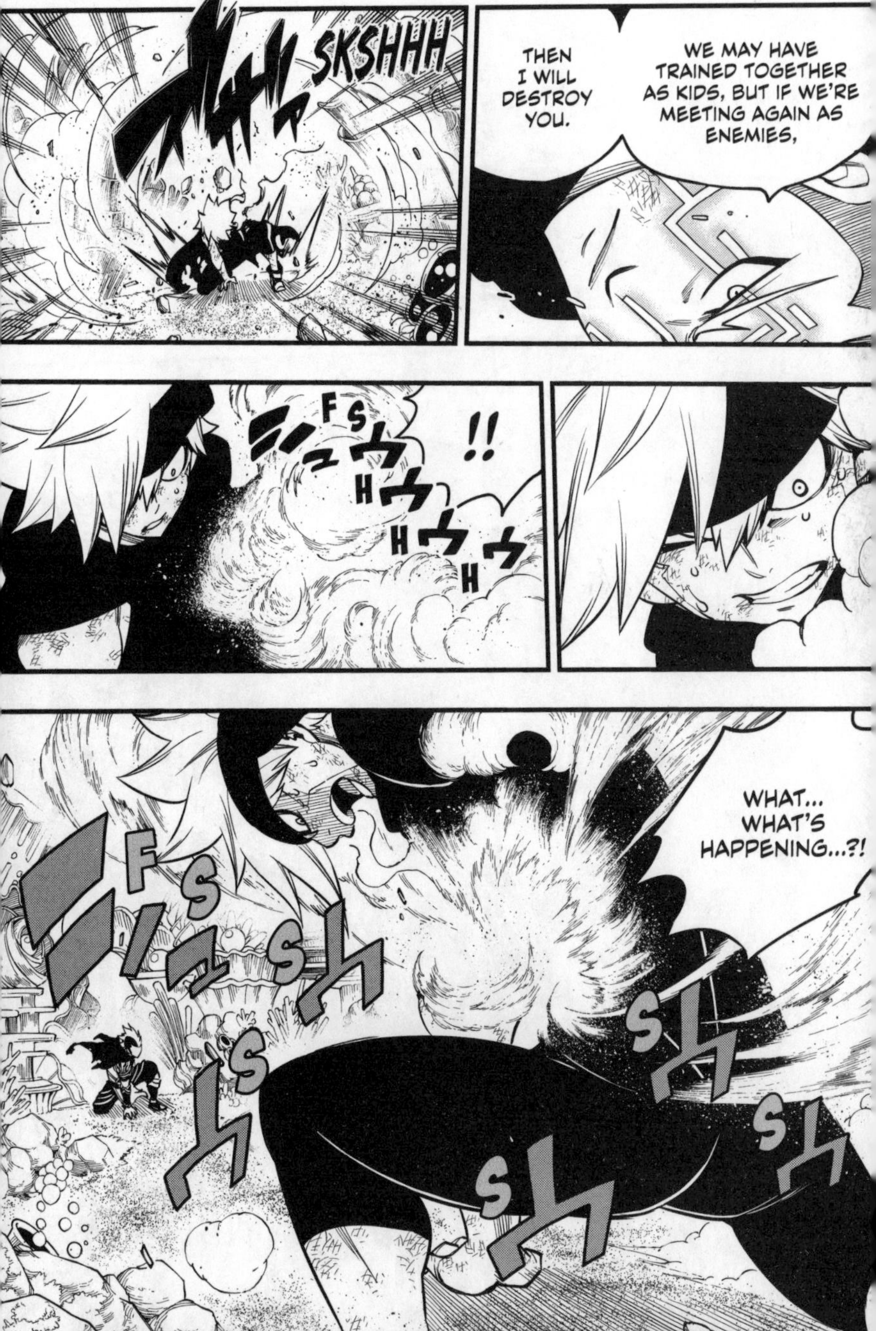
WE MAY HAVE TRAINED TOGETHER AS KIDS, BUT IF WE'RE MEETING AGAIN AS ENEMIES,
THEN I WILL DESTROY YOU.
SKSHHH
FSHHH
!!
FSSSSSSS
WHAT... WHAT'S HAPPENING...?!

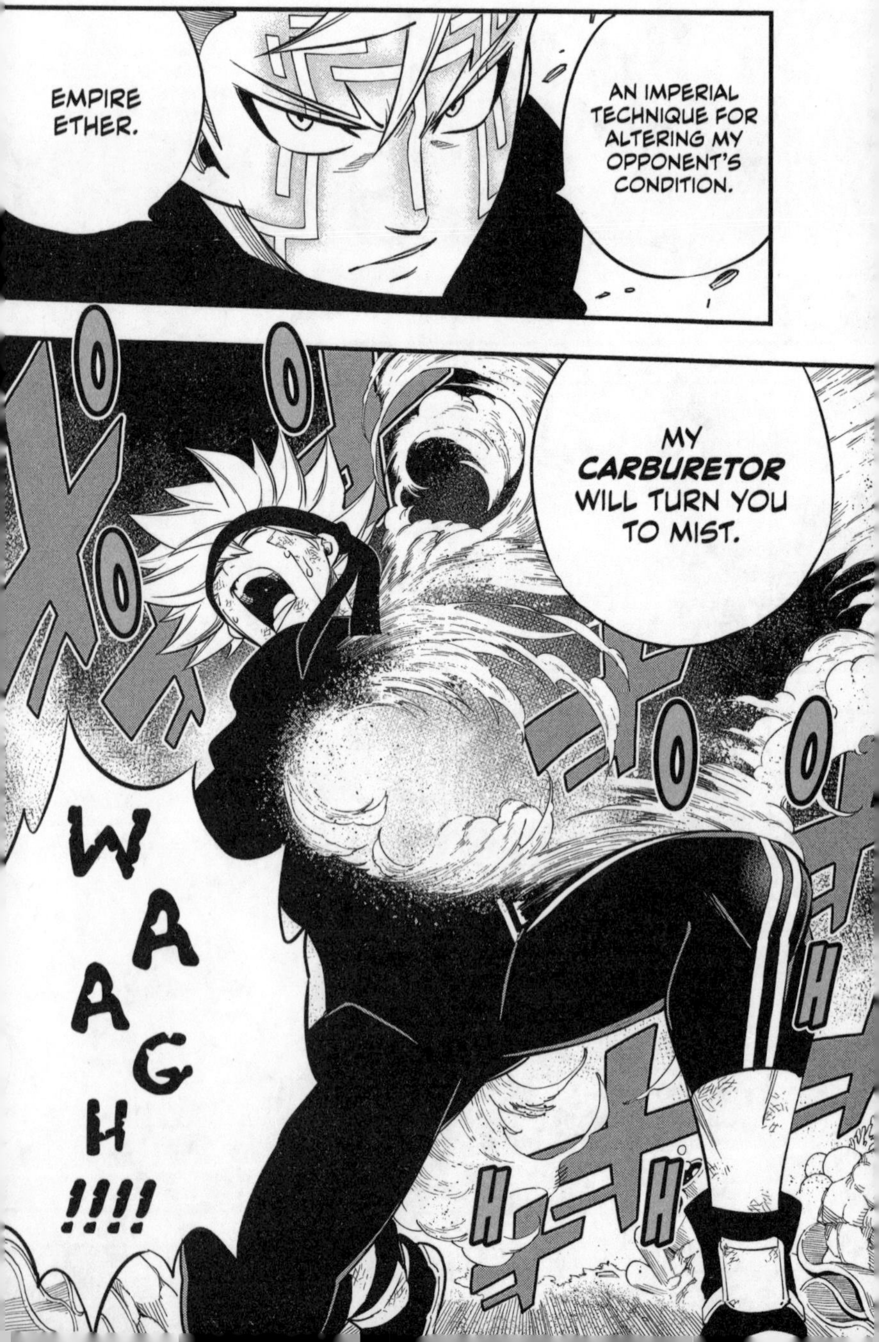
AN IMPERIAL TECHNIQUE FOR ALTERING MY OPPONENT'S CONDITION.
EMPIRE ETHER.
MY **CARBURETOR** WILL TURN YOU TO MIST.
WAAAGH!!!!

EDENS ZERO

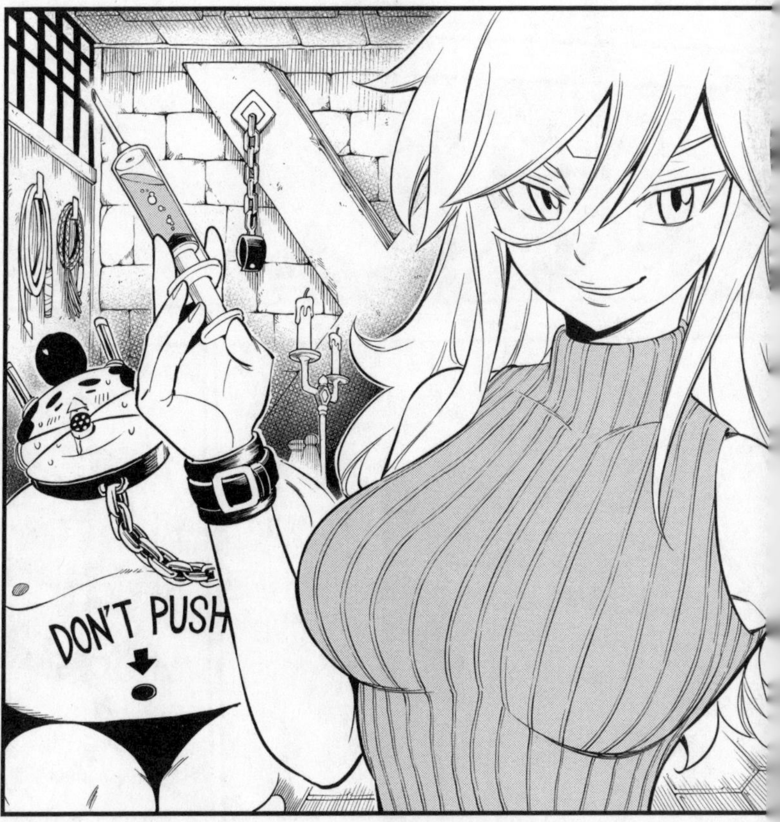
DON'T PUSH

CHAPTER 155: THE WINDS OF RUTHERFORD

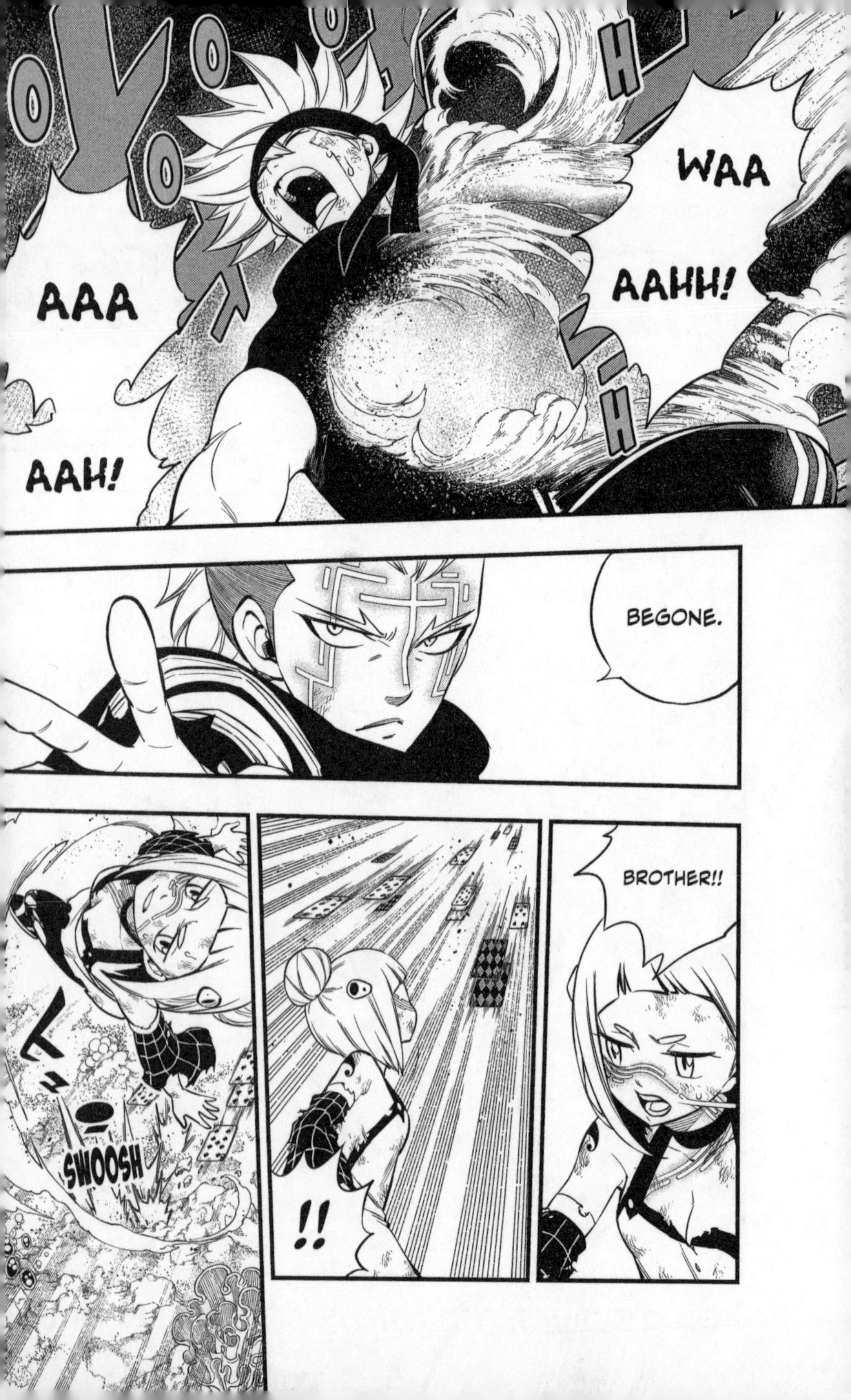
WAA AAHH!
AAA AAH!
BEGONE.
BROTHER!!
!!
SWOOSH

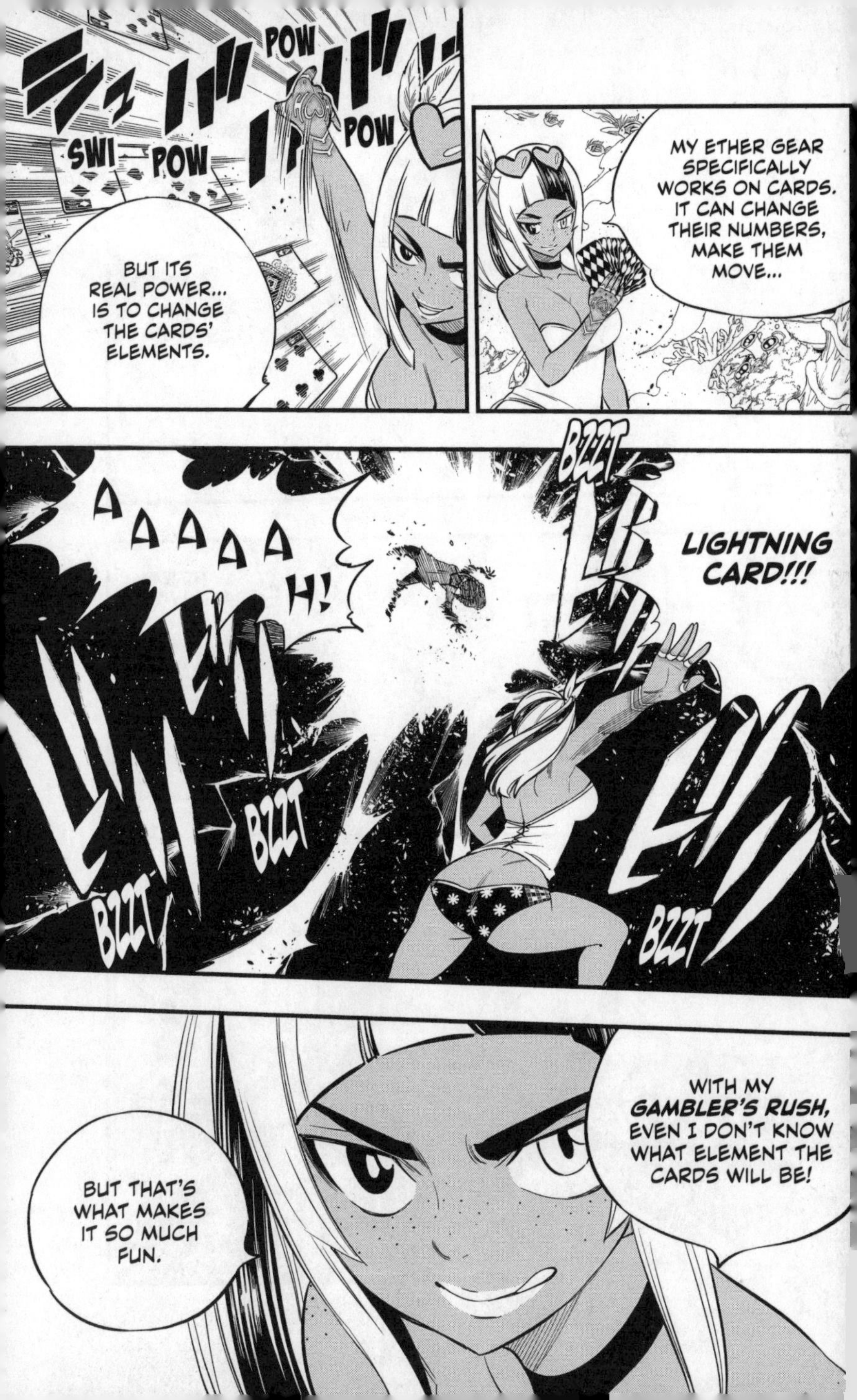

MY ETHER GEAR SPECIFICALLY WORKS ON CARDS. IT CAN CHANGE THEIR NUMBERS, MAKE THEM MOVE...
POW
POW
SWI
POW
BUT ITS REAL POWER... IS TO CHANGE THE CARDS' ELEMENTS.
BZZT
LIGHTNING CARD!!!
AAAAAAH!
BZZT
BZZT
BZZT
WITH MY *GAMBLER'S RUSH,* EVEN I DON'T KNOW WHAT ELEMENT THE CARDS WILL BE!
BUT THAT'S WHAT MAKES IT SO MUCH FUN.

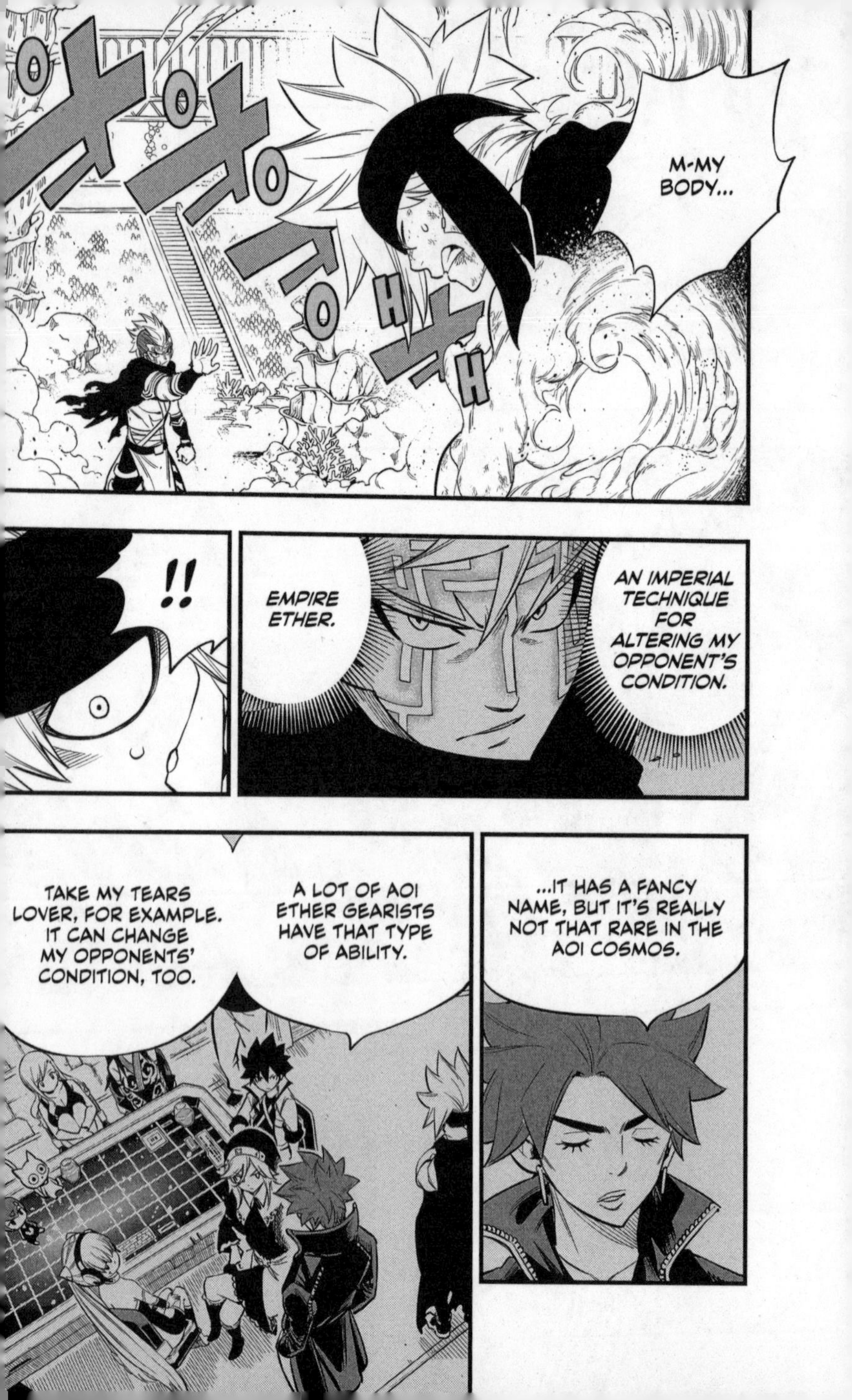
M-MY BODY...
AN IMPERIAL TECHNIQUE FOR ALTERING MY OPPONENT'S CONDITION.
EMPIRE ETHER.
!!
...IT HAS A FANCY NAME, BUT IT'S REALLY NOT THAT RARE IN THE AOI COSMOS.
A LOT OF AOI ETHER GEARISTS HAVE THAT TYPE OF ABILITY.
TAKE MY TEARS LOVER, FOR EXAMPLE. IT CAN CHANGE MY OPPONENTS' CONDITION, TOO.

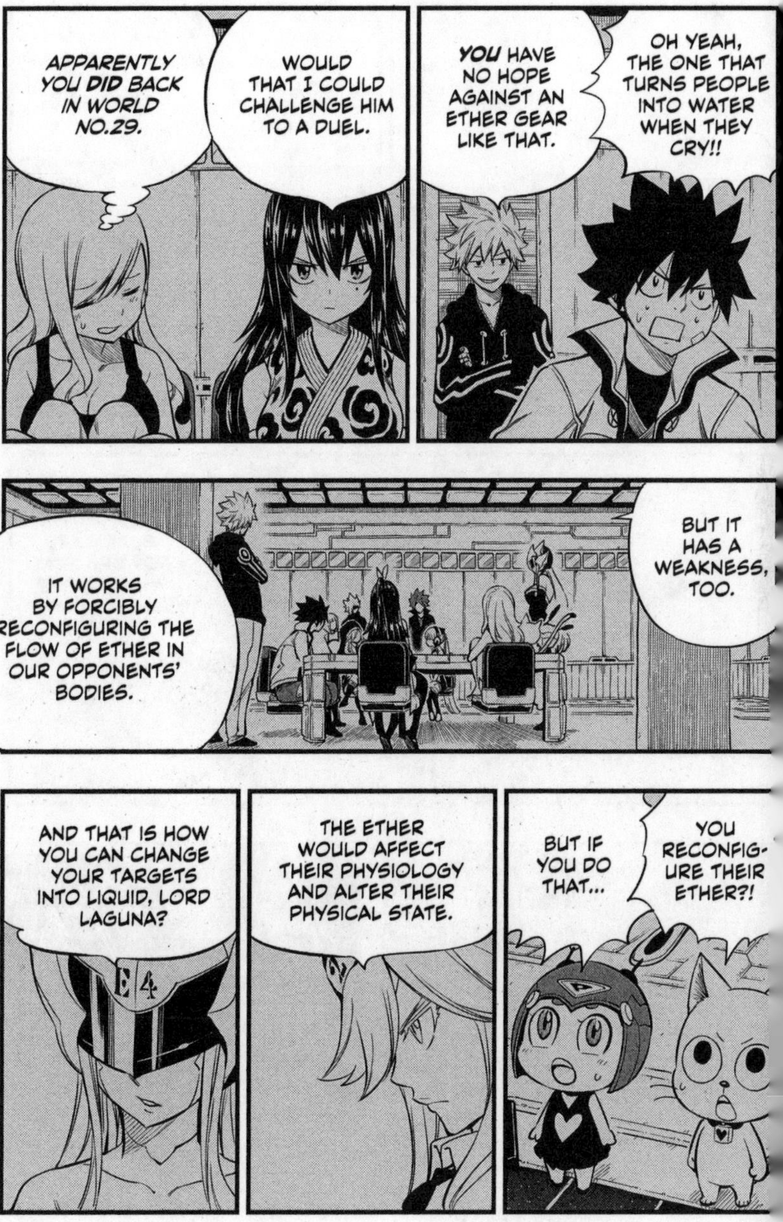
OH YEAH, THE ONE THAT TURNS PEOPLE INTO WATER WHEN THEY CRY!!
YOU HAVE NO HOPE AGAINST AN ETHER GEAR LIKE THAT.
WOULD THAT I COULD CHALLENGE HIM TO A DUEL.
APPARENTLY YOU DID BACK IN WORLD NO.29.
BUT IT HAS A WEAKNESS, TOO.
IT WORKS BY FORCIBLY RECONFIGURING THE FLOW OF ETHER IN OUR OPPONENTS' BODIES.
YOU RECONFIG-URE THEIR ETHER?!
BUT IF YOU DO THAT...
THE ETHER WOULD AFFECT THEIR PHYSIOLOGY AND ALTER THEIR PHYSICAL STATE.
AND THAT IS HOW YOU CAN CHANGE YOUR TARGETS INTO LIQUID, LORD LAGUNA?

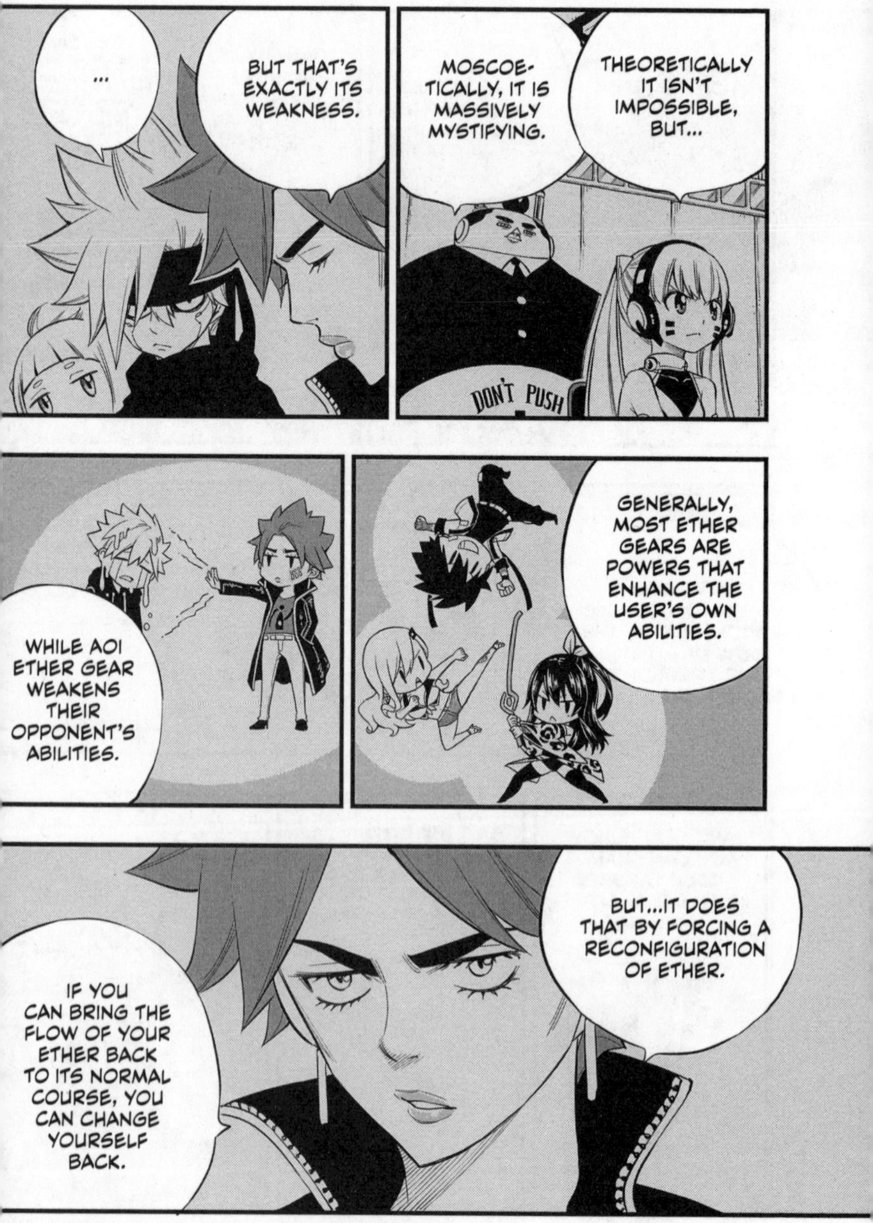
THEORETICALLY IT ISN'T IMPOSSIBLE, BUT...
MOSCOE-TICALLY, IT IS MASSIVELY MYSTIFYING.
DON'T PUSH
BUT THAT'S EXACTLY ITS WEAKNESS.
...
GENERALLY, MOST ETHER GEARS ARE POWERS THAT ENHANCE THE USER'S OWN ABILITIES.
WHILE AOI ETHER GEAR WEAKENS THEIR OPPONENT'S ABILITIES.
BUT...IT DOES THAT BY FORCING A RECONFIGURATION OF ETHER.
IF YOU CAN BRING THE FLOW OF YOUR ETHER BACK TO ITS NORMAL COURSE, YOU CAN CHANGE YOURSELF BACK.

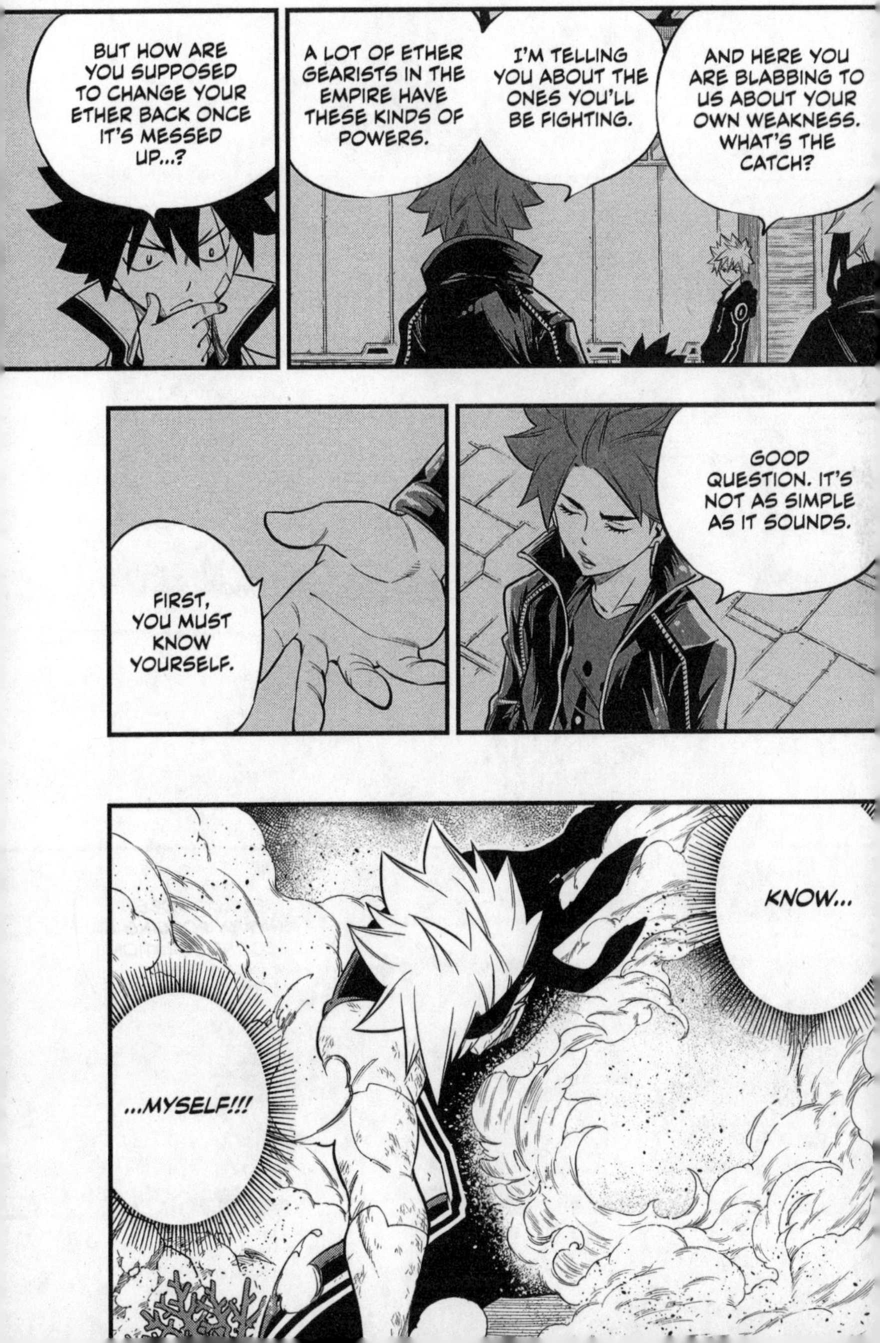
AND HERE YOU ARE BLABBING TO US ABOUT YOUR OWN WEAKNESS. WHAT'S THE CATCH?
I'M TELLING YOU ABOUT THE ONES YOU'LL BE FIGHTING.
A LOT OF ETHER GEARISTS IN THE EMPIRE HAVE THESE KINDS OF POWERS.
BUT HOW ARE YOU SUPPOSED TO CHANGE YOUR ETHER BACK ONCE IT'S MESSED UP...?
GOOD QUESTION. IT'S NOT AS SIMPLE AS IT SOUNDS.
FIRST, YOU MUST KNOW YOURSELF.
KNOW...
...MYSELF!!!

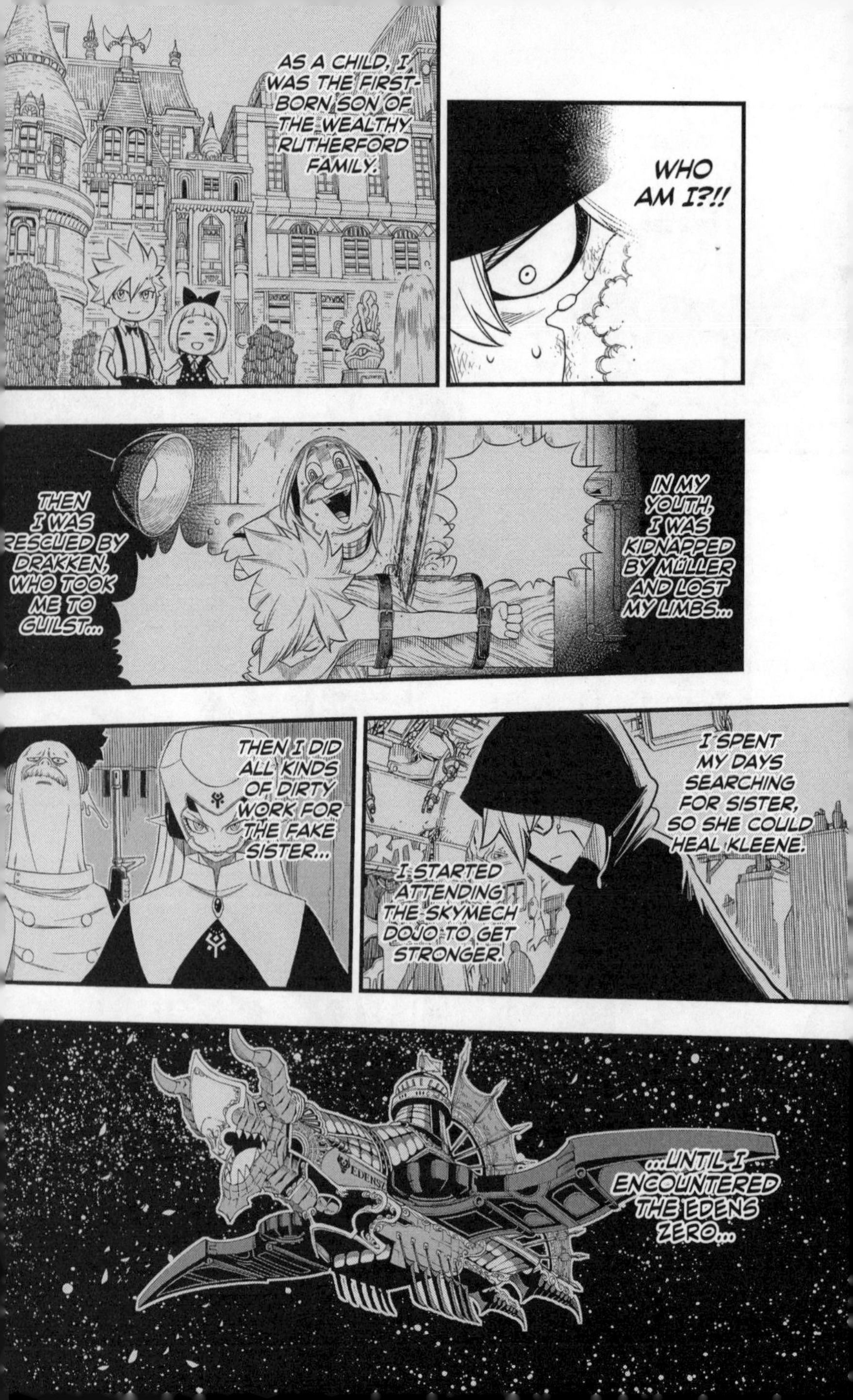
WHO AM I?!!
AS A CHILD, I WAS THE FIRST-BORN SON OF THE WEALTHY RUTHERFORD FAMILY.
IN MY YOUTH, I WAS KIDNAPPED BY MÜLLER AND LOST MY LIMBS...
THEN I WAS RESCUED BY DRAKKEN, WHO TOOK ME TO GUILST...
I SPENT MY DAYS SEARCHING FOR SISTER, SO SHE COULD HEAL KLEENE.
I STARTED ATTENDING THE SKYMECH DOJO TO GET STRONGER.
THEN I DID ALL KINDS OF DIRTY WORK FOR THE FAKE SISTER...
...UNTIL I ENCOUNTERED THE EDENS ZERO...

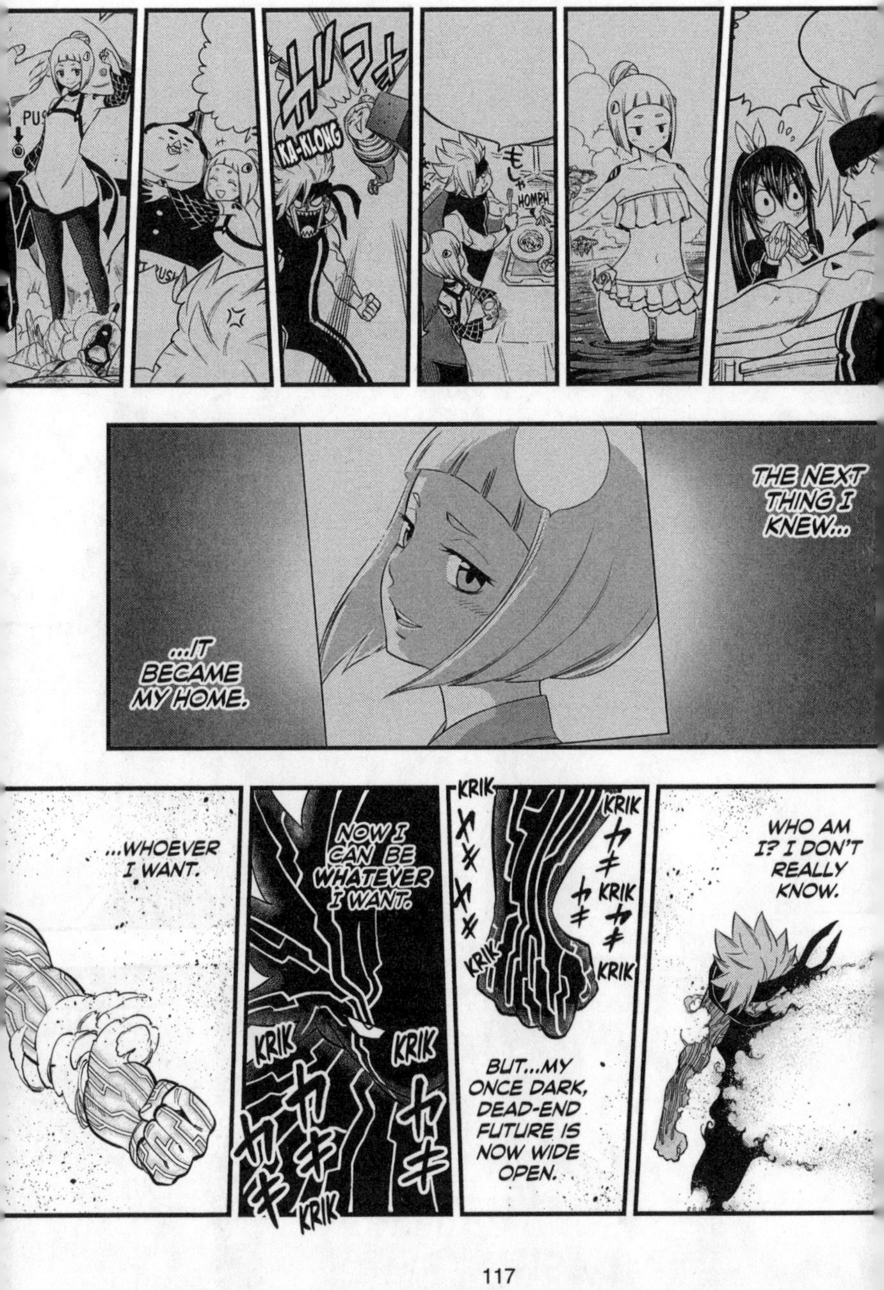
HOMPH
KA-KLONG
PUS
THE NEXT THING I KNEW...
...IT BECAME MY HOME.
WHO AM I? I DON'T REALLY KNOW.
KRIK
KRIK
KRIK
KRIK
BUT...MY ONCE DARK, DEAD-END FUTURE IS NOW WIDE OPEN.
NOW I CAN BE WHATEVER I WANT.
KRIK
KRIK
KRIK
...WHOEVER I WANT.

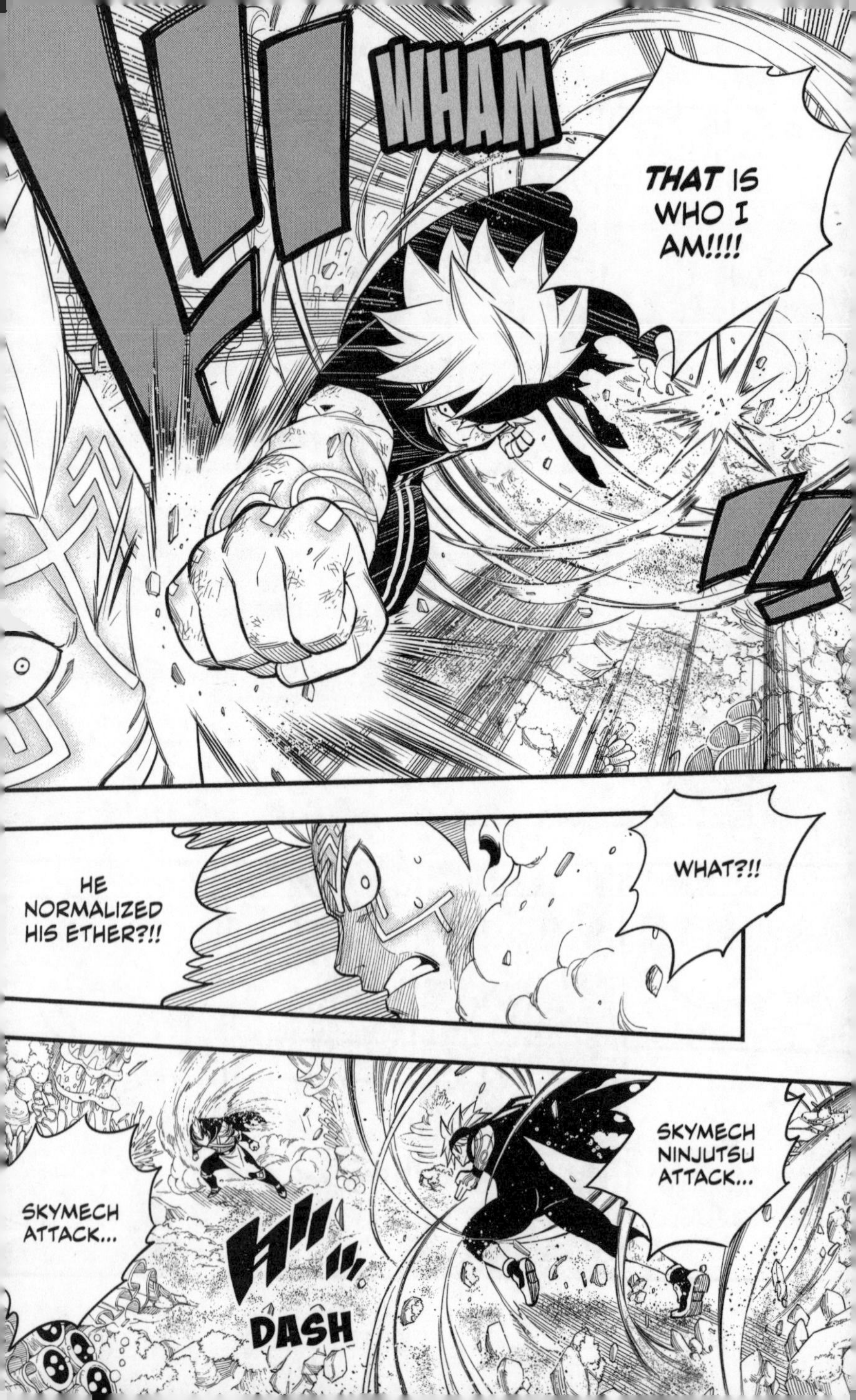
WHAM
THAT IS WHO I AM!!!!
WHAT?!!
HE NORMALIZED HIS ETHER?!!
SKYMECH NINJUTSU ATTACK...
SKYMECH ATTACK...
DASH

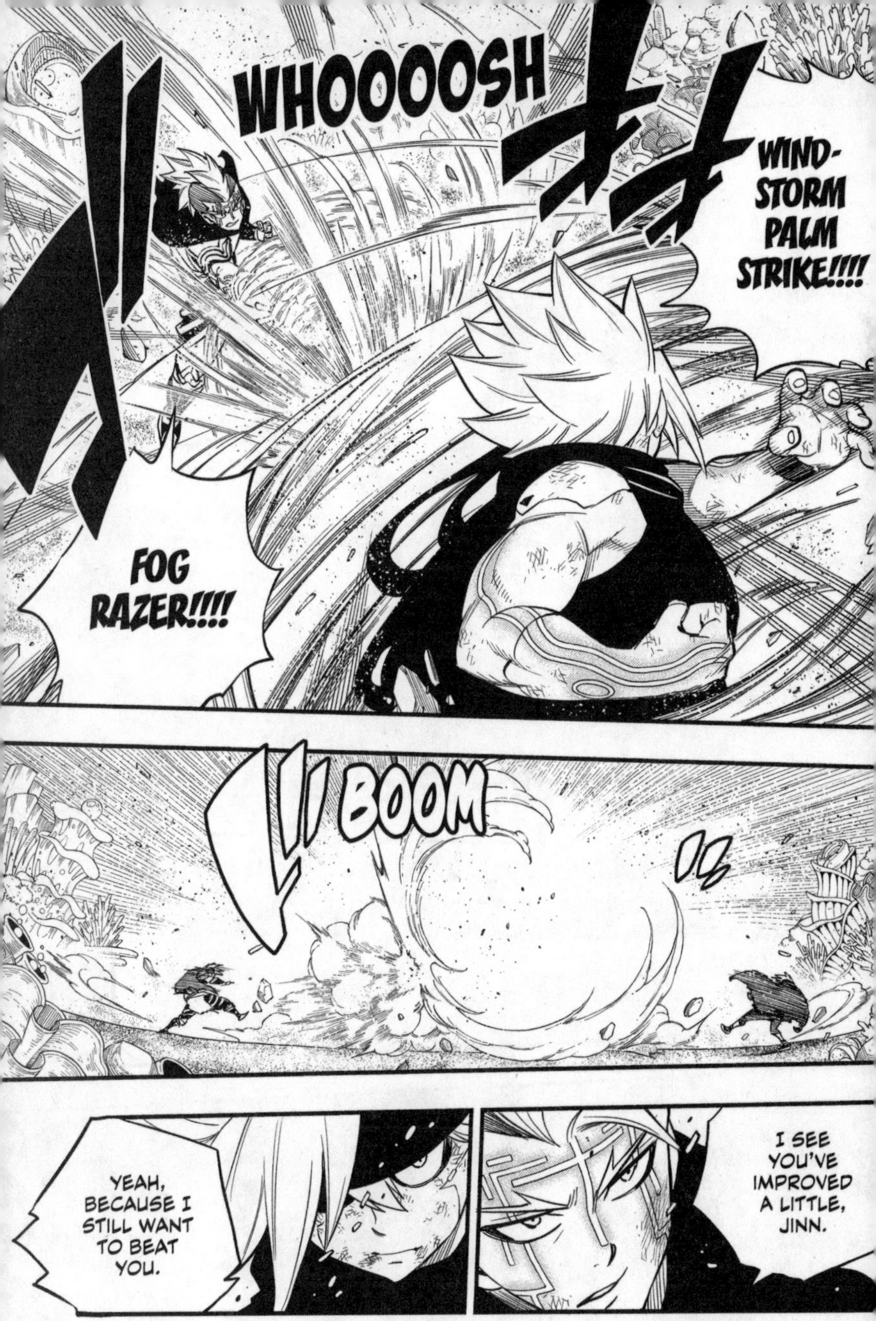
WHOOOOSH
WIND-STORM PALM STRIKE!!!!
FOG RAZER!!!!
BOOM
I SEE YOU'VE IMPROVED A LITTLE, JINN.
YEAH, BECAUSE I STILL WANT TO BEAT YOU.

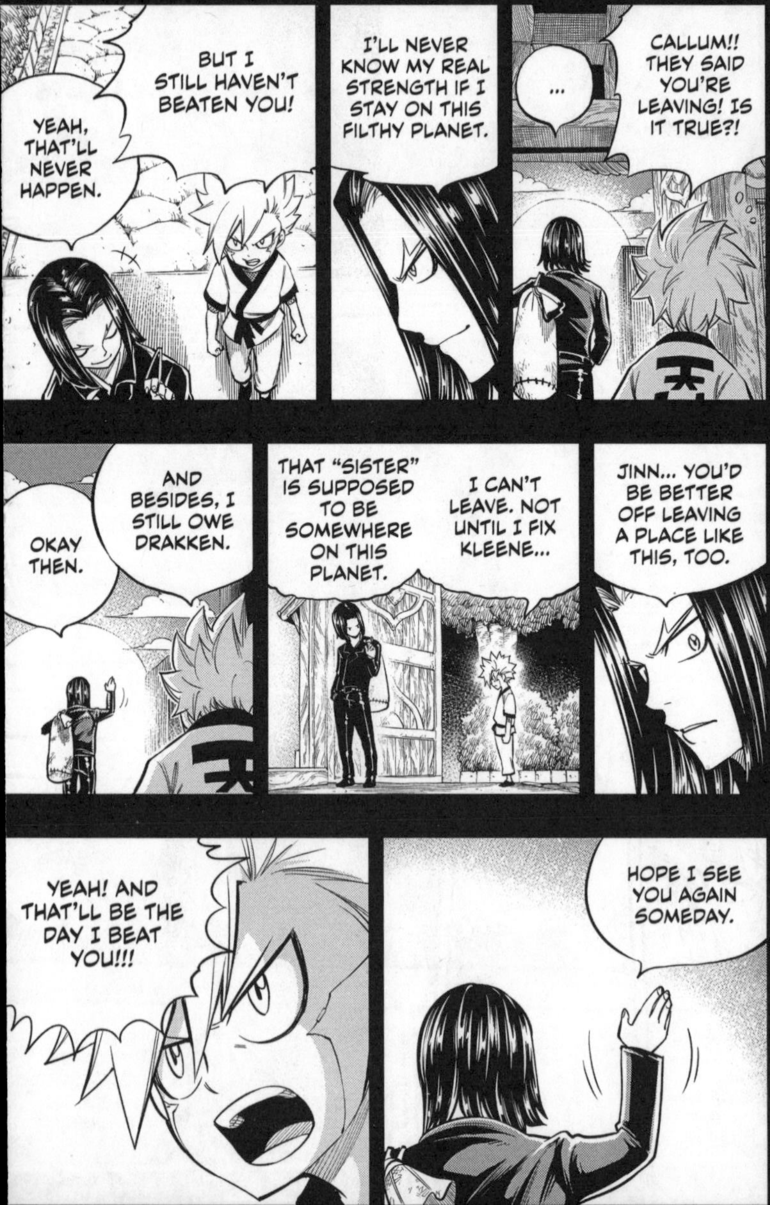

...
CALLUM!! THEY SAID YOU'RE LEAVING! IS IT TRUE?!
I'LL NEVER KNOW MY REAL STRENGTH IF I STAY ON THIS FILTHY PLANET.
BUT I STILL HAVEN'T BEATEN YOU!
YEAH, THAT'LL NEVER HAPPEN.
JINN... YOU'D BE BETTER OFF LEAVING A PLACE LIKE THIS, TOO.
I CAN'T LEAVE. NOT UNTIL I FIX KLEENE...
THAT "SISTER" IS SUPPOSED TO BE SOMEWHERE ON THIS PLANET.
AND BESIDES, I STILL OWE DRAKKEN.
OKAY THEN.
HOPE I SEE YOU AGAIN SOMEDAY.
YEAH! AND THAT'LL BE THE DAY I BEAT YOU!!!

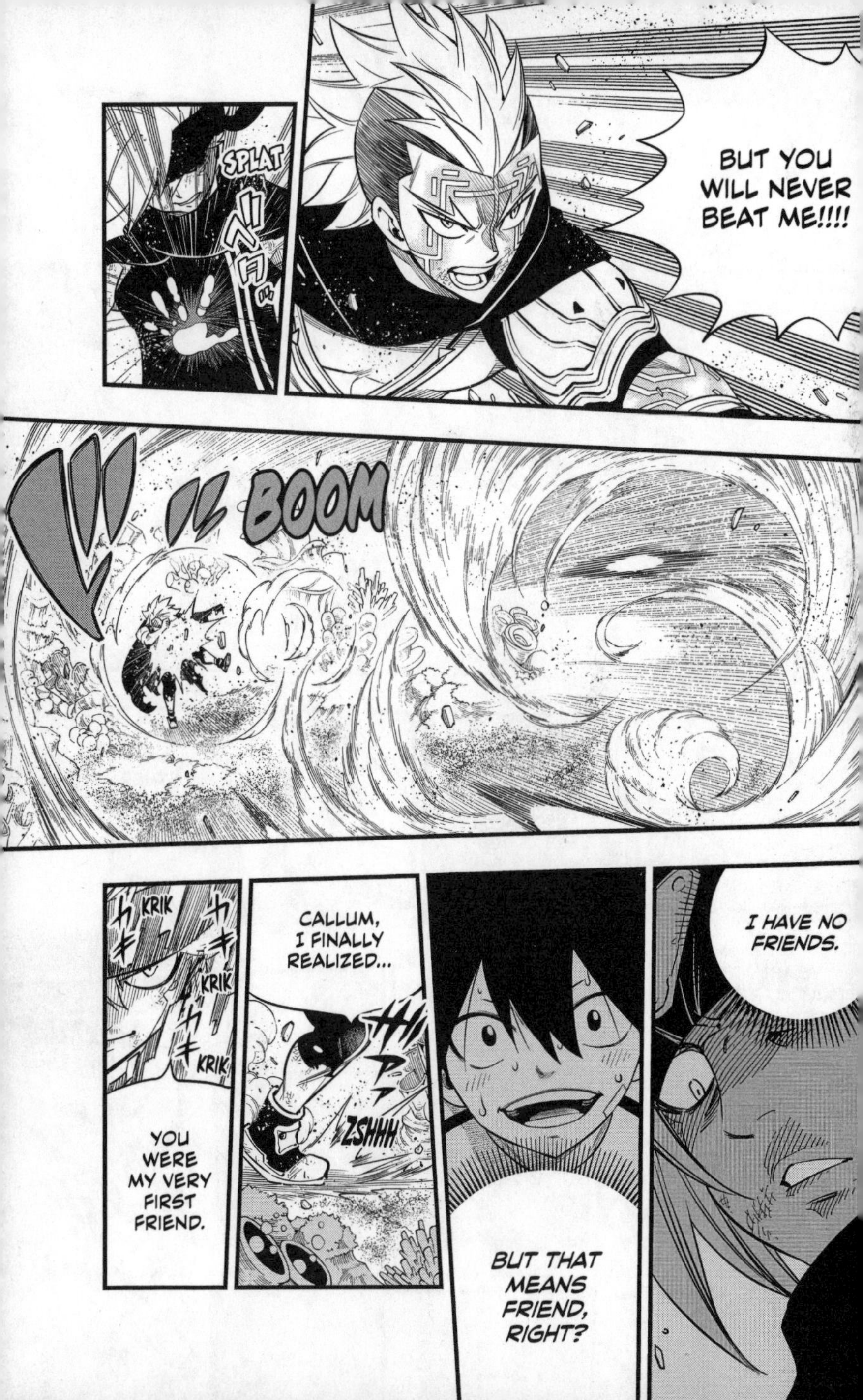

BUT YOU WILL NEVER BEAT ME!!!!
SPLAT
BOOM
I HAVE NO FRIENDS.
BUT THAT MEANS FRIEND, RIGHT?
CALLUM, I FINALLY REALIZED...
ZSHHH
KRIK
KRIK
KRIK
YOU WERE MY VERY FIRST FRIEND.

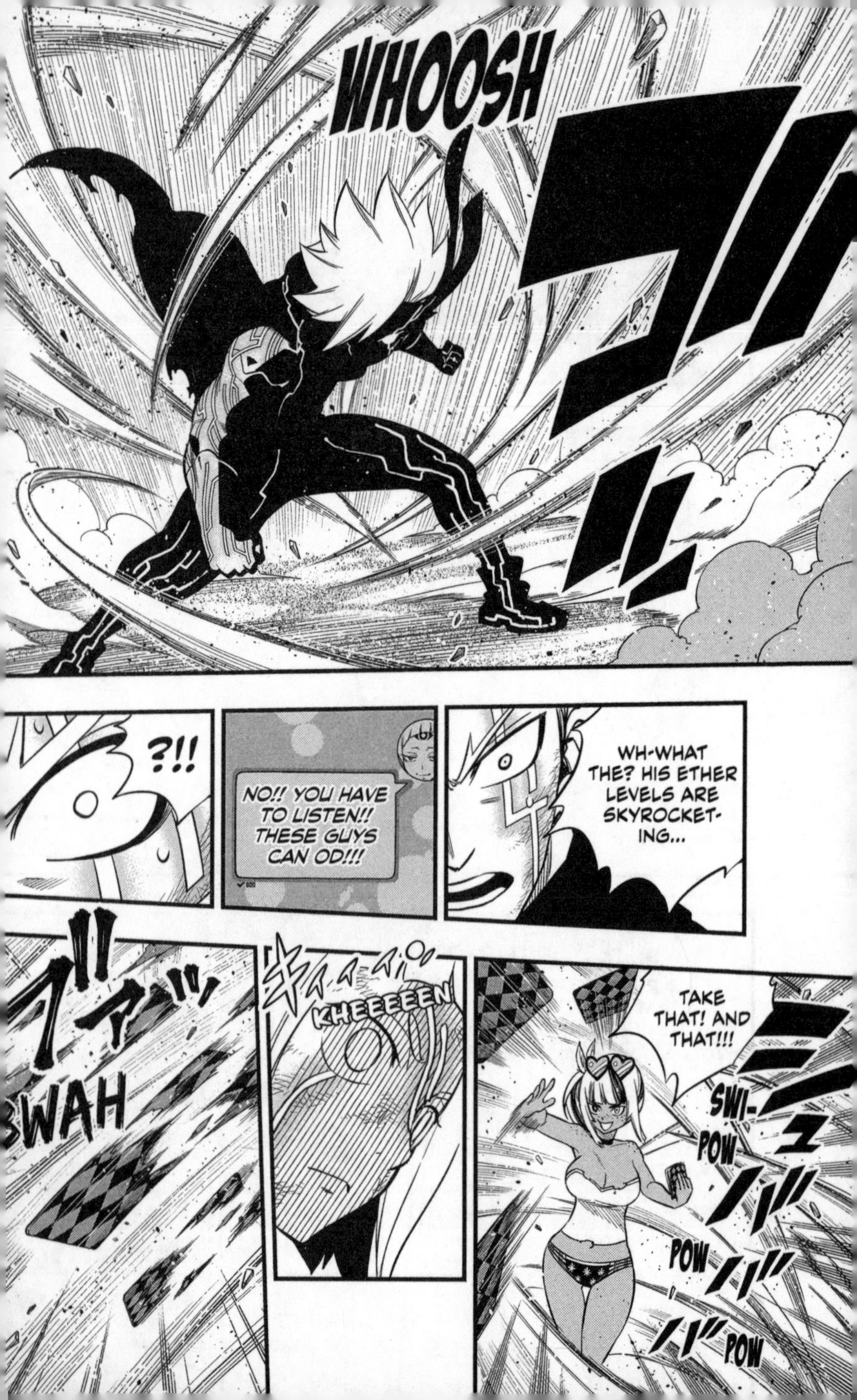
WHOOSH
WH-WHAT THE? HIS ETHER LEVELS ARE SKYROCKET-ING...
NO!! YOU HAVE TO LISTEN!! THESE GUYS CAN OD!!!
?!!
TAKE THAT! AND THAT!!!
SWI-
POW
POW
POW
KHEEEEEN
WAH

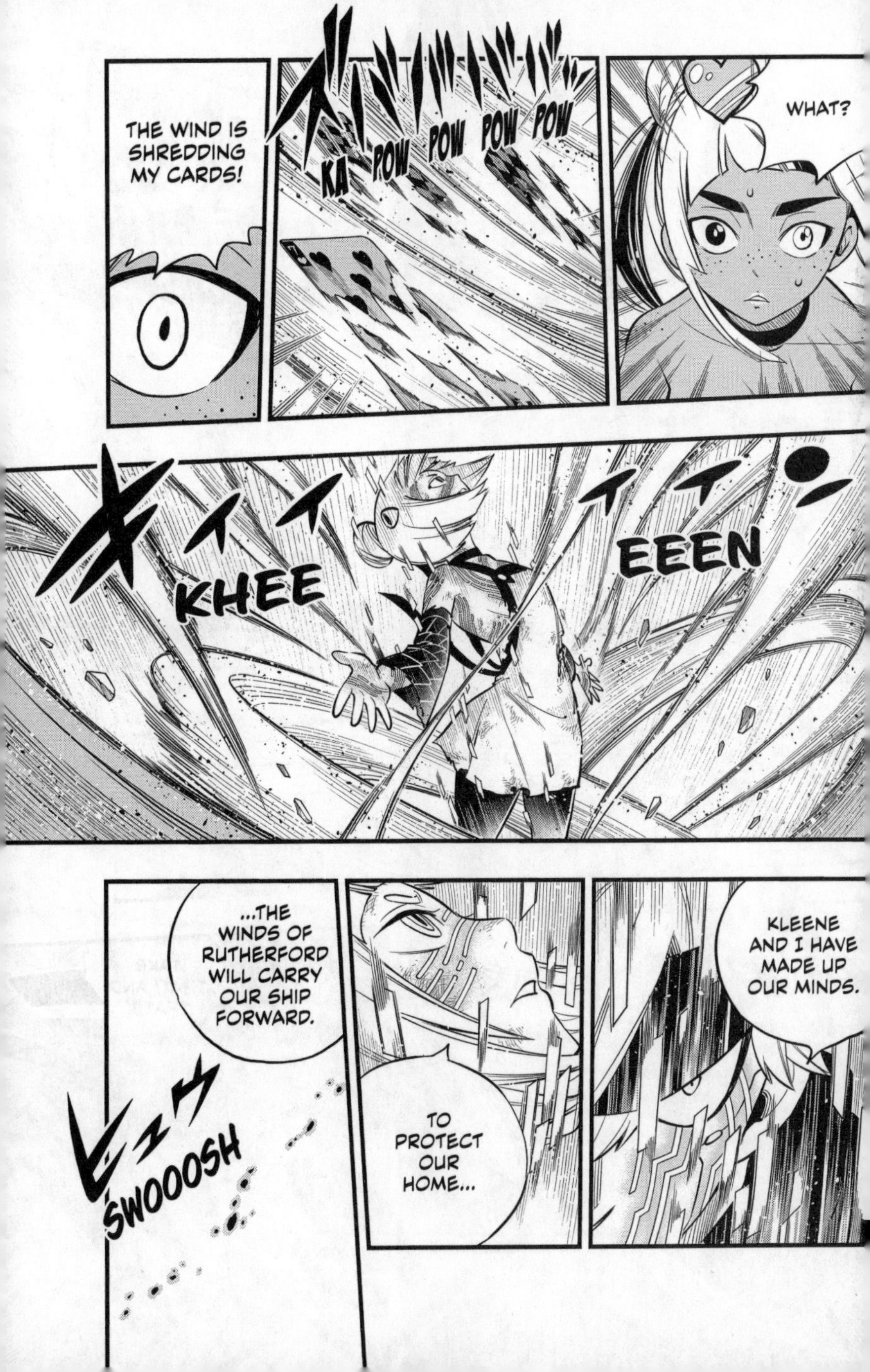
WHAT?
KA POW POW POW POW
THE WIND IS SHREDDING MY CARDS!
KHEE
EEEN
KLEENE AND I HAVE MADE UP OUR MINDS.
TO PROTECT OUR HOME...
...THE WINDS OF RUTHERFORD WILL CARRY OUR SHIP FORWARD.
SWOOOSH

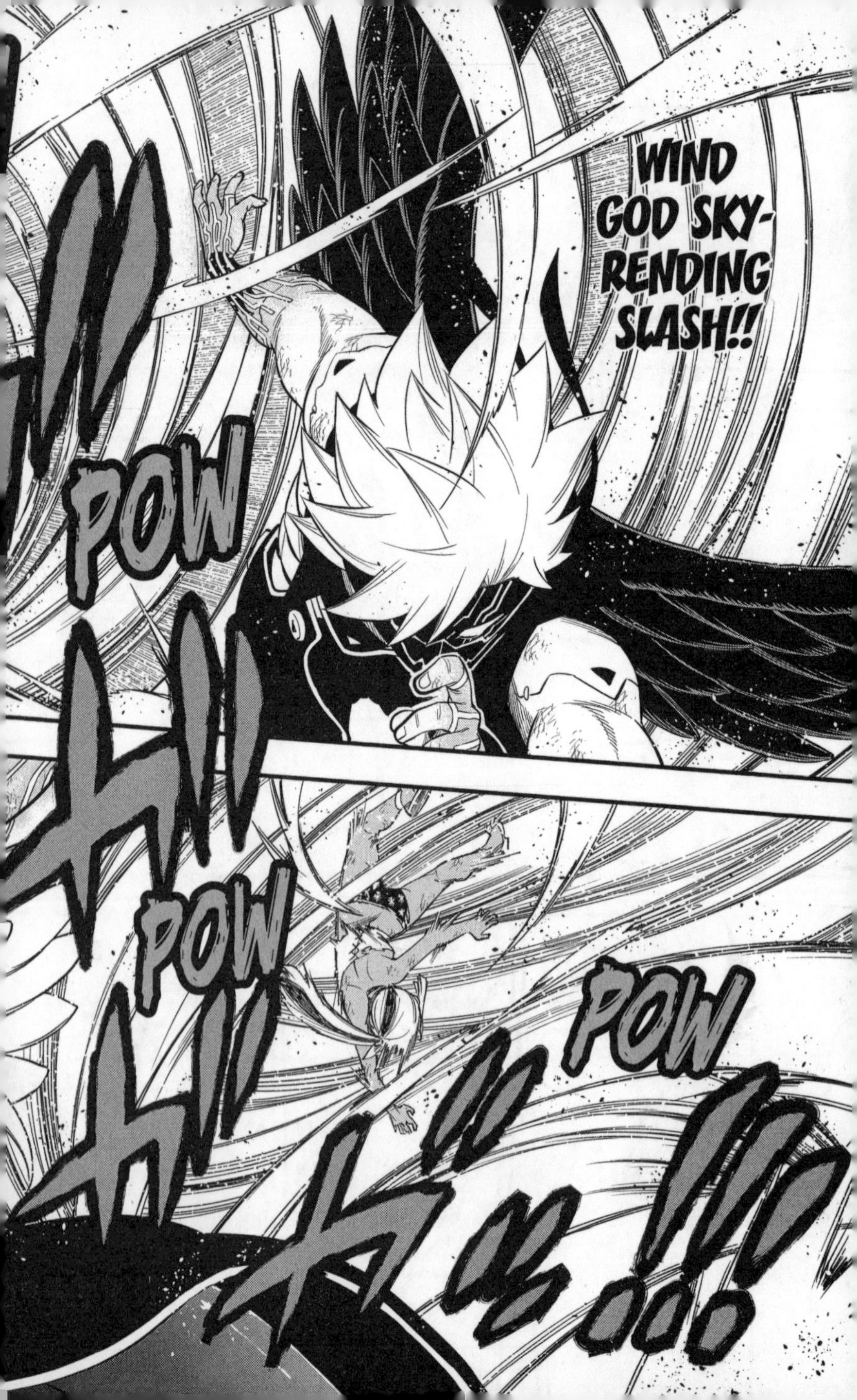
WIND GOD SKY-RENDING SLASH!!
POW
POW
POW

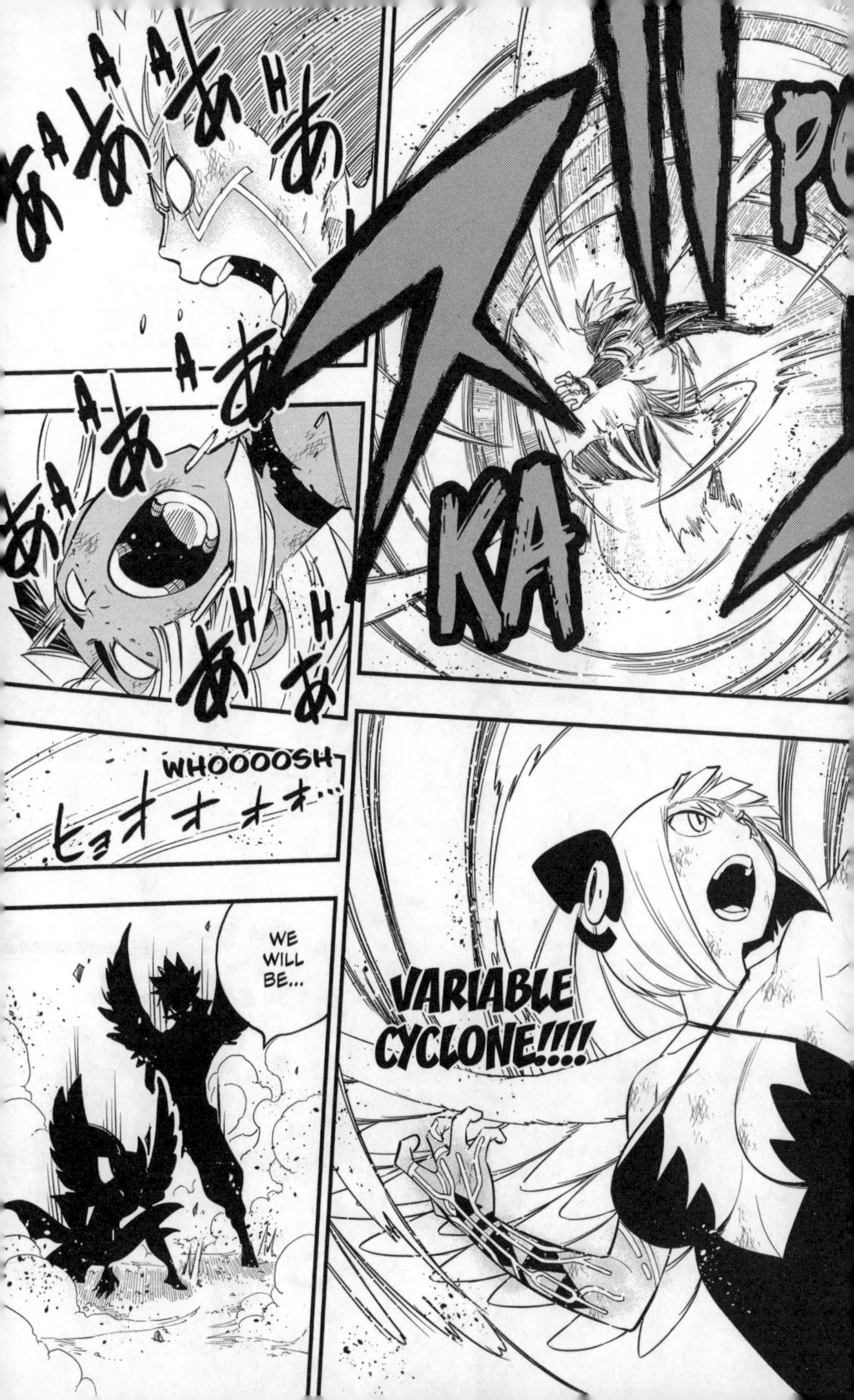
PO
KA
AAAH
ああああ
AAAHH
あああああ
VARIABLE CYCLONE!!!!
WHOOOOSH
ヒョオオオオ…
WE WILL BE...

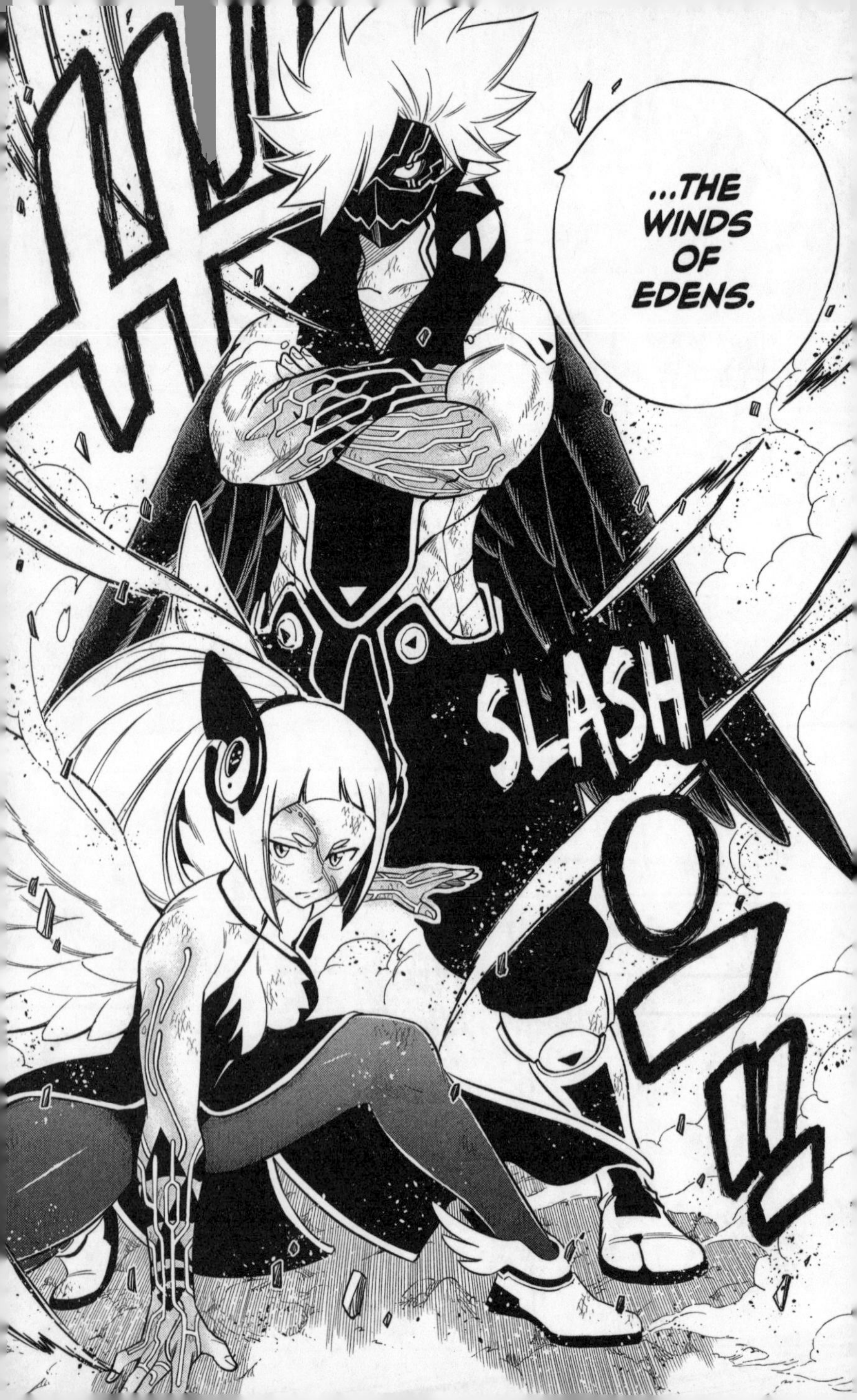
...THE WINDS OF EDENS.
SLASH

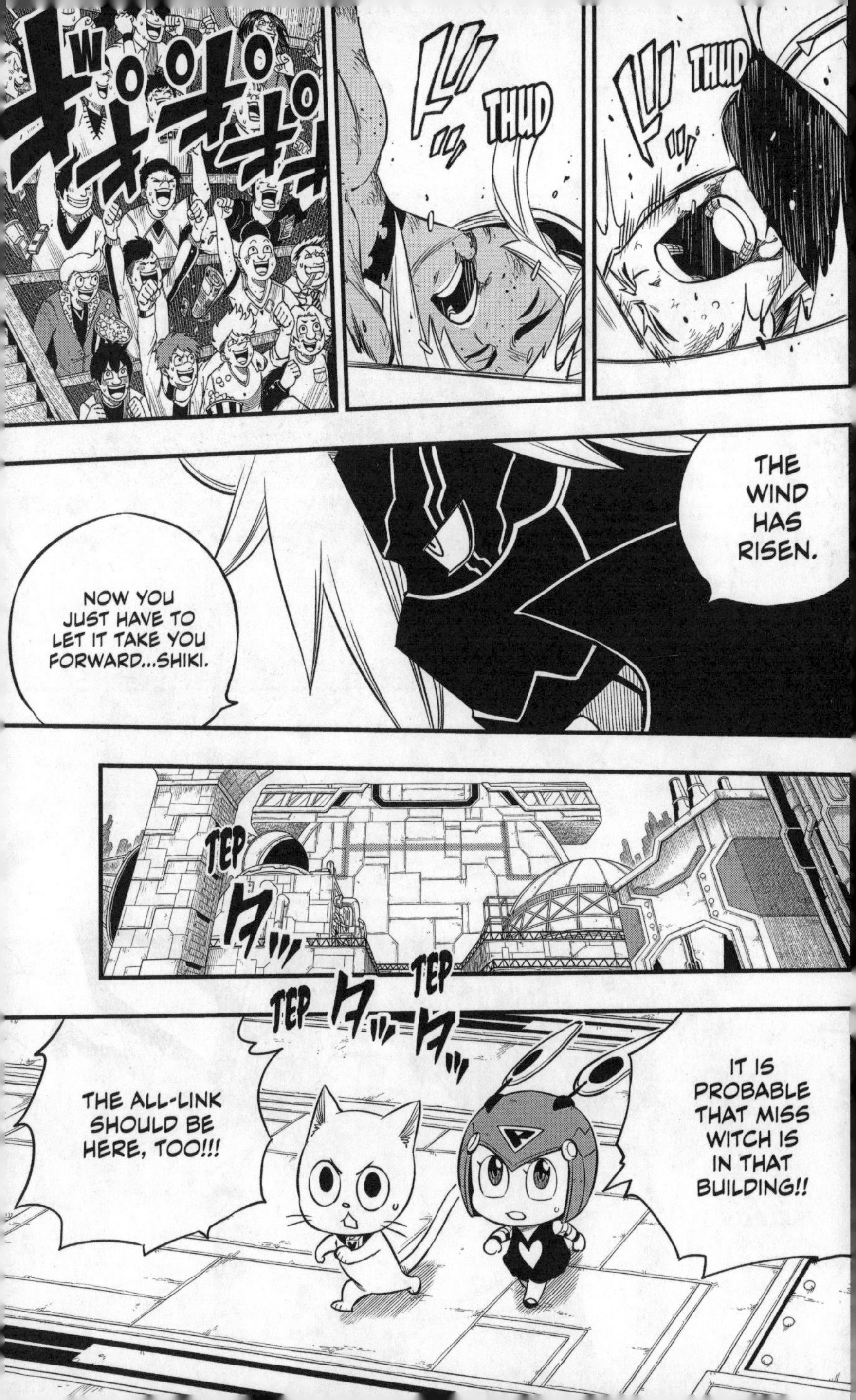
THUD
THUD
WOOOO
THE WIND HAS RISEN.
NOW YOU JUST HAVE TO LET IT TAKE YOU FORWARD...SHIKI.
TEP
TEP
TEP
IT IS PROBABLE THAT MISS WITCH IS IN THAT BUILDING!!
THE ALL-LINK SHOULD BE HERE, TOO!!!

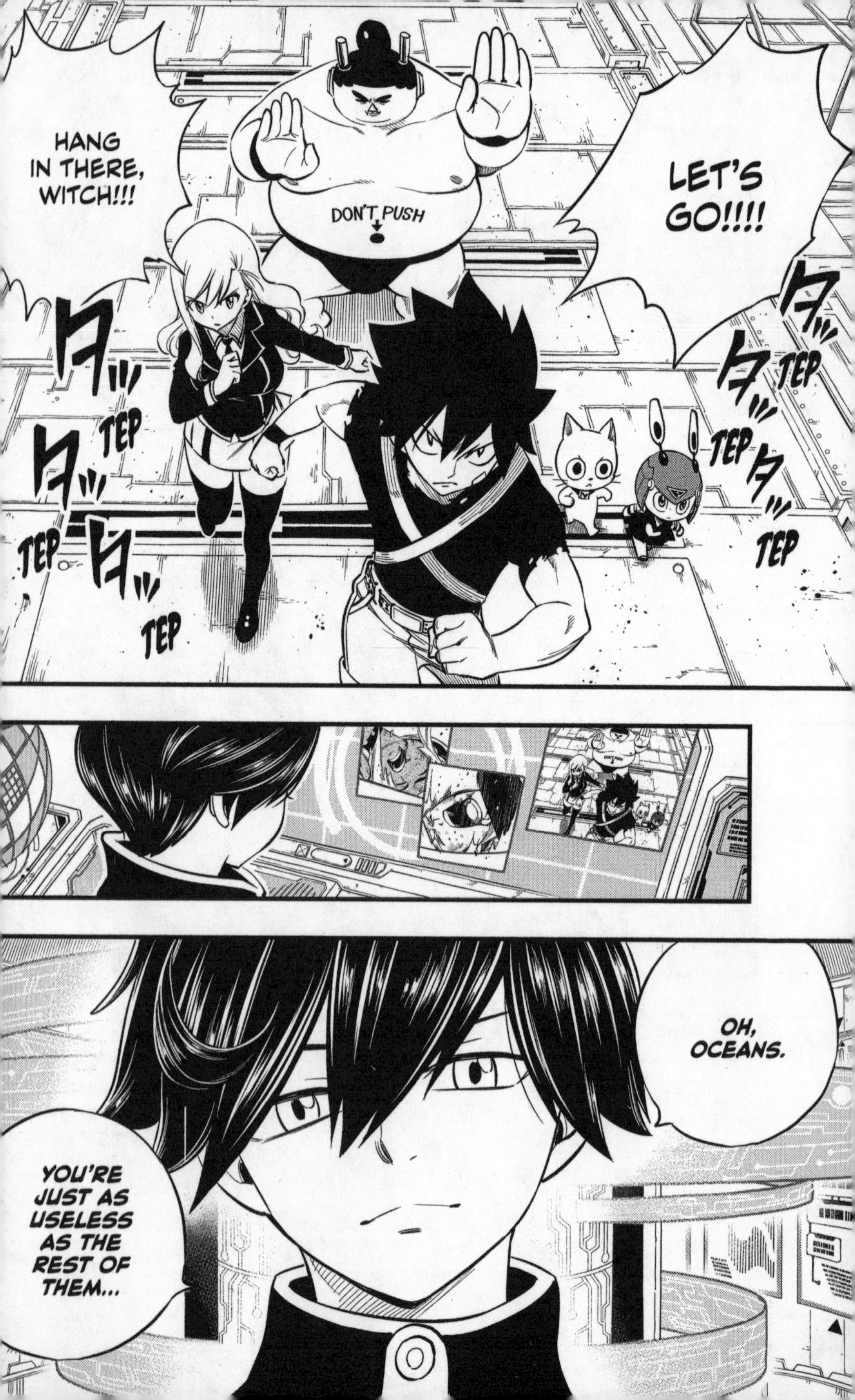
LET'S GO!!!!
TEP
TEP
TEP
HANG IN THERE, WITCH!!!
DON'T PUSH
TEP
TEP
TEP
OH, OCEANS.
YOU'RE JUST AS USELESS AS THE REST OF THEM...

EDENS ZERO

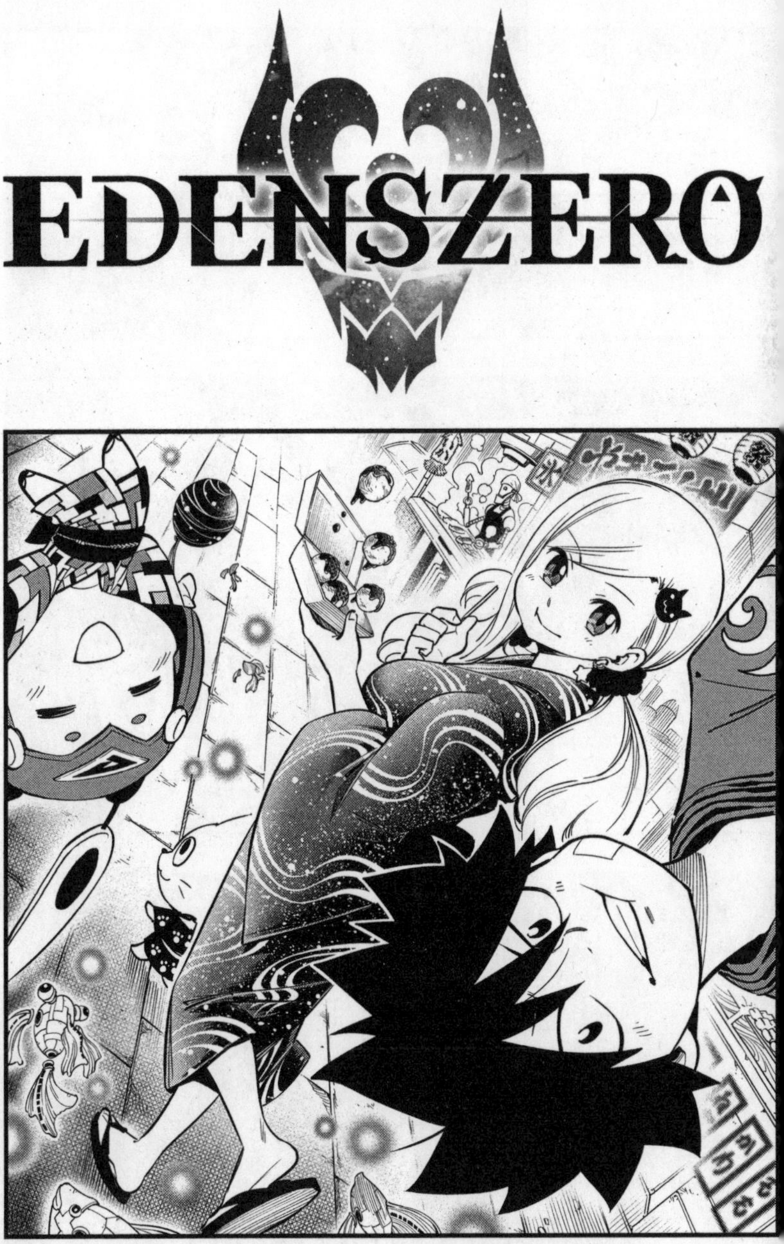

氷

CHAPTER 156: THE BEAST LORD

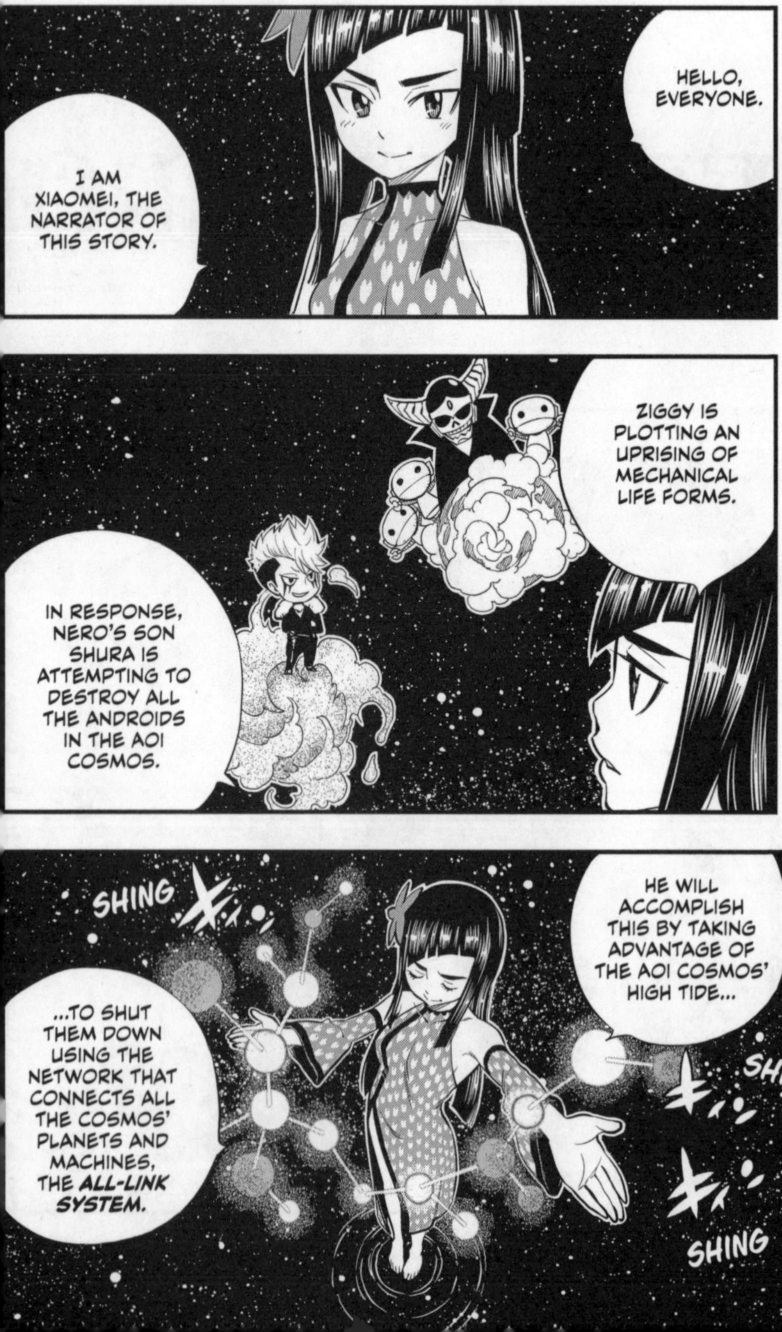
HELLO, EVERYONE.
I AM XIAOMEI, THE NARRATOR OF THIS STORY.
ZIGGY IS PLOTTING AN UPRISING OF MECHANICAL LIFE FORMS.
IN RESPONSE, NERO'S SON SHURA IS ATTEMPTING TO DESTROY ALL THE ANDROIDS IN THE AOI COSMOS.
HE WILL ACCOMPLISH THIS BY TAKING ADVANTAGE OF THE AOI COSMOS' HIGH TIDE...
SHING
SHING
SHING
...TO SHUT THEM DOWN USING THE NETWORK THAT CONNECTS ALL THE COSMOS' PLANETS AND MACHINES, THE ***ALL-LINK SYSTEM***.

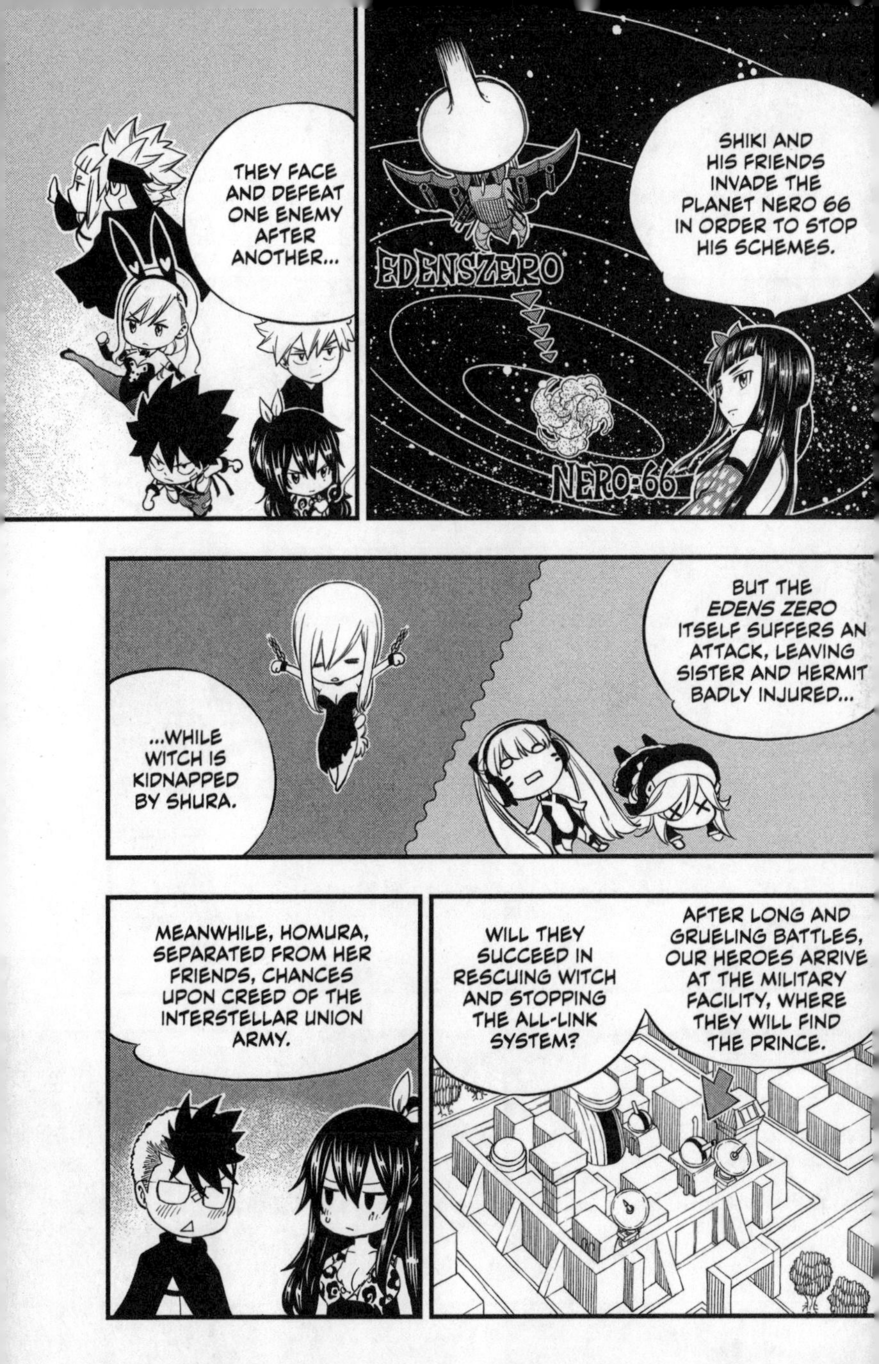
SHIKI AND HIS FRIENDS INVADE THE PLANET NERO 66 IN ORDER TO STOP HIS SCHEMES.
EDENSZERO
NERO-66
THEY FACE AND DEFEAT ONE ENEMY AFTER ANOTHER...
BUT THE *EDENS ZERO* ITSELF SUFFERS AN ATTACK, LEAVING SISTER AND HERMIT BADLY INJURED...
...WHILE WITCH IS KIDNAPPED BY SHURA.
AFTER LONG AND GRUELING BATTLES, OUR HEROES ARRIVE AT THE MILITARY FACILITY, WHERE THEY WILL FIND THE PRINCE.
WILL THEY SUCCEED IN RESCUING WITCH AND STOPPING THE ALL-LINK SYSTEM?
MEANWHILE, HOMURA, SEPARATED FROM HER FRIENDS, CHANCES UPON CREED OF THE INTERSTELLAR UNION ARMY.

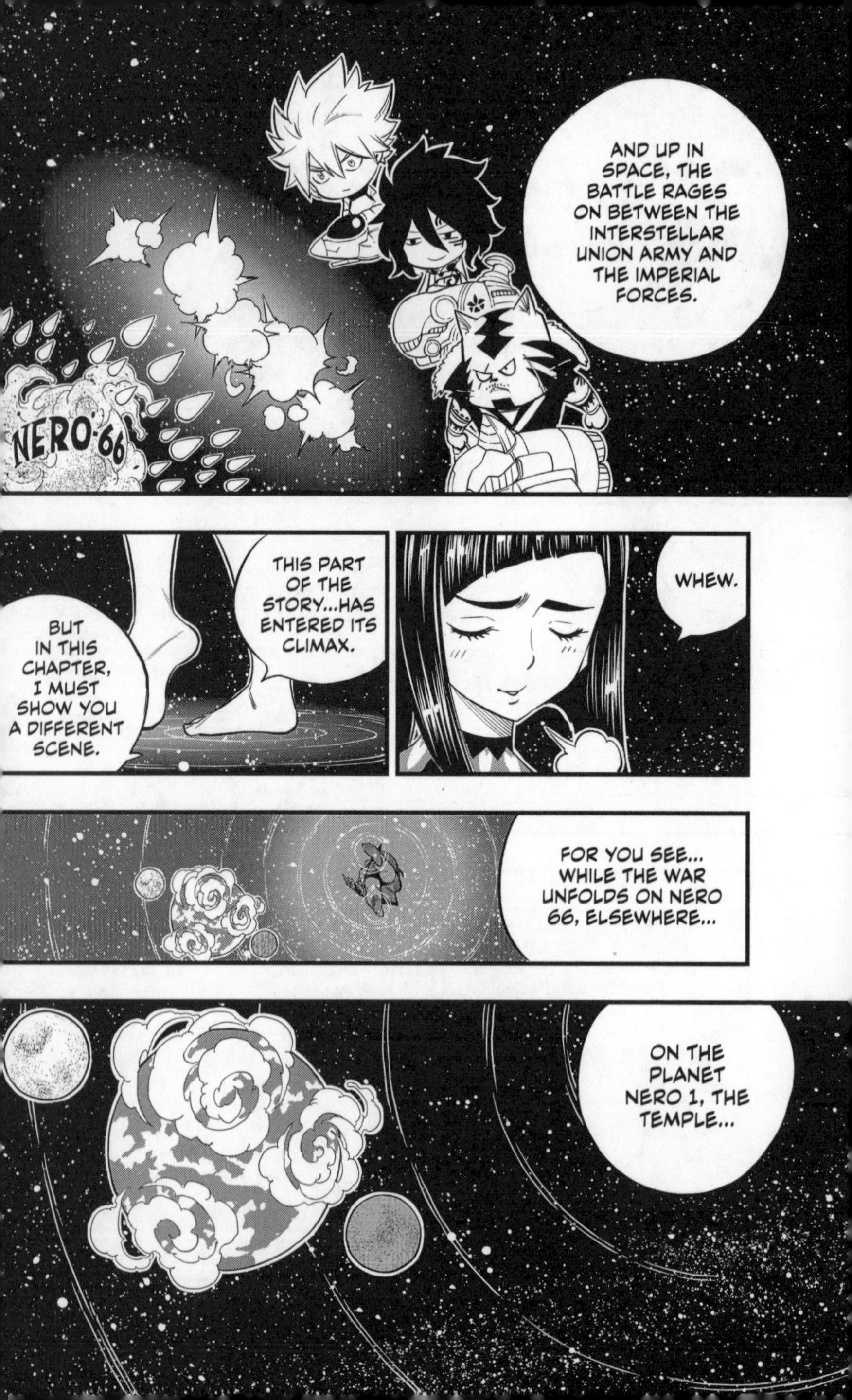
AND UP IN SPACE, THE BATTLE RAGES ON BETWEEN THE INTERSTELLAR UNION ARMY AND THE IMPERIAL FORCES.
NERO·66
WHEW.
THIS PART OF THE STORY...HAS ENTERED ITS CLIMAX.
BUT IN THIS CHAPTER, I MUST SHOW YOU A DIFFERENT SCENE.
FOR YOU SEE... WHILE THE WAR UNFOLDS ON NERO 66, ELSEWHERE...
ON THE PLANET NERO 1, THE TEMPLE...

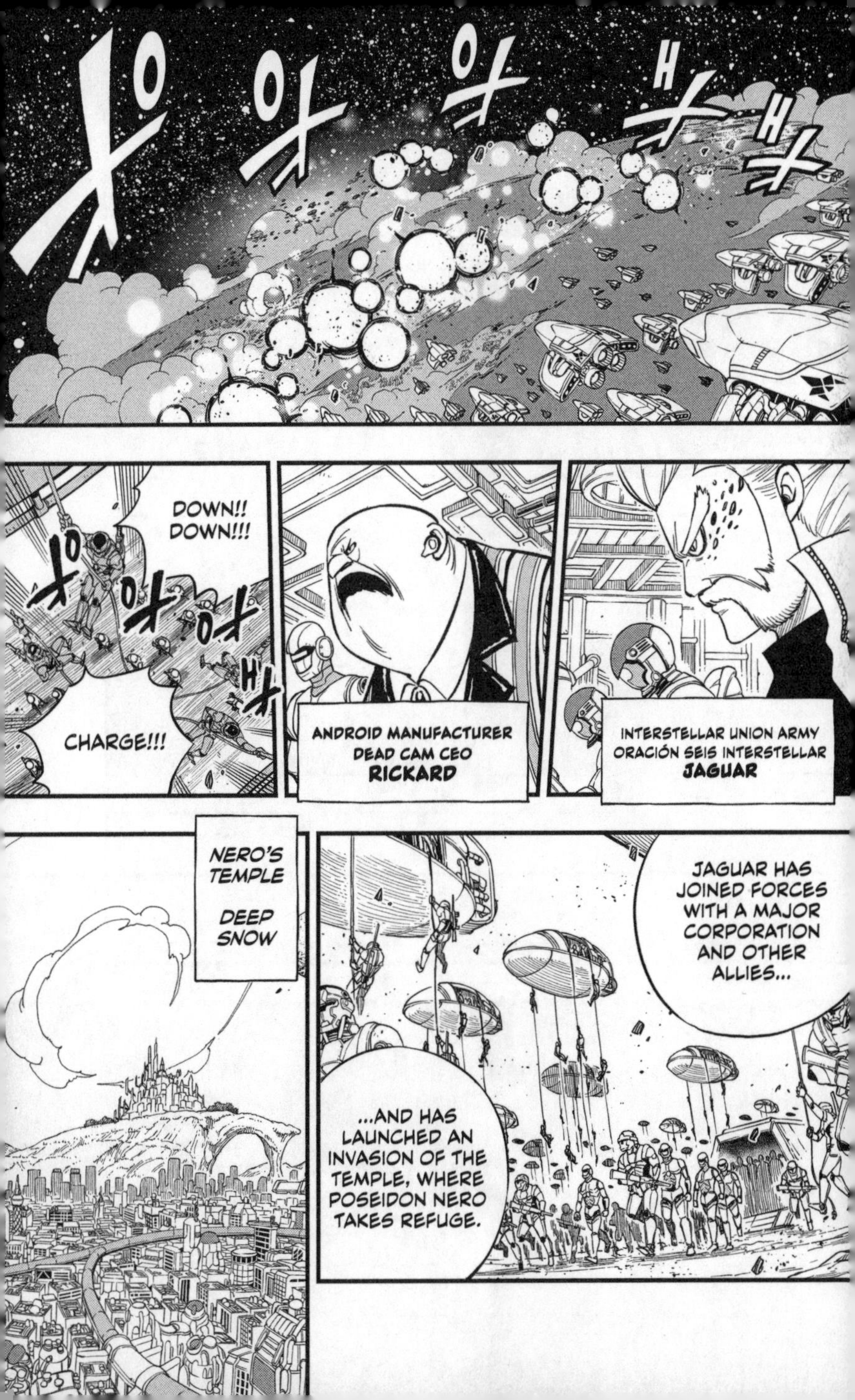
INTERSTELLAR UNION ARMY
ORACIÓN SEIS INTERSTELLAR
JAGUAR
ANDROID MANUFACTURER
DEAD CAM CEO
RICKARD
DOWN!! DOWN!!!
CHARGE!!!
JAGUAR HAS JOINED FORCES WITH A MAJOR CORPORATION AND OTHER ALLIES...
...AND HAS LAUNCHED AN INVASION OF THE TEMPLE, WHERE POSEIDON NERO TAKES REFUGE.
NERO'S TEMPLE
DEEP SNOW

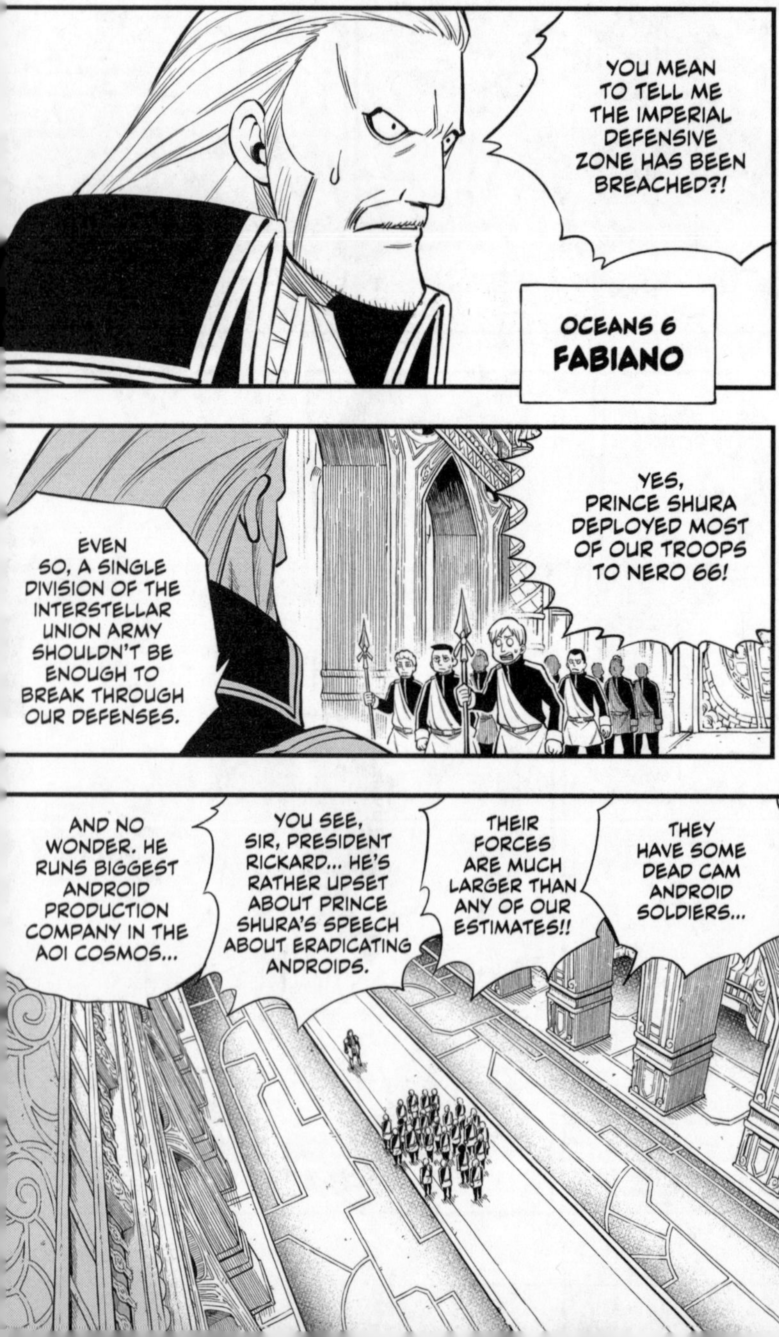
YOU MEAN TO TELL ME THE IMPERIAL DEFENSIVE ZONE HAS BEEN BREACHED?!
OCEANS 6
FABIANO
YES, PRINCE SHURA DEPLOYED MOST OF OUR TROOPS TO NERO 66!
EVEN SO, A SINGLE DIVISION OF THE INTERSTELLAR UNION ARMY SHOULDN'T BE ENOUGH TO BREAK THROUGH OUR DEFENSES.
THEY HAVE SOME DEAD CAM ANDROID SOLDIERS...
THEIR FORCES ARE MUCH LARGER THAN ANY OF OUR ESTIMATES!!
YOU SEE, SIR, PRESIDENT RICKARD... HE'S RATHER UPSET ABOUT PRINCE SHURA'S SPEECH ABOUT ERADICATING ANDROIDS.
AND NO WONDER. HE RUNS BIGGEST ANDROID PRODUCTION COMPANY IN THE AOI COSMOS...

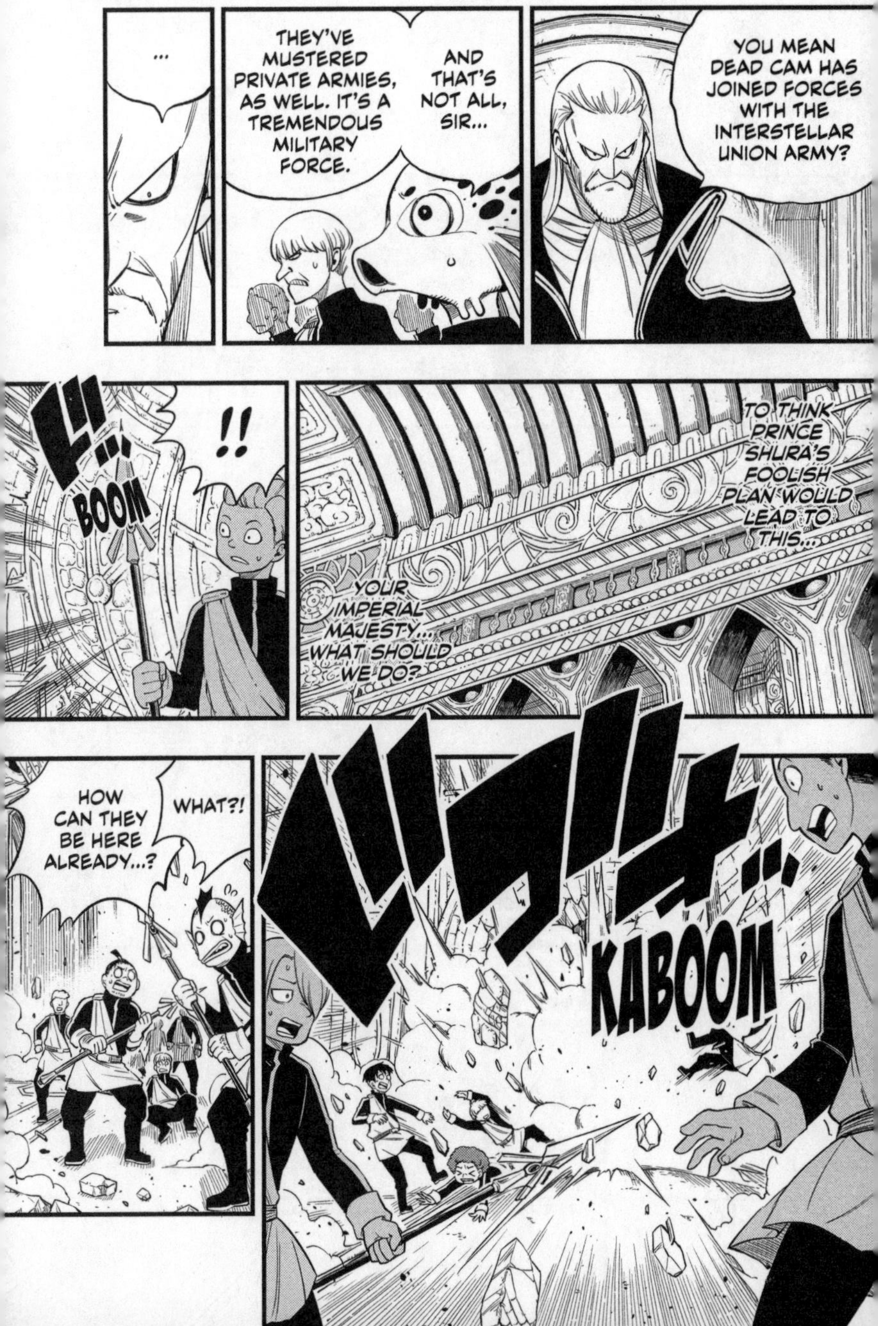
YOU MEAN DEAD CAM HAS JOINED FORCES WITH THE INTERSTELLAR UNION ARMY?
AND THAT'S NOT ALL, SIR...
THEY'VE MUSTERED PRIVATE ARMIES, AS WELL. IT'S A TREMENDOUS MILITARY FORCE.
...
TO THINK PRINCE SHURA'S FOOLISH PLAN WOULD LEAD TO THIS...
YOUR IMPERIAL MAJESTY... WHAT SHOULD WE DO?
!!
BOOM
KABOOM
WHAT?!
HOW CAN THEY BE HERE ALREADY...?

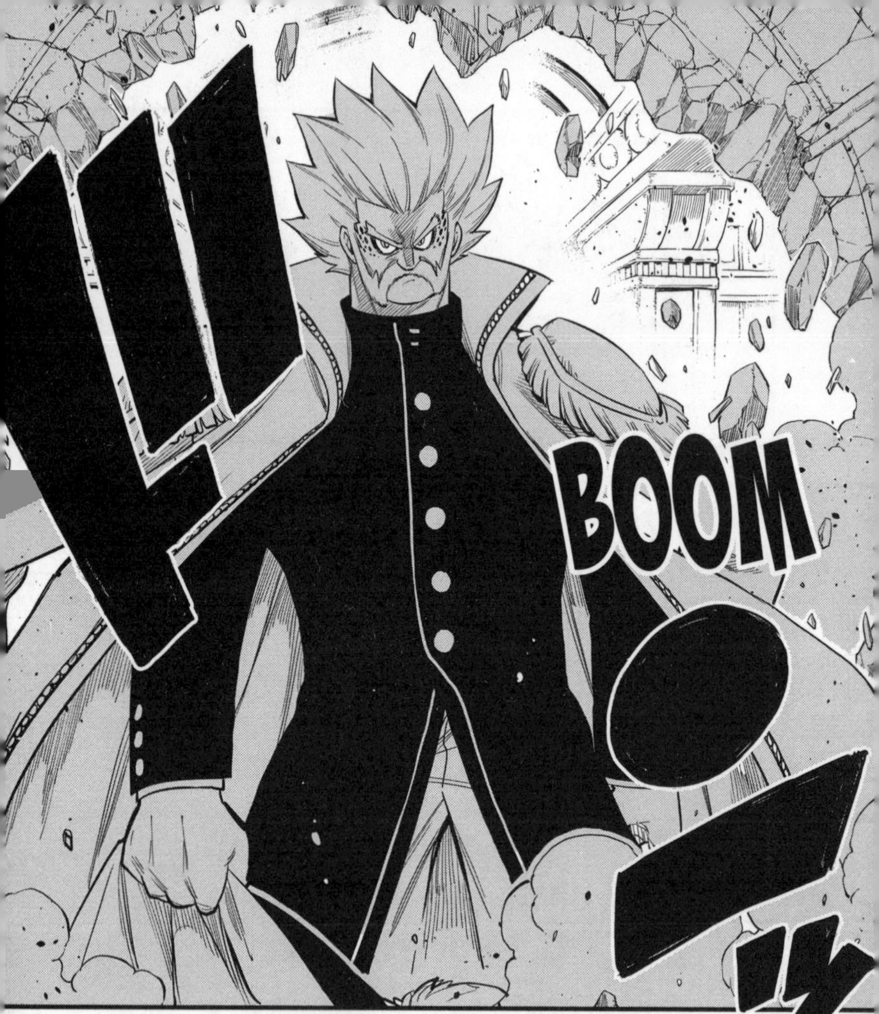
BOOM

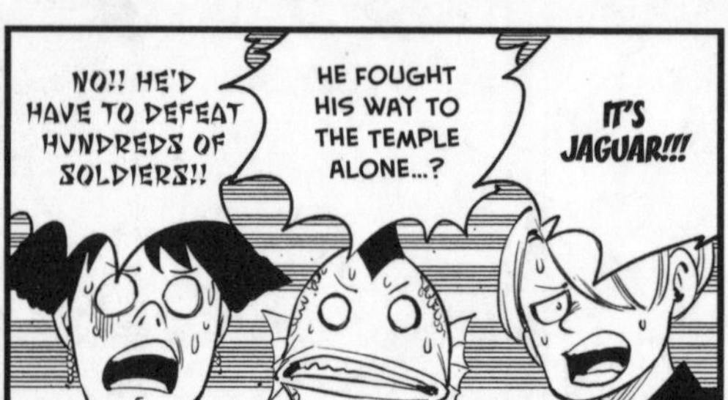
IT'S JAGUAR!!!
HE FOUGHT HIS WAY TO THE TEMPLE ALONE...?
NO!! HE'D HAVE TO DEFEAT HUNDREDS OF SOLDIERS!!

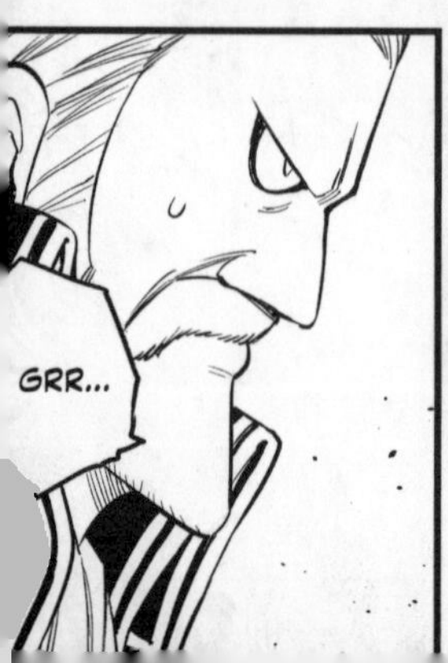
GRR...

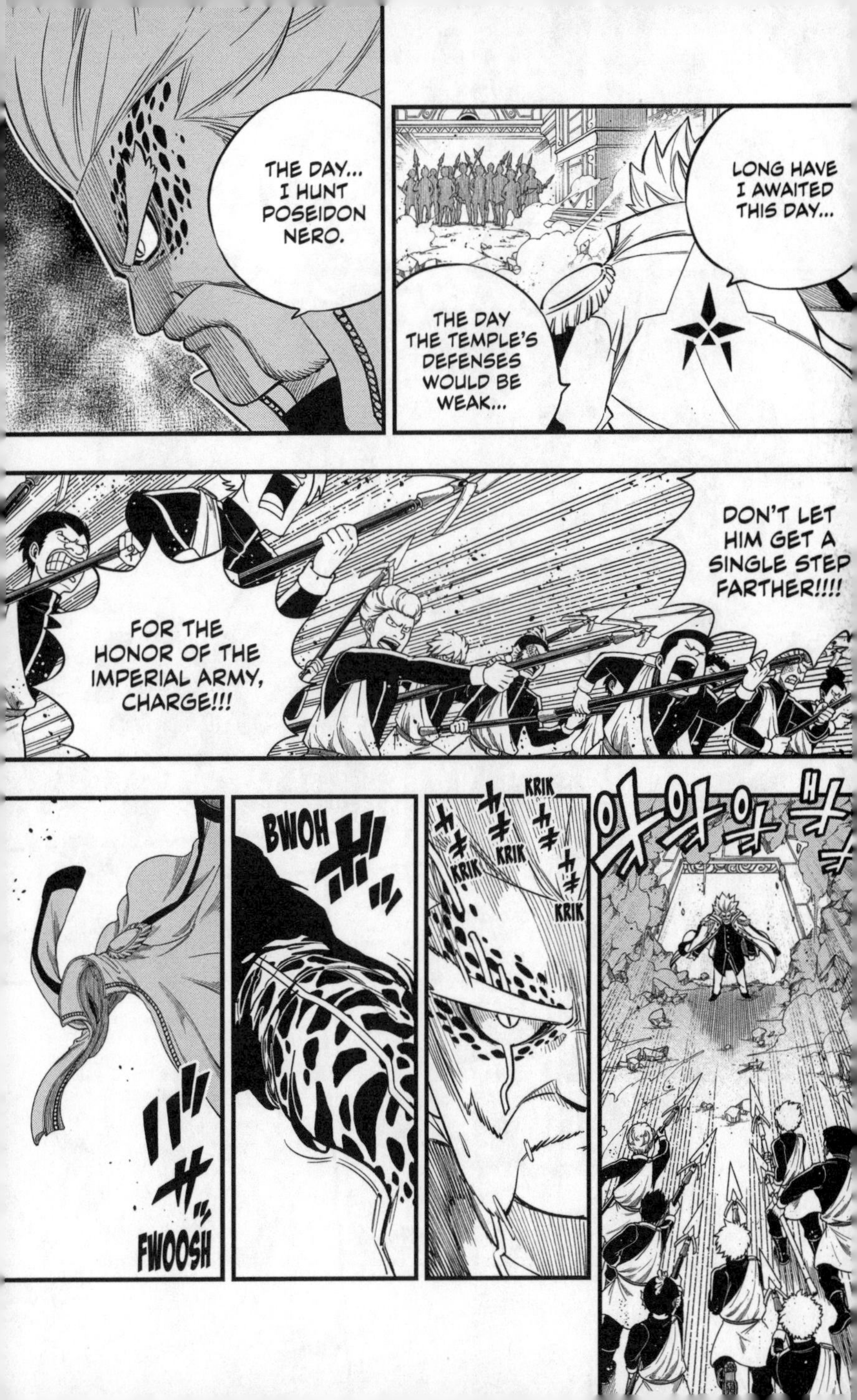
LONG HAVE I AWAITED THIS DAY...
THE DAY THE TEMPLE'S DEFENSES WOULD BE WEAK...
THE DAY... I HUNT POSEIDON NERO.
DON'T LET HIM GET A SINGLE STEP FARTHER!!!!
FOR THE HONOR OF THE IMPERIAL ARMY, CHARGE!!!
KRIK
KRIK
KRIK
KRIK
BWOH
FWOOSH

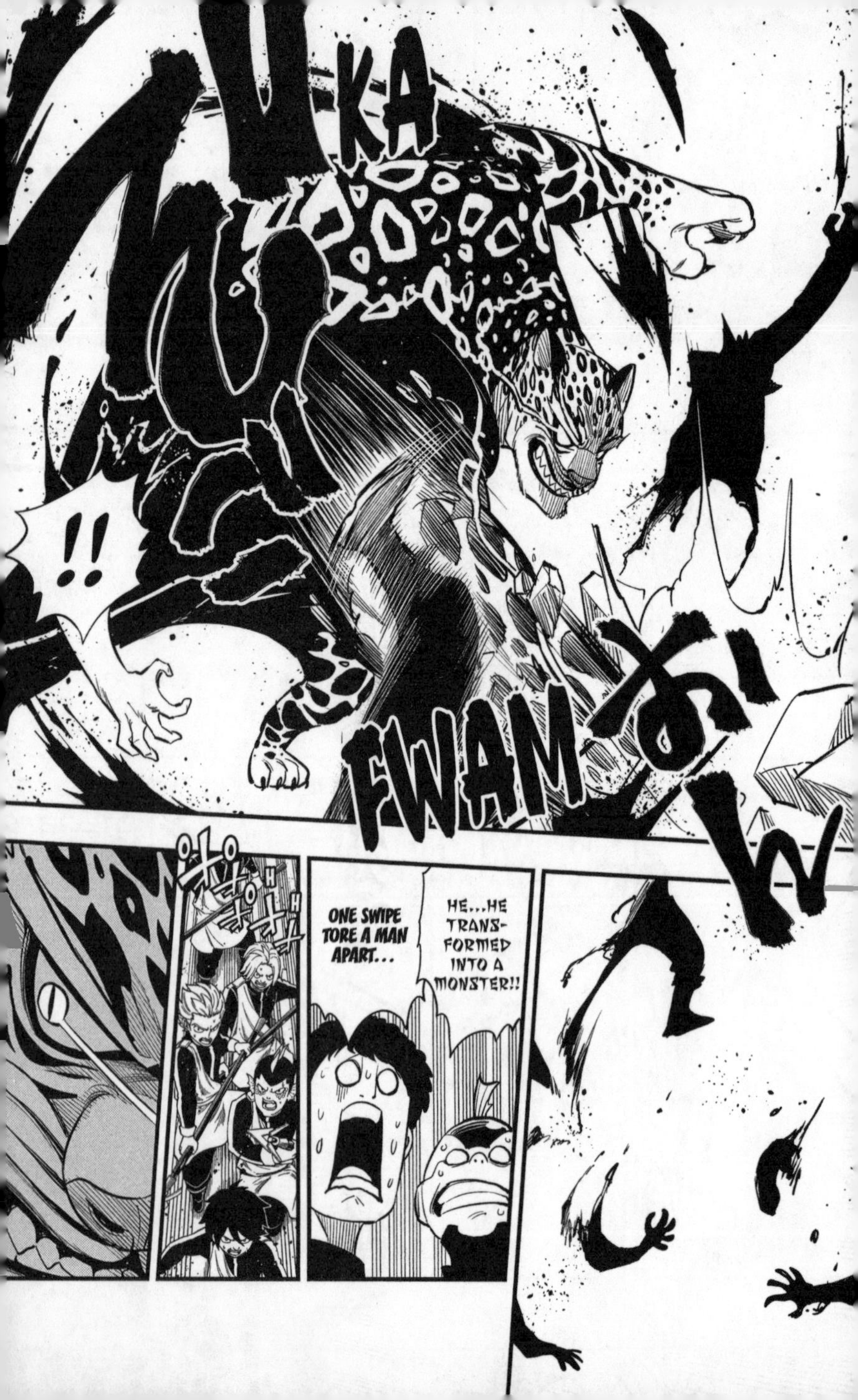
U-KA
!!
FWAM
HE...HE TRANSFORMED INTO A MONSTER!!
ONE SWIPE TORE A MAN APART...

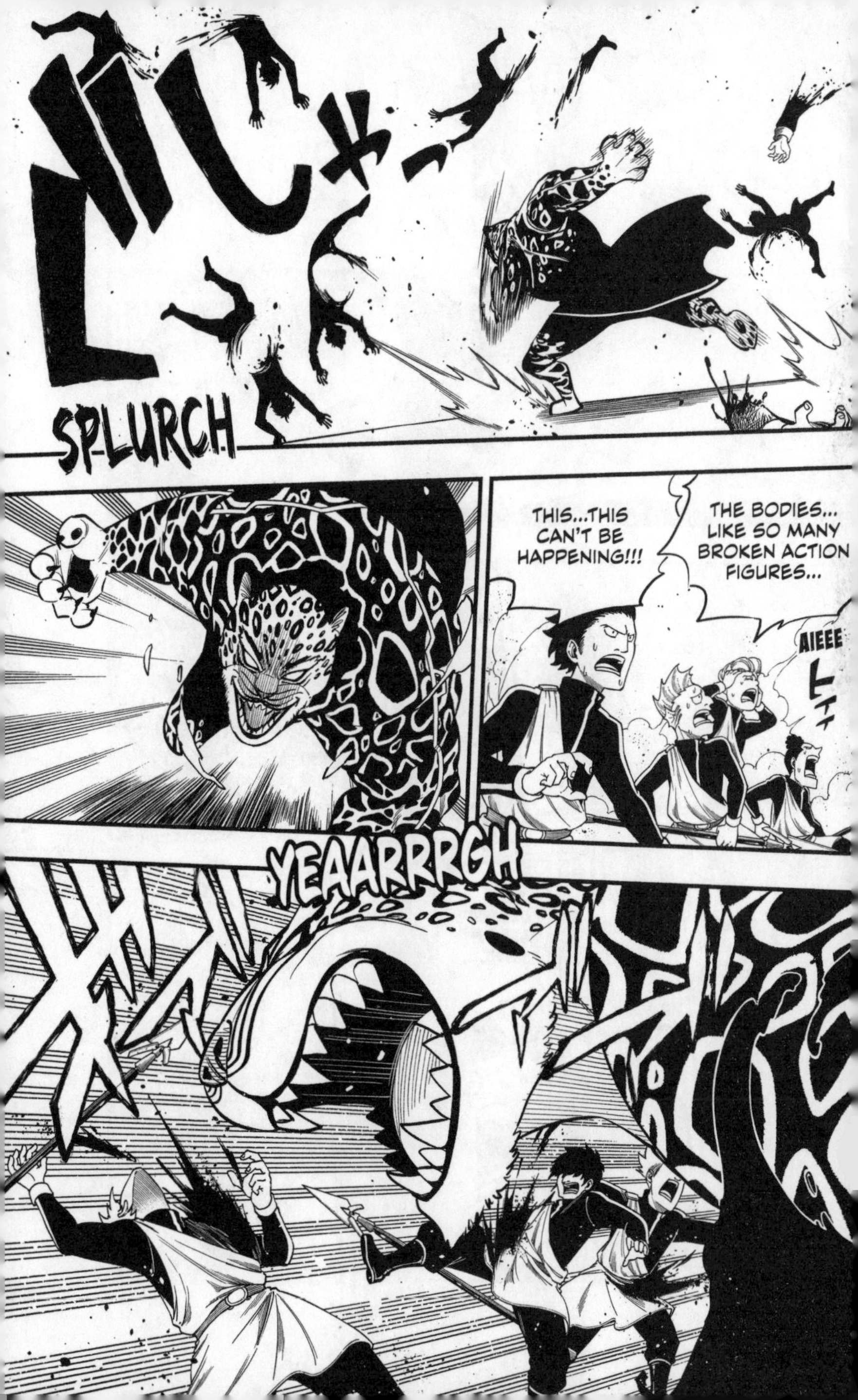
SPLURCH
THE BODIES... LIKE SO MANY BROKEN ACTION FIGURES...
THIS...THIS CAN'T BE HAPPENING!!!
AIEEE
YEAARRRGH

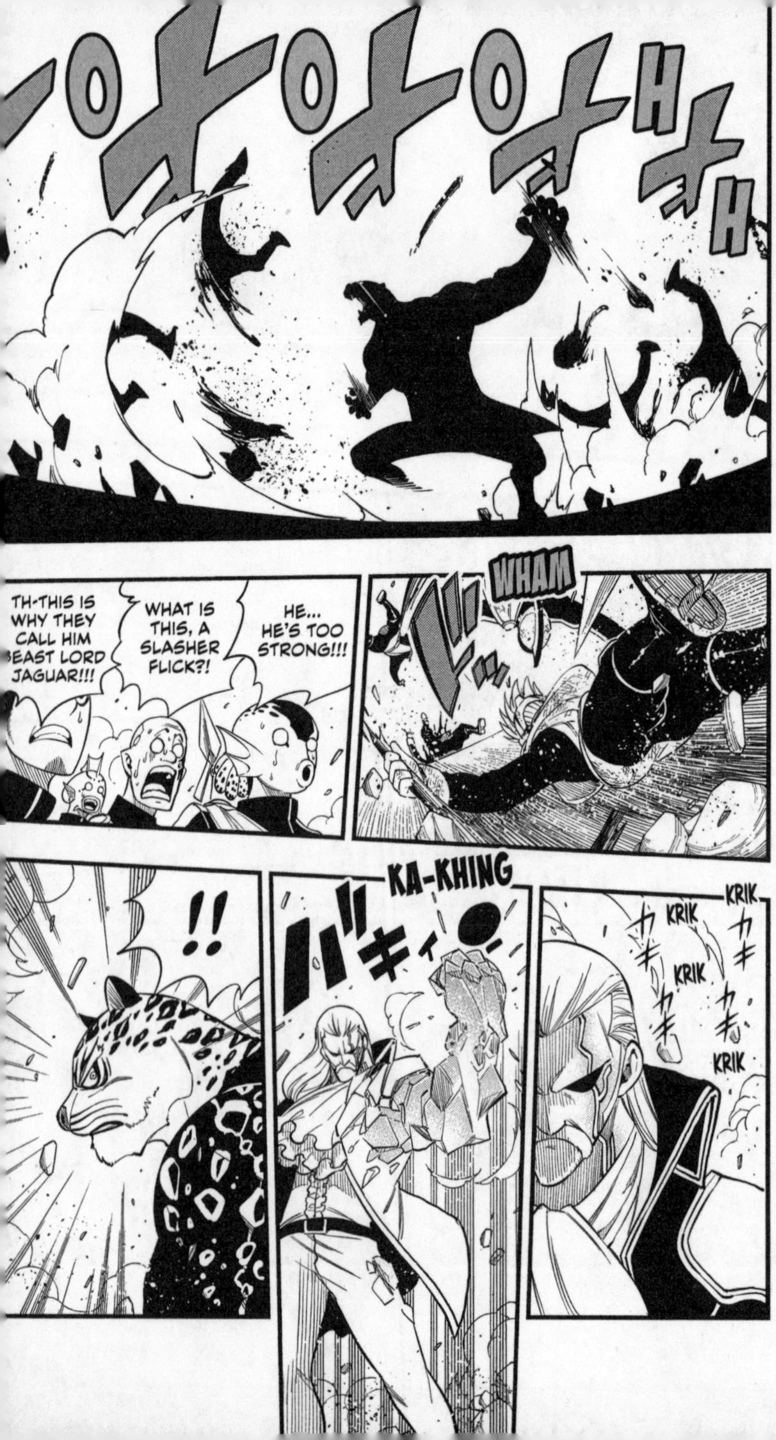
H
H
WHAM
HE... HE'S TOO STRONG!!!
WHAT IS THIS, A SLASHER FLICK?!
TH-THIS IS WHY THEY CALL HIM BEAST LORD JAGUAR!!!
KRIK
KRIK
KRIK
KRIK
KA-KHING
!!

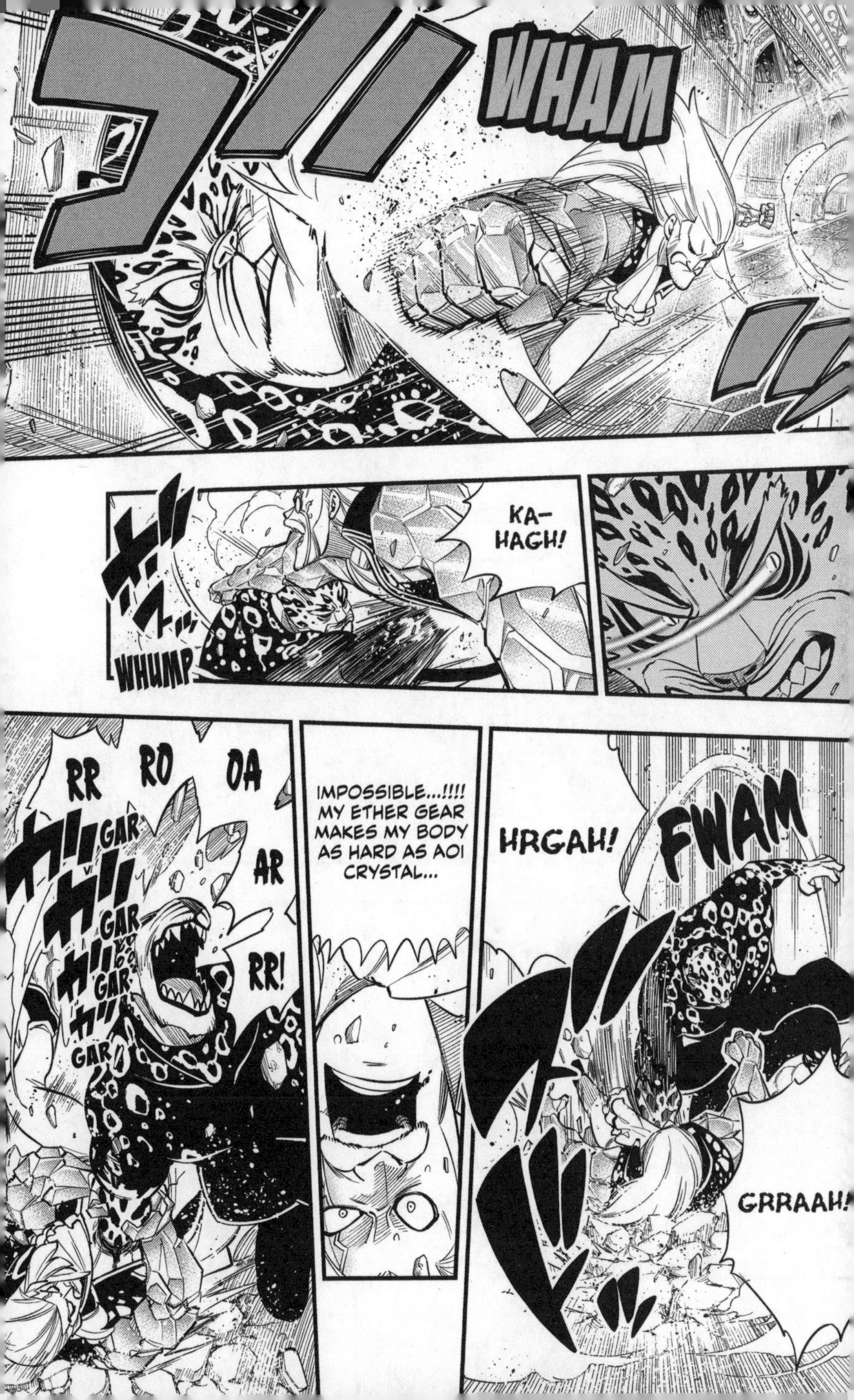
WHAM
KA-
HAGH!
WHUMP
FWAM
HRGAH!
GRRAAH!
IMPOSSIBLE...!!!!
MY ETHER GEAR
MAKES MY BODY
AS HARD AS AOI
CRYSTAL...
RR
RO
OA
AR
RR!
GAR
GAR
GAR
GAR

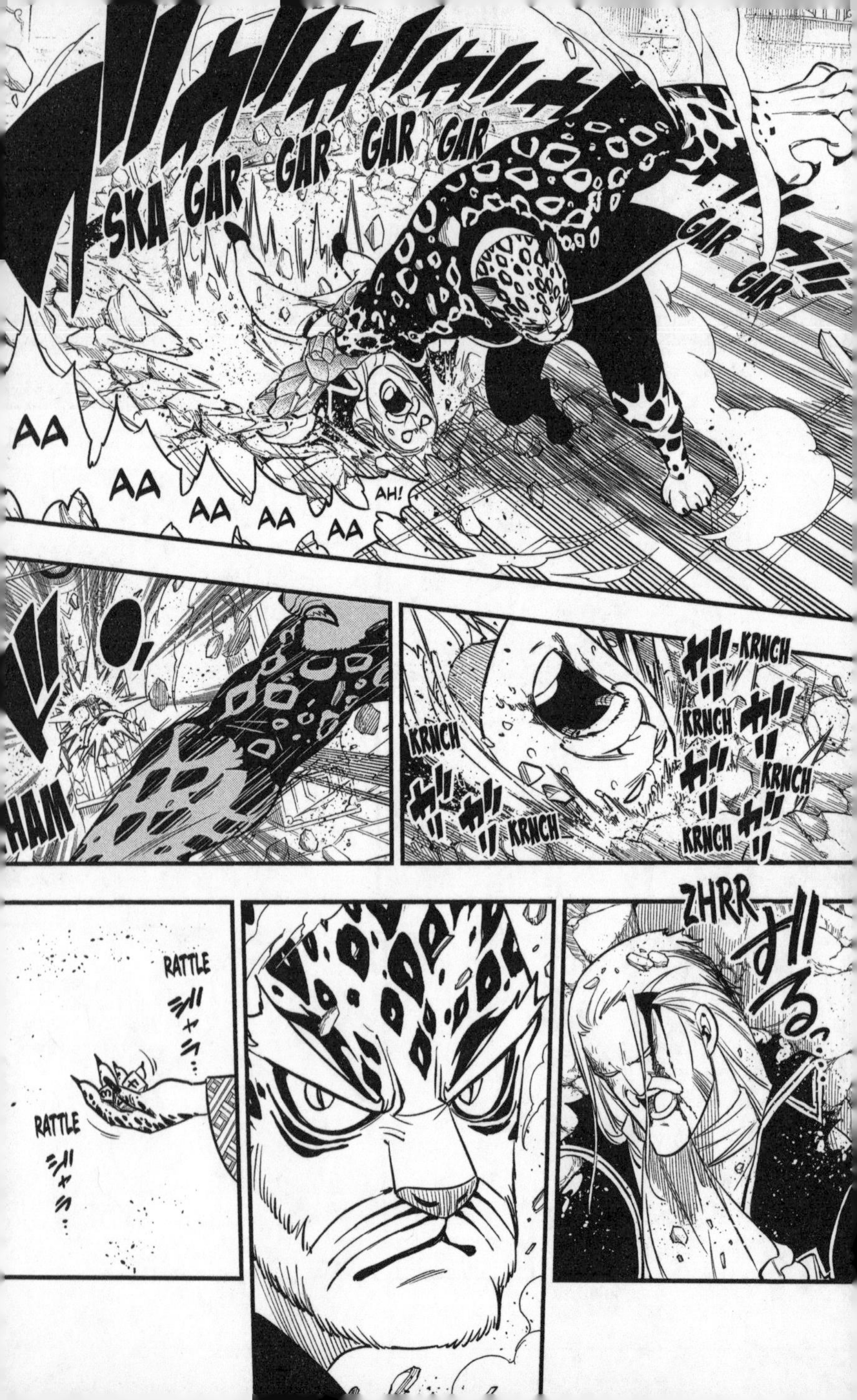
GAR
GAR
SKA GAR GAR GAR GAR
AH!
AA AA AA AA AA
KRNCH
KRNCH
KRNCH
KRNCH
KRNCH
KRNCH
HAM
ZHR-R
RATTLE
RATTLE

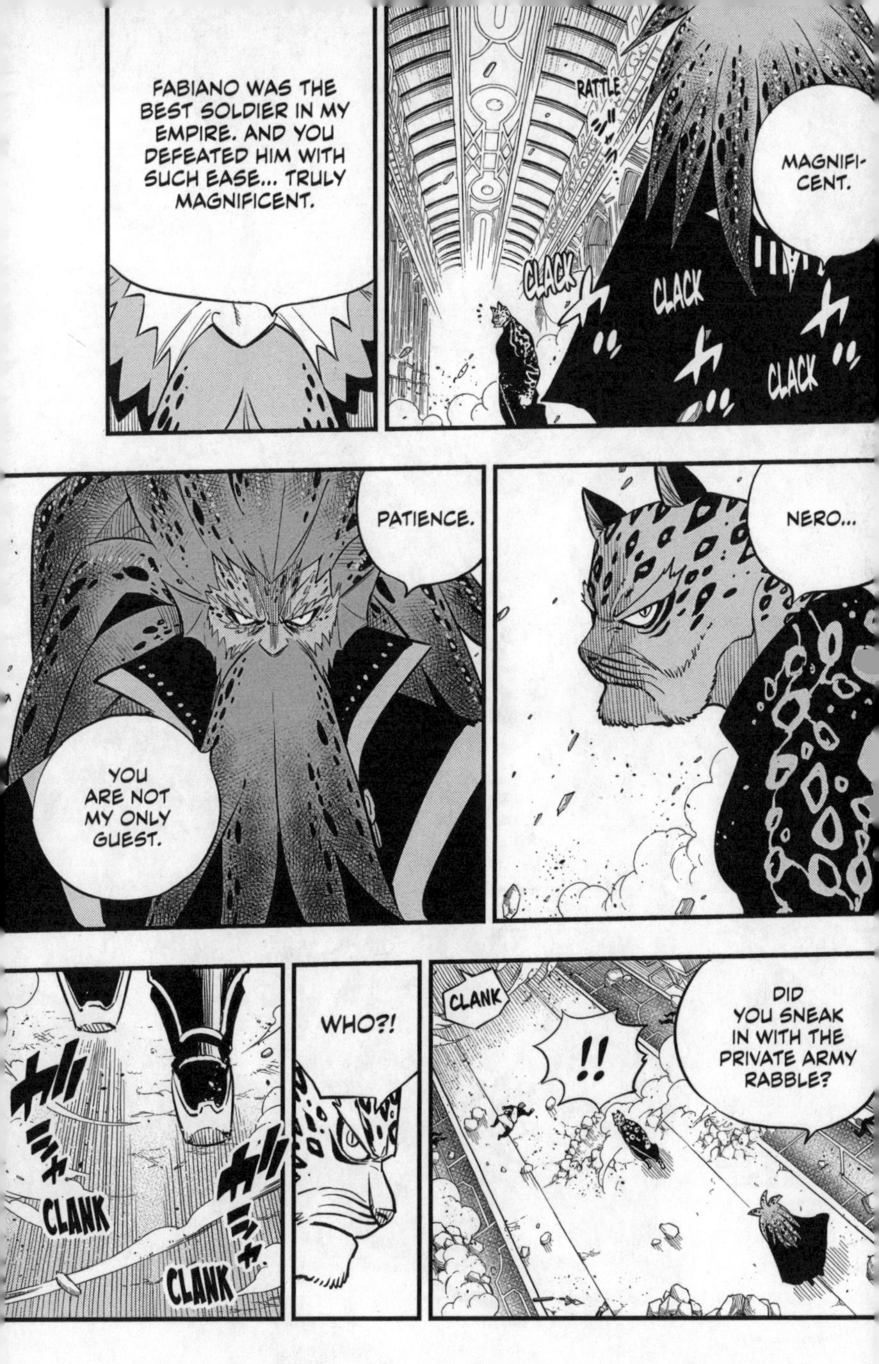
MAGNIFI-CENT.
RATTLE
CLACK
CLACK
CLACK
FABIANO WAS THE BEST SOLDIER IN MY EMPIRE. AND YOU DEFEATED HIM WITH SUCH EASE... TRULY MAGNIFICENT.
NERO...
PATIENCE.
YOU ARE NOT MY ONLY GUEST.
DID YOU SNEAK IN WITH THE PRIVATE ARMY RABBLE?
CLANK
!!
WHO?!
CLANK
CLANK

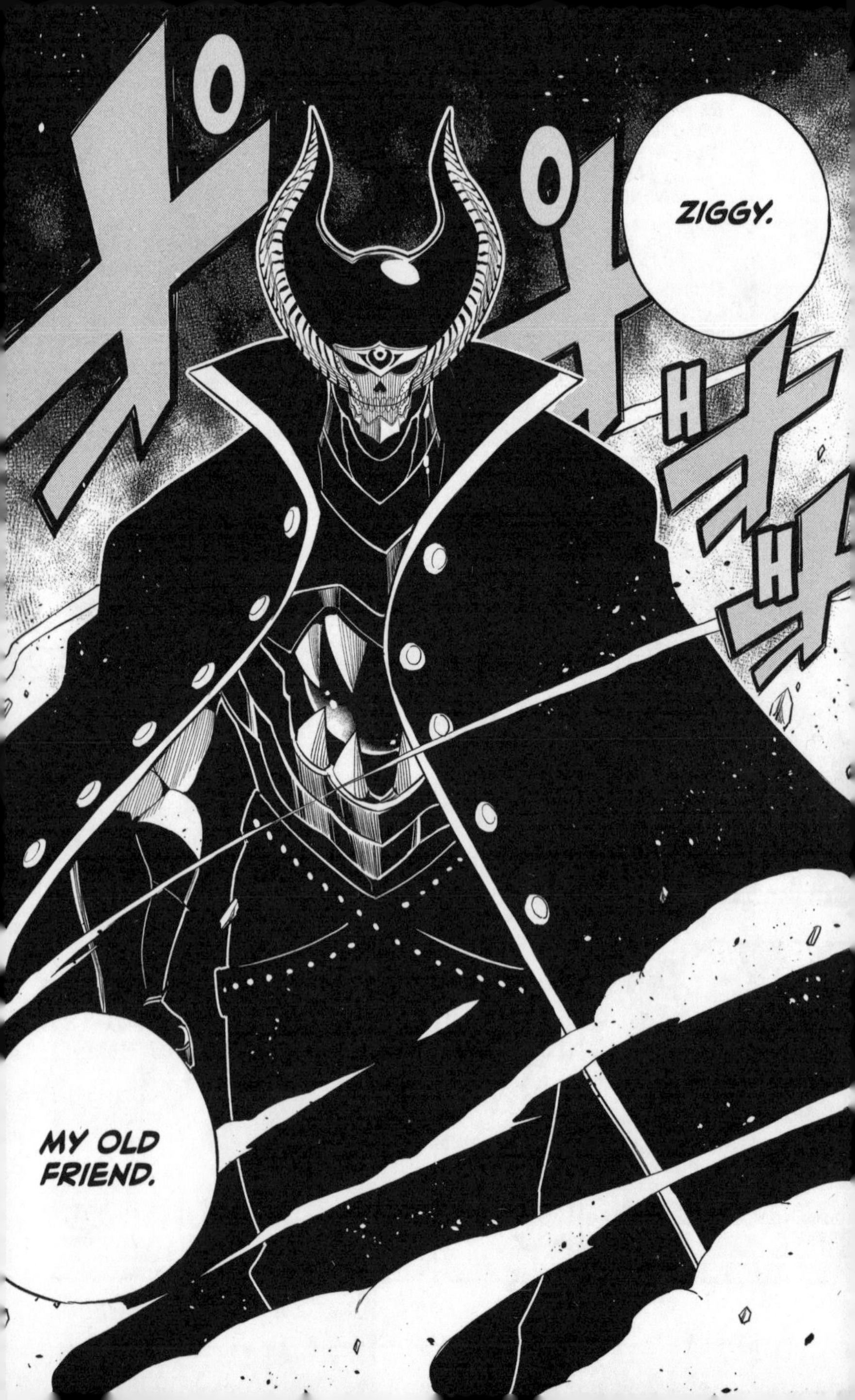
ZIGGY.
MY OLD FRIEND.

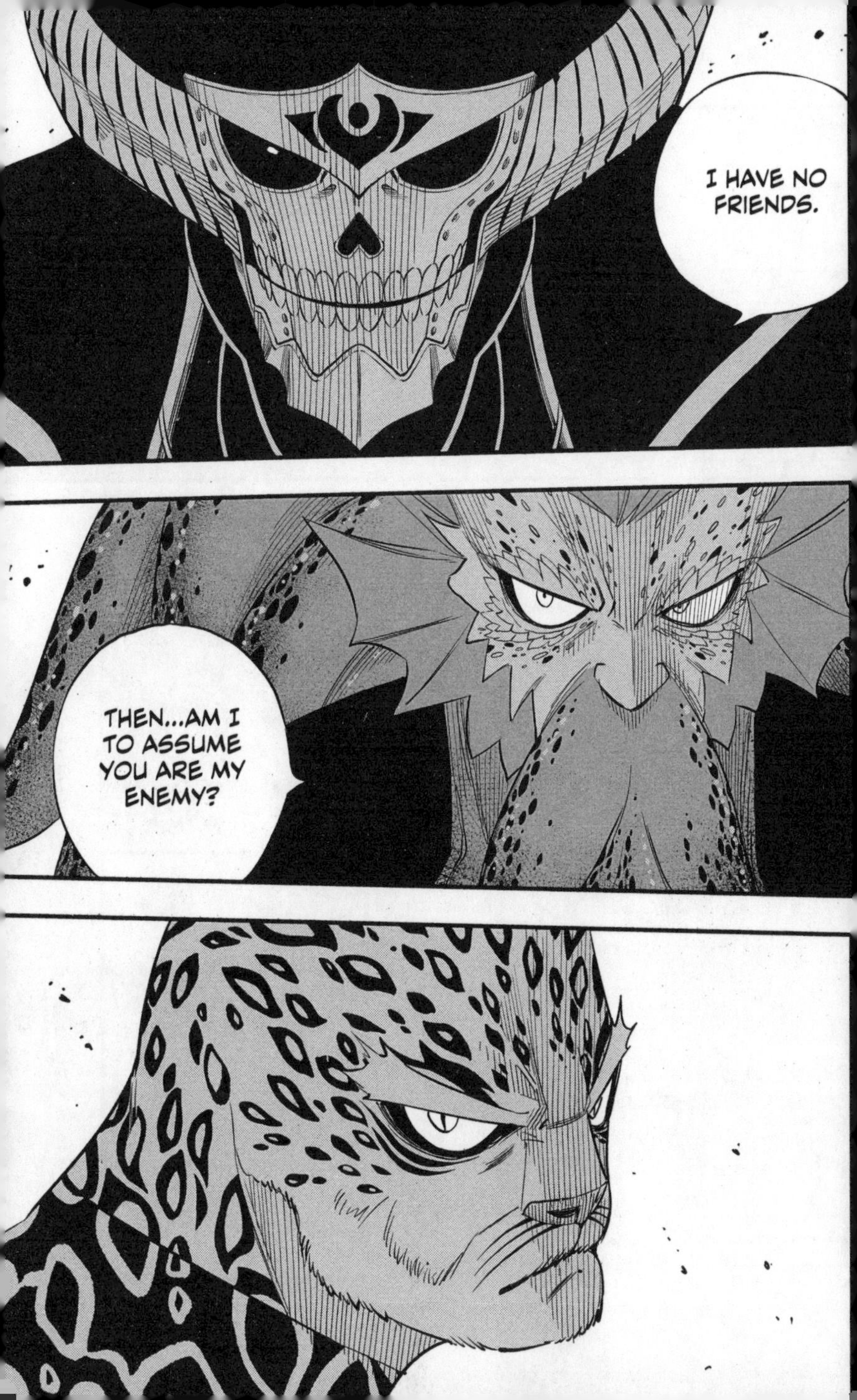
I HAVE NO FRIENDS.
THEN...AM I TO ASSUME YOU ARE MY ENEMY?

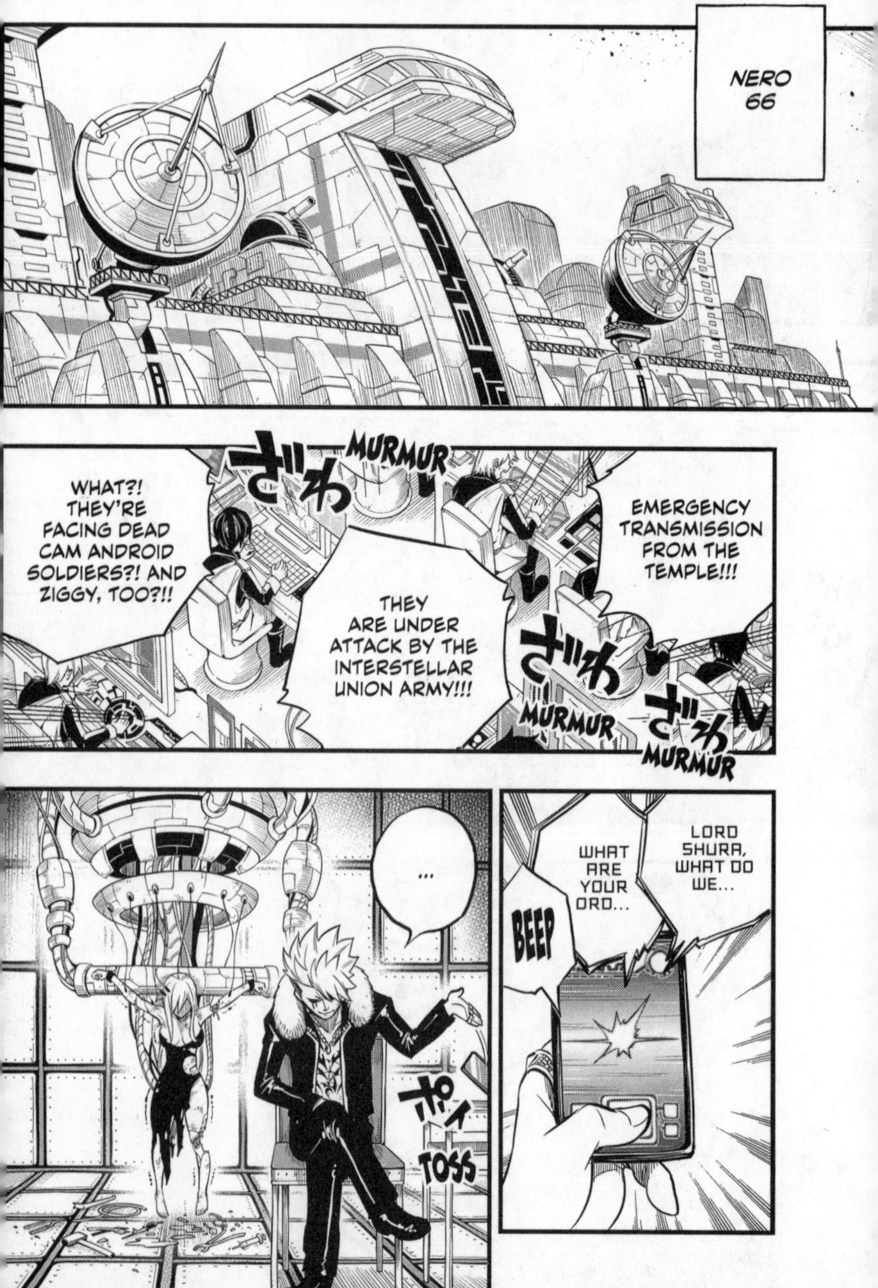

NERO 66
MURMUR
EMERGENCY TRANSMISSION FROM THE TEMPLE!!!
THEY ARE UNDER ATTACK BY THE INTERSTELLAR UNION ARMY!!!
WHAT?! THEY'RE FACING DEAD CAM ANDROID SOLDIERS?! AND ZIGGY, TOO?!!
MURMUR
MURMUR
LORD SHURA, WHAT DO WE...
WHAT ARE YOUR ORD...
BEEP
...
TOSS

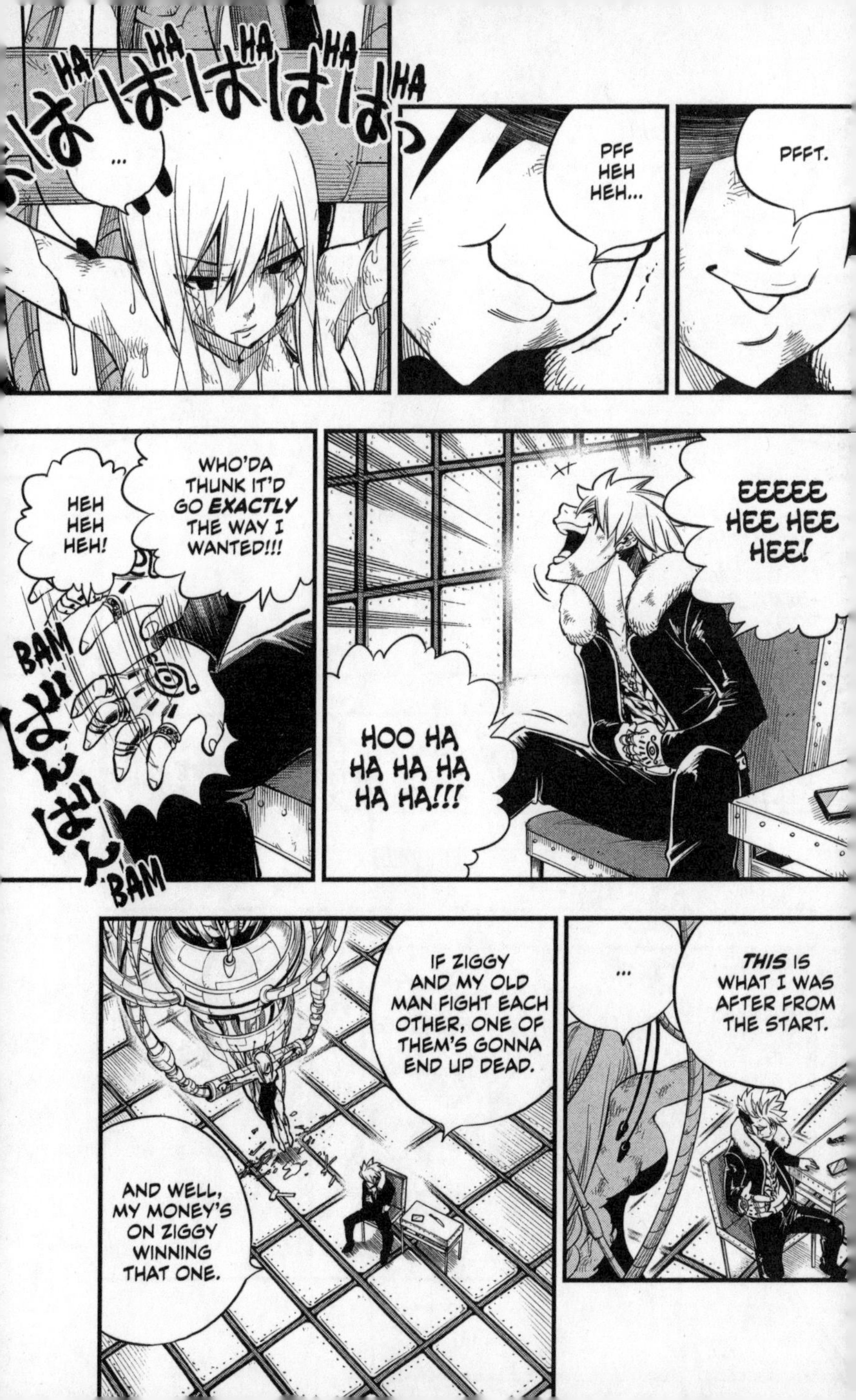
PFFT.
PFF HEH HEH...
HA HA HA HA HA
はははははっ
...
EEEEE HEE HEE HEE!
HOO HA HA HA HA HA HA!!!
WHO'DA THUNK IT'D GO *EXACTLY* THE WAY I WANTED!!!
HEH HEH HEH!
BAM
ばんばん
BAM
THIS IS WHAT I WAS AFTER FROM THE START.
...
IF ZIGGY AND MY OLD MAN FIGHT EACH OTHER, ONE OF THEM'S GONNA END UP DEAD.
AND WELL, MY MONEY'S ON ZIGGY WINNING THAT ONE.

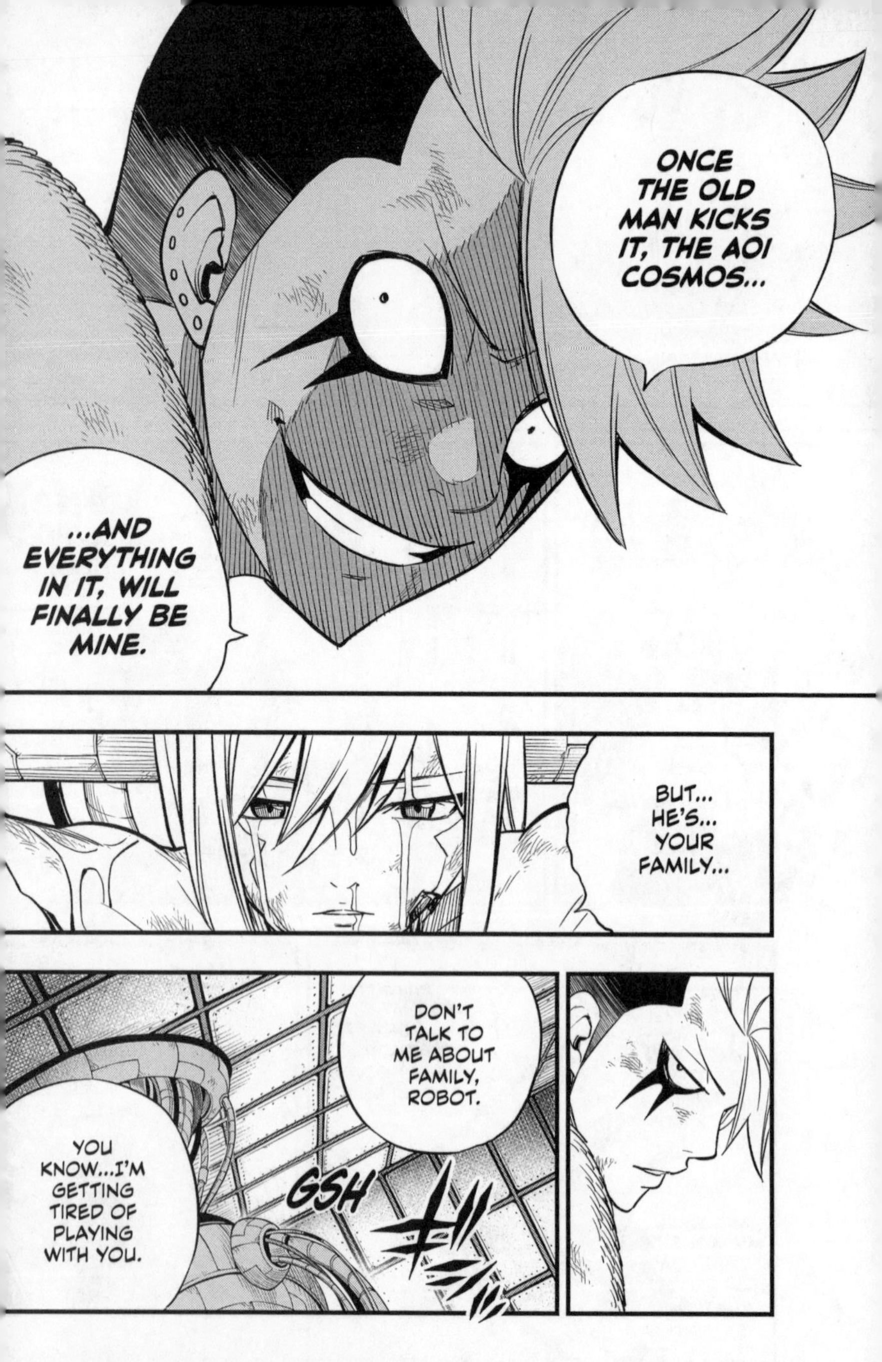

ONCE THE OLD MAN KICKS IT, THE AOI COSMOS...
...AND EVERYTHING IN IT, WILL FINALLY BE MINE.
BUT... HE'S... YOUR FAMILY...
DON'T TALK TO ME ABOUT FAMILY, ROBOT.
YOU KNOW...I'M GETTING TIRED OF PLAYING WITH YOU.
GSH

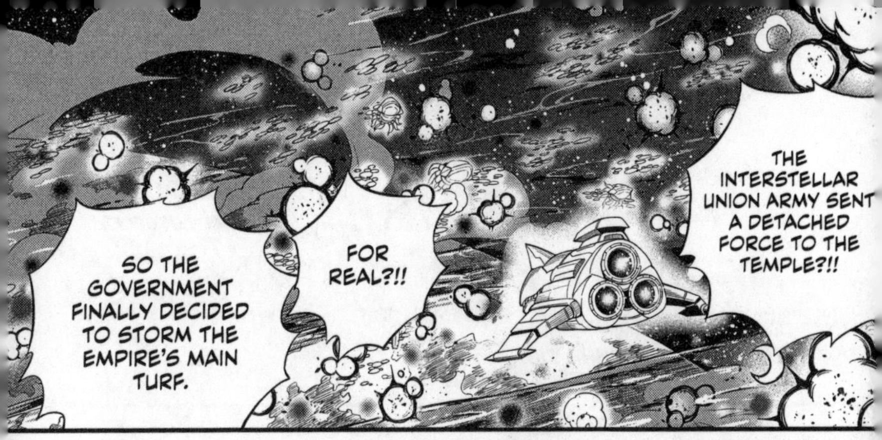
THE INTERSTELLAR UNION ARMY SENT A DETACHED FORCE TO THE TEMPLE?!!
FOR REAL?!!
SO THE GOVERNMENT FINALLY DECIDED TO STORM THE EMPIRE'S MAIN TURF.

EDENS ZERO

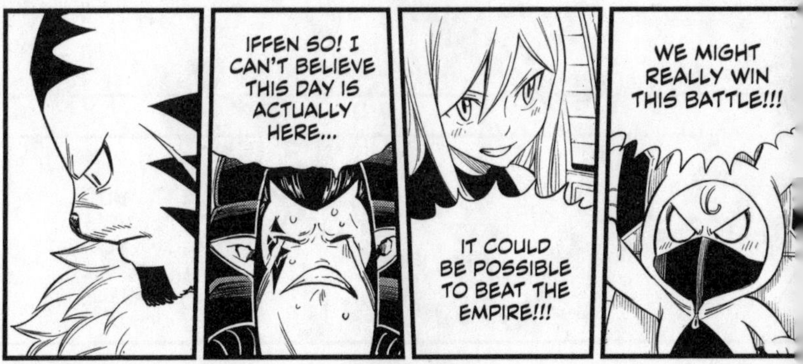
WE MIGHT REALLY WIN THIS BATTLE!!!
IT COULD BE POSSIBLE TO BEAT THE EMPIRE!!!
IFFEN SO! I CAN'T BELIEVE THIS DAY IS ACTUALLY HERE...

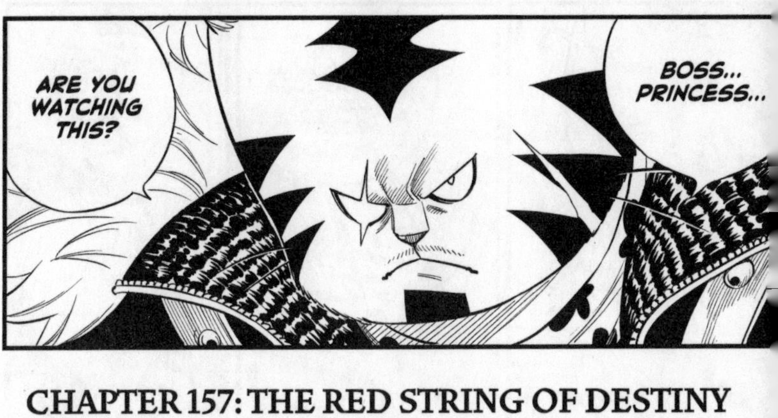
BOSS... PRINCESS...
ARE YOU WATCHING THIS?

CHAPTER 157: THE RED STRING OF DESTINY

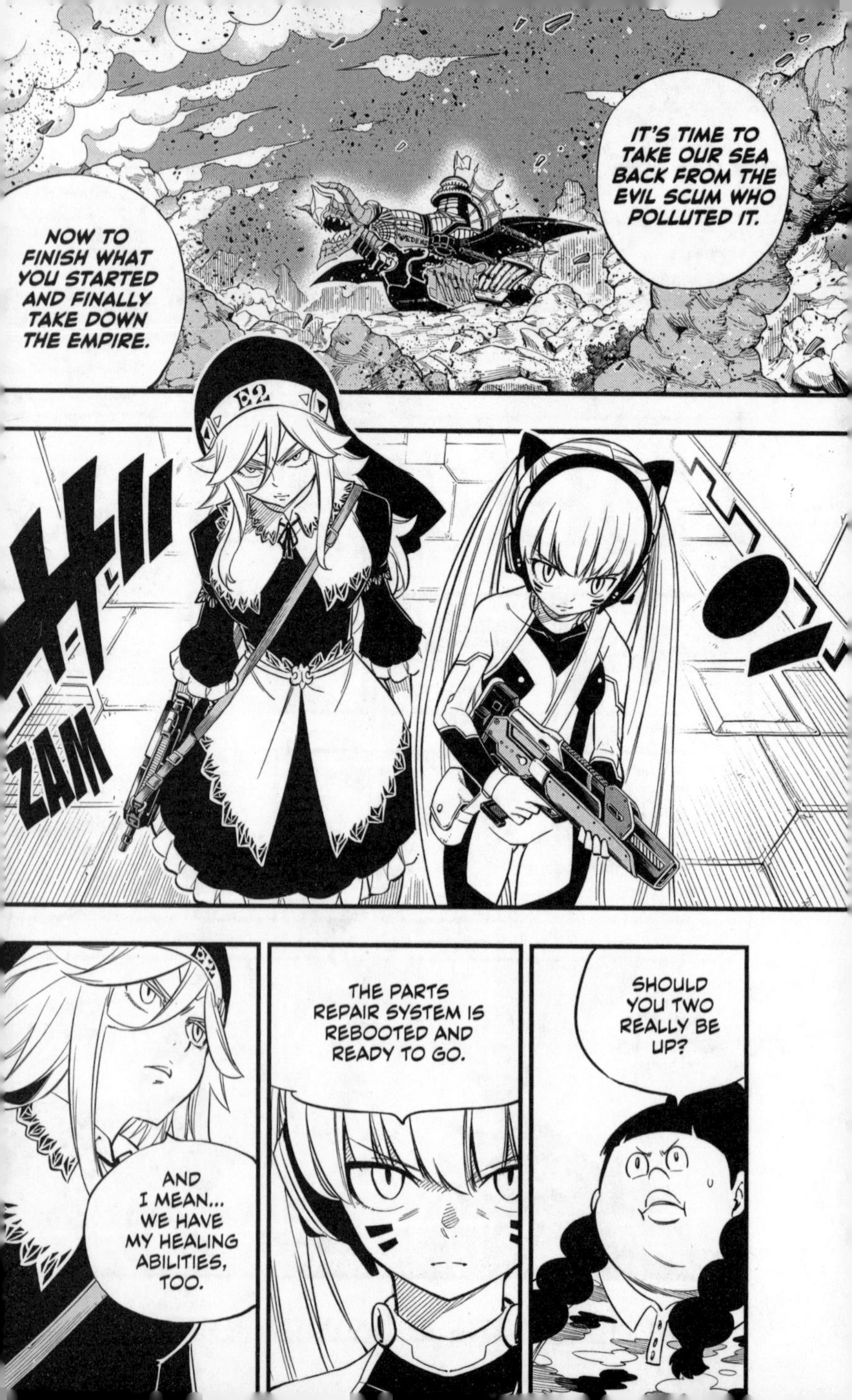
IT'S TIME TO TAKE OUR SEA BACK FROM THE EVIL SCUM WHO POLLUTED IT.
NOW TO FINISH WHAT YOU STARTED AND FINALLY TAKE DOWN THE EMPIRE.
ZAM
SHOULD YOU TWO REALLY BE UP?
THE PARTS REPAIR SYSTEM IS REBOOTED AND READY TO GO.
AND I MEAN... WE HAVE MY HEALING ABILITIES, TOO.

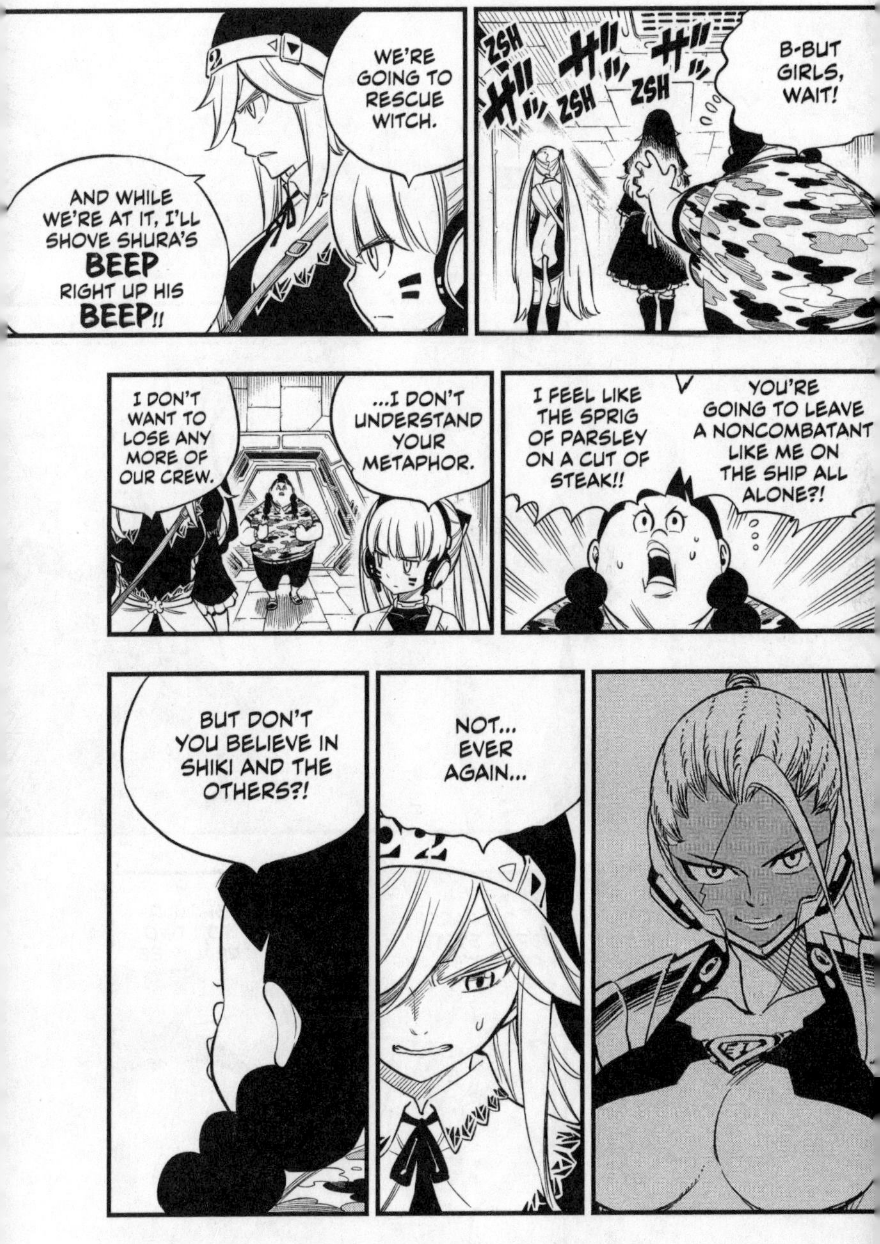
B-BUT GIRLS, WAIT!
ZSH
ZSH
ZSH
WE'RE GOING TO RESCUE WITCH.
AND WHILE WE'RE AT IT, I'LL SHOVE SHURA'S BEEP RIGHT UP HIS BEEP!!
YOU'RE GOING TO LEAVE A NONCOMBATANT LIKE ME ON THE SHIP ALL ALONE?!
I FEEL LIKE THE SPRIG OF PARSLEY ON A CUT OF STEAK!!
...I DON'T UNDERSTAND YOUR METAPHOR.
I DON'T WANT TO LOSE ANY MORE OF OUR CREW.
NOT... EVER AGAIN...
BUT DON'T YOU BELIEVE IN SHIKI AND THE OTHERS?!

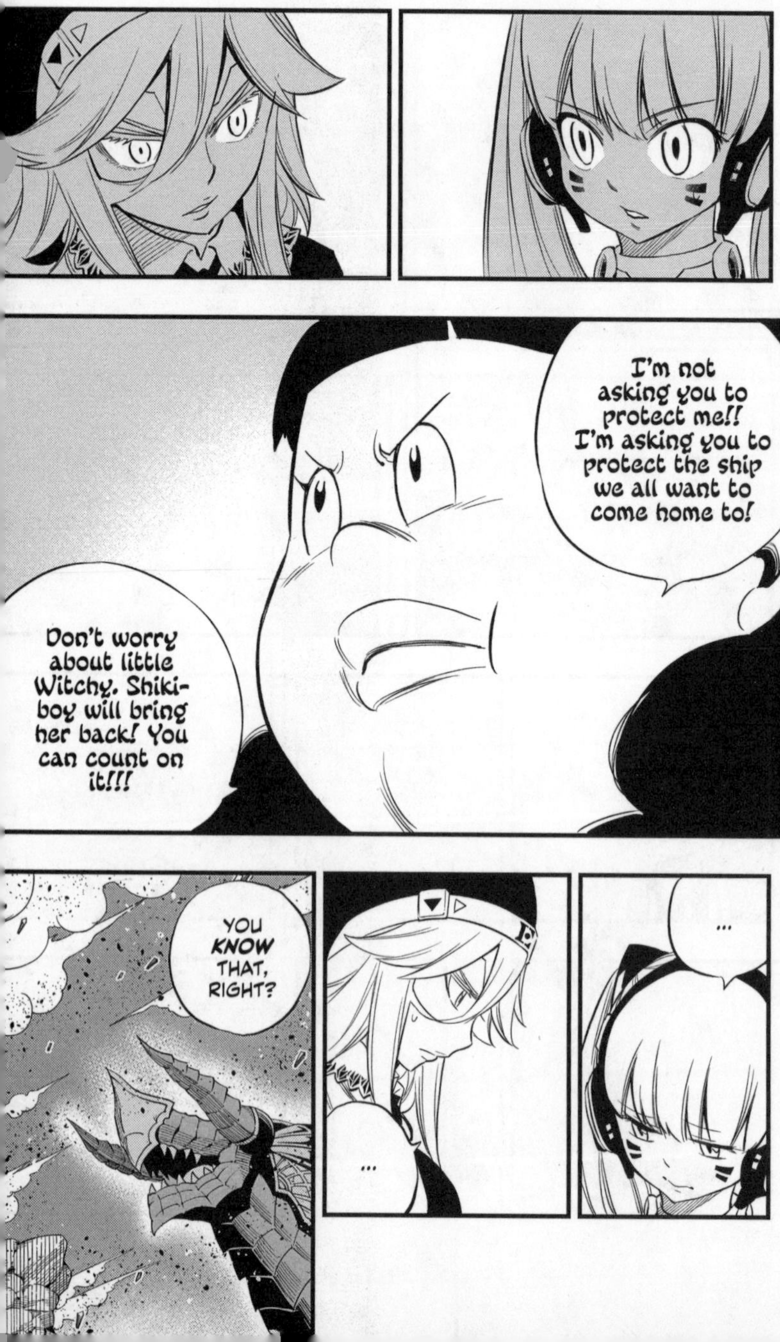
I'm not asking you to protect me!! I'm asking you to protect the ship we all want to come home to!
Don't worry about little Witchy. Shiki-boy will bring her back! You can count on it!!!
...
...
YOU KNOW THAT, RIGHT?

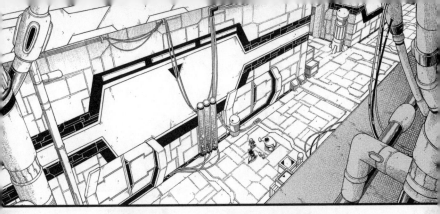

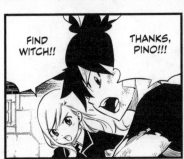

BEEP
BEEP
BEGINNING TO SCAN FOR LIFEFORMS!!!
THANKS, PINO!!!
FIND WITCH!!
IT'S FAINT BUT I HAVE A READING UP AHEAD A FEW HUNDRED METERS...
IDENTIFYING... IT'S WITCH'S LIFE SIGNATURE!!
LET'S HURRY!!!
MOSCOWITCH!!
DON'T PUSH

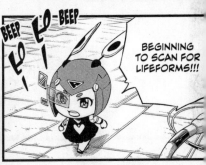

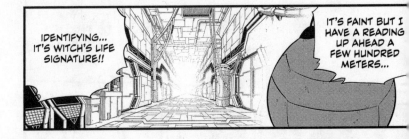

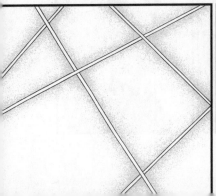

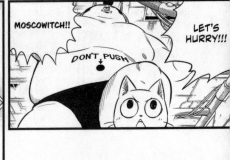

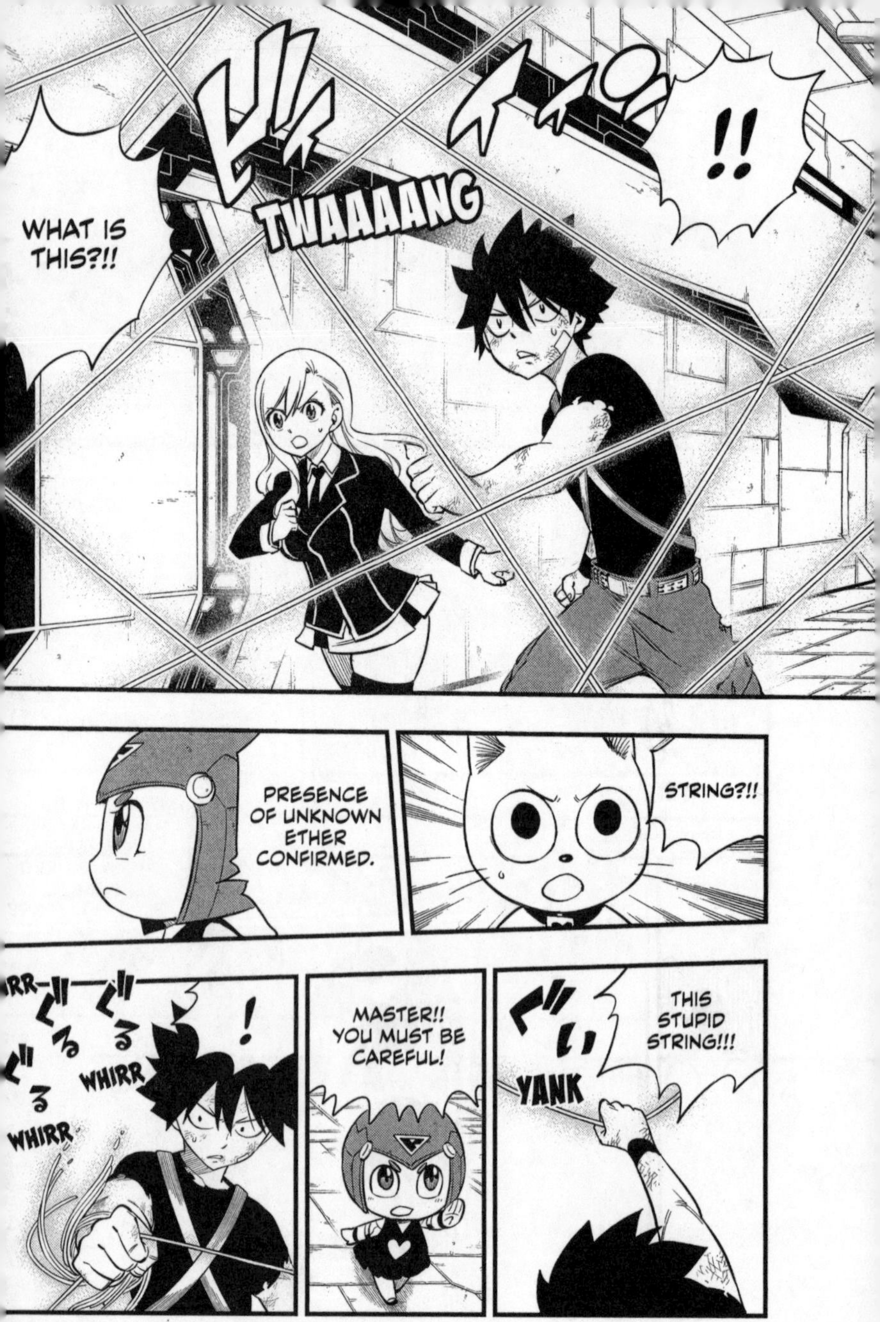
!!
TWAAAANG
WHAT IS THIS?!!
STRING?!!
PRESENCE OF UNKNOWN ETHER CONFIRMED.
THIS STUPID STRING!!!
YANK
MASTER!! YOU MUST BE CAREFUL!
!
WHIRR
WHIRR

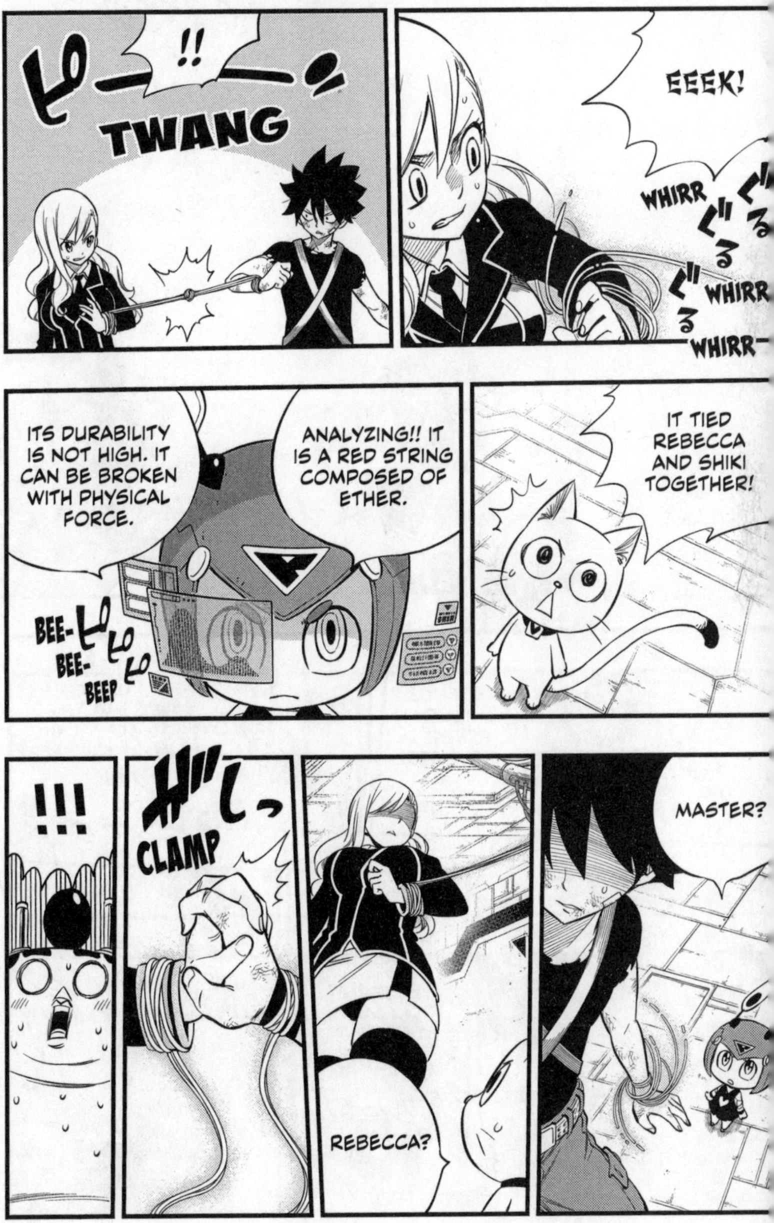
EEEK!
WHIRR
WHIRR
WHIRR
!!
TWANG
IT TIED REBECCA AND SHIKI TOGETHER!
ANALYZING!! IT IS A RED STRING COMPOSED OF ETHER.
ITS DURABILITY IS NOT HIGH. IT CAN BE BROKEN WITH PHYSICAL FORCE.
BEE- BEE- BEEP
MASTER?
REBECCA?
CLAMP
!!!

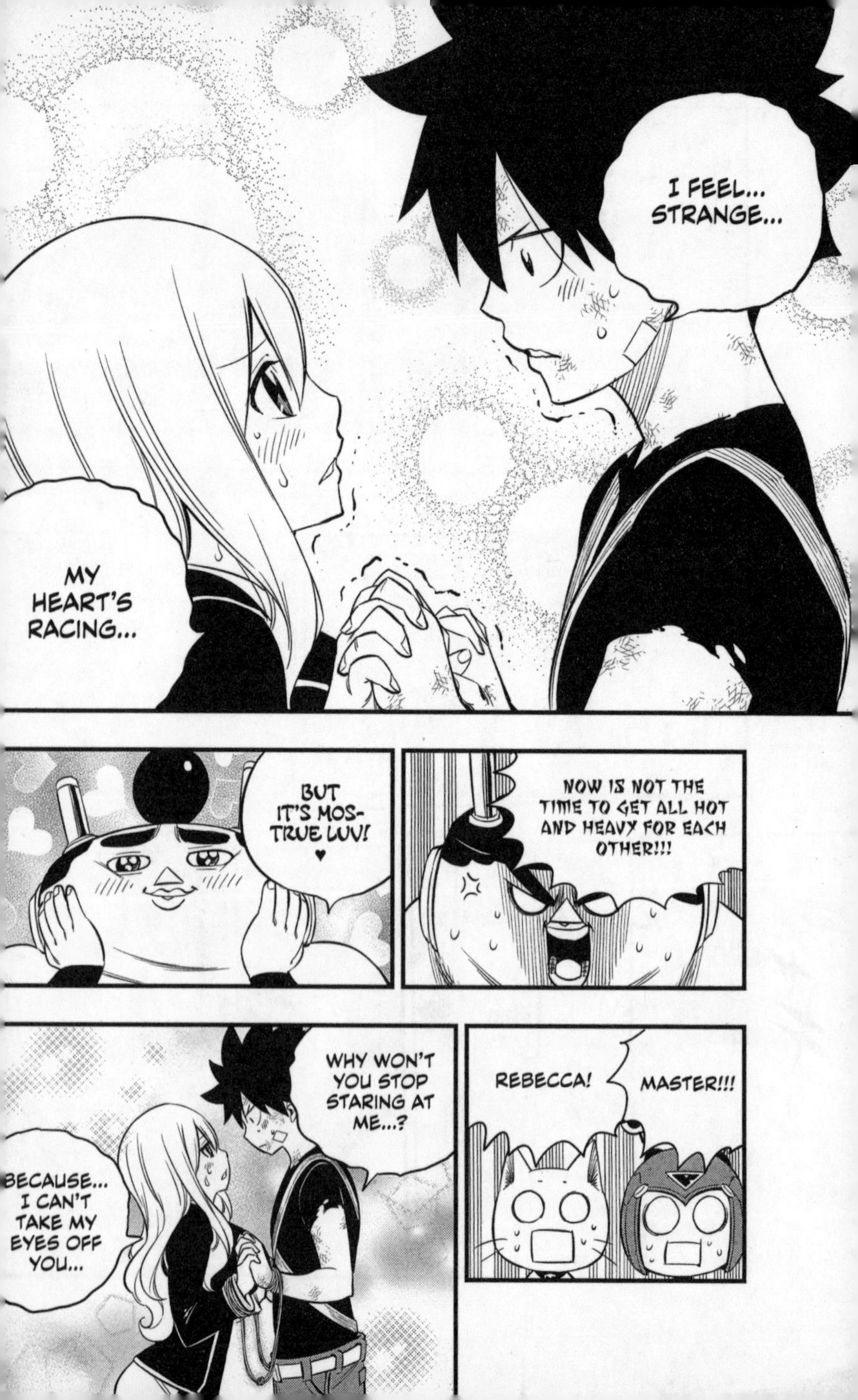
I FEEL... STRANGE...
MY HEART'S RACING...
NOW IS NOT THE TIME TO GET ALL HOT AND HEAVY FOR EACH OTHER!!!
BUT IT'S MOS-TRUE LUV! ♥
MASTER!!!
REBECCA!
WHY WON'T YOU STOP STARING AT ME...?
BECAUSE... I CAN'T TAKE MY EYES OFF YOU...

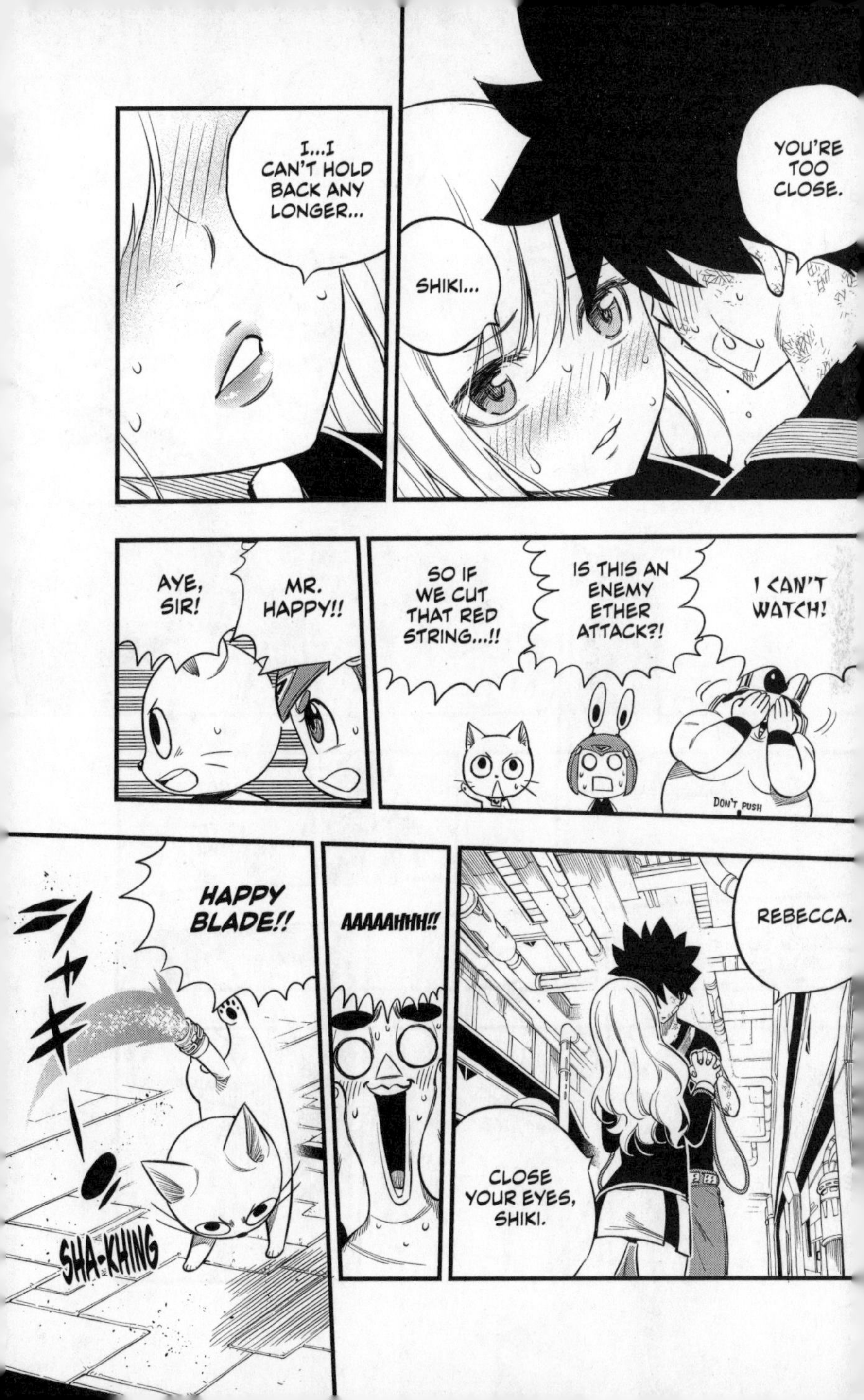
YOU'RE TOO CLOSE.
SHIKI...
I...I CAN'T HOLD BACK ANY LONGER...
I CAN'T WATCH!
IS THIS AN ENEMY ETHER ATTACK?!
SO IF WE CUT THAT RED STRING...!!
DON'T PUSH
MR. HAPPY!!
AYE, SIR!
REBECCA.
CLOSE YOUR EYES, SHIKI.
AAAAAHHH!!
HAPPY BLADE!!
SHA-KHING

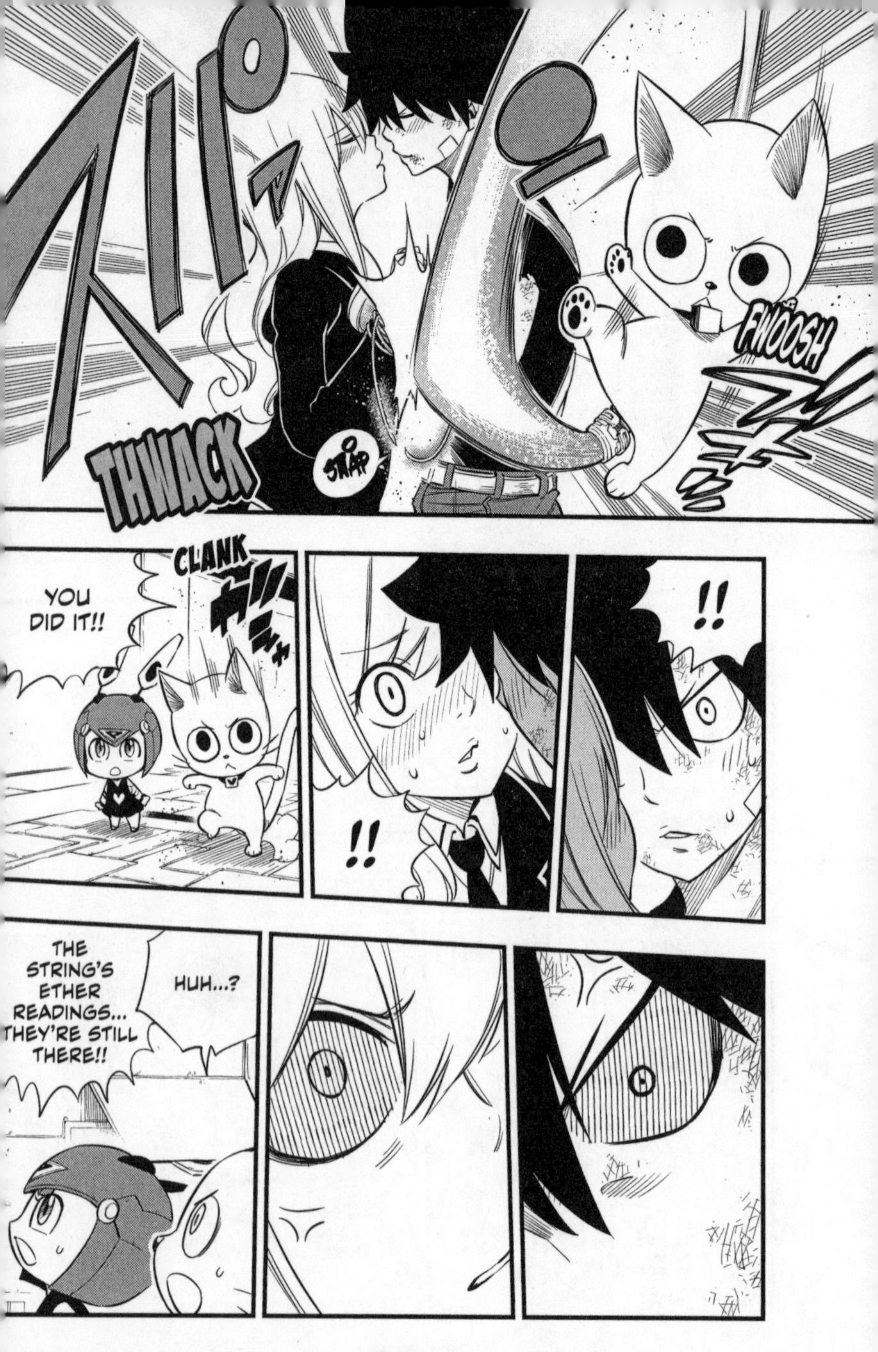
FWOOSH
THWACK
!!
!!
CLANK
YOU DID IT!!
HUH...?
THE STRING'S ETHER READINGS... THEY'RE STILL THERE!!

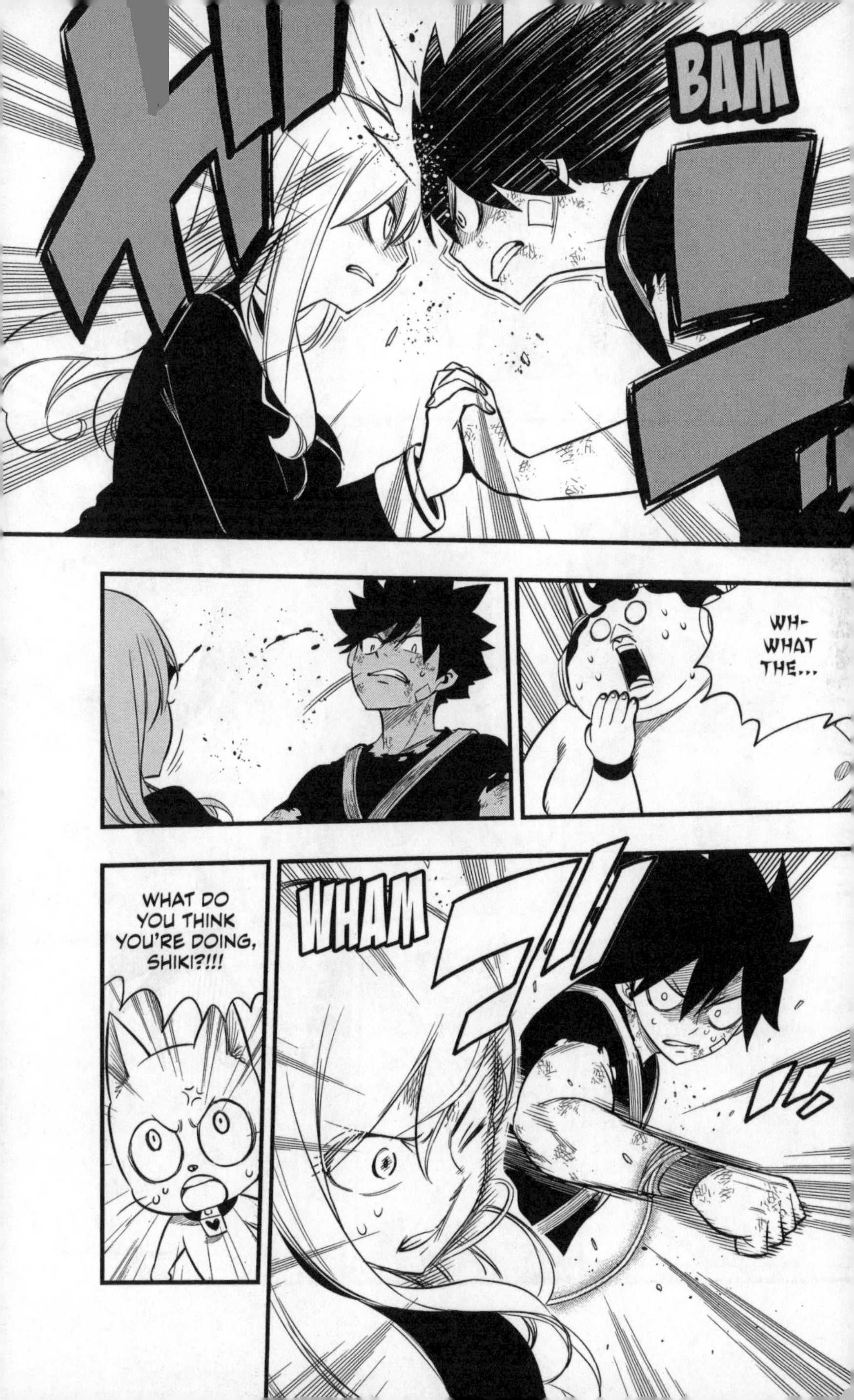
BAM
WH- WHAT THE...
WHAM
WHAT DO YOU THINK YOU'RE DOING, SHIKI?!!!

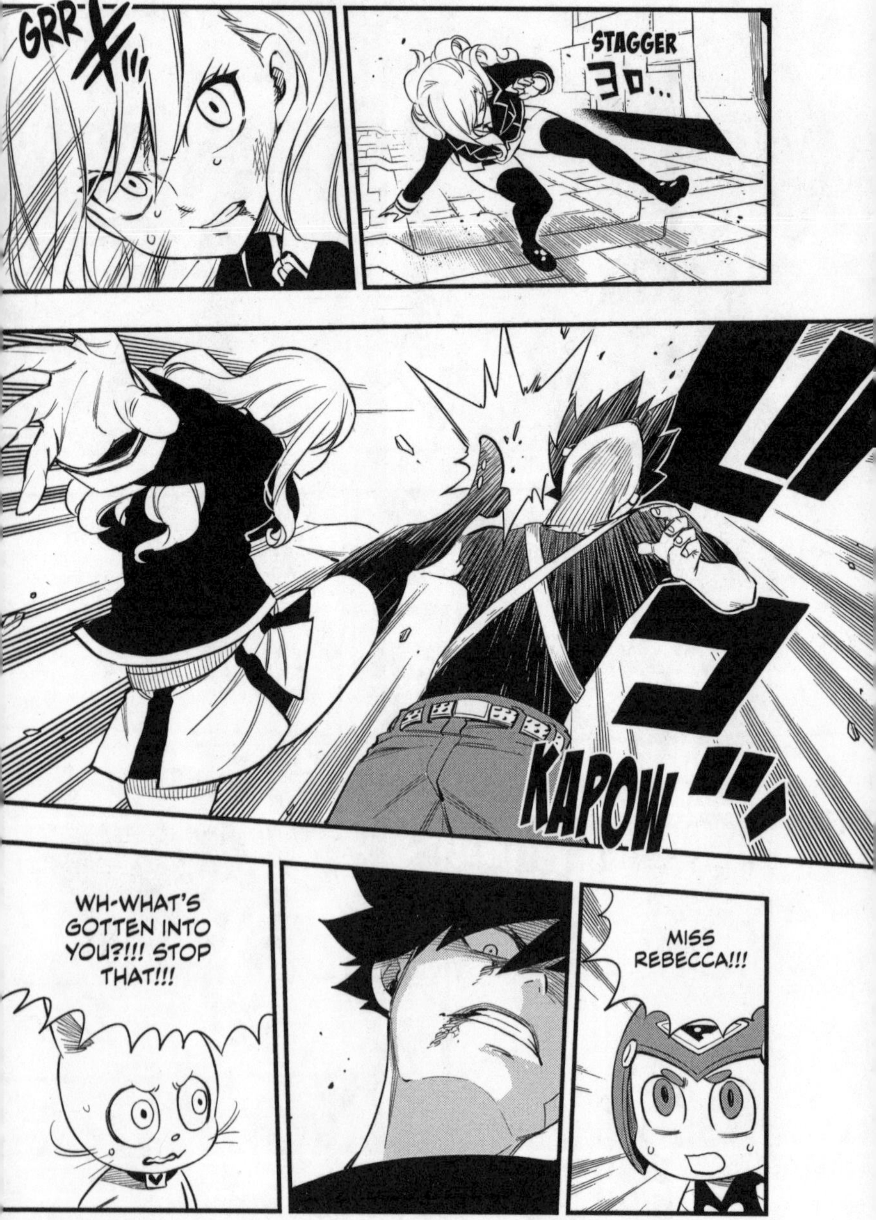
STAGGER
ヨロ...
GRR
KAPOW
MISS REBECCA!!!
WH-WHAT'S GOTTEN INTO YOU?!!! STOP THAT!!!

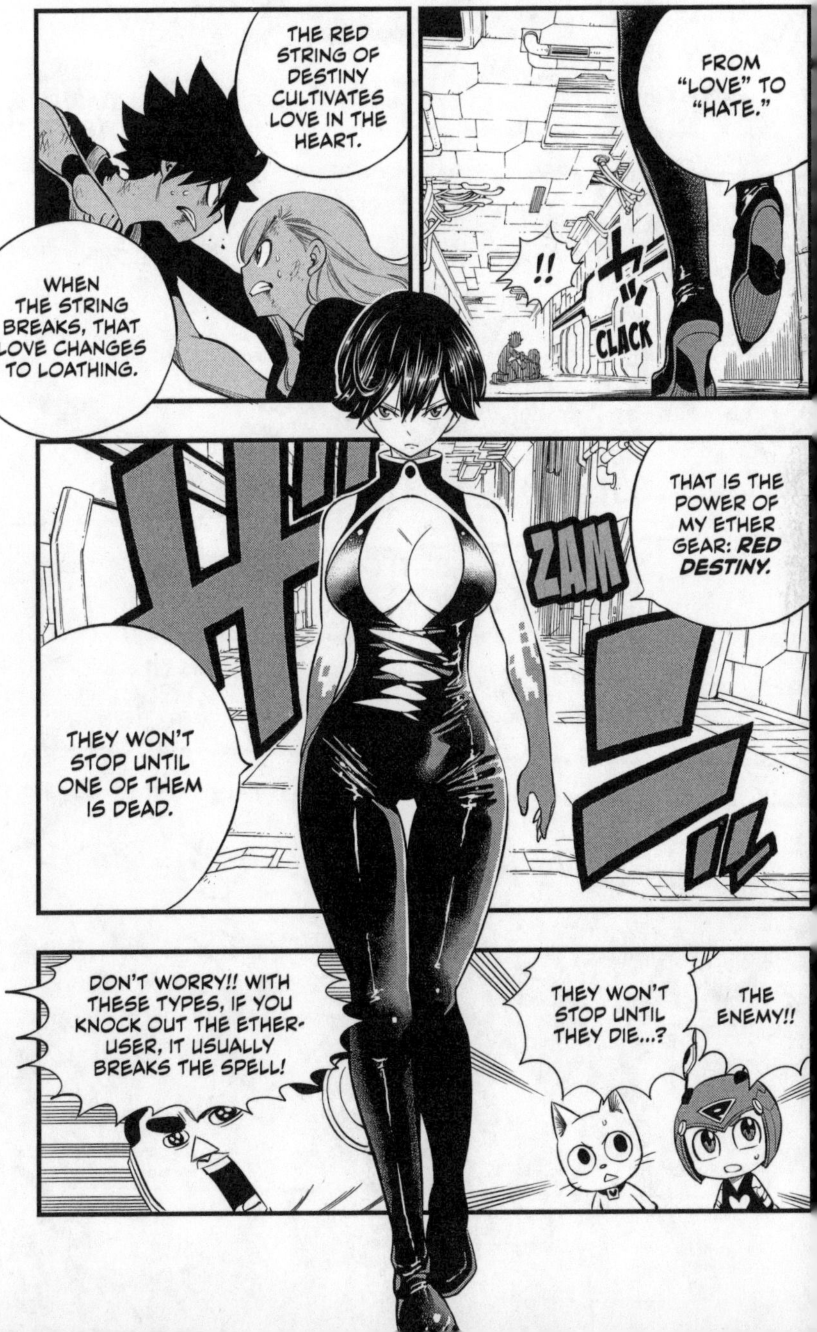
FROM "LOVE" TO "HATE."
!!
CLACK
THE RED STRING OF DESTINY CULTIVATES LOVE IN THE HEART.
WHEN THE STRING BREAKS, THAT LOVE CHANGES TO LOATHING.
ZAM
THAT IS THE POWER OF MY ETHER GEAR: *RED DESTINY.*
THEY WON'T STOP UNTIL ONE OF THEM IS DEAD.
THE ENEMY!!
THEY WON'T STOP UNTIL THEY DIE...?
DON'T WORRY!! WITH THESE TYPES, IF YOU KNOCK OUT THE ETHER-USER, IT USUALLY BREAKS THE SPELL!

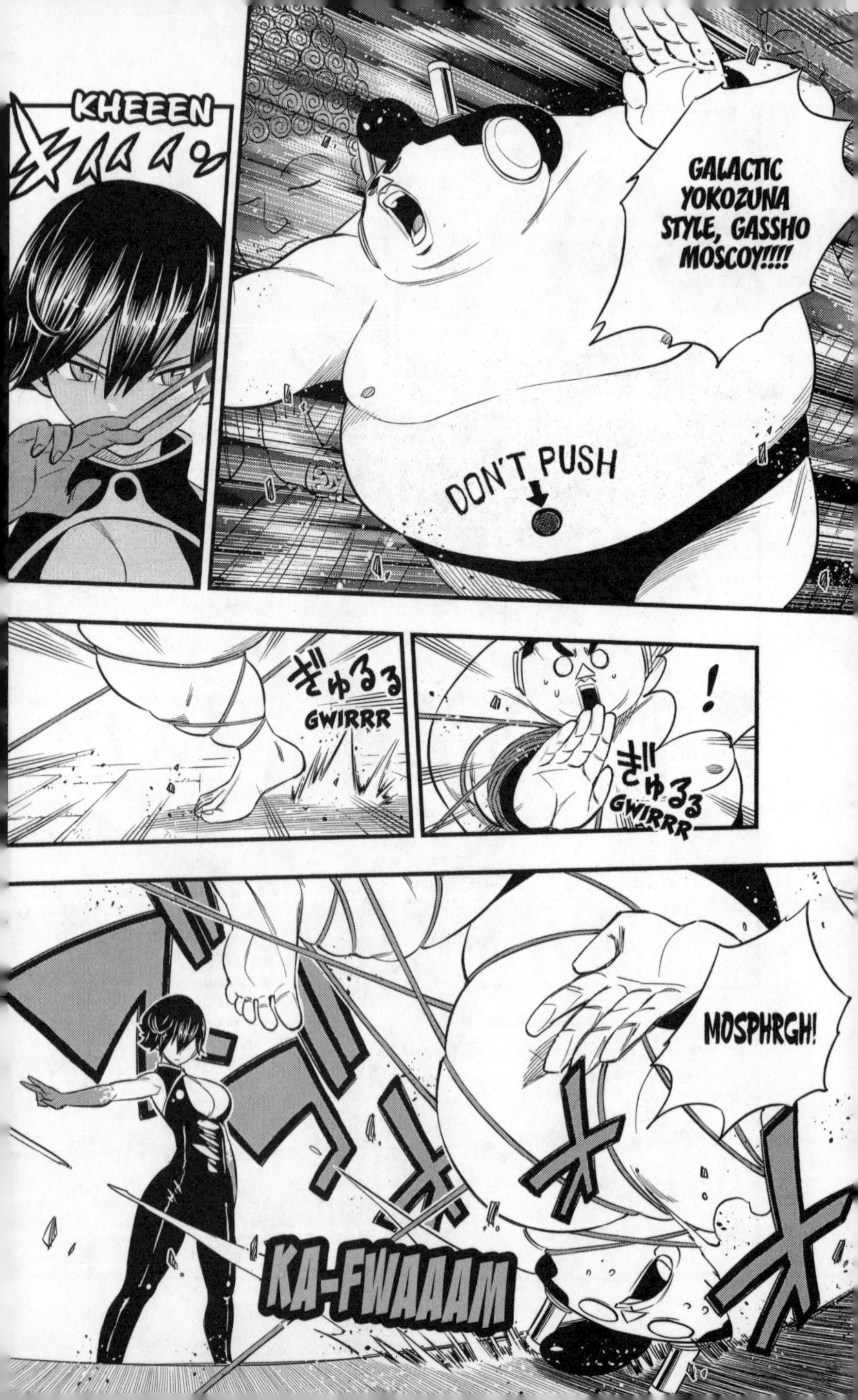
GALACTIC YOKOZUNA STYLE, GASSHO MOSCOY!!!!
DON'T PUSH
KHEEEN
!
ぎゅるる
GWIRRR
ぎゅるる
GWIRRR
MOSPHRGH!
KA-FWAAAM

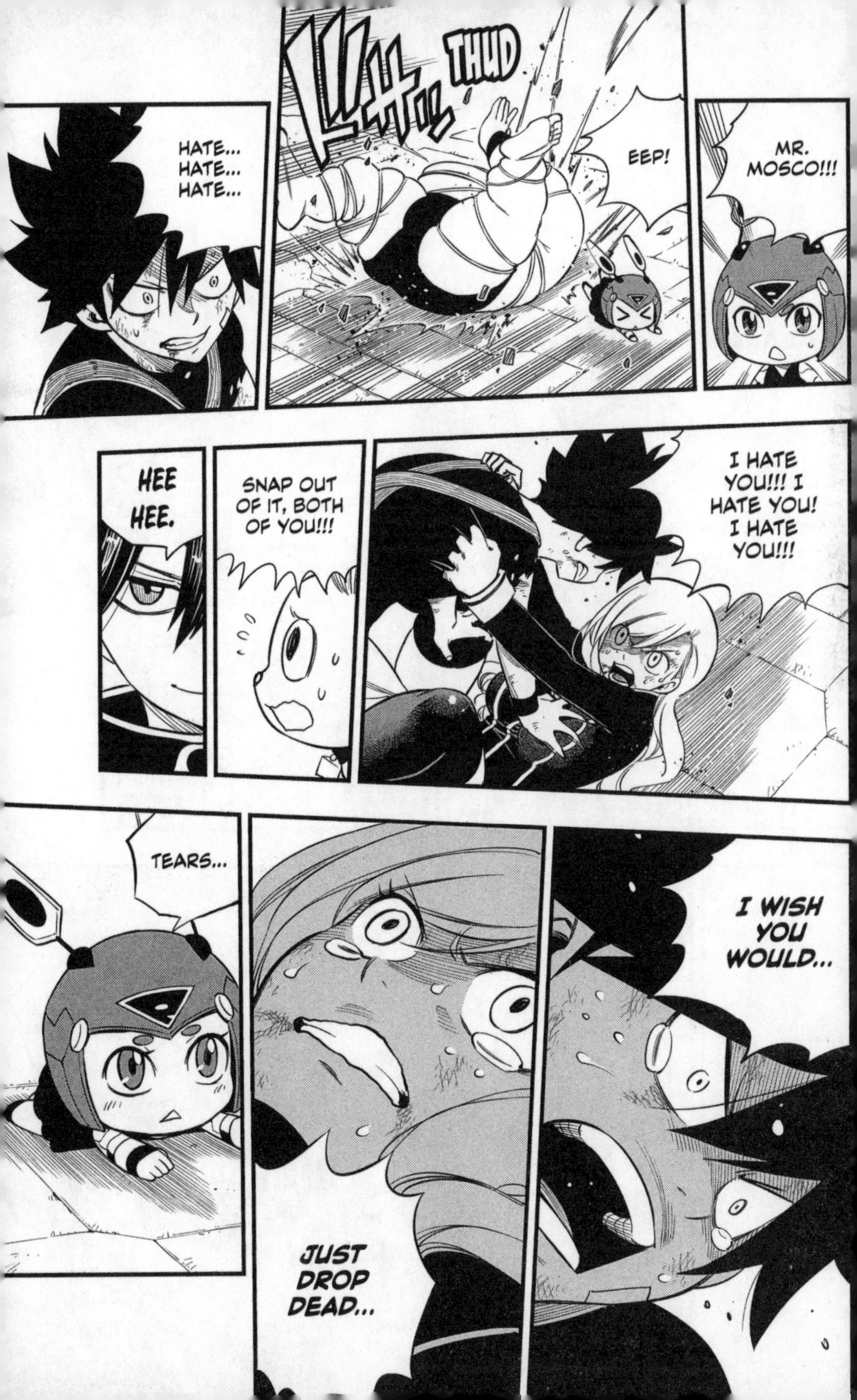
MR. MOSCO!!!
THUD
EEP!
HATE... HATE... HATE...
I HATE YOU!!! I HATE YOU! I HATE YOU!!!
SNAP OUT OF IT, BOTH OF YOU!!!
HEE HEE.
I WISH YOU WOULD...
JUST DROP DEAD...
TEARS...

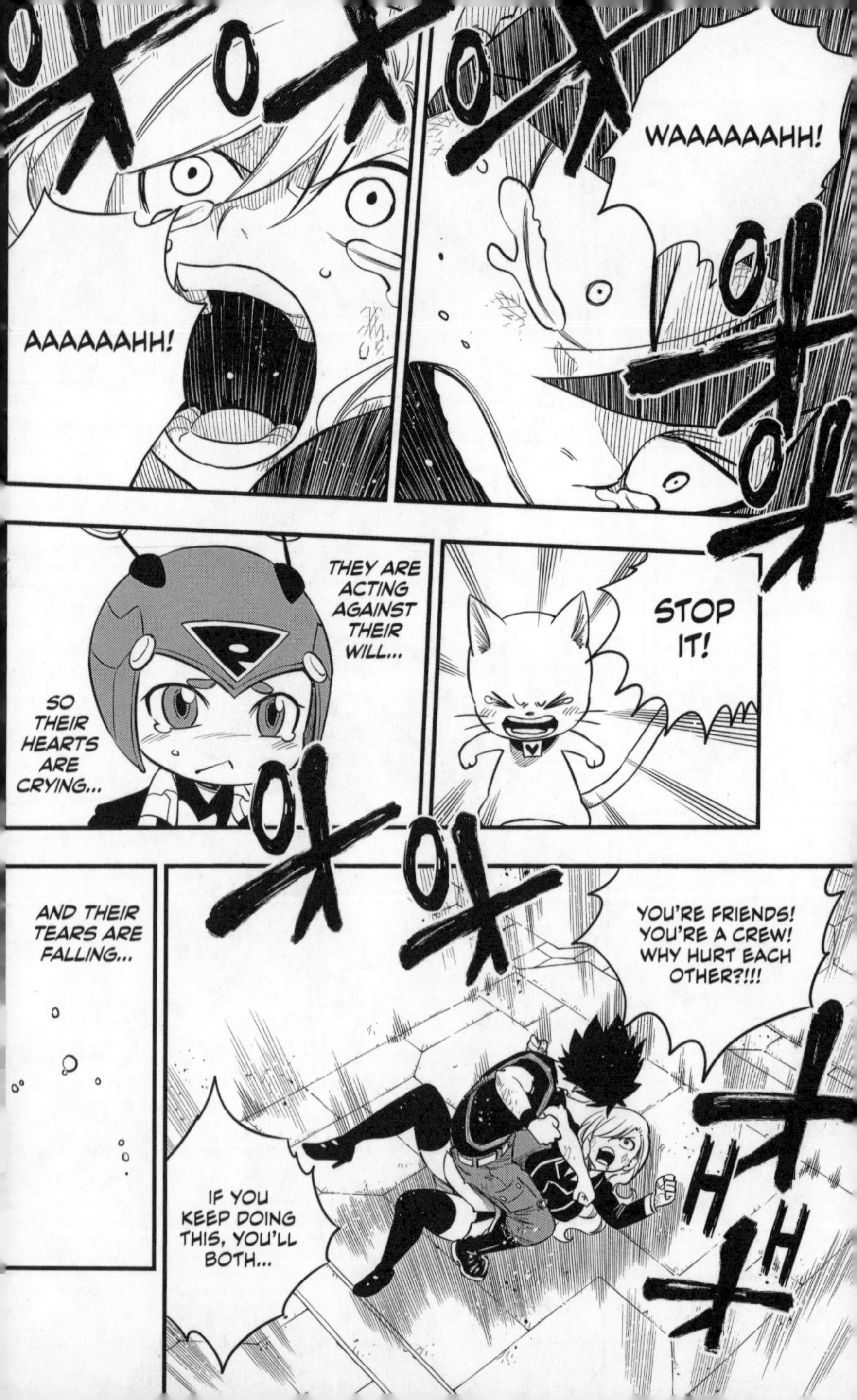
WAAAAAAHH!
AAAAAAHH!
STOP IT!
THEY ARE ACTING AGAINST THEIR WILL...
SO THEIR HEARTS ARE CRYING...
YOU'RE FRIENDS! YOU'RE A CREW! WHY HURT EACH OTHER?!!!
IF YOU KEEP DOING THIS, YOU'LL BOTH...
AND THEIR TEARS ARE FALLING...

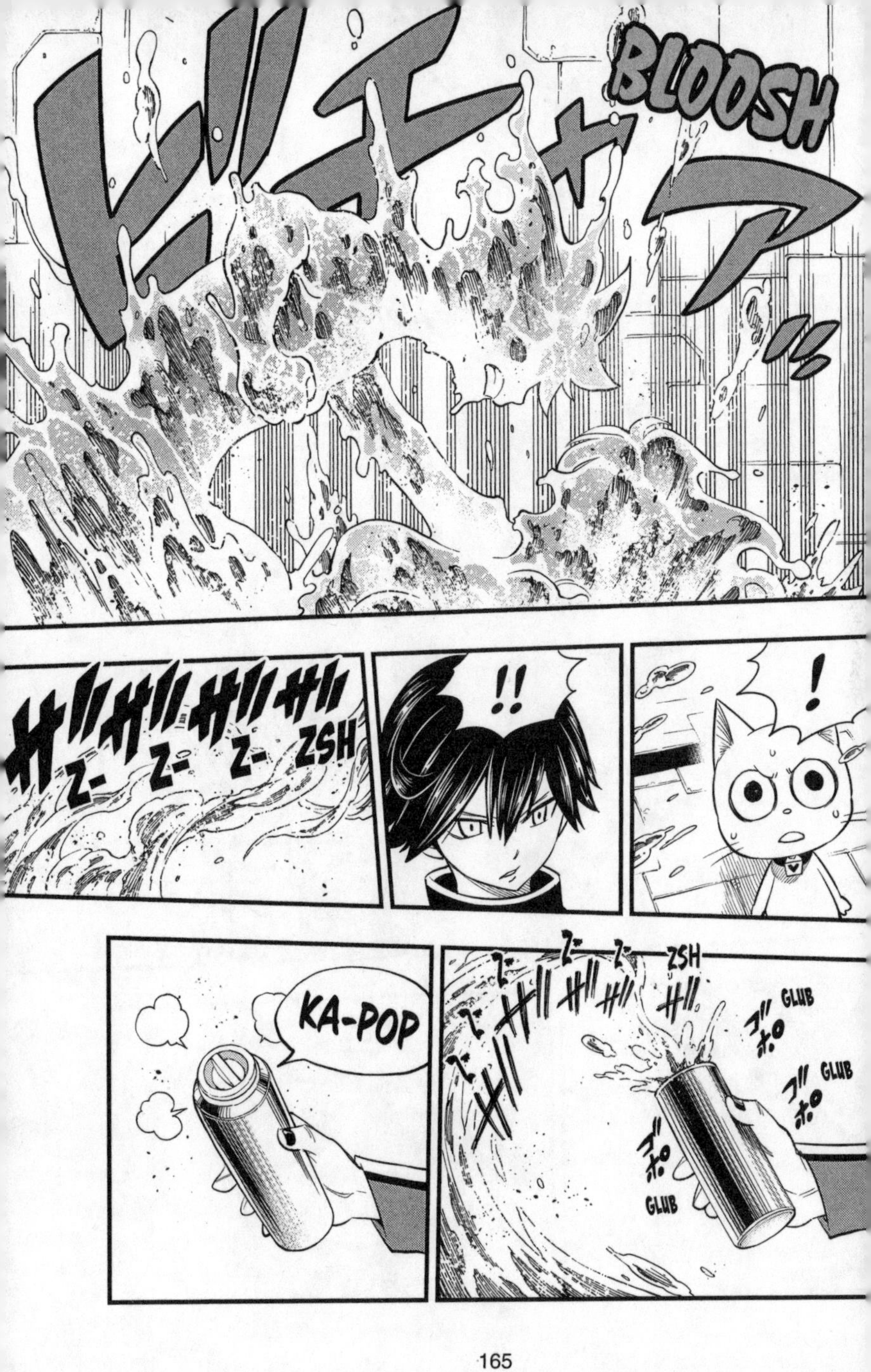
BLOOSH
!
!!
Z-
Z-
Z-
ZSH
ZSH
GLUB
GLUB
GLUB
KA-POP

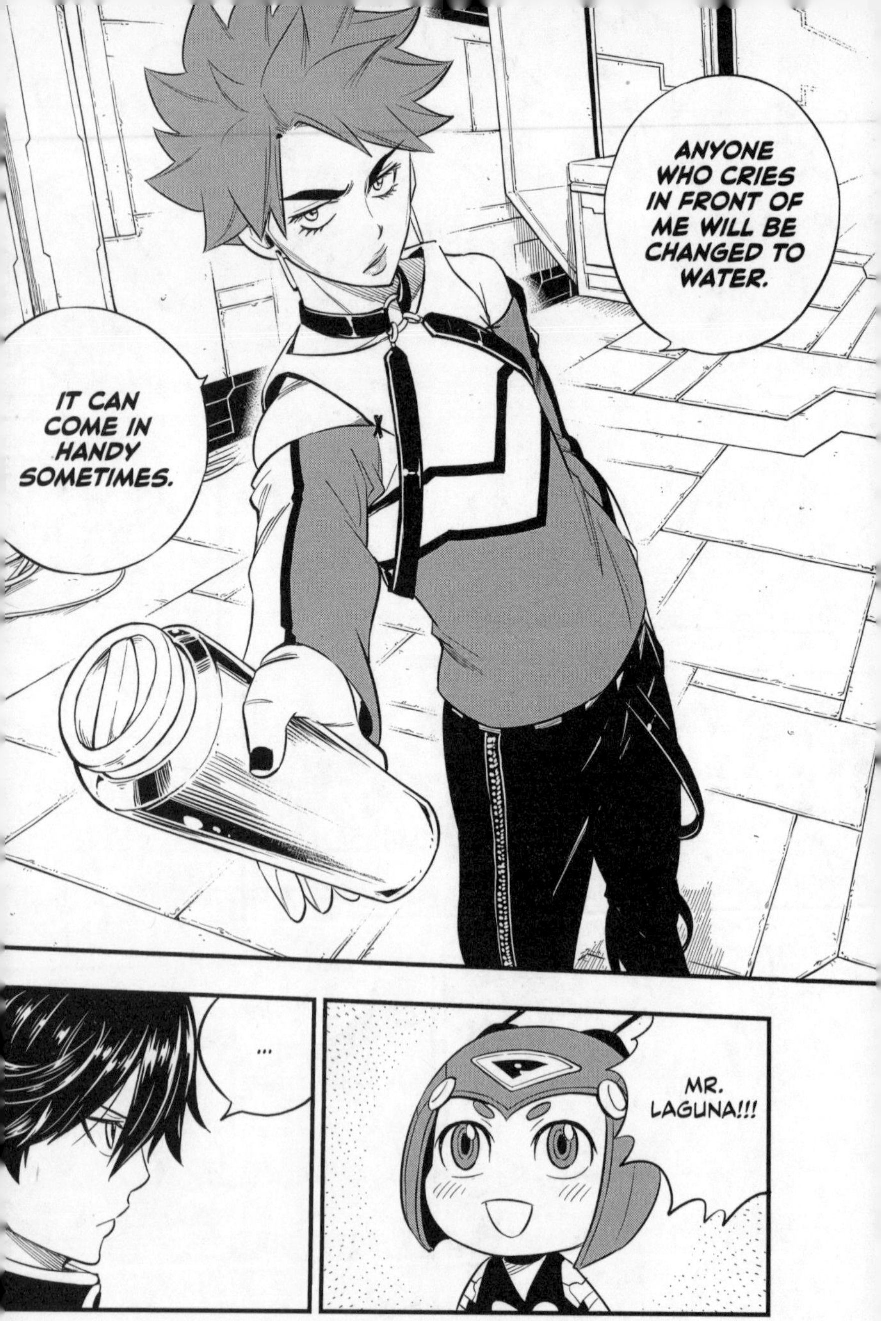
ANYONE WHO CRIES IN FRONT OF ME WILL BE CHANGED TO WATER.
IT CAN COME IN HANDY SOMETIMES.
MR. LAGUNA!!!
...

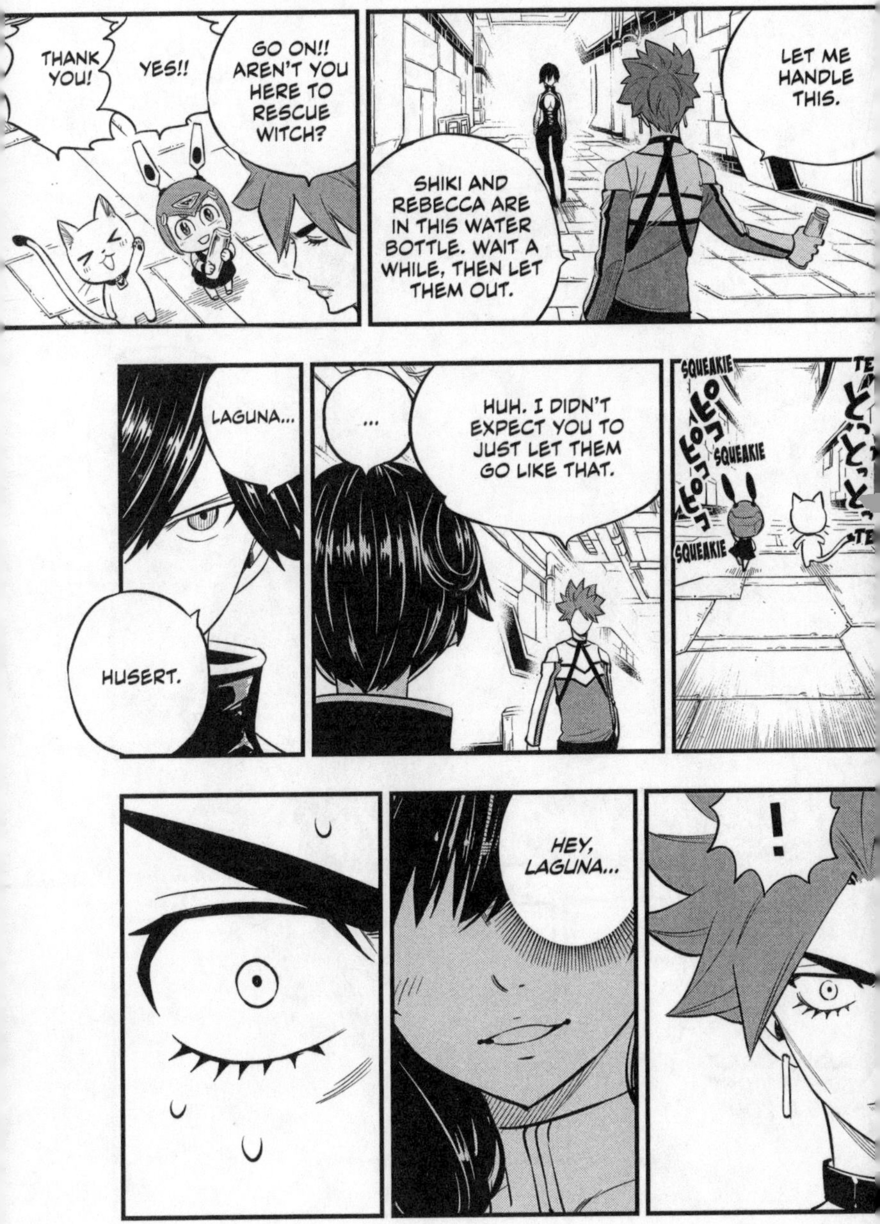
LET ME HANDLE THIS.
SHIKI AND REBECCA ARE IN THIS WATER BOTTLE. WAIT A WHILE, THEN LET THEM OUT.
GO ON!! AREN'T YOU HERE TO RESCUE WITCH?
YES!!
THANK YOU!
TE
とっとっとっ
TE
SQUEAKIE
ピョコピョコピョコ
SQUEAKIE
SQUEAKIE
HUH. I DIDN'T EXPECT YOU TO JUST LET THEM GO LIKE THAT.
...
LAGUNA...
HUSERT.
!
HEY, LAGUNA...

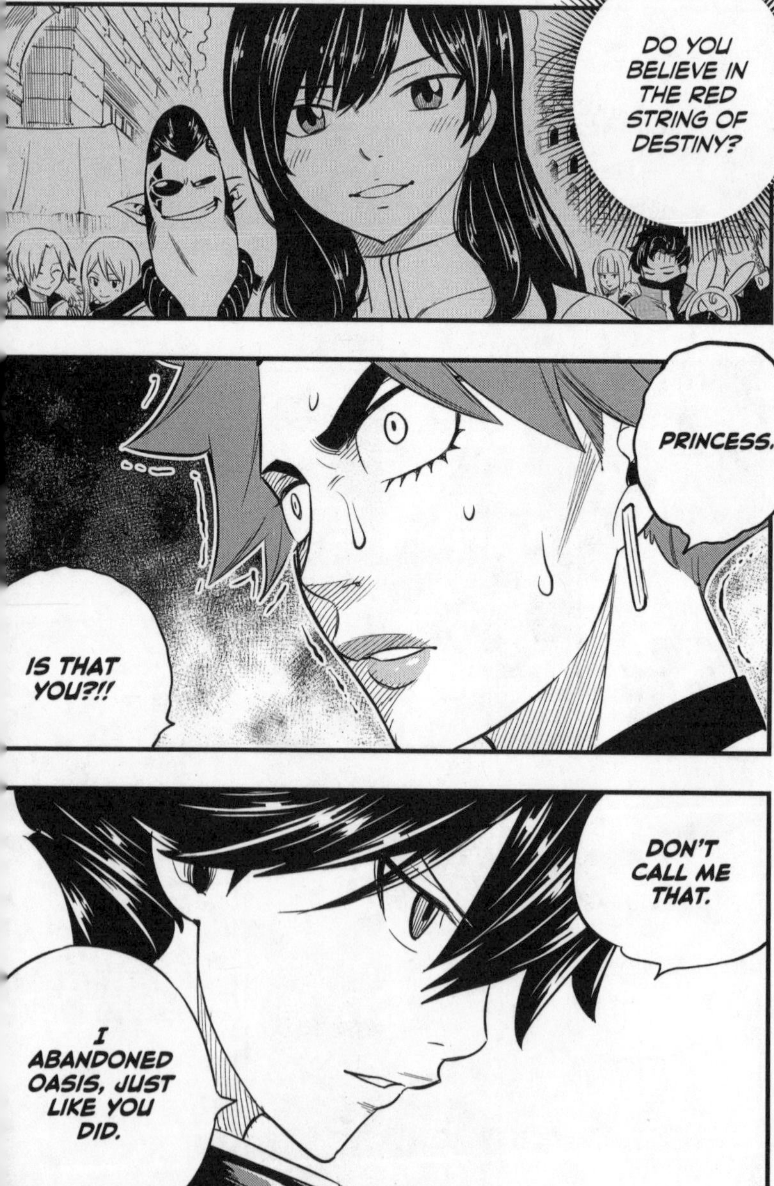
DO YOU BELIEVE IN THE RED STRING OF DESTINY?
PRINCESS...
IS THAT YOU?!!
DON'T CALL ME THAT.
I ABANDONED OASIS, JUST LIKE YOU DID.

EDENS ZERO

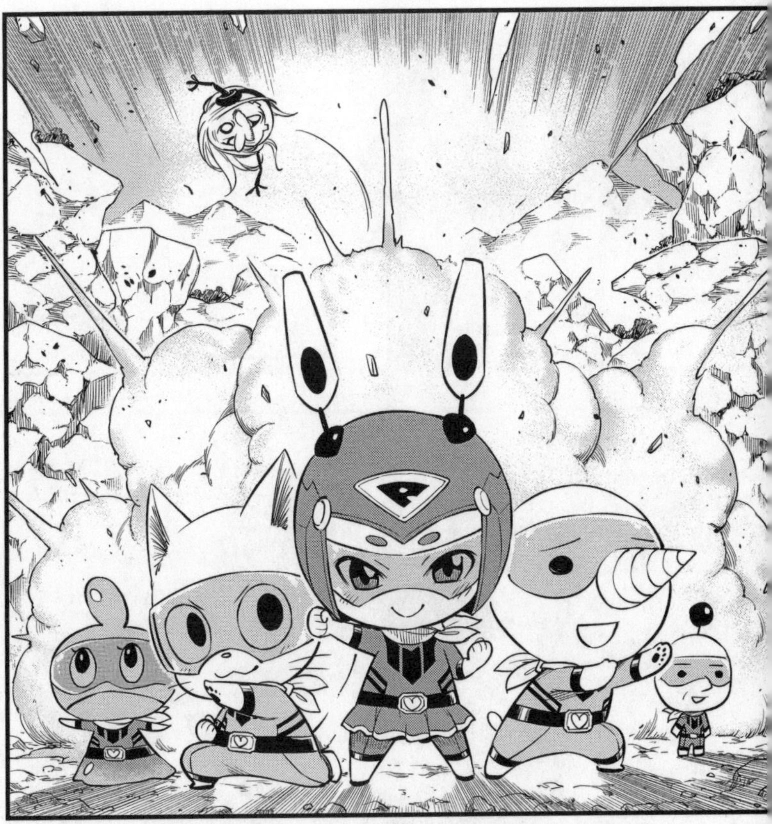

CHAPTER 158: THE MADNESS OF A MAN WHO KNOWS NO LOVE

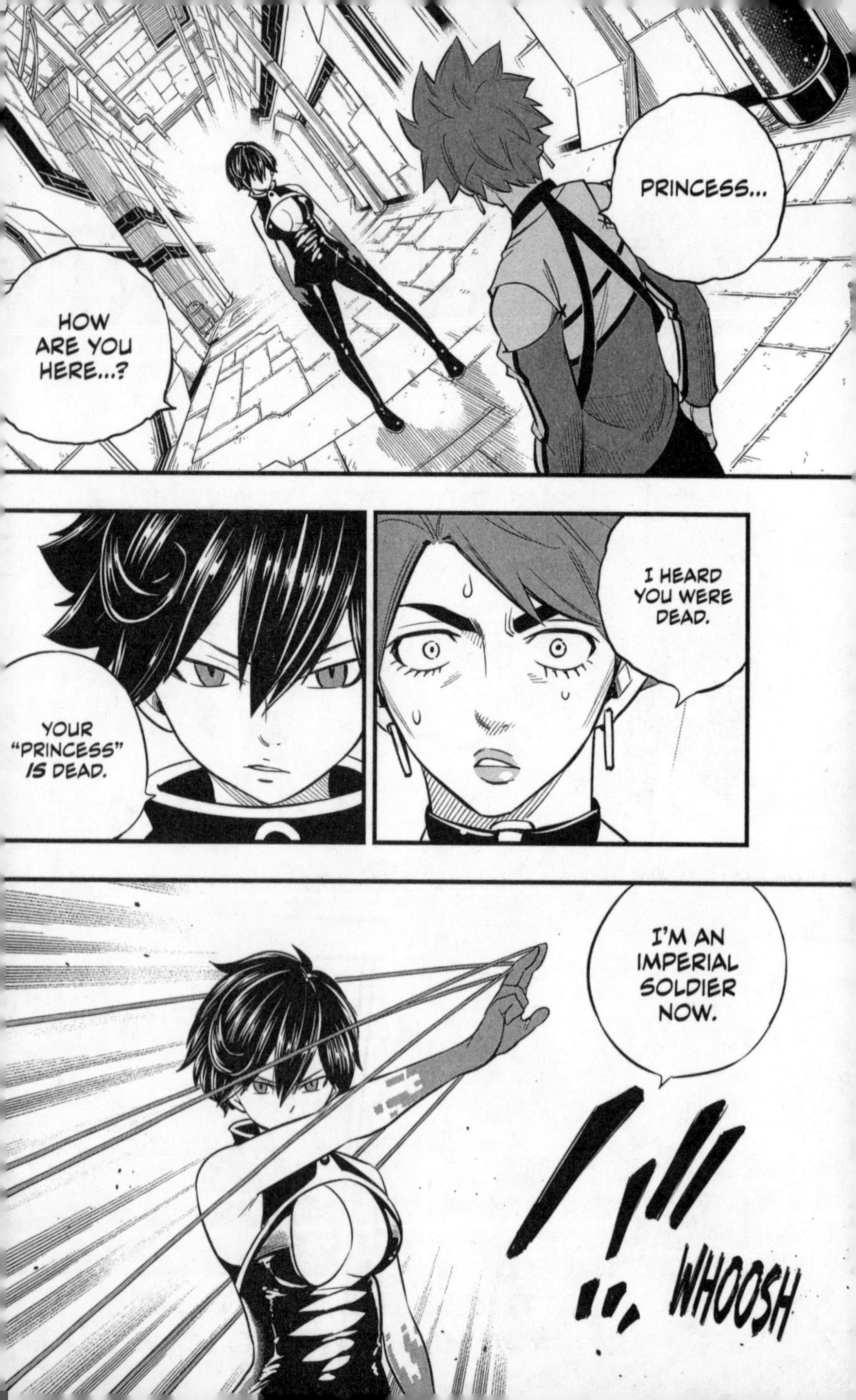
PRINCESS...
HOW ARE YOU HERE...?
I HEARD YOU WERE DEAD.
YOUR "PRINCESS" *IS* DEAD.
I'M AN IMPERIAL SOLDIER NOW.
WHOOSH

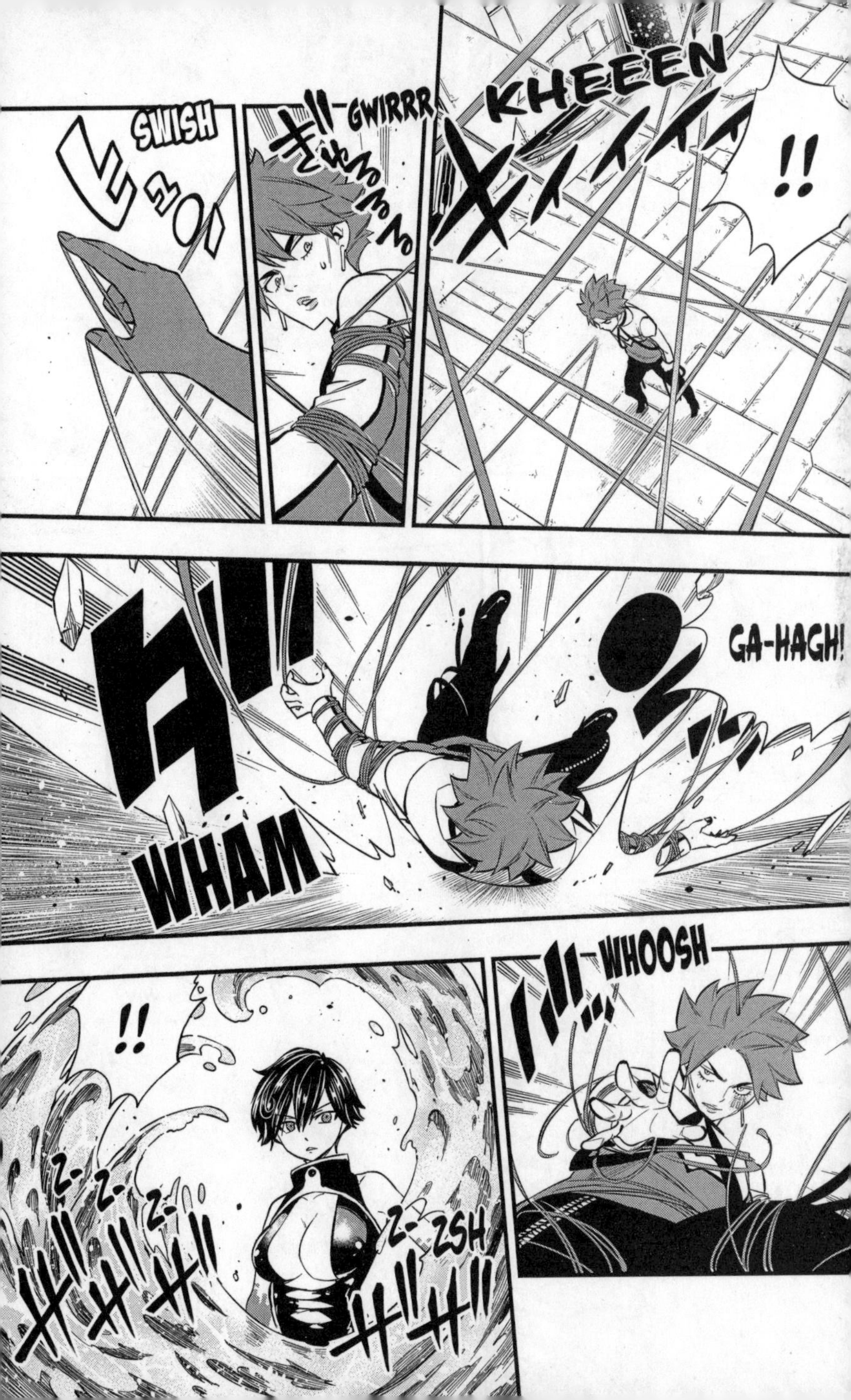
KHEEEN
!!
GWIRRR
SWISH
GA-HAGH!
WHAM
WHOOSH
!!
ZSH

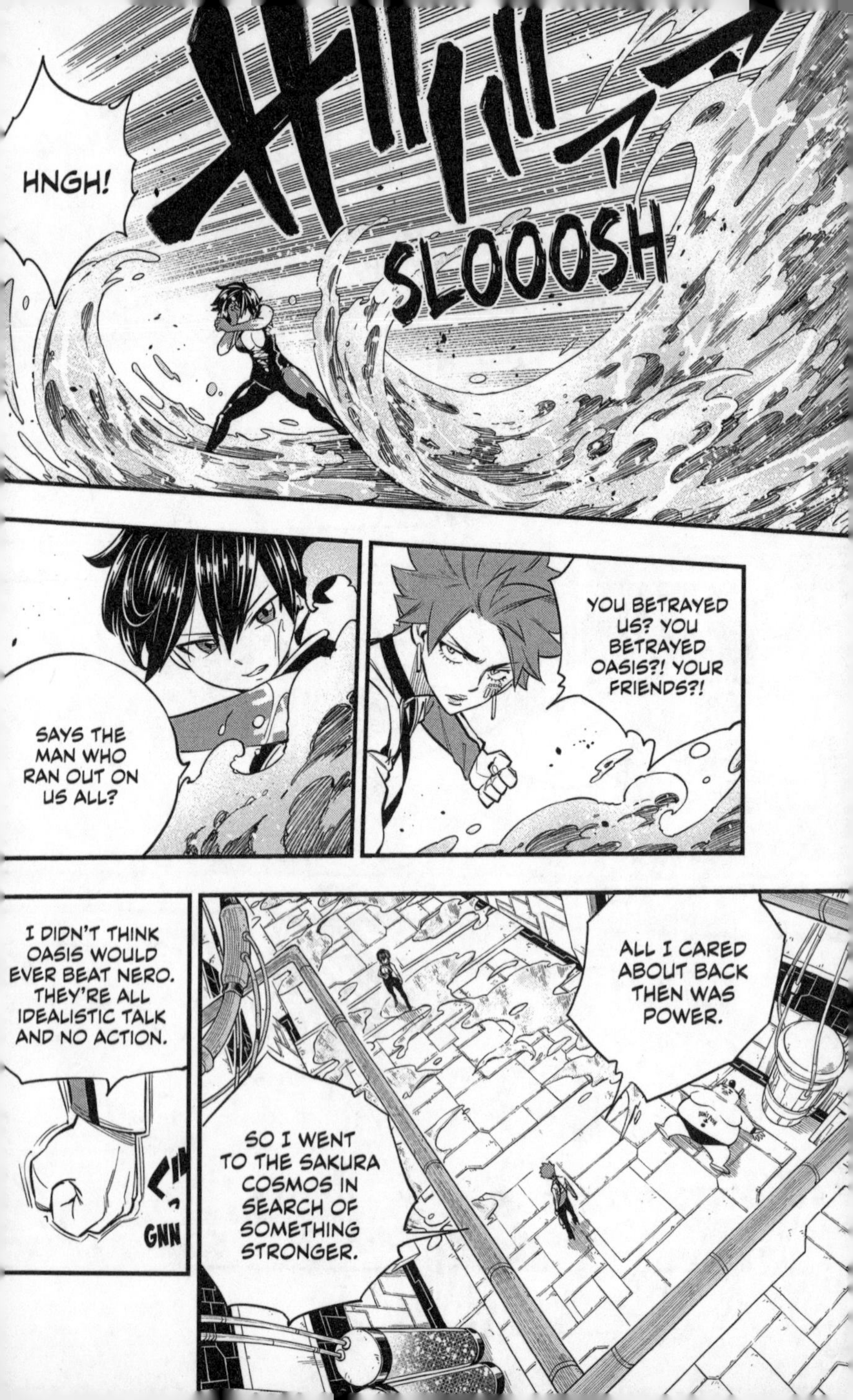
SLOOOSH
HNGH!
YOU BETRAYED US? YOU BETRAYED OASIS?! YOUR FRIENDS?!
SAYS THE MAN WHO RAN OUT ON US ALL?
ALL I CARED ABOUT BACK THEN WAS POWER.
SO I WENT TO THE SAKURA COSMOS IN SEARCH OF SOMETHING STRONGER.
I DIDN'T THINK OASIS WOULD EVER BEAT NERO. THEY'RE ALL IDEALISTIC TALK AND NO ACTION.
GNN

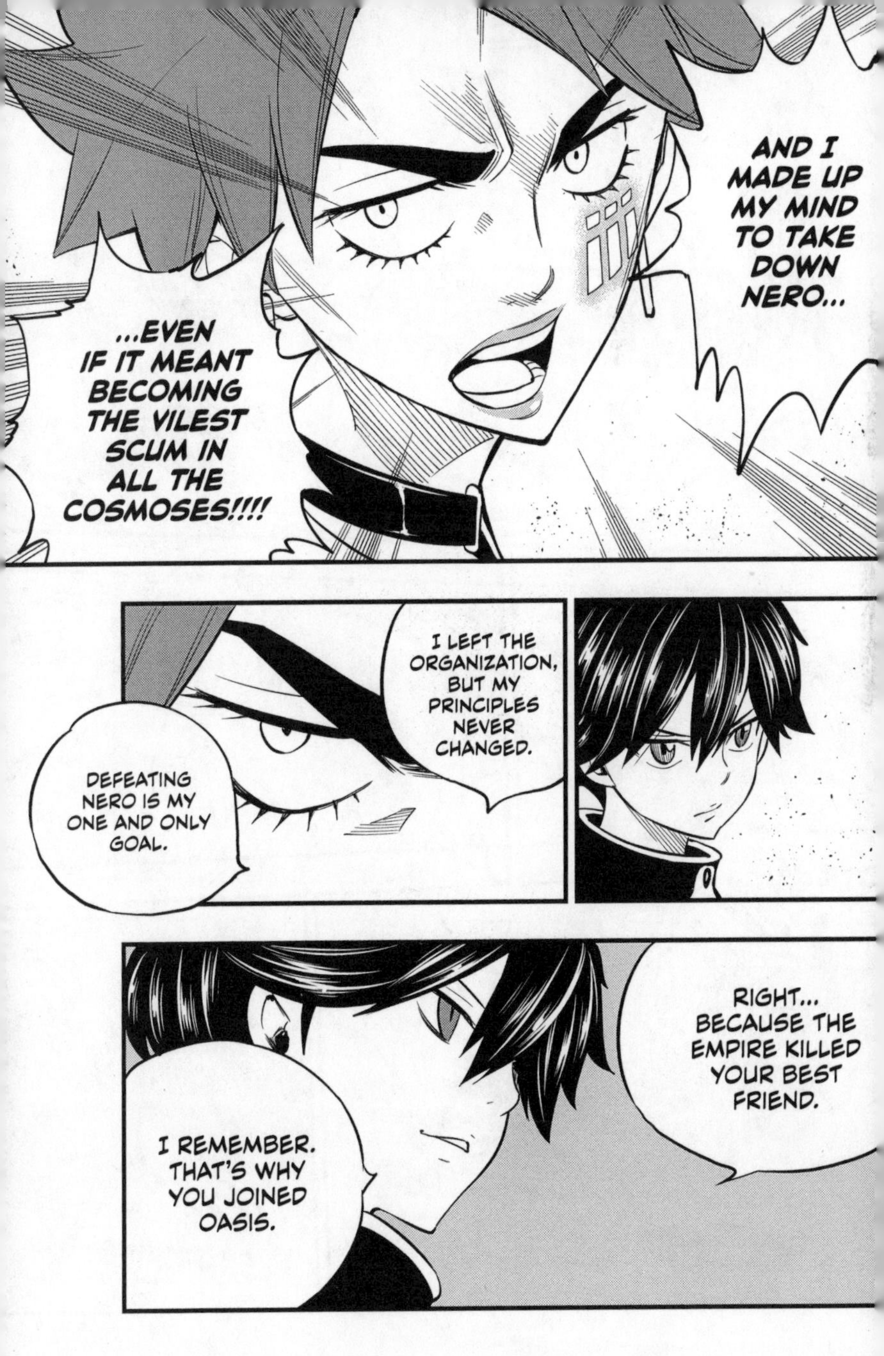
AND I MADE UP MY MIND TO TAKE DOWN NERO...
...EVEN IF IT MEANT BECOMING THE VILEST SCUM IN ALL THE COSMOSES!!!!
I LEFT THE ORGANIZATION, BUT MY PRINCIPLES NEVER CHANGED.
DEFEATING NERO IS MY ONE AND ONLY GOAL.
RIGHT... BECAUSE THE EMPIRE KILLED YOUR BEST FRIEND.
I REMEMBER. THAT'S WHY YOU JOINED OASIS.

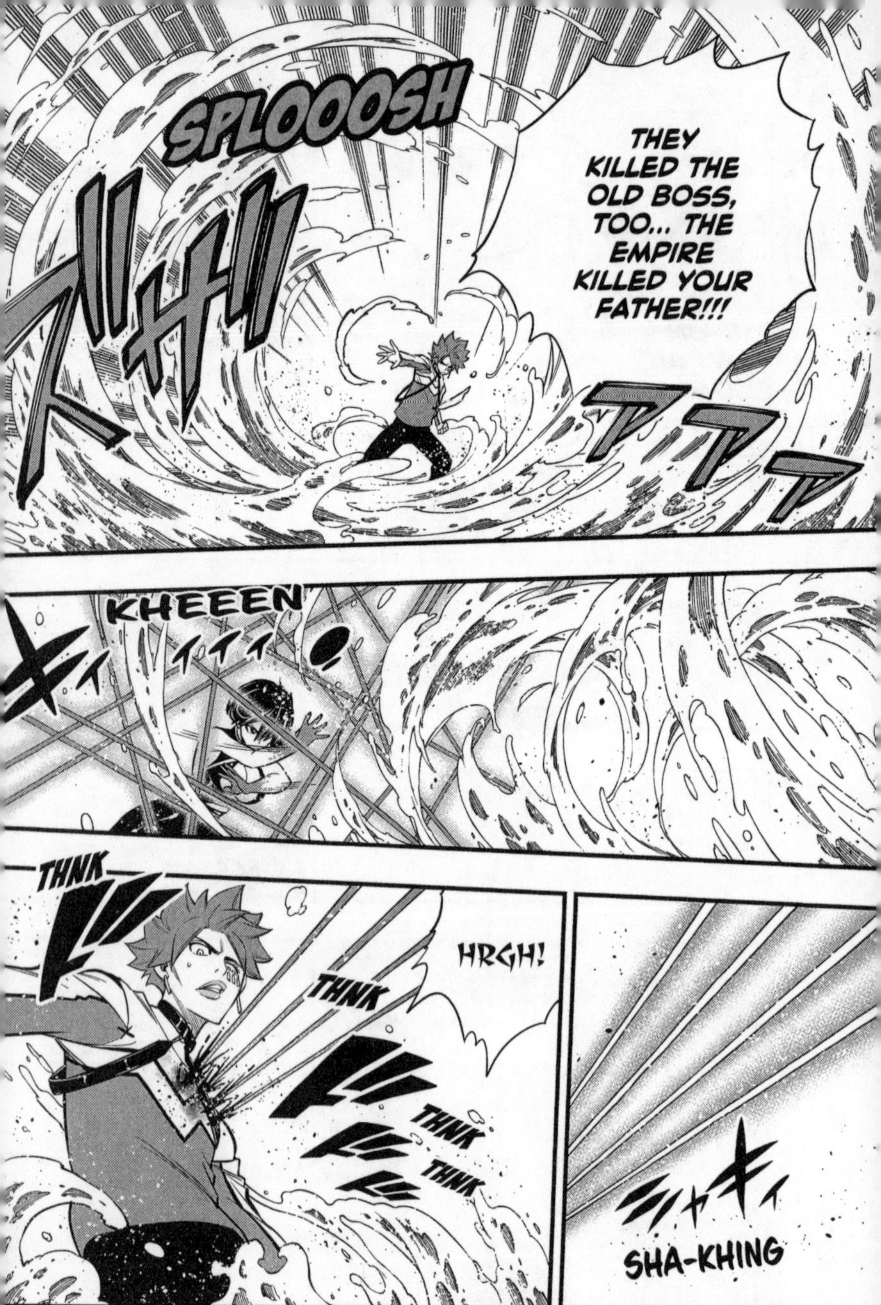
THEY KILLED THE OLD BOSS, TOO... THE EMPIRE KILLED YOUR FATHER!!!
SPLOOOSH
KHEEEN
SHA-KHING
HRGH!
THNK
THNK
THNK
THNK

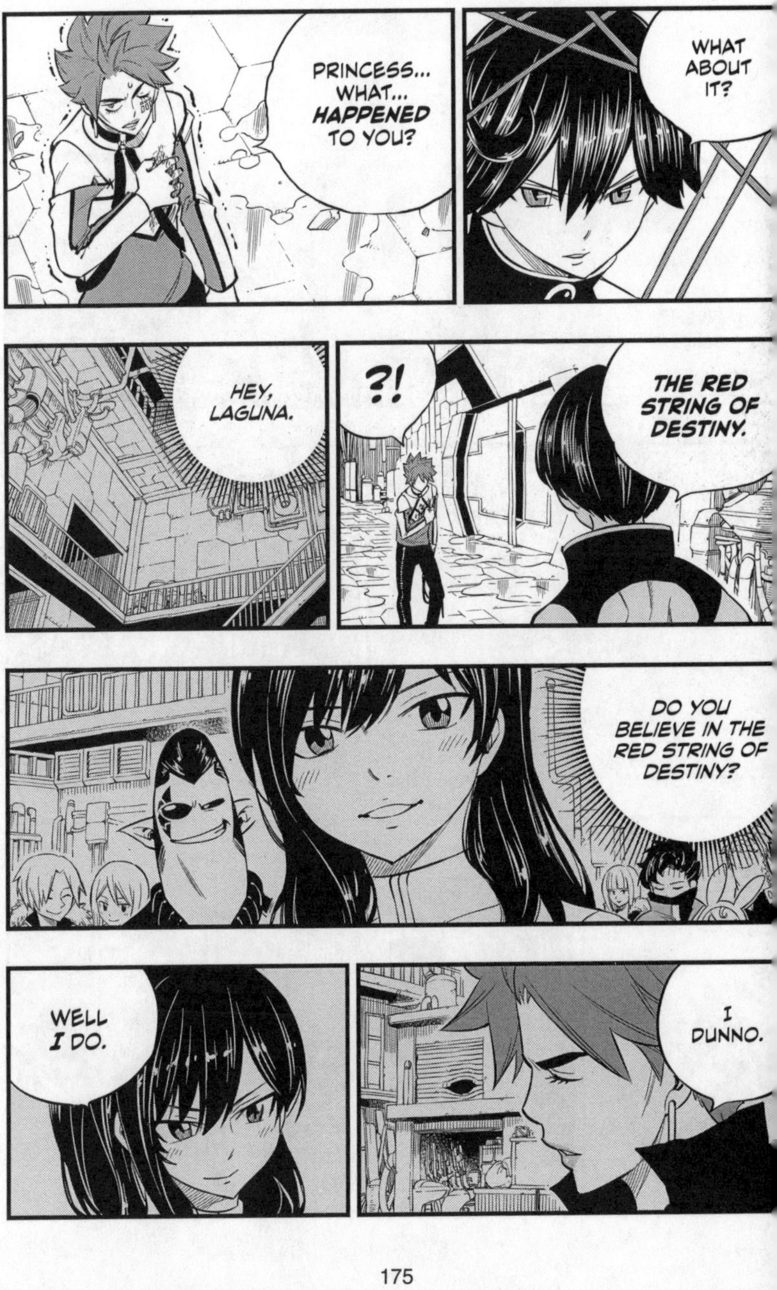
WHAT ABOUT IT?
PRINCESS... WHAT... HAPPENED TO YOU?
THE RED STRING OF DESTINY.
?!
HEY, LAGUNA.
DO YOU BELIEVE IN THE RED STRING OF DESTINY?
I DUNNO.
WELL I DO.

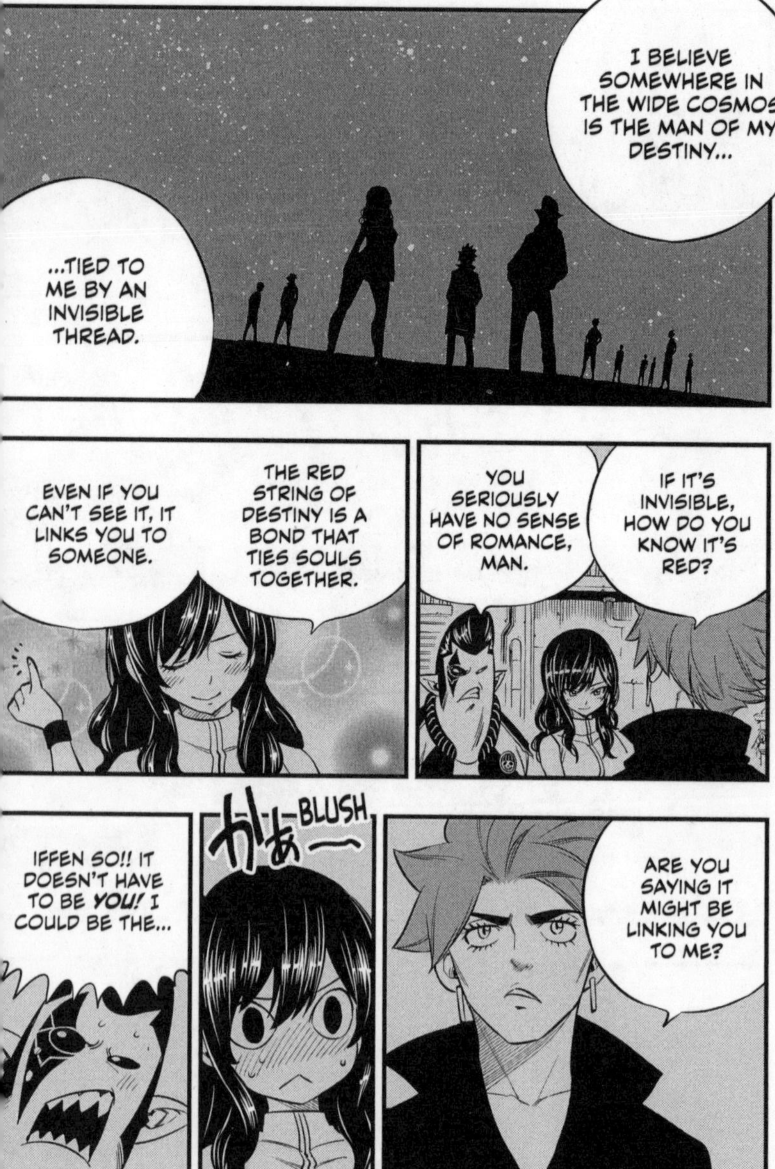
I BELIEVE SOMEWHERE IN THE WIDE COSMOS IS THE MAN OF MY DESTINY...
...TIED TO ME BY AN INVISIBLE THREAD.
IF IT'S INVISIBLE, HOW DO YOU KNOW IT'S RED?
YOU SERIOUSLY HAVE NO SENSE OF ROMANCE, MAN.
THE RED STRING OF DESTINY IS A BOND THAT TIES SOULS TOGETHER.
EVEN IF YOU CAN'T SEE IT, IT LINKS YOU TO SOMEONE.
ARE YOU SAYING IT MIGHT BE LINKING YOU TO ME?
かぁ〜
BLUSH
IFFEN SO!! IT DOESN'T HAVE TO BE *YOU!* I COULD BE THE...

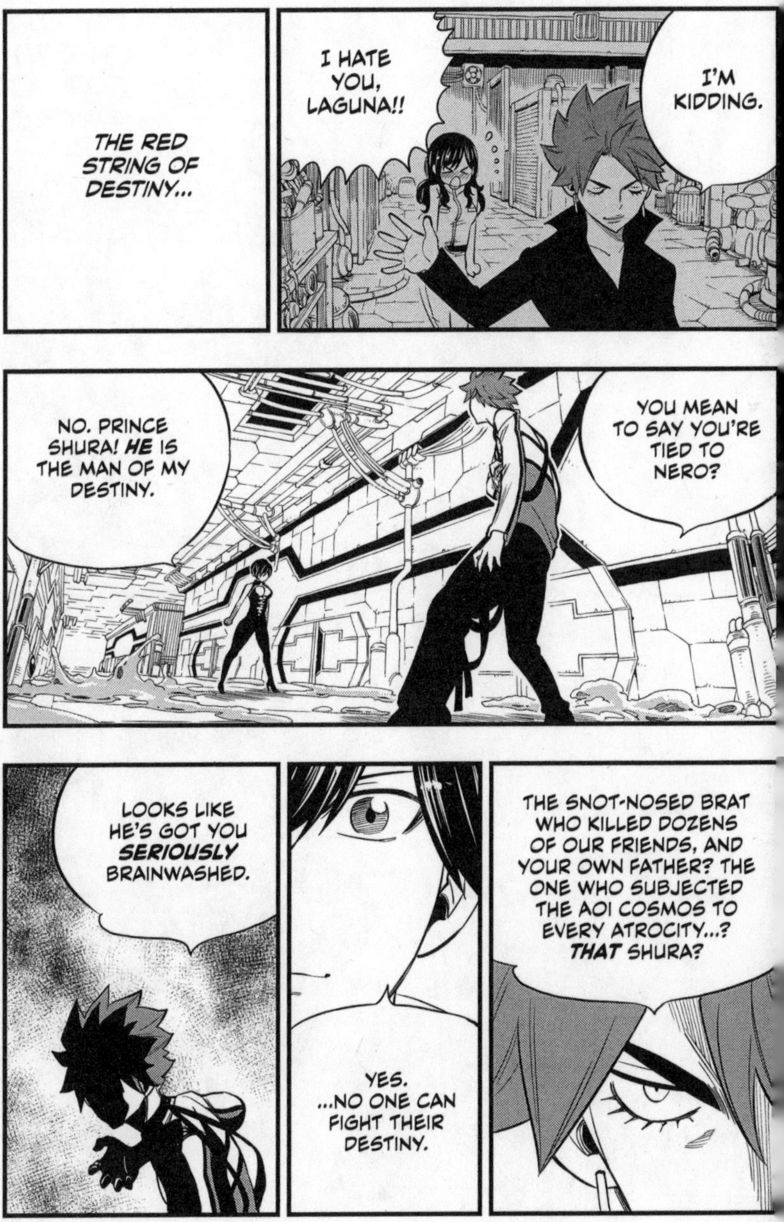
I'M KIDDING.
I HATE YOU, LAGUNA!!
THE RED STRING OF DESTINY...
YOU MEAN TO SAY YOU'RE TIED TO NERO?
NO. PRINCE SHURA! HE IS THE MAN OF MY DESTINY.
THE SNOT-NOSED BRAT WHO KILLED DOZENS OF OUR FRIENDS, AND YOUR OWN FATHER? THE ONE WHO SUBJECTED THE AOI COSMOS TO EVERY ATROCITY...? THAT SHURA?
YES. ...NO ONE CAN FIGHT THEIR DESTINY.
LOOKS LIKE HE'S GOT YOU SERIOUSLY BRAINWASHED.

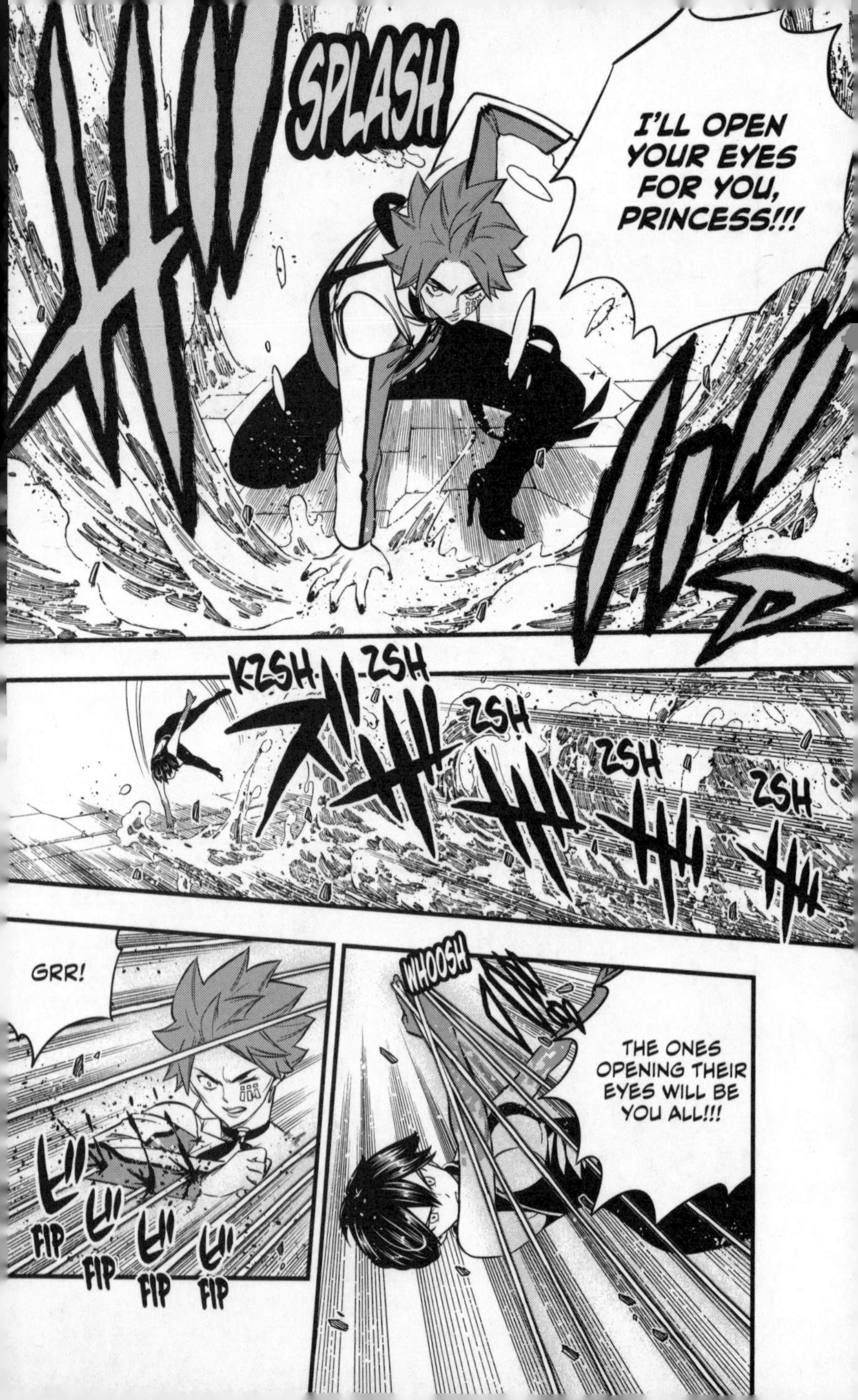
I'LL OPEN YOUR EYES FOR YOU, PRINCESS!!!
SPLASH
K-ZSH
ZSH
ZSH
ZSH
ZSH
WHOOSH
THE ONES OPENING THEIR EYES WILL BE YOU ALL!!!
GRR!
FIP
FIP
FIP
FIP

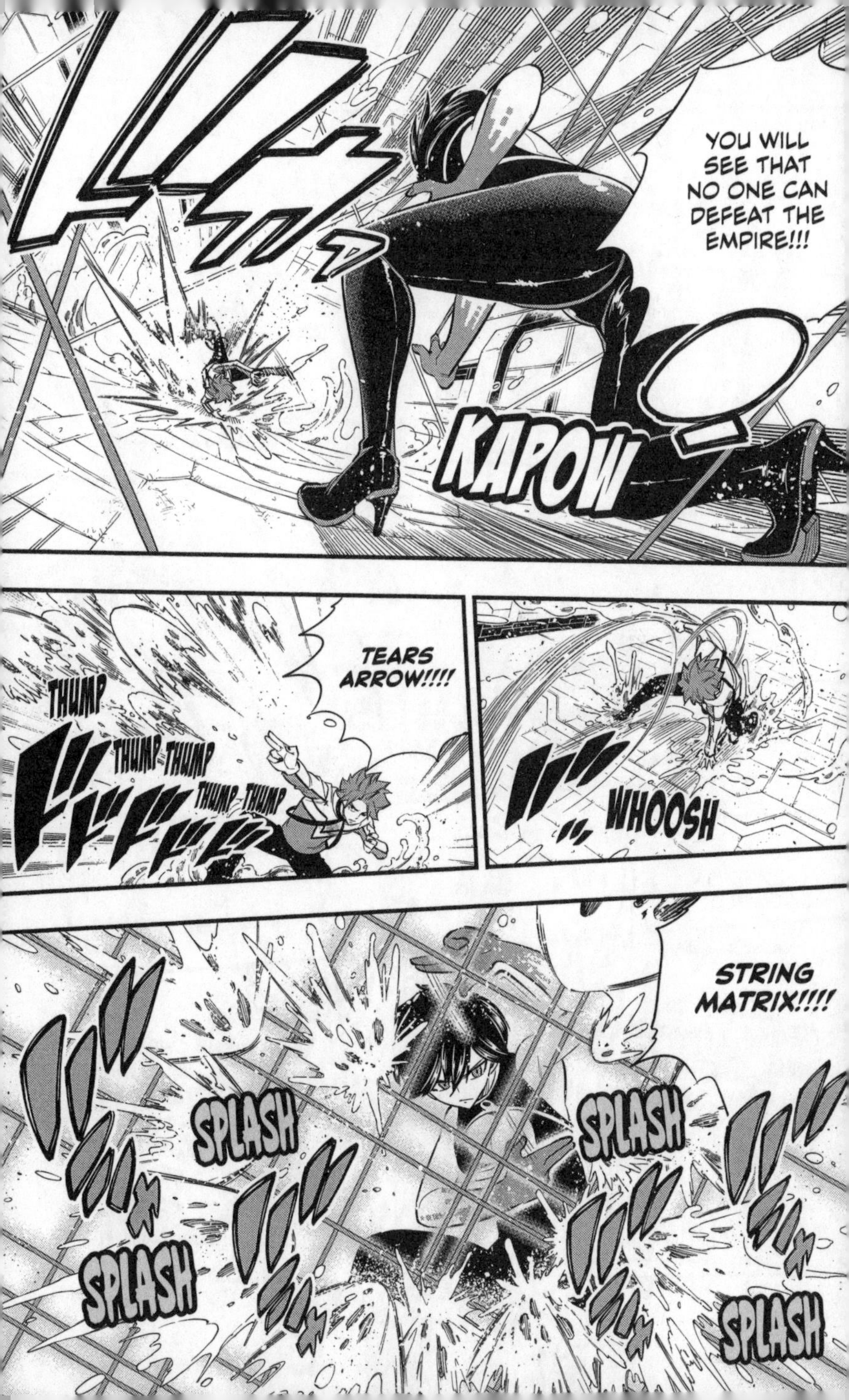
YOU WILL SEE THAT NO ONE CAN DEFEAT THE EMPIRE!!!
KAPOW
WHOOSH
TEARS ARROW!!!!
THUMP
THUMP THUMP
THUMP THUMP
STRING MATRIX!!!!
SPLASH
SPLASH
SPLASH
SPLASH

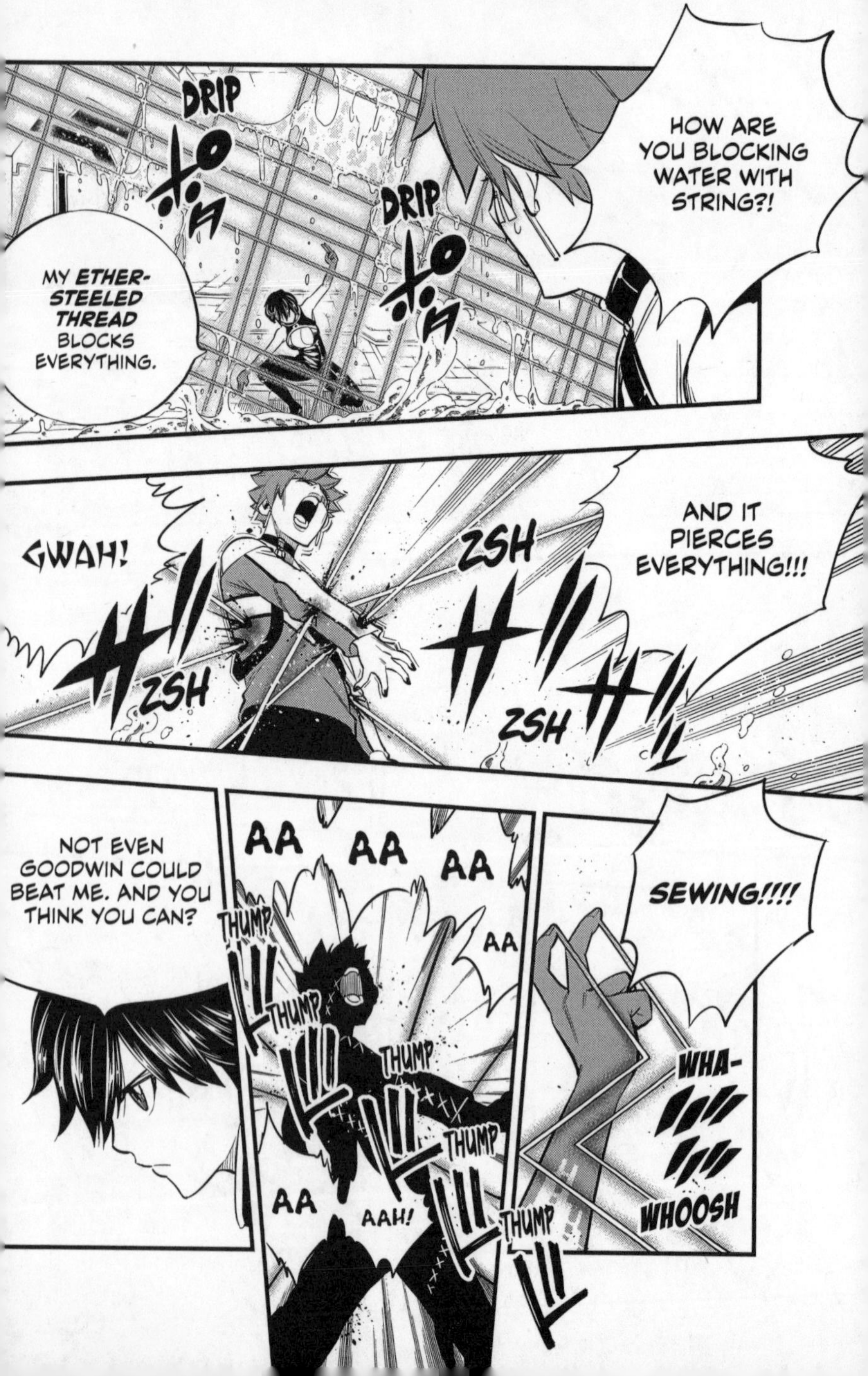
HOW ARE YOU BLOCKING WATER WITH STRING?!
DRIP
DRIP
MY *ETHER-STEELED THREAD* BLOCKS EVERYTHING.
AND IT PIERCES EVERYTHING!!!
ZSH
ZSH
ZSH
GWAH!
SEWING!!!!
WHA-
WHOOSH
AA
AA
AA
AA
THUMP
THUMP
THUMP
THUMP
THUMP
AA
AAH!
NOT EVEN GOODWIN COULD BEAT ME. AND YOU THINK YOU CAN?

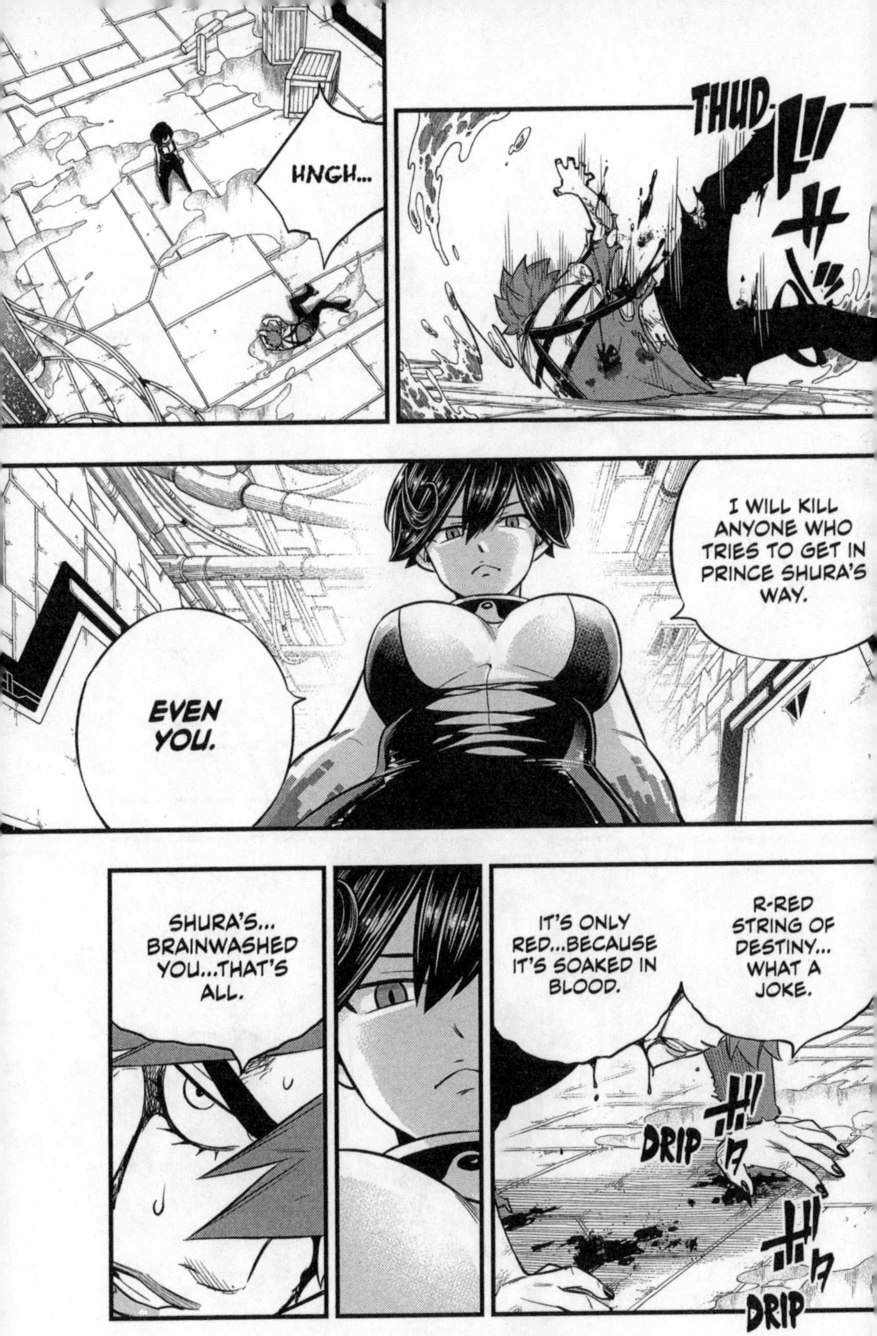
THUD
HNGH...
I WILL KILL ANYONE WHO TRIES TO GET IN PRINCE SHURA'S WAY.
EVEN YOU.
R-RED STRING OF DESTINY... WHAT A JOKE.
IT'S ONLY RED...BECAUSE IT'S SOAKED IN BLOOD.
DRIP
DRIP
SHURA'S... BRAINWASHED YOU...THAT'S ALL.

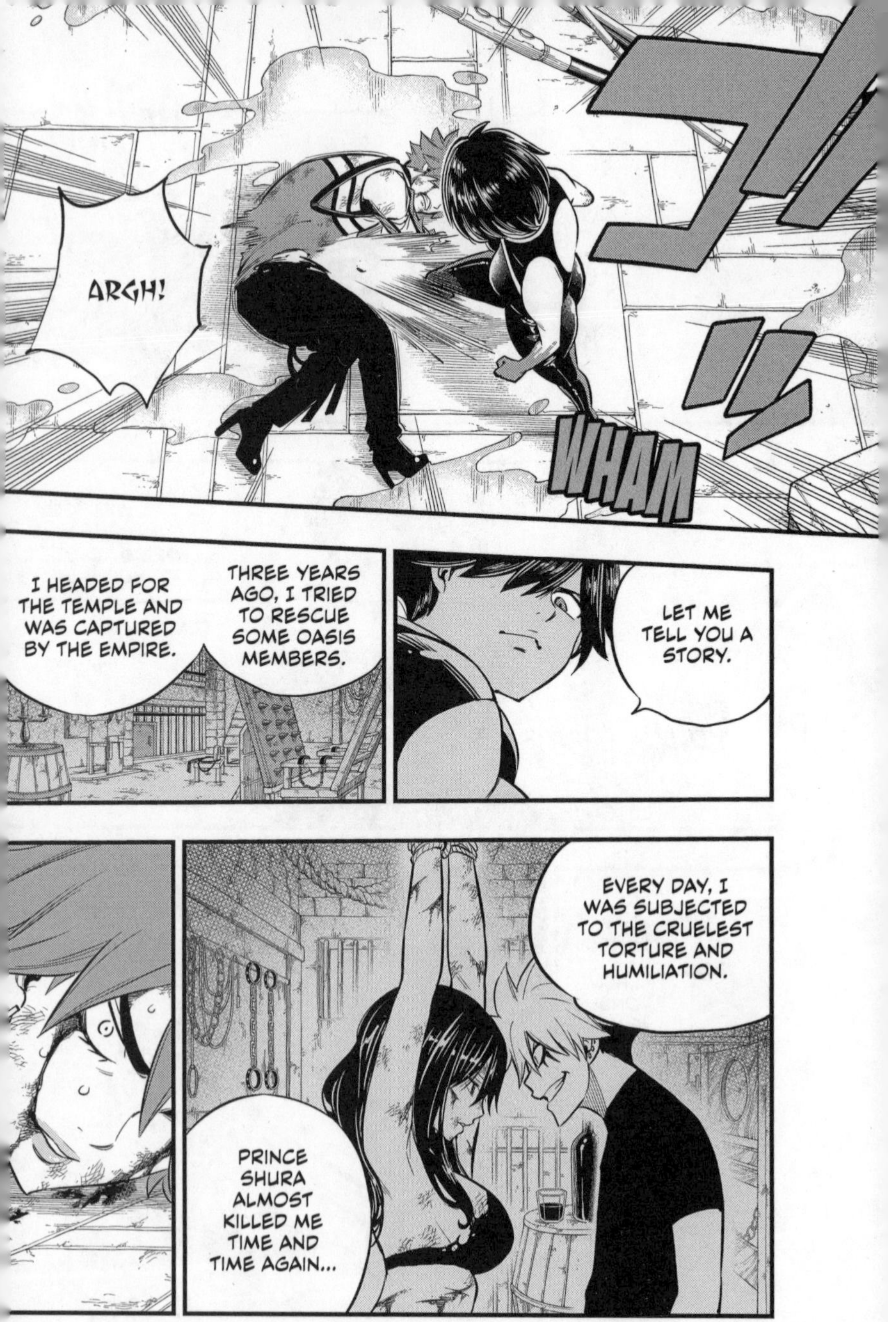
ARGH!
WHAM
LET ME TELL YOU A STORY.
THREE YEARS AGO, I TRIED TO RESCUE SOME OASIS MEMBERS.
I HEADED FOR THE TEMPLE AND WAS CAPTURED BY THE EMPIRE.
EVERY DAY, I WAS SUBJECTED TO THE CRUELEST TORTURE AND HUMILIATION.
PRINCE SHURA ALMOST KILLED ME TIME AND TIME AGAIN...

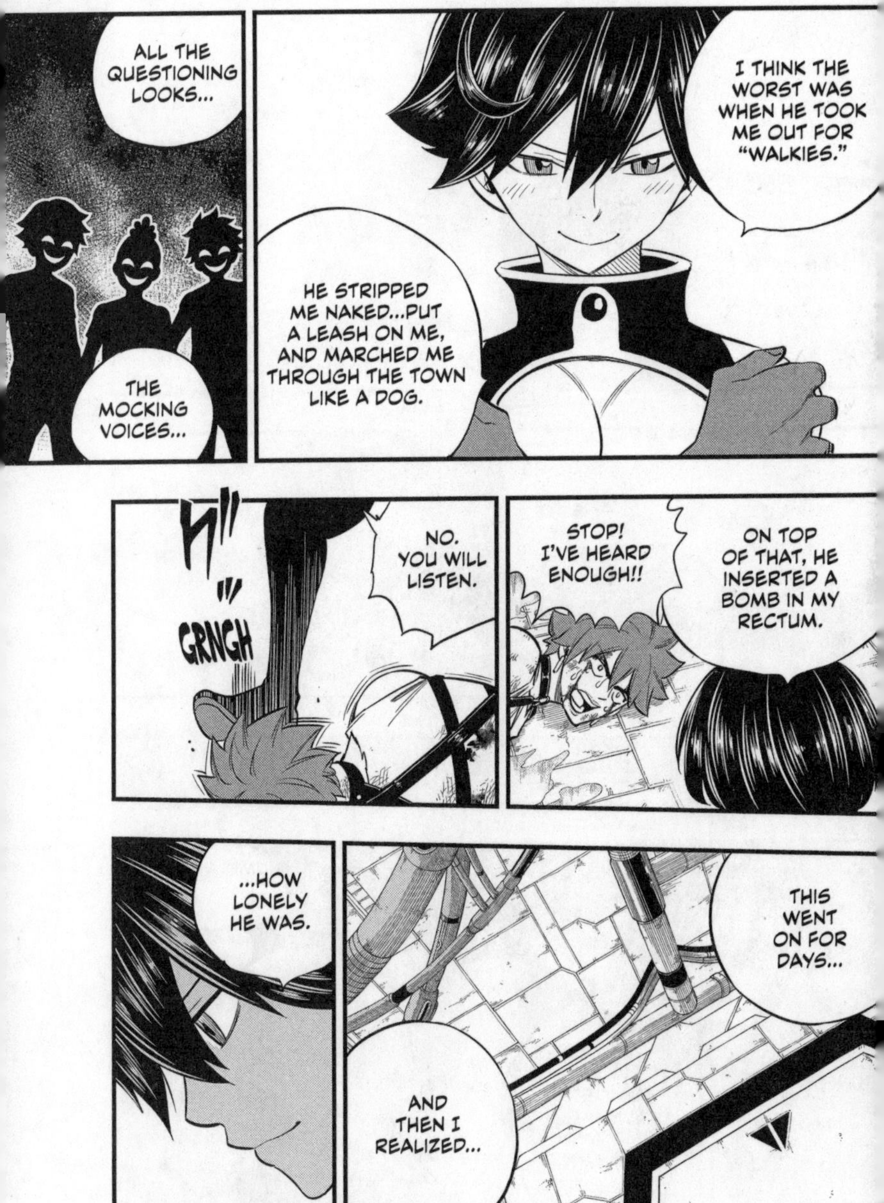
I THINK THE WORST WAS WHEN HE TOOK ME OUT FOR "WALKIES."
HE STRIPPED ME NAKED...PUT A LEASH ON ME, AND MARCHED ME THROUGH THE TOWN LIKE A DOG.
ALL THE QUESTIONING LOOKS...
THE MOCKING VOICES...
ON TOP OF THAT, HE INSERTED A BOMB IN MY RECTUM.
STOP! I'VE HEARD ENOUGH!!
NO. YOU WILL LISTEN.
GRNGH
THIS WENT ON FOR DAYS...
AND THEN I REALIZED...
...HOW LONELY HE WAS.

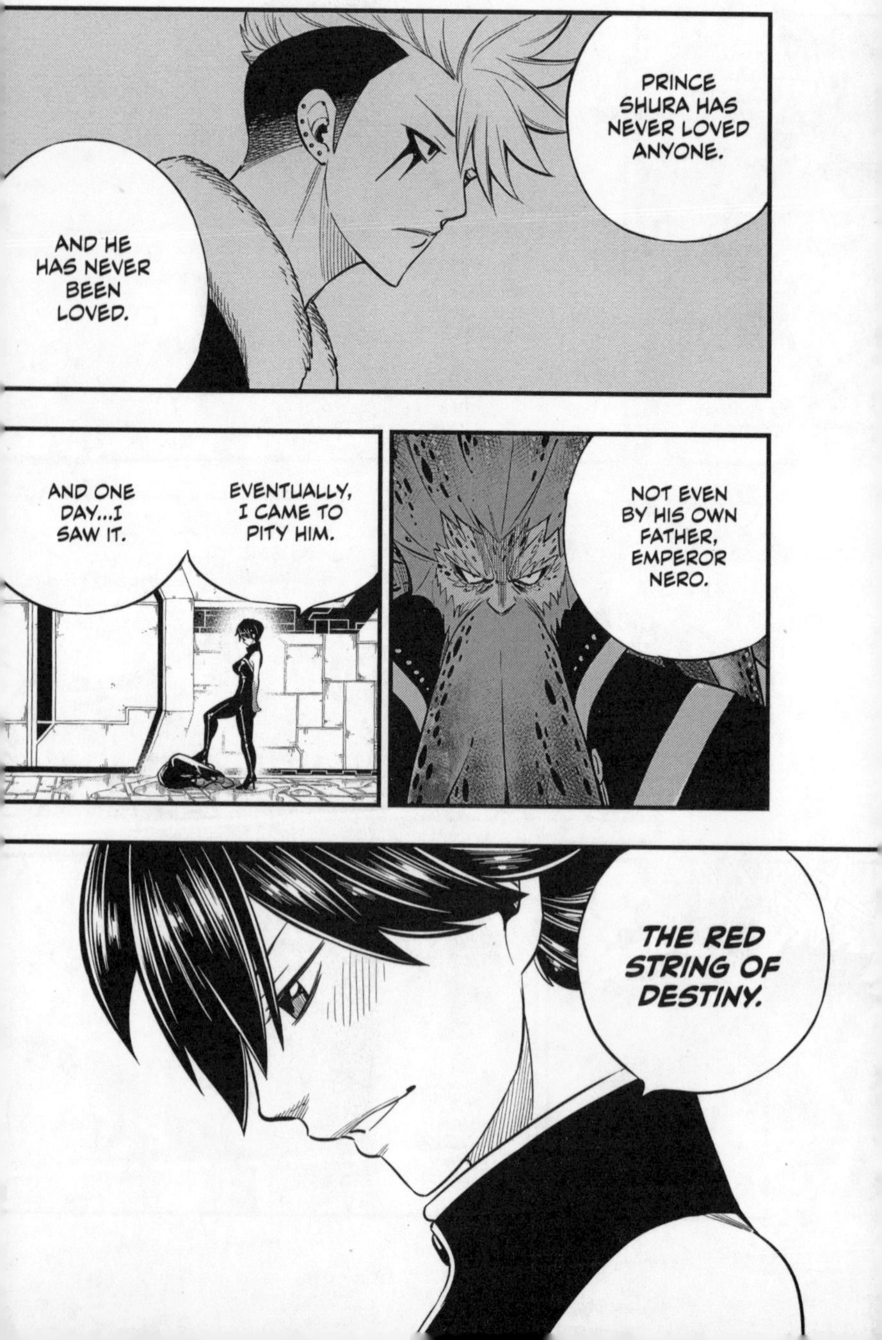
PRINCE SHURA HAS NEVER LOVED ANYONE.
AND HE HAS NEVER BEEN LOVED.
NOT EVEN BY HIS OWN FATHER, EMPEROR NERO.
EVENTUALLY, I CAME TO PITY HIM.
AND ONE DAY...I SAW IT.
THE RED STRING OF DESTINY.

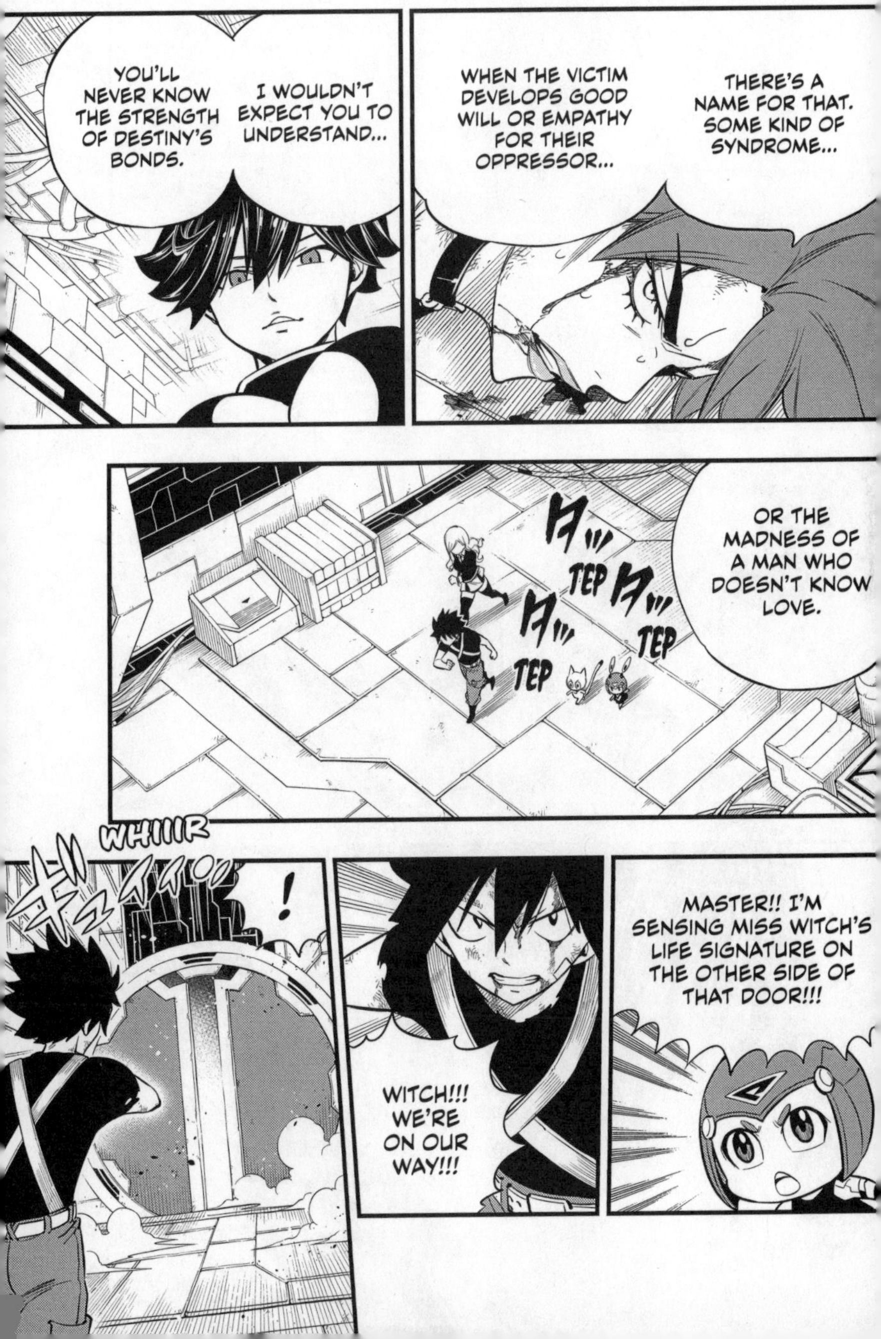
THERE'S A NAME FOR THAT. SOME KIND OF SYNDROME...
WHEN THE VICTIM DEVELOPS GOOD WILL OR EMPATHY FOR THEIR OPPRESSOR...
I WOULDN'T EXPECT YOU TO UNDERSTAND...
YOU'LL NEVER KNOW THE STRENGTH OF DESTINY'S BONDS.
OR THE MADNESS OF A MAN WHO DOESN'T KNOW LOVE.
TEP
TEP
TEP
MASTER!! I'M SENSING MISS WITCH'S LIFE SIGNATURE ON THE OTHER SIDE OF THAT DOOR!!!
WITCH!!! WE'RE ON OUR WAY!!!
WHIIIR
!

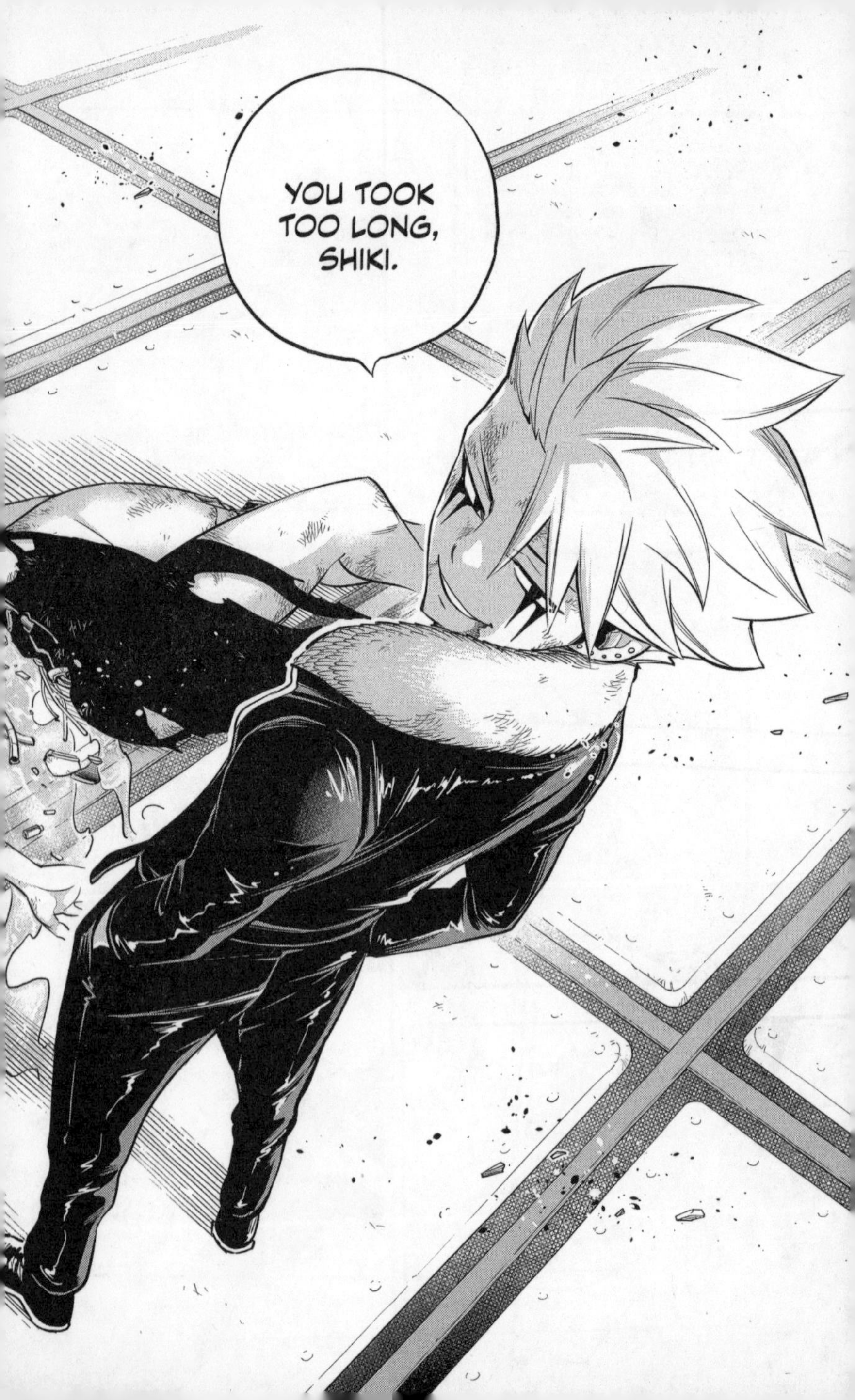
YOU TOOK TOO LONG, SHIKI.

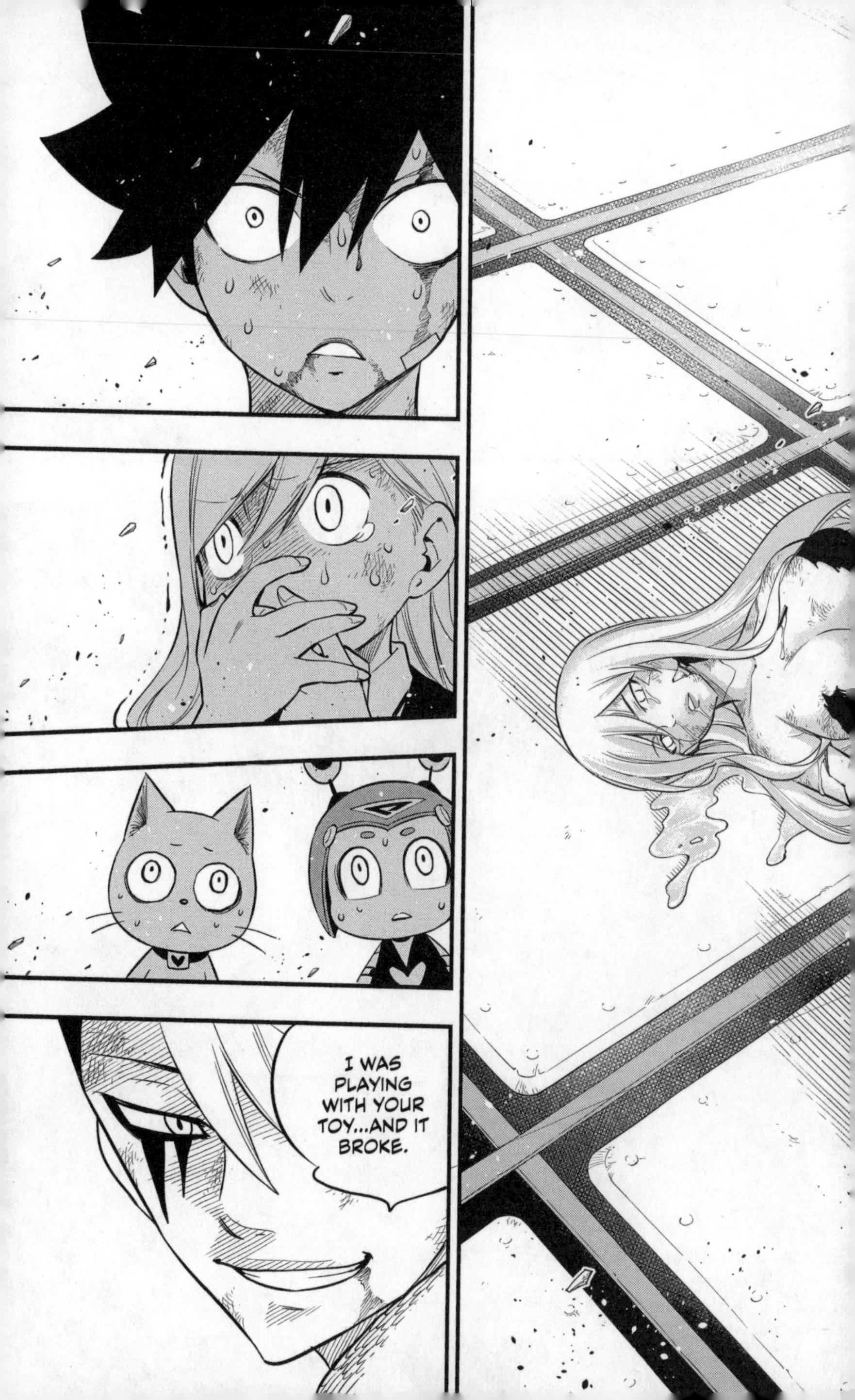
I WAS PLAYING WITH YOUR TOY...AND IT BROKE.

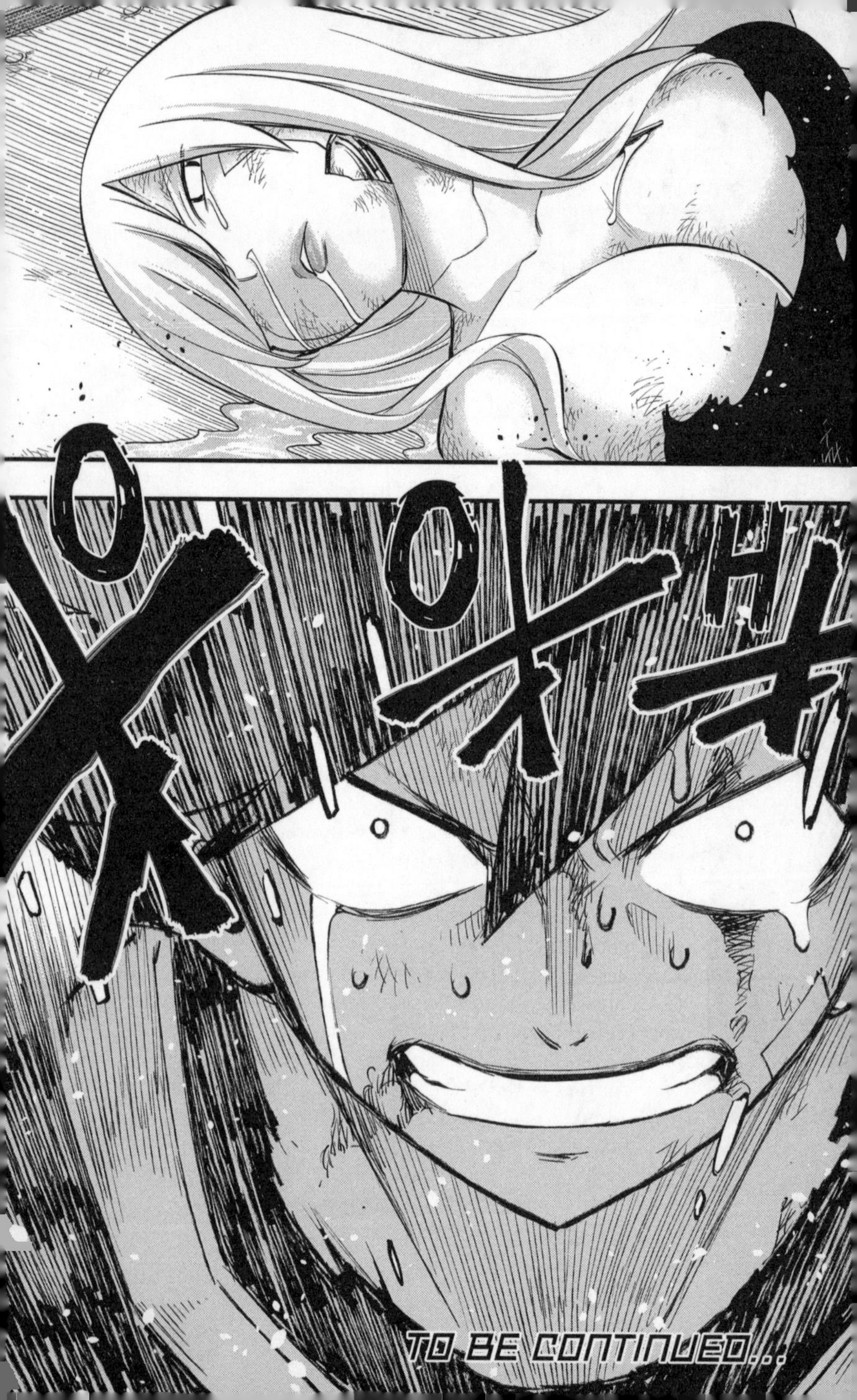
TO BE CONTINUED...

AFTERWORD

The other day, I did my second online autograph signing. Unlike last time, this one was an event specifically for Japan, but I'm thankful to say that a lot of people from overseas tuned in, too.

I didn't notice it at all during the event, but when it was over, it turned out I had been signing autographs for almost six hours, so I had a lot of people expressing their gratitude, like, "Thank you for spending so much time on this." But as someone who normally spends more than six hours a day drawing for work, I'm thinking, "I actually spent less time on that than what I'm used to." And unlike published manga and game illustrations and all that, where I have to really concentrate, the sketches I do for autographs are pretty close to rough drafts, so they're a lot easier to draw, which means it's not as tiring as you might think. It's actually pretty fun.

To be honest, getting to appear in media and stuff is not something I've really sought out. I'm basically very timid and shy. But I've been in a lot of events and stuff anyway. Usually it's because they tell me, "The fans will love to see you," and then I can't say no. So from now on, I want to actively participate in events where the fans would be happy to see me. If I have the time, of course.

Which reminds me, there were a lot of very unusual and specific requests at this last autograph session, and it was a lot of fun to draw them, but the ones that really stood out were the ones for male characters in bunny girl(?) outfits. I spent days after that thinking about how, wow, there's a demand for that kind of thing (ha ha).

As I wrote on Cover 2 (the cover flap), for a long time now, I've often gotten the question, "You really like bunny girls, don't you?" I'm sure there are a lot of opportunities for them to show up in manga (?). My answer to the question is a boring, "I like them, but they're not necessarily my most favorite costume," but it's true that I enjoy drawing them. A long time ago, I had my first encounter with a real bunny girl out on the street. I think she was advertising for some establishment, but I remember being so impressed that I went home and immediately drew a bunny girl.

This volume has a part where we have Rebecca in a bunny girl costume, but we're going to get into some serious developments, so we can't keep her in that outfit, can we?

Young characters and steampunk setting, like *Howl's Moving Castle* and *Battle Angel Alita*

Beyond the Clouds © 2018 Nicke / Ki-oon

A boy with a talent for machines and a mysterious girl whose wings he's fixed will take you beyond the clouds! In the tradition of the high-flying, resonant adventure stories of Studio Ghibli comes a gorgeous tale about the longing of young hearts for adventure and friendship!

A Kodansha Comics Trade Paperback Original
EDENS ZERO 18 copyright © 2021 Hiro Mashima
English translation copyright © 2022 Hiro Mashima

Published in the United States by Kodansha Comics, an imprint of Kodansha USA Publishing, LLC, New York.

Publication rights for this English edition arranged through Kodansha Ltd., Tokyo.

First published in Japan in 2021 by Kodansha Ltd., Tokyo.

ISBN 978-1-64651-570-7

Printed in the United States of America.

www.kodansha.us

9 8 7 6 5 4 3 2 1
Translation: Alethea Nibley & Athena Nibley
Lettering: AndWorld Design
Editing: David Yoo
Kodansha Comics edition cover design by Phil Balsman

Publisher: Kiichiro Sugawara

Director of publishing services: Ben Applegate
Director of publishing operations: Dave Barrett
Associate director of publishing operations: Stephen Pakula
Publishing services managing editors: Madison Salters, Alanna Ruse, with Grace Chen
Production manager: Jocelyn O'Dowd